HIDDEN HISTORY

Skyhorse Publishing books may be purchased in bulk at special discounts for sales promotion, corporate gifts, fund-raising, or educational purposes. Special editions can also be created to specifications. For details, contact the Special Sales Department, Skyhorse Publishing, 307 West 36th Street, 11th Floor, New York, NY 10018 or info@skyhorsepublishing.com.

Skyhorse® and Skyhorse Publishing® are registered trademarks of Skyhorse Publishing, Inc.®, a Delaware corporation.

Visit our website at www.skyhorsepublishing.com.

10 9 8 7 6 5 4

Library of Congress Cataloging-in-Publication Data
Jeffries, Donald, 1956-
  Hidden history : an encyclopedia of modern crimes, conspiracies, and cover-ups in American politics / Donald Jeffries.
     pages cm
  ISBN 978-1-62914-484-9 (hardback) -- ISBN 978-1-62914-984-4 (ebook) 1. United States--Politics and government--1945-1989. 2. United States--Politics and government--1989- 3. Official secrets--United States. 4. Political crimes and offenses--United States. 5. Conspiracies--United States. I. Title.
  E839.5.J45 2014
  973.92--dc23
                          2014025042

Cover design by Richard Rossiter
Cover photos from the Public Domain

Print ISBN: 9781510705371
Ebook ISBN: 9781510710887

Printed in the United States of America

HIDDEN HISTORY

AN EXPOSÉ OF MODERN CRIMES, CONSPIRACIES, AND COVER-UPS IN AMERICAN POLITICS

DONALD JEFFRIES

SKYHORSE PUBLISHING

To my children, John and Julianna

May they help to build a better world

CONTENTS

FOREWORD

D on Jeffries's *Hidden History* may be one of the most important books of our time. Jeffries has the audacity to provide an alternate narrative for the most important events in our nation's recent history. It's a narrative the mainstream media suppresses and the federal government seeks to deny.

Whether it is the assassination of John F. Kennedy, the murders of Dr. Martin Luther King and Senator Robert Kennedy, the Vietnam War, Watergate, Iran-Contra, the attempted assassination of Ronald Reagan, the Oklahoma City bombing, the downing of TWA Flight 800, the Clinton scandals or facts about Barrack Obama, Don Jeffries provides a taut, compelling case for a new view of our history—one that is both breathtaking and thought-provoking.

When the mainstream media calls journalists like Don Jeffries (and yours truly) "conspiracy theorists" they don't mean it as a compliment. Put aside the labels. Don Jeffries's work stands on its own. He presents, as Sgt. Joe Friday used to say on the popular TV show *Dragnet*, "just the facts." Indeed, Jeffries's work is meticulously researched and sourced, not to mention that in all cases his presentation is more *logical* than the lies served up by the government and its Greek chorus, the media.

Perhaps it is because *Hidden History* spans such a broad swath of our recent history that the book is hard to pigeonhole and has yet to receive the attention it so richly deserves. In the 1960s, suppressing the truth about historical events was much easier. There were only three TV networks and a handful of "national" newspapers. If it wasn't reported there it simply did not happen. Now, with the advent of the internet and the proliferation of talk radio and the growth of daring publishers like Skyhorse, hiding the truth is no longer so easy for the powers that be. In 1963 we only had the Zapruder film. Today, JFK's murder would be recorded by dozens of cell phone cameras.

I myself spent forty years in the corroded inner workings of the two-party system. I consider myself a political insider, having worked on a senior level in nine American presidential campaigns, from Richard Nixon to Donald Trump, and been a top aide in both the US House and Senate. I've seen the sausage being made. Yet I learned much I did not know in *Hidden History*. Jeffries connects the dots in a way that makes you sit bolt upright and say "AHA." Thus is the incandescence of Don Jeffries's work.

Don Jeffries comes at these events with no ideological agenda. He regards the events of history with a clear eye. He is driven only by the facts and only goes where the facts lead. The sheer size of the events he retells from an honest, fact-based point of view is stunning in itself. There is so much to digest in *Hidden History* that, if you are like me, you will have trouble putting it down until you have consumed it.

There are many fine works on the Kennedy assassination, the murder of MLK, Watergate, the Clinton impeachment, and the like, but if you seek one book to connect these events in the flow of history, to see how they are related, you have it in your hands in *Hidden History*. Read it and pass it on to your children. It's time for the truth, and Don Jeffries gives us the unvarnished version.

ROGER STONE
New York City
July 6, 2016

INTRODUCTION

Conspiracy
1. An agreement to perform together an illegal, wrongful, or subversive act.
2. An agreement between two or more persons to commit a crime or accomplish a legal purpose through illegal action.
3. A joining or acting together, as if by sinister design.

Abraham Lincoln's secretary of state, William Seward, was notorious for having a bell on his desk, which he claimed he could ring to have any American citizen arrested. Historians have never provided an accurate estimate for the number of Americans the Lincoln administration incarcerated, but they generally believe it to have been at least fourteen thousand. Lincoln suspended the writ of habeas corpus, permitting those who disagreed with his wartime policies to be thrown into makeshift prisons without reason or explanation. However, Lincoln's undeniable curtailment of civil liberties hasn't kept the "court historians," as renegade scholar Harry Elmer Barnes referred to them, from ranking him as our greatest president.

Another president highly rated and esteemed by establishment historians is Franklin D. Roosevelt. Even some mainstream scholars now acknowledge that FDR knew about the Japanese attack on Pearl Harbor in advance. Roosevelt's famous comment "In politics, nothing happens by accident. If it happens, you can bet it was planned that way" is a strong endorsement of the conspiratorial view of history.

We stand today on the brink of economic destruction. The housing market remains stagnant. Unemployment is obviously far higher than the officially reported figures of 6 to 7 percent, which factor in only those filing for unemployment benefits. As I was completing this book, there were alarming reports disseminated by the media that a hundred million Americans of working age were without jobs. This amounts to a staggering true unemployment rate of 36.3 percent. While some of those are willfully unemployed, such as stay-at-home parents, retirees, and high school students, there is no question that the real rate must still be at least somewhere in the

25-percent range. Student loan debt is quickly surpassing credit card debt in volume. The cost of living continues to surge, while the vast majority of American workers receive little or no yearly wage increase. Our industry has practically left our shores, leaving us incapable of manufacturing anything of substance. Although the US population increased by 10 percent during the first decade of the twenty-first century, 5,500,000 manufacturing jobs were lost during the same time period. The sad reality is America doesn't make much of anything anymore. The income disparity has grown to such an extent that the richest four hundred citizens presently possess more aggregate wealth than the bottom 50 percent of all Americans combined. If present trends continue, the United States is rapidly on the way to Third World nation status.

According to 2011 statistics from the Organization for Economic Cooperation and Development, America ranks twenty-eighth in life expectancy worldwide, behind countries like Chile and Greece, despite the fact our citizens pay more for health care than any other country. In contrast to all the government-run health-care systems the United States was compared with, Americans actually pay more taxes for health care than citizens do in most countries. (*Daily Mail UK*, November 24, 2011). Other research paints an even bleaker picture. In a recent joint study by Columbia University and the World Health Organization, the United States had fallen to forty-ninth in life expectancy worldwide, whereas in 1960 it had ranked fifth. Just as damningly, the United States ranks forty-first in infant mortality rate, according to the World Health Organization. America was tied in this category with Qatar and ranked behind countries like San Marino, Singapore, Montenegro, Slovenia, Monaco, Estonia, Croatia, Brunei Darussalam, and the dreaded Cuba. The United States does, however, rank first in categories such as obesity and childhood poverty among industrialized countries, and it has the seventh highest cancer rate in the world. Childhood cancer rates have been increasing steadily for the past twenty years, according to environmental public health expert Dr. Richard Clapp. (*Environment News Service*, January 26, 2011). In 2008, the Centers for Disease Control revealed that type 2 diabetes rates had risen 90 percent in America since 1997.

America also has more people imprisoned than the leading thirty-five European countries combined. The United States has twice as many citizens in prison as China, the world's foremost totalitarian society, even though they have four times the number of people. Vivien Stern, a research fellow at the prison studies center in London, expressed the view that the American incarceration rate has made the United States "a rogue state, a country that has made a decision not to follow what is a normal Western approach." (*New York Times*, April 23, 2008). And many of these prisons are now privately run.

In April 2012, two judges in Pennsylvania pled guilty to sentencing children to juvenile detention facilities in return for cash payoffs. The judges received $2.6 million from PA Childcare and Western PA Childcare, the corporations that ran the detention centers and were given a stipend for each inmate they housed. Meanwhile, the *Wall Street Journal* recently reported that projects to repave thousands of roads across America have been abandoned due to lack of funds. America's public transportation systems are a joke compared to that of many nations with only a fraction of our wealth. While Americans pay enough to support a well-run, socialist state, our leaders allocate resources in such a way that they receive almost nothing of substance in return for their tax dollars.

Who is responsible for the incredible mess the present-day generation of Americans find themselves in? In this book, I hope to show exactly how this happened. A series of deadly, inexplicable decisions by our elected leaders and corporate executives have paved the way to the crisis we must deal with now. Corruption has grown entrenched, like an inoperable disease, in nearly every organ of the establishment. We must heed the words of one of America's greatest statesmen, Thomas Jefferson: "Single acts of tyranny may be ascribed to the accidental opinion of a day. But a series of oppressions, begun at a distinguished period, and pursued unalterably through every change of ministers [administrations], too plainly proves a deliberate systematic plan of reducing us to slavery." The American people have been dealing with just such a "series of oppressions" now for well over a century, and there can be little doubt that it is the result of a "deliberate systematic plan." The best word to describe it is *conspiracy*.

Much of the information and analysis here will be new to readers; a huge part of the reason such high-level incompetence and corruption have flourished is because of the pathetic "efforts" of the mainstream media. Establishment journalists have long ignored or distorted the truth about scandalous and outrageous behavior on the part of the influential and powerful. The recent conduct of the establishment press toward the truly surging Ron Paul presidential campaign is a perfect illustration of this. They have attempted to manipulate public perception about Rep. Paul, much as they have long been manipulating the truth about our electoral process and countless other important aspects of our society.

As the great eccentric writer Charles Fort once said, "One measures a circle, beginning anywhere." Thus, while our problems began long before 1963, we will start with the 1963 assassination of President John F. Kennedy in Dallas.

CHAPTER ONE

THE MOTHER OF ALL CONSPIRACIES: THE ASSASSINATION OF JOHN FITZGERALD KENNEDY

"We were at war with the national security people."
—Kennedy aide Arthur Schlesinger Jr.

Before the assassination of President John F. Kennedy, the very word *conspiracy* was seldom used by most Americans. The JFK assassination was the seminal national event in the lives of the Baby Boomer generation. We've heard all the clichés about the loss of our innocence, and the beginning of public distrust in our government's leaders, being born with the events of November 22, 1963, but there's a good deal of truth in that. President Kennedy tapped into our innate idealism and inspired a great many people, especially the young, like no president ever had before.

John F. Kennedy was vastly different from most of our elected presidents. He was the first president to refuse a salary. He never attended a Bilderberg meeting. He was the first Catholic to sit in the Oval Office, and he almost certainly wasn't related to numerous other presidents and/or the royal family of England, as is often the case. He was a genuine war hero, having tugged an injured man more than three miles using only a life preserver's strap between his teeth, after the Japanese had destroyed the boat he commanded, *PT-109*. This selfless act seems even more courageous when one takes into account Kennedy's recurring health problems and chronic bad back. He was an intellectual and an accomplished author who wrote many of his memorable speeches. He would never have been invited to dance naked with other powerful men and worship a giant owl, as so many of our leaders do every sun'mer at Bohemian Grove in California.

Close JFK aide Arthur Schlesinger Jr., in his book on the Kennedy presidency, *A Thousand Days*, wrote that Kennedy was not part of what he called the "New York establishment": "In particular, he was little acquainted with the New York financial and legal community—that arsenal of talent which had so long furnished a steady supply of always orthodox and often able people to Democratic as well as Republican administrations. This community was the heart of the American establishment. Its household deities were Henry Stimson and Elihu Root; its present leaders, Robert Lovett and John J. McCloy; its front organizations, the Rockefeller, Ford and Carnegie foundations and the Council on Foreign Relations; its organs, the *New York Times* and *Foreign Affairs*."

By November 1963, John F. Kennedy had collected a slew of powerful enemies who had equally powerful motives to want him removed from the Oval Office. Kennedy was the first and only president to attempt to rein in organized crime. He held a mutual animosity with the CIA, telling friend and Secretary of the Navy Paul "Red" Fay that he wanted to see the agency "shattered into a thousand pieces." During 1963, he was engaged in a series of increasingly vitriolic exchanges with then Israeli president David Ben-Gurion over the issue of Israel developing nuclear weapons. Big business, especially the oil companies, had good reason to oppose him. He had stood up to US Steel and was attempting to eliminate the oil industry's long-cherished depletion allowance. There are strong indications that, influenced by his father, former Ambassador to England Joseph P. Kennedy, JFK understood the true nature of the Federal Reserve and was planning to strip its control of the money supply. Finally, the military mistrusted him because, unlike most presidents before him and all presidents afterward, he rejected every overture toward war during his administration. In this vein, with National Security Action Memorandum 263, he laid the groundwork for withdrawing the first one thousand advisors from Vietnam, and he planned to have them all out by 1965.

Kennedy's April 1961 speech in which he railed against secret societies, and secrecy in government in general, was unlike any speech ever given by another president. While his presidential peers would cling to their "national security" blankets, JFK espoused openness and a free flow of information. His June 1963 speech at American University, in which he pleaded for world peace and declared that our sworn enemies "breathe the same air" as we do, was profound and timeless. Compared to the empty rhetoric and unoriginal slogans of other politicians, JFK's words of wisdom stand out in stark contrast.

The JFK assassination itself has been dissected to pieces by obsessed researchers like me. Suffice to say that a few days of intense study of the available record will convince any honest person, beyond any reasonable doubt, that Lee Harvey Oswald was not responsible for the crime. The cover-up was so clear and obvious in nature, and so shabbily constructed, that the conclusion is inescapable that the conspirators who killed him wanted the kind of controversy that soon exploded, shortly after the first wave of private citizens began to look at the data.

Because of the fact that no honest inquiry into the crime ever took place, and the mainstream media from the outset was content to merely pass along the increasingly absurd official findings, we can be sure about very few things associated with the events of November 22, 1963. We know that President Kennedy was shot and killed by a fusillade of bullets as he rode in an open limousine down Elm Street in Dallas, Texas. We also know that his alleged assassin, Lee Harvey Oswald, was murdered himself two days later in the basement of Dallas Police headquarters, in the midst of what was a strangely public and totally unnecessary transfer, by low-level mobster and nightclub operator Jack Ruby. Although there were more than seventy law enforcement officers at the scene, for some reason Oswald's front was left entirely unprotected. Given the circumstances, and the fact the alleged assassin was now silenced forever, it was only natural to suspect that Oswald had been shot to stop him from telling what he knew.

To avoid becoming mired in the minutia of this case, we will scrutinize the most obvious indicators of conspiracy. The most important thing to remember here is that the assassination of a sitting US president was never properly investigated by any authoritative body. The Dallas Police, while exhibiting the predictable kind of incompetence expected of local law enforcement, were quickly pushed out of the way by federal officials. JFK's body was, in fact, basically stolen and illegally transported out of Texas by the Secret Service; at the time, political assassination was not a federal crime, and thus the authorities in Dallas had legal jurisdiction.

On November 25, 1963, the day after Oswald was gunned down by Ruby, Assistant Attorney General and Rhodes scholar Nicholas Katzenbach sent a memo to Bill Moyers, aide to new president Lyndon B. Johnson (and later a well-known journalist). The memo clearly delineated the future official policy concerning this issue: "The public must be satisfied that Oswald was the assassin; that he did not have confederates who are still at large; and that the evidence was such that he would have been convicted at trial." Furthermore, Katzenbach went on to state, "Speculation about Oswald's motivation ought to be cut off. . . ." Could they have been any bolder? One would expect an honest Justice Department official to say something like, "With the death of the primary suspect, no stone must be left unturned in uncovering the truth about the assassination of President Kennedy." This illuminating memo alone, in my view, proves that the highest government officials had no interest in ascertaining the truth about the death of John F. Kennedy—which is tantamount, of course, to saying they were involved in covering up the crime.

The same Bill Moyers had fielded a phone call on November 24, with Oswald's body still warm, from an Establishment stalwart, Yale Law School Dean Eugene Rostow. Rostow suggested that a blue ribbon commission should be formed to investigate the assassination. In another phone conversation that day, FBI Director J. Edgar Hoover told LBJ aide Walter Jenkins that "Katzenbach thinks that the President might appoint a Presidential Commission of three outstanding citizens to make a determination." Hoover also foretold the exact sentiments to be expressed by Katzenbach in his memo, when he mentioned the need for having "something issued so we can convince the public that Oswald is the real assassin." The next day, influential journalist Joseph Alsop strongly urged President Johnson to appoint a commission.

Such a commission, not surprisingly, was subsequently established. Named after its chairman, Supreme Court Chief Justice Earl Warren, the Warren Commission would set new standards for incompetence and willful disregard for the truth. There were no members that could be described as even lukewarm supporters of John F. Kennedy. One appointee was shocking: Allen Dulles, the former CIA director whom JFK had fired after the Bay of Pigs. Another notable member was future president Gerald Ford. The FBI had already conducted its own superficial "investigation," and the Warren Commission rubber-stamped it, basically constructing a hugely flawed prosecutorial brief against Oswald. Much of the official record compiled by the Commission consisted of irrelevant material, such as photos of Oswald's pubic hair or the dental X-rays of Jack Ruby's mother. As an early critic noted about these X-rays, they would not have been germane even if Jack Ruby had bitten Oswald to death.

Questions surround nearly every aspect of the assassination. The chain of possession regarding each piece of evidence was tainted beyond repair. The presidential limousine, which represented the literal crime scene, was taken over by officials immediately after JFK's body was carried into Parkland Hospital and tampered with. The Secret Service apparently cleaned up the limousine, washing away crucial evidence in the process. Obviously, whatever bullet fragments or other material that was purportedly found there became immediately suspect because of this. On November 26, the windshield on the presidential limo was replaced.

The supposed murder weapon—a cheap, Italian Mannlicher-Carcano rifle with a defective scope, allegedly ordered by Oswald through a post office box registered to his purported alias, Alex Hidell—is similarly troublesome. The two Dallas officers who discovered the rifle on the sixth floor of the Texas School Book Depository building, Seymour Weitzman and Eugene Boone, both swore in separate affidavits that the weapon was a German Mauser. As was to become all too common in this case, they would later each claim to be "mistaken" in a curiously identical manner.

In fact, as late as midnight on November 22, Dallas District Attorney Henry Wade would refer to the rifle as a Mauser when speaking to the press. Local WFAA television reported the weapon found as both a German Mauser and an Argentine Mauser. NBC, meanwhile, described the weapon as a British Enfield. In an honest court, the Carcano would not even have been permitted into the record, because no reliable chain of possession for it existed. Legally speaking, the rifle found on the sixth floor was a German Mauser, and no one claimed Oswald owned a weapon of that kind.

Seymour Weitzman would also discover some interesting footprints; upon being told the shots had come from "the wall" on the grassy knoll, Weitzman scaled it and reported, "We noticed numerous kinds of footprints that did not make sense because they were going different directions. . . ." (*Warren Commission Hearings and Exhibits*, Vol. 7, p. 106). This supports the statement of witness S. M. Holland, who told the Commission that ". . . there was a station wagon backed up toward the fence, about the third car down, and a spot, I'd say 3 foot by 2 foot, looked to me like somebody had been standing there for a long period. I guess if you could count them about a hundred foottracks in that little spot, and also mud up on the bumper of that station wagon."

Holland went on to say there had been "mud on the bumper in two spots," and it was as if someone had "cleaned their foot, or stood up on the bumper to see over the fence." (*Hearings and Exhibits*, Vol. 6, pp. 245–246). Witness Richard C. Dodd, who was with Holland, verified his claims to researcher Mark Lane (Dodd was not called as a witness by the Warren Commission), adding that he also saw numerous cigarette butts along with the muddy footprints. Holland told Lane he saw cigarette butts as well; both of their interviews appeared in Lane's film *Rush to Judgment*, based on his best-selling book.

The almost pristine, intact "magic" bullet was found on a stretcher at Parkland Hospital by engineer Darrell Tomlinson, after which it was passed around to several people, none of whom seemed the least bit interested. Incredibly enough, it was eventually carried out of Dallas in the coat pocket of Secret Service agent Richard Johnsen, who took it back to Washington, D.C. Afterward, the first three men who handled the bullet at Parkland could not identify it as the one placed into evidence as Commission Exhibit 399. In a document released by the Assassinations Record and Review Board (ARRB) in 1996, it was revealed that Gerald Behn, the agent in charge of the White House detail, who wasn't even in Dallas, stated he was a part of the chain of custody for this "magic" bullet, something not previously reported, further muddying the waters.

When researcher Vince Palamara interviewed agent Richard Johnsen in 1992, Johnsen told him that he didn't recall ever having possession of CE399! The record already showed that Johnsen had never initialed the bullet he carried in his coat pocket (and incredibly neither did anyone else who handled it at Parkland Hospital). Is it plausible that someone would forget perhaps the most important moment of his professional career, when he personally transported such a historical piece of evidence? On the contrary, wouldn't one be expected to brag about such a thing to his family and friends? Needless to say, a competent defense attorney would have a field day picking apart these kinds of gaping holes in the chain of custody.

Warren Commission counsel Arlen Specter badgered Darrell Tomlinson repeatedly during his testimony, but Tomlinson refused to state definitively that the stretcher he'd found the "magic" bullet on had been Connally's. At one point, he advised Specter, ". . . I'm not going to tell you something I can't lay down and sleep at night with either." (*Warren Commission Hearings and Exhibits*, Vol. 6, pp. 128–134).

On an all too familiar note, Tomlinson later reported receiving an ominous phone call from the FBI. ". . . Saturday morning, after the assassination, the FBI woke me up on the phone and told me to keep my mouth shut," Tomlinson told researcher Ray Marcus in a 1967 interview. Tomlinson had initially given the bullet to his supervisor, O. P. Wright, who told author Josiah Thompson that the bullet he handled "had a pointed tip," while the "magic" bullet's tip was rounded. When shown a picture of CE399, Wright exclaimed, "Is that the bullet I was supposed to have had?" (*Six Seconds in Dallas* by Josiah Thompson, p. 175).

In 1993, researcher Wallace Milam interviewed Wright's widow, Elizabeth Goode Wright, who in 1963 was the director of nursing at Parkland Hospital. She told Milam that actually two bullets had been found at Parkland on the day of the assassination, and her husband had found a *third* unfired bullet on a gurney, which he never reported or turned over to the authorities. Mrs. Wright showed this .38 caliber missile to Milam, and he noticed that it just happened to have the same manufacturer's case markings as two of the four shell casings did that were allegedly discovered at the scene of Dallas Police Officer J. D. Tippit's murder and later matched to the pistol taken from Oswald at the Texas Theater. (*Murder in Dealey Plaza*, edited by James H. Fetzer, p. 93).

The legitimacy of Oswald's alleged alias, Alex Hidell, is tainted beyond repair by the nature of the Selective Service card supposedly found on him after his arrest in the Texas Theater. This card bore a photograph of Lee Harvey Oswald but the name of Alex Hidell. The problem is real Selective Service cards never had photos on them, so the card would have been worthless as a means of identification. It was perfect, however, for instantly associating Oswald with the Hidell alias. Oswald apparently only used this alias twice— once to order the unreliable rifle later dubiously tied to the assassination, and once to order the revolver allegedly used to kill Officer Tippit. The authorities claimed Oswald utilized a P.O. Box, under Hidell's name, for just this purpose. Critics quickly pointed out how senseless this would have been, as anyone could have purchased better, cheaper weapons on virtually every street corner in 1963 Dallas, with no convenient trail left behind.

The chain-of-possession problems crop up repeatedly in this case. For instance, the three empty rifle shells found under the alleged sixth floor sniper's window by Detective Richard Sims (they had no fingerprints on them) were placed in an unsealed envelope by Lieutenant J. C. Day, signed by him, and returned to Sims. Day at first told the Warren Commission he'd marked all three shells at the scene, which would have been normal procedure, but he later admitted he was in error and had actually not marked any until ten o'clock that night, when he marked two, but not all three of them.

The third shell, for some unexplained reason, was missing. Lieutenant Day, in typical Dallas Police fashion, brushed this off by saying, "I didn't examine it too close at that time." (*Warren Commission Hearings and Exhibits*, Vol. 4, p. 249). Day's Dallas Police report dated November 22, 1963, clearly refers to "2 spent hulls from 6th floor window." Day's signature on this report is followed by Officer R. L. Studebaker's, demonstrating he witnessed the transfer of evidence from Day to FBI agent Vincent Drain. The FBI receipt for this evidence states, "2 spent hulls found at School Book Depository."

Author Noel Twyman covered this issue extensively in his excellent 1997 book *Bloody Treason*. The third shell entered into evidence bore the identification of Captain George Doughty, Day's superior. There is a great deal of confusing material about these shells in the official record. Lieutenant Day was also asked about the condition of one of the shells, which was flattened out on the small end, but could only respond "No, sir, I don't" to the question of whether or not he could remember if it was that way when the shells were originally discovered. (*Hearings and Exhibits* Vol. 4, pp. 253–255). Day attempted to clarify things in two different affidavits, dated May 7, 1964, and June 23, 1964, but their belated nature detracted from their credibility.

Then there was the pistol said to have been found on Oswald when he was arrested in the Texas Theatre, the one that he allegedly used to kill Officer Tippit. Officer N. M. McDonald admitted he didn't mark the revolver until later at the police station (*Warren Report*, p. 304). Detective Bob Carroll, a special service bureau detective who was one of many seemingly displaced law enforcement personnel who happened to be at the theater when Oswald was arrested, testified that when he saw Oswald and McDonald struggling and realized the alleged assassin was brandishing a gun in his direction, ". . . I reached out and jerked the pistol away and stuck it in my belt, and then I grabbed Oswald." (*Hearings and Exhibits* Vol. 7, p. 20). When they got into the police car, he gave the revolver to Sergeant Gerald L. Hill. Carroll then stated that Hill unloaded the weapon, but was not certain of the time. Carroll was not asked when he put his mark on the revolver. It is mind-boggling to imagine what these severe chain-of-possession problems would have meant in the hands of any halfway competent public defender.

Texas Governor John Connally had been riding in the limousine, seated in front of JFK, and was struck in the back with a nonfatal wound. Once future senator Arlen Spector invented the preposterous single-bullet theory, Connally's clothing became a key piece of evidence. Unfortunately, the governor's clothing wasn't exactly handled properly, either. For unknown reasons, Texas congressman Henry Gonzalez—who would later be one of those pushing hardest in Congress for a new investigation into the assassination—took Connally's clothes back to his office, where they hung in his closet for at least a week. Thereafter, the governor's wife, Nellie Connally, laundered them, rendering them meaningless as evidence. This is the way all of the crucial evidence in this case was handled.

There are many obvious indications of conspiracy and cover-up relating to the murder of Kennedy. The chief autopsy surgeon, the eminently underqualified Dr. James J. Humes, acknowledged burning "certain preliminary draft notes" as well as his first draft of the autopsy report in his home fireplace. JFK autopsy photographer John T. Stringer reported that the Secret Service confiscated his film, in violation of standard procedure, and purposefully ruined the film of Corpsman Floyd Riebe, who was taking pictures of those in the morgue for posterity, by exposing it to light. The FBI admitted destroying a "threatening" note from Oswald by flushing it down a toilet.

During reenactments for *Life* magazine and then the Warren Commission, the first done a few weeks after JFK's death, surveyor Joe West found that the Stemmons Freeway sign, which blocked JFK from view during the crucial moment when shots were first fired, had been moved some ten feet since the assassination. Warren Commission member John J. McCloy mentioned, during a December 16, 1963, executive session, "You see this sign here, someone has suggested that this sign has now been removed. Why I don't know." Emmett Hudson, groundskeeper at Dealey Plaza, gave the following testimony to the Warren Commission:

Mr. LIEBELER: There are two signs in picture No. 18, one says, "R.L. Thornton Freeway, keep right." and the other one says, "Fort Worth Turn-pike, keep right."
Mr. HUDSON: There were two of them that wasn't too far apart right through here—them signs was—one was right along in here and the other one was either further up, I guess. It's not in that picture—I don't believe. Now, they have moved some of those signs. They have moved the R.L. Thornton Freeway sign and put up a Stemmons sign.
Mr. LIEBELER: They have? They have moved it?
Mr. HUDSON: Yes, sir.
Mr. LIEBELER: That might explain it, because this picture here, No. 18, was taken after the assassination and this one was taken at the time— No. 1.
(*Warren Commission Hearings and Exhibits*, Vol. 7, p. 562).

Note that Commission counsel Wesley Liebeler was not the least bit curious about Hudson's disclosure regarding the missing sign. That was par for the course during the Warren Commission's "investigation." There has been speculation for years that a bullet went through or nicked the sign, which would provide a plausible explanation for its mysterious removal. Hudson revealed other things in his testimony: the shrubbery and hedges in the area had been trimmed, and in fact all three road signs had been moved. This obviously impacted the government's reconstruction of events, for which they actually used an entirely different make of automobile. (*Crossfire* by Jim Marrs, p. 456).

The Department of Defense "routinely" destroyed an Army Intelligence file on Oswald in 1971. Oswald's Office of Naval Intelligence file was "routinely" destroyed as well. As late as 1993, the Secret Service destroyed records that the ARRB was trying to obtain. There was an absurd series of "backyard" photographs of Oswald, holding the weapons that allegedly killed JFK and Officer Tippit, with some visible Communist newspapers thrown in for good measure, that were found in the garage of Mrs. Ruth Paine's home. Oswald's wife, Marina, along with the children, lived with Paine in an unconventional arrangement, while Lee stayed in a rooming house during the week. Researchers have convincingly contended that these implausible pictures are fakes. The negatives, held by the Dallas Police, disappeared.

In 1970, researcher Jim Marrs interviewed Robert and Patricia Hester, who worked at the National Photo Lab in Dallas. They told Marrs that they'd been very busy developing photographs for both the Secret Service and the FBI on the night of the assassination. They particularly recalled seeing color transparencies of the backyard photos, including one in which there was no figure in the picture. A "ghost image" backyard photo was discovered in the 1980s, featuring a surreal white outline of Oswald's body. This photo, along with *ten* others that were taken in the backyard without a figure, was found in the files of the Dallas Police Department. One of the most believable statements attributed to Oswald during his unrecorded interrogation sessions was his vehement reaction when first shown the backyard photos. Oswald is alleged to have declared that they were fakes, and he could prove it.

The original police reports of Oswald's arrest in the Texas Theatre are not available. The police never bothered to record the names of those who were attending the movie at the time of Oswald's arrest, so we have no way of knowing exactly who witnessed it. The presidential limousine Kennedy was riding in was rebuilt shortly after the assassination. The Warren Commission included an exhibit in their records listed as Oswald's birth certificate, but it is not a birth certificate. The original one has never been found. Finally, John F. Kennedy's brain is officially missing. Seriously. You couldn't make this stuff up.

A grotesque anecdote involving JFK's missing brain was discovered by the Assassinations Records and Review Board (ARRB). An April 1, 1997, ARRB memo concerned the allegations of former Secret Service agent James Mastrovito. Mastrovito had been in charge of the Secret Service's JFK assassination file during the 1970s. He told the ARRB that "about 3 or 4 years later" after the assassination, he had been given a small vial with a label indicating it contained a piece of President Kennedy's brain, by his supervisor, first chief of the intelligence division Walter Young. Young had received it from someone at the Armed Forces Institute of Pathology. The ARRB memo reveals that "Mastrovito said he destroyed the vial and its contents in a machine that destroys food." I think we can safely say it's not proper protocol to obliterate a president's brain with a food processor.

A small Minox camera was found in Oswald's Marines sea bag during a search conducted by Dallas Police at the Paine residence. Detectives Gus Rose and R. S. Stovall reported the camera was loaded with film. The police inventory of Oswald's property taken from the Paine home, made on November 26, 1963, listed "one Minox camera" as item 375. This list was witnessed by Warren De Brueys, the New Orleans FBI agent who'd been assigned to monitor Oswald during the spring and summer of 1963. The FBI property list would later describe item 375 as a "Minox light meter." Rose told the *Dallas Morning News* (in the June 15, 1978, edition), "[The FBI] were calling it a light meter, I know that. But I know a camera when I see it. . . . The thing we got at Irving out of Oswald's sea bag was a Minox camera. No question about it. They tried to get me to change the records because it wasn't a light meter. . . ."

The reason for the official concern about all this is that the German-made Minox was famous as a "spy" camera used by both sides during World War II. The *Dallas Morning News* discovered, in 1978, that the Minox camera was not available to the public in 1963. *Dallas Morning News* reporter Earl Golz also discovered that Minox did not sell a light meter in the United States in 1963. In 1979, a Freedom of Information Act suit forced the FBI to release about twenty-five photographs, which the Bureau matter-of-factly reported to have been taken with a Minox camera belonging to Oswald. (*Dallas Morning News*, August 7, 1978). In Jesse Curry's 1969 book *JFK Assassination File*, there is a photograph, on page 113, of Oswald's property taken from the Paine residence. Assorted Minox camera equipment, including a telephoto lens, is clearly pictured.

Obviously, to own a spy camera in 1963 one must have been some sort of spy. Critics have long suspected Oswald of being affiliated in some manner with intelligence work. His defection to Russia and incomprehensibly easy repatriation to the United States, at the height of the Cold War, not to mention his slew of connections to assorted characters of all political stripes, have convinced most researchers that he was much more than a minimum-wage-earning "loser," as the official story maintains.

Nothing expresses the clear nature of conspiracy better than Jack Ruby's Warren Commission testimony. Ruby was one of the rare witnesses who appeared before Chief Justice Earl Warren himself, and the result was an embarrassment to Warren. With a good deal of irrelevant exchanges omitted, here are the highlights of this bizarre session, taken from the *Warren Commission's Hearings and Exhibits*, Vol. 5, pp. 186–205:

> **RUBY:** . . . Gentlemen, unless you get me to Washington, you can't get a fair shake out of me. If you understand my way of talking, you have got to bring me to Washington to get the tests. Do I sound dramatic? Off the beam?
>
> **WARREN:** No; you are speaking very, very rationally, and I am really surprised that you can remember as much as you have remembered up to the present time. . . .
>
> **RUBY:** Unless you can get me to Washington, and I am not a crackpot, I have all my senses—I don't want to evade any crime I am guilty of. . . .
>
> **RUBY:** My reluctance to talk—you haven't had any witness in telling the story, in finding so many problems?
>
> **WARREN:** You have a greater problem than any witness we have had.
>
> **RUBY:** I have a lot of reasons for having those problems.
>
> **WARREN:** I know that. . . . I only want to hear what you are willing to tell us, because I realize that you still have a great problem before you, and I am not trying to press you.
>
> **RUBY:** If you request me to go back to Washington with you right now, that couldn't be done, could it?
>
> **WARREN:** No; it could not be done. It could not be done. There are a good many things involved in that, Mr. Ruby.
>
> **RUBY:** Gentlemen, my life is in danger here. Not with my guilty plea of execution. Do I sound sober enough to you as I say this?
>
> **WARREN:** You do. You sound entirely sober.
>
> **RUBY:** . . . I may not live tomorrow to give any further testimony . . . the only thing I want to get out to the public, and I can't say it here, is with authenticity, with the sincerity of the truth of everything and why my act

was committed, but it can't be said here. . . . Chairman Warren, if you felt that your life was in danger at the moment, how would you feel? Would you be reluctant to go on speaking, even though you request me to do so?

WARREN: I think I might have some reluctance if I was in your position, yes; I think I would. I think I would figure it out very carefully as to whether it would endanger me or not. . . . I want you to feel absolutely free to say that the interview is over.

RUBY: What happens then? I didn't accomplish anything.

WARREN: No; nothing has been accomplished.

RUBY: Well, then you won't follow up with anything further?

WARREN: There wouldn't be anything to follow up if you hadn't completed your statement.

RUBY: You said you have the power to do what you want to do, is that correct?

WARREN: Exactly.

RUBY: Without any limitations?

WARREN: . . . We have the right to take testimony of anyone we want in this whole situation. . . .

RUBY: But you don't have a right to take a prisoner back with you when you want to?

WARREN: No; we have the power to subpoena witnesses to Washington if we want to do it, but we have taken the testimony of 200 or 300 people, I would imagine, here in Dallas without going to Washington.

RUBY: Yes; but those people aren't Jack Ruby.

WARREN: No; they weren't . . . unless you had indicated not only through your lawyers but also through your sister, who wrote a letter addressed either to me or Mr. Rankin saying that you wanted to testify before the Commission, unless she had told us that, I wouldn't have bothered you.

RUBY: . . . . with your power that you have, Chief Justice Warren, and all these gentlemen, too much time has gone by for me to give you any benefit of what I may say now. . . . At that time when you first got the letter and I was begging Joe Tonahill and the other lawyers to know the truth about me, certain things that are happening now wouldn't be happening at this particular time.

WARREN: This story was given by a lawyer by the name of Mark Lane, who is representing Mrs. Marguerite Oswald, the mother of Lee Harvey Oswald, and it was in the paper, so we subpoenaed him, and he testified that someone had given him information to the effect that a week or two before President Kennedy was assassinated, that in your Carousel Club you and Weismann and Tippit, Officer Tippit, the one who was killed, and a rich oil man had an interview or conversation for an hour or two. And we asked him who it was that told him, and he said that it was confidential, and he couldn't tell at the moment, but that he would find out for us. . . .

RUBY: Isn't that foolish? If a man is patriotic enough in the first place, who am I to be concerned if he wasn't an informer. I am incarcerated, nothing to be worried about anyone hurting me.

WARREN: . . . I did feel that our record should show that we would ask you the question and that you would answer it, and you have answered it.

RUBY: No; I am as innocent regarding any conspiracy as any of you gentlemen in the room. . . .

This was riveting stuff, and it drew the close attention of the private citizens (like Mark Lane, mentioned by Warren) who began sifting through the morass of testimony shortly after the volumes were published. Ruby also told the Commission, "Who else could have timed it so perfectly by seconds. If it were timed that way, then someone in the police department is guilty of giving the information as to when Lee Harvey Oswald was coming down." Warren and his fellow commissioner, future president Gerald Ford, who was also on hand for Ruby's testimony, were so disinterested in questioning this important witness that Ruby reminded them at one point, "You can get more out of me. Let's not break up too soon."

Jack Ruby was clearly disturbed to some degree; he also rambled on quite a bit about how all Jews were going to be blamed for his act, for instance. However, it's undeniable that he was extremely anxious to be taken to Washington, so that he could tell them *something* he felt unable to tell them in Dallas. It's also crystal clear that Warren and the others fabricated lame excuses as to why they couldn't make that happen. Remember, at one point, Warren informed Ruby that the only reason they called him to testify at all was because of his sister's letter requesting it!

There is an unforgettable video of Jack Ruby, still readily available on the Internet, taken shortly after he was granted a new trial, in which he stated the following: "The world will never know the true facts of what occurred, my motives. . . . The people had, that had so much to gain, and had such an ulterior motive for putting me in the position I'm in, will never let the true facts come above board to the world." Ruby is then asked by a reporter, "Are these people in very high positions, Jack?" Ruby replies, "Yes." In yet another video, Ruby directly implicates Lyndon Johnson when he tells reporters, "When I mentioned about Adlai Stevenson, if he was vice president there would never have been an assassination of our beloved President Kennedy . . . the answer is the man in office now."

The notion that Ruby was compelled spontaneously to shoot Oswald, out of his desire to prevent Jacqueline Kennedy from having to testify at Oswald's trial, is ludicrous. From newsreel footage, we know that Ruby posed as a reporter and attended District Attorney Henry Wade's press conference at Dallas Police headquarters on the night of the assassination. Ruby even corrected Wade when he stated that Oswald had been a member of the anti-Castro group Free Cuba Committee by shouting, "Henry, that's the Fair Play for Cuba Committee," referring to the pro-Castro organization that the authorities would tie Oswald to, which was under the directorship of his supposed alias, Alex Hidell.

Dallas Police Officer Billy Grammer reported receiving a phone call in the early morning hours of November 24, 1963, warning that Oswald was going to be killed. The voice was familiar to him, but he couldn't place it. When he saw his old friend Jack Ruby (Ruby was well known to most of the Dallas Police) shoot Oswald later that morning, he immediately realized the voice had belonged to him. Grammer swore out an affidavit that Ruby had made the call threatening Oswald's life.

Ruby was seen at Parkland Hospital only an hour or so after the assassination by newsman Seth Kantor. Kantor was quite familiar with Ruby, and certainly didn't mistake him for someone else. Wilma May Tice, a friend of Jack's sister Eva, also saw Ruby at Parkland the day of the assassination, but in typical fashion the Commission chose to believe Ruby over these disparate witnesses who corroborated each other. Mrs. Tice's testimony was nearly as incredible as Ruby's in its own way, as it illustrated again just what kind of an "investigation" was being conducted. The counsel deposing her is Burt Griffin. Here are some pertinent excerpts, from the *Warren Commission's Hearings and Exhibits*, Vol. 15, pp. 388–396:

GRIFFIN: Would you rather think about this? There is no reason why you have to make a decision today about it.

TICE: . . . . Well go ahead and ask me whatever you want to ask me now, whatever it is you want to know.

GRIFFIN: . . . . Do you have any reservations about testifying?

TICE: I don't know if it is going to cause any more trouble than it already has. I don't see how it could.

GRIFFIN: Let me put it this way. Would you prefer not to testify? . . . Mrs. Tice, did you know that Jack himself has denied very vehemently he was out at the hospital?

TICE: Yes; I know he denied that, and I hated to say that I saw him out there, . . .

GRIFFIN: Do you think you could have been mistaken about the man you saw?

TICE: It could have been somebody else that looked like Jack, named Jack; yes.

GRIFFIN: I want to ask one other question. That is, there was a newspaper report that you received a threat of some sort before you came here. Do you know anything about that?

TICE: Well, I don't know if it was a threat or I don't know now—I don't know what you are talking about. Are you talking about when I was barricaded in the house?

GRIFFIN: . . . I was just informed by someone in this US attorney's office that one of the daily newspapers here had carried an article that you had been threatened. . . .

TICE: They said that I had been threatened, but what the paper said is not what—I got a telephone call, and some man told me on the telephone that it would pay me to keep my mouth shut.

GRIFFIN: Did you recognize the voice on the telephone?

TICE: I never heard that voice before in my life, that I know of. . . . Well, that is all I know. And as far as the phone calls, the rest of them didn't say anything. They just hung up.

GRIFFIN: Did you get more than one phone call?

TICE: Yes, sir; I got several phone calls that were just—whenever I wouldn't answer the phone any more, and our little niece had been there, and she is 14 and I would tell her to answer the telephone, and she answered the telephone, and they would hang up.

GRIFFIN: Well, I want to thank you again very much for coming. . . .

Yeah, no need for further questioning there. . . . The official record is full of this—page after page wasted on meaningless background material, coupled with the premature dismissal of those like Wilma Tice, when further interrogation was clearly needed. Tice would tell the FBI about a phone call to her home the very day she received a letter from the Warren Commission. The anonymous caller told her, "It would pay you to keep your mouth shut." She also reported that on another occasion, a ladder had been "wedged against the bottom of the door" at the back of her house, making it impossible to open the door from the inside without force. (*Hearings and Exhibits*, Vol. 25, pp. 224–225).

As we've seen, Tice wasn't the only witness who described receiving threats, and most people are familiar with the number of unnatural deaths that occurred among those connected to the events in Dallas following the assassination. Still others would claim that the information they gave to the FBI hadn't been recorded accurately, and/or that the testimony published by the Warren Commission didn't reflect what they'd actually said.

Richard Carr, a steelworker who was watching the motorcade from a lofty perch on the courthouse building under construction, told researchers Gary Shaw and Larry Harris that the FBI had paid a threatening visit to him after he'd reported seeing such things as a heavyset man on the sixth floor of the TSBD just before the shooting, two men running from the back of the TSBD minutes after the assassination—where they got into a Nash Rambler station wagon, which left in such a hurry that one of its doors was still open—then the same heavyset man again, once Carr had gone down to ground level, walking quickly in an eastward direction on Commerce Street and looking back over his shoulder as he went.

In a taped interview, Carr stated: "The FBI came to my house—there were two of them—and they said they heard I witnessed the assassination and I said I did. They told me, 'If you didn't see Lee Harvey Oswald up in the School Book Depository with a rifle, you didn't witness it.' I said, 'Well, the man I saw on television that they tell me is Lee Harvey Oswald was not in the window of the School Book Depository. That's not the man.' And [one of the agents] said I better keep my mouth shut. He did not ask me what I saw, he told me what I saw."

Shortly after this encounter with the FBI, Carr's home was raided by Dallas Police looking for "stolen articles." The law enforcement officers ransacked Carr's home while they held him and his wife at gunpoint. The day after the raid, Carr received an anonymous phone call warning him to "get out of Texas." Carr eventually moved to Montana in an effort to avoid any further harassment (or worse), but even there he once found dynamite in his car and was shot at on another occasion. Carr testified for Jim Garrison at the Clay Shaw trial in New Orleans, but afterward was attacked by two men in Atlanta, who stabbed him in the back and left arm. Carr killed one of the attackers but was not indicted after turning himself in.

There were other cases of intimidation by the authorities. Warren Reynolds was employed by a car lot close to the scene of the Tippit shooting.

On January 21, 1964, he told the FBI that he could not identify the fleeing man he'd seen at close range as Oswald. Two days after his FBI interview, he was shot through the head in his office, but survived. As Reynolds would tell the Warren Commission, a month later someone attempted to kidnap his ten-year-old daughter. In addition, his family received the usual threatening phone calls. Reynolds grew fearful of even taking his nightly walks. By the time he testified to the Warren Commission in July, Reynolds had gotten the message, and he said there was "no question" in his mind that the man he'd seen fleeing the Tippit murder scene was Lee Harvey Oswald.

Counsel Wesley Liebeler seemed unduly concerned with convincing Reynolds that his shooting had not been connected to the assassination in some way. Liebeler also attempted to dismiss any notions that the death of Nancy J. Mooney—a stripper who was the girlfriend of Darrell Wayne Garner, the man police arrested for the shooting of Reynolds—was suspicious. (*Hearings and Exhibits*, Vol. 11, pp. 434–441). Mooney, also known as Betty McDonald, had supposedly worked for Jack Ruby's Carousel Club, and had provided Garner with an alibi. Eight days later, Mooney was arrested for "disturbing the peace" and was found hanged to death two hours later in her cell. Garner would continue to deny shooting Reynolds, before dying of an alleged heroin overdose on January 24, 1970. In another odd connection, Warren Reynolds was friends with General Edwin Walker, the right winger whom Oswald's widow, Marina, rather dubiously claimed Oswald had fired a shot at in April 1963.

Waitress Helen Markham was one of the Warren Commission's star witnesses, and like the others, was practically bereft of any credibility. The following snippet from her testimony will illustrate just how valid her identification of Oswald as the killer of Officer Tippit was:

BALL: Did you recognize anyone in the lineup?
MARKHAM: No, sir.
BALL: You did not? Did you see anybody—I have asked you that question before—did you recognize anybody from their face?
MARKHAM: From their face, no.
BALL: Did you identify anybody in these four people?
MARKHAM: I didn't know nobody.
BALL: I know you didn't know anybody, but did anybody in that lineup look like anybody you had seen before?
MARKHAM: No. I had never seen none of them, none of these men.
BALL: No one of the four?

MARKHAM: No one of them.
BALL: No one of all four?
MARKHAM: No, sir.
BALL: Was there a number two man in there?
MARKHAM: Number two is the one I picked.
(*Hearings and Exhibits*, Vol. 3, pp. 310–311).

Early critic Vince Salandria and his brother-in-law Harold Feldman went to Dallas in June 1964 to talk to Helen Markham. Accompanying them was Oswald's mother, Marguerite, who had been very vocal in defending her son, and in all reality should probably be credited with being the first "conspiracy theorist" associated with the assassination. They found Markham and her husband in their apartment, and according to Salandria, "I've never seen that kind of terror. Their teeth were actually chattering." Marguerite asked, "You've been threatened, haven't you?" Mr. Markham replied, "Yes, please go away!" The Markham's adult son, Bill, followed them to the car, and after attempting to get money for information he claimed to have, eventually told them that the Secret Service had warned his parents that there would be trouble for them if they talked to outsiders. (*Praise from a Future Generation* by John Kelin, pp. 76–77).

Acquilla Clemons, who reported she saw two men at the scene of the Tippit slaying, neither of them Oswald, alleged that a man with a gun came to her home afterward and told her to keep quiet. Ed Hoffman, the deaf mute who belatedly came forward and claimed to have seen two men with a rifle behind the Pickett fence on the grassy knoll, claimed he was warned by an FBI agent to keep quiet "or you might get killed." Book Depository Superintendent Roy Truly was evidently fearful until his death because of intimidation from authorities. Truly's wife, Mildred, wouldn't mention the assassination, even with relatives. Sandy Speaker was the supervisor for a construction crew working across the street from the Book Depository on November 22, 1963, which included Warren Commission star witness Howard Brennan. He refused to talk about the assassination for many years. However, in a 1987 interview with author Jim Marrs, he reported that he had received a frightening phone call from coworker and friend A. J. Millican in 1964, in which Millican advised him never to discuss the assassination. Millican told Speaker he'd just received an anonymous phone call threatening his life, as well as the lives of his wife and her sister. The caller had mentioned Speaker and urged Millican to tell him to keep quiet as well. In Speaker's words, "That call really shook me up because Millican was a former boxing champ

25

of the Pacific fleet. He was a scrapper, a fighter. But he was obviously scared to death. And I still don't know how they got my name because I was never interviewed by the FBI, the Secret Service, the police or anyone. They must be pretty powerful to have found out about me." (*Crossfire* by Jim Marrs, p. 319). They must be indeed.

On the day of the assassination, Lee Bowers was on duty in the railroad tower, overlooking the parking lot and grassy knoll area, just west of the Book Depository building. Bowers reported seeing men he didn't recognize in the area of the stockade fence, where many have speculated an assassin or assassins were planted. He also told the Warren Commission about three strange cars driving near his tower somewhere between noon and the time of the assassination. Most notably, Bowers described the driver of one of these cars as holding "a mike or microphone or something," a decidedly unusual feature for automobiles of that era. (*Hearings and Exhibits*, Vol. 6, pp. 285–286). Bowers would also tell researcher Mark Lane that he'd seen "a flash of light or smoke" in the vicinity at the time of the shooting. Bowers was among all the mysterious deaths connected to this case, dying in a one-car crash on August 9, 1966.

Bowers's friend Walter Rischel would later tell reporter Maury Terry, on a May 6, 1992, broadcast of the syndicated television show *Now It Can Be Told*, that Bowers was afraid to reveal everything he knew. Rischel stated that Bowers had maintained in private that he'd seen two men get out of a car carrying rifles, and later saw both men fire shots. Of special interest is Rischel's claim that Bowers mysteriously disappeared for about two days, shortly before his death. When he returned, Bowers was missing one of his fingers, giving a nonsensical excuse for it. On the same program, reporter Craig Rivera informed the audience and his brother Geraldo that Bowers's death certificate was missing, no autopsy had been performed, and the insurance company supposedly hadn't paid the claim because they didn't believe the death was accidental.

The record is replete with witnesses reporting that they were intimidated by various authorities. Could all of them, unconnected and unknown to each other, be having the same fantasies? And if the threats were real, the obvious question is: why would any law enforcement officer at any level, or any anonymous phone caller, for that matter, threaten someone if the assassination was the result of a random act by a lone nut that was no longer alive? But this is akin to asking why any information about the murder of John F. Kennedy was ever withheld, let alone still withheld after fifty years, on the grounds of "national security" if Lee Harvey Oswald was a minimum-wage loser, with no conspirators, who was out to impress his estranged wife.

Julia Ann Mercer was a potentially crucial witness who provided the authorities with unwanted information. About an hour before the assassination, Mercer had witnessed a man exiting a pickup truck carrying a rifle, who proceeded to walk up the grassy knoll. She also saw three police officers nearby who showed no curiosity about this. She got a good look at the driver, and when shown a series of mug shots by the FBI the day after the assassination, one of those she selected had the name "Jack Ruby" written on the back. When Ruby shot Oswald, she immediately recognized him and remembered the name and contacted the FBI again. She told New Orleans District Attorney Jim Garrison, when she met with him in early 1968, regarding the copies of her statements that had been printed in the Warren Commission's volumes of Hearings and Exhibits, "These all have been altered. They have me saying just the opposite of what I really told them."

The Dallas Sheriff's office changed her statement as well, even falsely filing a notarized affidavit swearing that Mercer couldn't identify the driver, despite the fact she never appeared before a notary. "See that notarized signature?" she told Garrison. "That's not my signature either." (*On the Trail of the Assassins* by Jim Garrison, pp. 251–254). Years later, during the House Assassinations Committee investigation, Garrison contacted them and urged them to interview Mercer. He told them he feared for her safety, cognizant of all the witness deaths associated with the case, but would be happy to furnish them with her married name and address if they were interested. Garrison never heard back from them, but he was dismayed to later read a brief note in their published hearings about them being "unable to contact" Mercer.

Another witness associated with Ruby's killing of Oswald was Dallas Police Sergeant Patrick Dean. I am aware that many have suspected Dean of helping Ruby access the Dallas Police Department basement, just before he shot Oswald. I think his testimony can be seen in an entirely different light, however. Dean requested to be heard by the Commission itself after being previously deposed by the aforementioned counsel Burt Griffin. Aside from Dean's damning indictment of counsel Griffin, wherein he described what went on during the "off the record" portion of his appearance (the testimony taken by the Warren Commission is liberally sprinkled with these curious "off the record" discussions), the sergeant also mentioned one of the many unwanted films of the assassination.

Dean alleged that Griffin had called him a liar for saying that Jack Ruby had told him he entered the basement via the main street ramp. Even more telling was Dean's assertion that Griffin had bluntly informed him: "Jack Ruby did not tell you that he had thought or planned to kill Oswald two nights prior." Dean also mentioned that Griffin had alluded to the fact that "he would help me and that he felt that I would probably need some help in the future." Then, unsolicited by the disinterested Commission members (which in this case actually included Earl Warren himself), Dean spoke of receiving a phone call from a man in Victoria, Canada, who ". . . had a reel of movie film that he had taken the day of the assassination and that these—or the camera was on the President at the time of the assassination and he described to me the position as to where he was, which was across and in trajectory of the line of fire, and that he felt in addition to the assassination that he had gotten the School Book Depository." Dean had mentioned this to Griffin in his earlier testimony and indicated that the FBI had been given the man's name as well. Predictably, when Dean finished bringing up this unwanted subject once again, Chief Counsel J. Lee Rankin didn't even acknowledge the matter, as is seen in this exchange:

DEAN: . . . This man told me that he had read something about my testimony and that he asked me would it be all right for him to send it to me, and I told him, "Yes," and I said I was supposed to go back to the Warren Commission and he could send it to me, and I would make it available for them. This was just additional information that I told Mr. Griffin that I was—this is an example—I was there to help them in any way I could.
RANKIN: Now, the differences in your testimony that Mr. Griffin was discussing with you off the record, you have gone into that in detail on the record, haven't you, in your deposition?
(*Hearings and Exhibits*, Vol. 5, pp. 254–258).

Dean was referring to Canadian Ralph Simpson here. Like much of the photographic record from that day, Simpson's film—if it truly showed anything of significance—was unwanted by the authorities and remains shrouded in mystery. From Dean's testimony, it is unclear if he ever received the film, and if so whether he gave it to the Commission.

Another Canadian, Norman Similas, told a similar story, although he claimed one of his pictures captured the Texas School Book Depository building's sixth floor window at the moment shots were being fired, and that it revealed two figures there. The film has never been seen by the public—if it ever existed. I had an interesting email exchange with Similas in February 2004, but I was left a bit confused by it all. He mentioned that publisher John Bassitt "lost the negs to what was the most newsworthy story in the last 100 years" and claimed that shortly thereafter Bassitt "became the head of the Canadian version of the CIA." I did a bit of research and discovered that John Bassett was indeed a prominent figure in Canadian journalism, and coincidentally was a good friend of Robert Kennedy and even a pallbearer at his funeral. There was no mention in his *New York Times* obituary of any affiliation with the intelligence community.

Similas was nothing if not interesting. In his rather disjointed style, he told me, ". . . the photo editor died a month after loosing [sic] the film the reporter for the Newspaper that gave the negs to the photo editor left the newspaper very shortly there after if I could believe the photo editor who died. . . . You can understand that I tried on many occations [sic] to find him to get the negs . . . I have not seen or heard of any body calling the radio station in Hamilton Ontario that aired my eyewitness account at aprox 25 mins after the shooting, I think the station call letters were CHML . . . I stand by this and the story that KG Armstrong wrote for LIBERTY magazine and do not believe his story that he gave to the RCMP. . . ." In his last email reply to me, Similas stated, "I had no less than 60 hours of telephone conversations with Mark Lane and he proved everything that I told him to be the truth. . . ." I emailed Mark Lane about this, and he told me he had "no recollection" of it, and that the fact he didn't write about Similas tended to indicate he'd been unable to verify his claims.

The authorities were desperate to dismiss any claims that Oswald and Ruby knew each other. Dallas District Attorney Bill Alexander admitted, early on, that the Dallas Police had received "about 100" reports of a connection between Oswald and Ruby. (*Dallas Morning News*, November 26, 1963). William D. Crowe, who went by the stage name of Bill DeMar, was an entertainer who had performed at Ruby's Carousel Club. He told the Associated Press on November 25, 1963, that he was "positive" he'd seen Oswald in the club and he had even participated in his memory act, about a week before the assassination. By the time he testified to the Warren Commission, Crowe was much less certain of this. Crowe did tell counsel Leon Hubert that he'd been advised at one point by "American News" or "American Broadcasting" to "make myself scarce or to hide out or to move" due to the fact "my life would be in danger." Crowe also mentioned that the Carousel Club's drummer, Bill Willis, "seemed to remember Lee Harvey Oswald sitting in the front row" at the club one night. (*Hearings and Exhibits*, Vol. 15, pp. 105–111).

Carousel Club master of ceremonies Wally Weston claimed that he'd punched Oswald after the future alleged assassin called him a "communist" during his act. Weston described an angry Jack Ruby grabbing Oswald and telling him, "You son of a bitch, I told you never to come in here." (*New York Daily News*, July 18, 1976). Weston was married to Ruby's stripper Bobbie Louise Meserole, who danced under the name of Shari Angel. Angel would verify this story to British researcher Ian Griggs in a 1994 interview. When Griggs asked her if Oswald had ever been in the Carousel Club, Angel replied, "Oh, yeah," and told him that she'd ". . . seen him about three or four times in the club."

An FBI report dated February 3, 1976, described a meeting of Carousel Club employees that took place a few weeks after the assassination. The memo quoted stripper Kathy Kay as saying "she had danced with the man who shot President Kennedy about one month before the shooting, which was about a week before Weston slugged the customer who called him a Communist." A September 21, 1976, FBI report echoed this, stating that Weston "could establish that Jack Ruby and Lee Harvey Oswald knew each other before the assassination of President Kennedy and that Kathy Kay, a former stripper at the Carousel Club, could corroborate his story."

A December 11, 1963, Dallas Police Department report described Oswald being witnessed driving Jack Ruby's car on several occasions. The source was a mechanic named William J. Chesher, who had worked on Ruby's car and claimed that "Oswald had brought Ruby's car to his garage for repairs." When detectives attempted to question Chesher further about this in April 1964, they discovered he'd died of a heart attack on March 31, 1964. According to researcher John Armstrong, Ruby employee Clyde Limbaugh claimed to have seen Oswald in Ruby's office three times. Ruby's stripper Janet Conforto, aka "Jada," told the *Dallas Times-Herald* that she'd seen Oswald in the Carousel Club. Ruby stripper Karen Lynn Bennett, aka "Little Lynn," told FBI agent Roger Warner, on November 24, 1963, that "she was under the impression that Lee Harvey Oswald, Jack Ruby and other individuals unknown to her were involved in a plot to assassinate President Kennedy."

Dallas attorney Carroll Jarnagin was in the Carousel Club on October 4, 1963, discussing a legal case with one of Ruby's strippers. Jarnagin knew Jack Ruby well, and claimed to have overheard him talking with a man he later recognized as Oswald. At one point, the man told Ruby, "Don't use my real name. I'm going by the name of O. H. Lee," which was the alias Oswald allegedly used at his rooming house. Jarnagin also described hearing the two men boldly speculating about Oswald assassinating Governor John

Connally. Jarnagin's notes of the conversation were later reproduced as Warren Commission Exhibit 2821.

A March 4, 1964, FBI report concerned the claims of Fort Worth Judge J. C. Duvall. Duvall stated that Jack Ruby's bookkeeper and bartender Roy Pike had told him, "Oswald had been seen at Ruby's place of business on numerous occasions and had been there just recently." Pike, who used the alias Tommy Ryan, denied this, declaring that "he had no knowledge of any association between Ruby and Oswald. . . ." A March 6, 1964, FBI report detailed the relationship between Judge Duvall and George DeMohrenschildt, Lee Harvey Oswald's refined, much older, and well-connected "friend." Duvall met DeMohrenschildt and his wife, Jeanne, in January 1963, through his position as director of the Good Neighbor Council. Duvall also described discussing Oswald's attempts to have his dishonorable discharge from the military changed to an honorable one during a February 1963 dinner with the DeMohrenschildts. DeMohrenschildt even asked Duvall to intercede on Oswald's behalf.

Rose Cheramie was discovered on the side of a road in Louisiana by the state police on November 20, 1963. She'd been struck by a car but not seriously injured. Police Lieutenant Francis Fruge reported that Cheramie had told him that the companions who had abandoned her were going to "kill Kennedy." Fruge dismissed her comments as the ramblings of a drug addict. After the assassination, Cheramie told Fruge she'd once been a stripper for Jack Ruby and laughingly dismissed a newspaper headline about there being no evidence of a link between Oswald and his murderer by saying Oswald and Ruby "had been shacking up for years. . . . They were bed-mates." Fruge called Dallas Police Captain Will Fritz, but he was "not interested" in this information. Cheramie joined the lengthy list of unnatural deaths in this case when she was killed in an accident in Big Sandy, Texas, on September 4, 1965.

Studying the twenty-six volumes of Hearings and Exhibits produced by the Warren Commission was not an easy task. As Commission member Allen Dulles, former director of the CIA, would remind the others serving on the Commission, "But nobody reads. Don't believe people read in this country. There will be a few professors that will read the record. . . . The public will read very little." (September 6, 1964, Warren Commission internal memo). The government made it difficult for those who wanted to research its record to do so. It printed only a modest number of the twenty-six volumes, and one had to buy the entire set together, at a prohibitive price. The testimony was "disorganized with scientific precision," to quote critic Harold Weisberg. Another critic, Sylvia Meagher, described studying the volumes as "tantamount to a search for information in the *Encyclopedia Britannica* if the contents were untitled, unalphabetized, and in random sequence."

Questions abound about every aspect of the shoddy, incomplete autopsy of President Kennedy, done at Bethesda Naval Hospital. The indefatigable early researcher Harold Weisberg accurately called it an autopsy "unworthy of a bowery bum." Much of the medical evidence indicates that shots came from the front of the limousine, and of course Oswald was allegedly firing from the rear. There is the statement of Parkland doctor Kemp Clark, for example, in the November 27, 1963, *New York Times*, that a bullet had struck Kennedy in the area of the necktie knot and "ranged downward in his chest, and did not exit." Even more specific was the statement of Dallas doctor Robert Shaw, who told *New York Herald Tribune* reporter Martin Steadman on November 27, 1963, that a bullet entered Kennedy's throat from the front, "coursed downward into his lung [and] was removed in the Bethesda Naval Hospital where the autopsy was performed."

These comments lend credence to a mysterious reference in the official record, wherein FBI agents James Sibert and Francis O'Neill signed a receipt dated November 22, 1963, stating, "We hereby acknowledge receipt of a missile removed by Commander James J. Humes, MC, USN on this date." The official story is that the only "missile" located was the "magic bullet" supposedly found on a stretcher at Parkland Hospital. Yet another letter of receipt, from the Protective Research Section of the Treasury Department, dated November 26, 1963, lists among a number of items received from JFK's personal physician, Admiral George Burkley, "One receipt from FBI for a missile removed during examination of the body." And there were the remarks of Dr. Malcolm Perry, who performed a tracheotomy on JFK at Parkland that unfortunately destroyed the particulars of the bullet wound in his throat, and said three times at his initial press conference that the hole looked like a wound of entrance. Perry's remarks were widely disseminated in the mainstream media; UPI, for instance, reported on November 22, 1963, that Perry had said, "There was an entrance wound below the Adam's apple." Needless to say, honest investigators would have been consumed with investigating these questions.

On August 21, 2012, in a column for Lew Rockwell's website, Dr. Donald W. Miller, who'd worked alongside Dr. Perry at the University of Washington, revealed that Perry had informed him, fifteen years after the fact, that "the bullet wound in Kennedy's neck was, without question, a wound of entrance, irrespective of what he had told the Warren Commission." Perry also allegedly told another colleague, Dr. Robert Artwohl, the same thing in

1986. Perry had been badgered into changing his testimony about the throat wound by Secret Service agent Elmer Moore. Moore later felt remorse about this, telling friend Jim Gochenaur that "I regret what I had to do with Perry." (*JFK and the Unspeakable* by James W. Douglass, pp. 309–310).

Every medical witness to JFK's wounds at Parkland Hospital in Dallas described a massive blowout in the back of his head. Exit wounds are invariably larger than entrance wounds, so this was yet another solid indication that at least one shot had been fired from the front. How, then, does one explain the fact that the existing autopsy photos show no huge hole, and in fact reveal the rear of Kennedy's head to be intact? The x-rays show a huge hole on the upper right side of JFK's skull, extending nearly to his hairline. Pictures and eyewitness testimony indicated that Kennedy's face appeared to be undamaged. These conflicts in the medical evidence, which should not exist, helped inspire researcher David Lifton's body-alteration theory, detailed in his 1980 book *Best Evidence*. Lifton found discrepancies in not only the wounds but in the descriptions of the casket Kennedy was transported out of Dallas in, as well as how his body was wrapped.

In June 1999, a bizarre story broke in the press; the bronze casket used to transport JFK's body from Dallas had later been dumped in the Atlantic Ocean, allegedly at the behest of the Kennedy family. The article declared that in February 1966, the casket, which had been at the National Archives, was loaded with bags of sand, drilled with holes, and loaded into a pine box, which was also drilled with holes. The Air Force was in control of this rather incomprehensible project, and the drop supposedly took place several miles off the Maryland-Delaware coastline. (BBC News, June 2, 1999). Whatever this incident meant, it certainly doesn't seem like standard operating procedure.

The Warren Commission failed to call the most essential witnesses imaginable; for example, Admiral George Burkley, JFK's personal physician. Burkley had been in the motorcade, was with JFK at Parkland Hospital, was on *Air Force One* accompanying the body back to Washington, was at Bethesda Naval Hospital for the substandard autopsy, and was the official recipient of all the medical evidence. Meanwhile, the same brilliant legal staff managed somehow to track down Anne Boudreaux, a woman who knew someone who'd been the infant Oswald's babysitter, *and had never even met the Oswalds*. They also deposed Viola Peterman, who'd been a neighbor of the Oswalds in the past but hadn't seen or spoken to any of them for many years. The "testimony" of these "witnesses" gives new meaning to the word *irrelevant*. The entire record is overtly padded, as one wades through page after page of pointless exchanges about a witness's childhood, school record, etc.

However, the failure to properly interrogate witnesses on matters of real importance—as Kevin Costner's Jim Garrison character referred to when he demanded "Ask the question!" in Oliver Stone's film *JFK*, is glaring. There are no innocent explanations for any of this. It has become common for many in the research community to subscribe to the belief that the Warren Commission cover-up was a "benign" one, perhaps nothing more than a reluctance to delve into certain sensitive areas. I would suggest that going to the lengths of locating obscure witnesses, while overlooking the most obvious ones, demonstrates that the Warren Commission members were acutely aware of what they were doing.

Those entrusted to protect President Kennedy in Dallas—his Secret Service detail—failed to respond at all to the sound of gunfire. There is an existing film clip of one agent—probably Henry Rybka—at Love Field, as the limousine prepares to leave for downtown Dallas, being waved off his post by agent in charge Emory Roberts. Rybka throws up his arms in frustration, as if to say, "What the . . . ?" No one was ever able to question Rybka about this curious episode, as he died quite young in 1975, long before this film had been scrutinized. Roberts behaved in a questionable manner that day, at one point evidently stopping agent John Ready from charging toward the limousine after the shots rang out. Later, he would usurp his superior, Roy Kellerman, who was sitting in the passenger seat of the limousine at the time of the assassination (and also showed a complete dereliction of duty) by taking charge at Parkland Hospital. Roberts died before his time as well, in the late 1960s. John Ready died just before this book was published; I had tried earlier to contact him about this, but he didn't respond to a message I left on his answering machine.

Researchers had tried to contact members of Henry Rybka's family for years without success. I was able to track down Rybka's granddaughter, Kathleen Rybka, and had a nice phone conversation with her in May 2012. She was aware of the controversy surrounding her grandfather but told me she didn't know if he was the Secret Service agent in question. She was very cordial, and said her family had been worried that her grandfather had been shot himself that day, but had very little information to offer. She informed me that her father would be the one to talk to, and gave me his email address. She also said she'd be sure to tell him I'd called, and to look for my email. Two days later, I sent Henry W. Rybka, son of Secret Service agent Henry J. Rybka, a long email detailing my questions. He never replied. After a few weeks, I tried telephoning Kathleen Rybka again and left a message on her answering machine. She didn't call me back. I emailed Henry Rybka one more time, pleading with him to at least verify whether or not his father was the agent seen waving his arms in frustration in the film, but again I did not receive a response. I could only conclude that Rybka's son felt uncomfortable answering a simple inquiry about his father, nearly fifty years after the fact, leading naturally to speculation that his unresponsiveness was not due to his father being mistaken for someone else.

Not satisfied, I contacted researcher William Law, author of the important book *In the Eye of History*. William had interviewed many witnesses in the past, and I gave him Henry Rybka's phone number. After some initial difficulty, William managed to speak with Rybka. Rybka assured him that the agent in the film was not his father, but Donald Lawton. He seemed adamant about this, stating that the figure was six feet tall, while his father was only five foot seven. William and I each found it implausible to believe the agent's height could be determined from that film footage. He said his father never talked much about the assassination, until he sat him down in 1970 and questioned him about it. Rybka's father told him, "You'll find out in the next few years, and the truth will all come out." Rybka incorrectly believed his father had testified before the Warren Commission, and clearly was now a believer in the official story. As he had informed William, "They got it right." Rather curiously, Rybka volunteered, without any prompting, that there was never any pressure on his family from the government to keep quiet.

The most obvious agent who failed to perform as expected that day was limousine driver William Greer. Not only did Greer fail to react to gunfire in the appropriate manner—i.e., by instantly accelerating out of the situation—he actually slowed down or perhaps even totally stopped the car and turned around to watch the final head shot. Texas senator Ralph Yarborough, who was riding in the motorcade, criticized the lack of response on the part of the Secret Service agents this way in a sworn affidavit to the Warren Commission, dated July 10, 1964: "I don't want to hurt anyone's feelings but for the protection of future presidents, they should be trained to take off when a shot is fired."

Researcher Vince Palamara has done invaluable work on the Secret Service. When he interviewed Greer's son Richard on September 17, 1991, and asked him what his father had thought of JFK, the younger Greer did not respond. When Palamara repeated the question, Greer answered, "Well, we're Methodists . . . and JFK was Catholic." Greer also told Palamara, "My father certainly didn't blame himself. . . . My father had absolutely no survivor's guilt." (*Survivor's Guilt* by Vince Palamara, beginning of Chapter 8).

Nearly sixty witnesses testified that the motorcade had either stopped or substantially slowed down at the time of the shooting. More witnesses, all identically "mistaken" in the exact same way. Greer, a Secret Service veteran, had to have been extensively trained to accelerate instantly at the sound of gunfire. Instead, he either slowed or stopped the car and turned around twice to look at Kennedy. Privately, Jacqueline Kennedy was extremely critical of Greer, telling her personal assistant, "He might just as well have been Miss Shaw!" in reference to Maud Shaw, nanny to John-John and Caroline. (*My Life with Jacqueline Kennedy* by Mary Barelli Gallagher, p. 342). She would also advise Gallagher to "get yourself a good driver so that nothing ever happens to you." (Ibid, p. 351).

The idea that Oswald was a communist or even a committed Marxist was contradicted by every Marine, with a single exception, who served with him at El Toro Marine Base in California, where the future alleged assassin was stationed from November 1958 until September 1959. It was noted that he was intelligent, and a reader, but his fellow Marines all testified that Oswald, in their presence, never displayed any communist sympathies and did not criticize capitalism. Peter Francis Connor stated: "He claimed to be named after Robert E. Lee, whom he characterized as the greatest man in history." (*Hearings and Exhibits*, Vol. 8, p. 317).

Only Kerry Thornley, of all his fellow Marines, testified to Oswald's interest in communism. Thornley was a very interesting character himself, and it isn't much of a surprise to learn that his testimony is separated from all the other Marine affidavits in the *Hearings and Exhibits*, and that he was granted the high honor of testifying before the Warren Commission itself. His testimony in Volume 11 took up thirty-three pages, which is a clear anomaly considering the other Marines stationed with Oswald at El Toro were mostly reduced to half-page affidavits. If there is an innocent explanation for Thornley's conflicting testimony, it may perhaps be due to the fact that he served with Oswald for a shorter period of time than many of the others who testified, and didn't even live on the same part of the base at El Toro. At any rate, his testimony should be read with a skeptical mind. (*On the Trail of the Assassins* by Jim Garrison, pp. 50–53).

As for the question of Oswald's palm print, which magically appeared on the Mannlicher-Carcano that was alleged to be the murder weapon, even those who were participants in the bogus official inquiry scoffed at it. For instance, commission counsel Wesley J. Liebeler is quoted, in an internal FBI memo dated August 28, 1964 (but not released until 1968), that ". . . there is a serious question in the minds of the Commission as to whether the palm impression that has been obtained from the Dallas Police Department is a legitimate palm impression removed from the rifle barrel or whether it was obtained from some other source and that for this reason the matter needs to be resolved." Of course, neither Liebeler nor any of his colleagues was about to "resolve" anything. In 1984, FBI agent Vincent Drain, who handled the Mannlicher-Carcano for the FBI, stated in an interview with author Henry Hurt: "All I can figure is that it [Oswald's print] was some kind of cushion because they were getting a lot of heat by Sunday night. You could take the print off Oswald's card and put it on the rifle. Something like that happened." (Ibid, p. 113).

Researchers have always been understandably baffled that while no prints were initially found on the rifle by FBI technicians—not even partial ones—a palm print traced to Oswald appeared later after the rifle had been returned to the Dallas police. Paul Groody, the Texas mortician who embalmed Oswald, would tell astonished researchers that government agents came into his funeral home and fingerprinted Oswald's corpse, leaving black residue on his fingertips. This evidence, in conjunction with the fact that a "nitrate" test given to Oswald on the evening of the assassination revealed no traces of nitrate, and thus was solid proof he hadn't shot a rifle on November 22, clearly tended to exculpate, not incriminate, Oswald.

Not only was the rifle supposedly found on the sixth floor of the Book Depository originally "misidentified" as a German Mauser, there was evidently at least one other weapon discovered by the Dallas Police. A film taken by Dallas Cinema Associates, showing the Book Depository shortly after the assassination, caught police officers in the act of bringing down a rifle from the roof above the sixth floor. The officers are seen climbing down the fire escape, gingerly transporting a weapon that, as a high-ranking officer held it high for everyone to see, clearly does not have a sight mounted on it. The problem here is that the Mannlicher-Carcano *did* have a sight (defective though it was). Whatever this scene, captured on film, meant, it didn't help the official thesis and was, like so much other conflicting evidence, ignored and never explained. (Ibid, p. 115).

Fort Worth Star-Telegram reporter Thayer Waldo claimed to have observed a group of high-ranking Dallas police huddling together in conversation about a half hour after the assassination. This was about the same time the aforementioned film was taken. When he questioned a secretary who was aware of what was being discussed, she informed him that they had found a rifle on the "roof of the school book depository." (*Hearings and Exhibits*, Vol. 15, p. 5). Confusing things further, a November 25, 1963, CIA memo would state, ". . . employed in this criminal attack is a Model 91 rifle, 7.35 caliber, 1938 modification . . . the description of a Mannlicher-Carcano rifle in the Italian and foreign press is in error. It was a Mauser." (*Warren Report*, p. 546–548). And Mark Lane pointed out the obvious during his Warren Commission testimony when he held the Carcano up and said, "Although I am personally not a rifle expert, I was able to determine that it was an Italian carbine because printed indelibly upon it are the words 'Made Italy' and 'caliber 6.5.' I suggest it is very difficult for a police officer to pick up a weapon which has printed upon it clearly in English 'Made Italy. Cal 6.5,' and then the next day draft an affidavit stating that that was in fact a German Mauser 7.65 millimeters." (*Hearings and Exhibits*, Vol. 5, pp. 560–561). The term "reasonable doubt" doesn't quite seem strong enough to describe this kind of "evidence."

One of the most overt indicators of conspiracy is the November 8, 1963, letter Oswald allegedly wrote to a "Mr. Hunt," whom researchers logically associated with either wealthy right wing oil magnate H. L. Hunt or notorious CIA spymaster E. Howard Hunt. The letter reads:

Dear Mr. Hunt,

I would like information concerding [sic] my position.
I am asking only for information. I am suggesting that we discuss the matter fully before any steps are taken by me or anyone else.

Thank you,
Lee Harvey Oswald.

The letter had been sent to researcher Penn Jones Jr. from an anonymous source in Mexico City, in 1975. Was the letter a forgery? Handwriting experts concluded it had been written by Oswald, but the circumstances under which it was obtained were certainly questionable. If the letter is legitimate, it strongly indicates Oswald was concerned about something other than his lowly paid job in the Texas School Book Depository when he referred to his "position" and the "steps" that were to be "taken." The date of the letter fits perfectly into a conspiracy scenario as well, being written exactly two weeks before the assassination of JFK.

How can one innocently explain Commission Exhibit 1365 (Vol. 22, p. 617)? The exhibit purports to be a copy of the front page of the November 22, 1963, edition of the *Dallas Morning News*. However, there is a large gray area on the front page, where the subject matter should have been. What was the subject matter? Merely a diagram of the presidential motorcade route. Now the cynical among us may suggest that the area was "grayed out" by someone because the route clearly showed that the motorcade was scheduled to stay on Main Street straight through Dealey Plaza, without making a right onto Houston and then taking that deadly 120-degree left turn onto Elm Street. Of course, this raises many questions, even without considering the fact that someone affiliated with the Warren Commission "grayed out" all the pertinent information. How could Lee Harvey Oswald, or any other lone assassin in wait, have planned to shoot the president from the Book Depository building, when the best information available to him would have revealed the motorcade wasn't passing directly by there? (Ibid, pp. 118–119).

Oswald was never placed in the sixth floor window of the Texas School Book Depository building, where the authorities would claim all the shots were fired from. The best evidence indicates that at the time of the shooting, he was either on the first floor (he supposedly told Dallas Police Captain Will Fritz he was there, but as noted earlier, since none of Oswald's interrogation sessions, unbelievably enough, were recorded, anything he is alleged to have said is questionable), or quite possibly in the doorway entrance to the building, looking out at the motorcade with other spectators, captured on film by photographer James Altgens at the precise instant JFK can be seen to be reacting to gunfire by grabbing his throat. The record shows Oswald was a "rather poor shot," according to the Marines themselves, and none of the genuine experts used in reconstructions, all done under more favorable conditions, by the FBI, CBS News, and others over the years, have been able to duplicate his feat. He had no rational motive, and boasted a decidedly murky background that effectively invited speculation over the extent of his intelligence connections.

Bonnie Ray Williams, one of Oswald's Texas School Book Depository coworkers, ate lunch on the sixth floor on the day of the assassination. He told the Warren Commission that he left the sixth floor at around 12:20: "That is one of the reasons I left—because it was so quiet." He denied that he'd stated he left at 12:05, as was indicated in his FBI report. He didn't see Oswald or anyone else, and Kennedy was shot only ten minutes later, at 12:30 p.m. Carolyn Arnold, meanwhile, told the *Dallas Morning News* in 1978 that she, like so many others, had been misquoted in her original FBI report. Her FBI statement indicated she had caught a "fleeting glimpse" of someone she thought was Oswald on the first floor of the TSBD, although she couldn't be sure. She told the *News*, however, that she'd actually reported that she definitely saw Oswald, sitting in the second floor lunchroom eating, at a time between 12:15 and as late as 12:25 p.m. As Dallas Police Chief Jesse Curry would later acknowledge, no one could place Oswald in that sixth floor window with a gun.

The authorities would claim, without any evidence whatsoever, that Oswald left the TSBD after the assassination, at 12:33 p.m. They had to do this in order to get him to the spot where Dallas Police Officer J. D. Tippit would be slain in time for him to have committed the act. According to the official version of events, Oswald left the building on foot, then caught a bus going *back* toward the Book Depository, left the bus when it became mired in traffic, and took a cab going in the *opposite* direction (after offering to let a woman waiting go first, in the manner of all fleeing assassins) *past* his rooming house, and then walked back to it. He supposedly obtained a pistol there and took off on foot, where he is alleged to have encountered Officer Tippit and shot him, then wound up in the Texas Theatre.

Although Julia Postal, the cashier, didn't see him enter the theater, unusually attentive shoe salesman Johnny Brewer claimed to have seen Oswald sneak in without paying, and alerted the authorities. An impressive contingent of law enforcement personnel descended upon the theater in short order, a curious reaction that Jim Garrison analyzed by saying, "One would think that the DPD would have kept a few officers back in reserve when answering a call for a guy sneaking into a movie without paying." The president of the United States had just been shot, barely an hour earlier, and yet all these law enforcement resources were spent on apprehending someone whose alleged crime was sneaking into a movie theater without a ticket!

While the authorities invented a fantastic, irrational flight from his workplace for Oswald, they had a very solid lead to pursue, which they totally ignored. Deputy Roger Craig had reported seeing a man resembling Oswald running down the slope outside the Book Depository just after the assassination, and then entering a Rambler station wagon. (Things fell apart for Craig, the Dallas Sheriff's Department's Man of the Year in 1960, after the assassination, as his testimony contradicted many aspects of the official story. He became yet another unnatural death connected to this case, when he allegedly killed himself on May 15, 1975.) Marvin Robinson was directly behind this Rambler station wagon when it abruptly stopped to pick up the man running down the grass. Robinson's employee, Roy Cooper, was following him in another vehicle and reported seeing the exact same thing. Helen Forrest also witnessed the man running to the Rambler and stated,

"If it wasn't Oswald, it was his identical twin." Still another witness, James Pennington, saw a man he would identify as Oswald getting into the Rambler. These were all separate, corroborating statements, and they represented perhaps the best lead the authorities had, in terms of trying to locate and capture the real killers of John F. Kennedy.

Instead, they relied upon a series of comical witnesses to buttress their ridiculous post-assassination timeline. One of these witnesses, taxi driver William Whaley (who later became the first Dallas cab driver to die in a car wreck while on duty since the 1930s), aptly summed things up when he told the Warren Commission, "I don't want to get you mixed up and get your whole investigation mixed up through my ignorance, but a good defense attorney could take me apart." (*Hearings and Exhibits*, Vol. 11, p. 432).

The man seen running and entering a Rambler station wagon may have been Oswald, or it could have been one of the "fake" Oswalds that had been encountered by witnesses in the weeks before the assassination. Given the nature of these encounters, critics have logically speculated that the conspirators were attempting to frame Oswald ahead of time. To give one example of these "Oswald" sightings, take the case of Albert Guy Bogard. Bogard was a car salesman who had waited on someone identifying himself as Lee Oswald on November 9, 1963. The real Oswald supposedly didn't have a license, but this guy took Bogard on a high-speed, memorable test drive. He also said that Oswald informed him he was going to be coming into some money, and would return and pay cash at that time. (*Hearings and Exhibits*, Vol. 10, pp. 352–356). Bogard's fellow salesman Eugene Wilson heard "Oswald" add the inflammatory comment that maybe he needed to go back to Russia, "where they treat workers like men." (*High Treason* by Harrison Livingstone and Robert J. Groden, p. 132). Bogard was found dead in his car at Mt. Zion Cemetery in Louisiana on February 15, 1966. The official cause of death was determined to be suicide. In the trunk of Bogard's car were a stack of newspapers, all with headlines about the JFK assassination.

Another notable "Oswald" impersonation occurred when three men, two Cubans and an American, visited the home of Cuban exile Sylvia Odio in late September 1963. One of the men was introduced as "Leon" Oswald. The next day, Odio received a phone call from one of the Cubans, "Leopoldo," who elaborated about the quiet American "Leon Oswald." Leopoldo told Odio that "Oswald" was *loco*," and had declared that "Cubans didn't have any guts," and that Kennedy "should have been killed after the Bay of Pigs." Odio was an impeccable witness, and the Warren Commission couldn't discredit her. The incident represented a bold example of how Oswald was being set up as the patsy.

In January 1976, Odio was interviewed by Gaeton Fonzi (later to work with the House Assassinations Committee and author of the book *The Last Investigation*), then an investigator for the Senate Committee chaired by Senator Frank Church. Odio reported that counsel Wesley Liebeler had taken her to dinner prior to her Warren Commission testimony, and at one point he stated, "Well, you know if we do find out that this is a conspiracy you know we have orders from Chief Justice Warren to cover this thing up." Fonzi expressed astonishment that Liebeler had said this, but Odio assured him. "Yes, sir, I could swear on that," she said. Liebeler also invited her up to his room, joked about how good-looking she was, and, in Odio's words, "he made advances, yes. . . ."

Concerns about Lee Harvey Oswald had actually been raised years *before* the assassination. FBI Director J. Edgar Hoover asked the State Department for current information on Oswald on June 3, 1960, since "there is a possibility that an imposter is using Oswald's birth certificate." In March 1961, the Passport Office informed the State Department that "it has been stated that there is an imposter using Oswald's identification data. . . ." Discrepancies in the reporting of Oswald's height and weight have been analyzed by numerous critics, and inspired John Armstrong to develop the "two Oswalds" theory, which he delineated in his book *Harvey and Lee*. Another researcher, film expert Jack White, produced extensive studies showing the many physical differences in the available photographs of Lee Harvey Oswald.

There are perplexing questions about the schools Oswald attended. Frank Kudlaty, assistant principal at Stripling Junior High in Fort Worth, Texas (and in one of those coincidences, a former college classmate of researcher Jack White), provided Oswald's ninth grade records to the FBI on November 23, 1963. The FBI, however, later denied any knowledge of them, and the "official" timeline as stated by the Warren Commission is that Oswald attended Beauregard Junior High in New Orleans that year. Robert Oswald publicly said that his brother Lee went to Stripling, and Armstrong found many former Stripling students who remembered Oswald living directly across the street from the school. To further cloud the issue, Warren Commission Exhibit 1413 documents Oswald attending schools in New Orleans and New York simultaneously in 1953–54! Armstrong discovered other things, like the fact the tax ID numbers on Oswald's W-2 forms from three different employers weren't issued until January 1964, in an obvious post-assassination forgery.

An FBI memo sent to both the White House and the Secret Service on November 23, 1963, disclosed, "The CIA advised that on October 1, 1963, an extremely sensitive source had reported that an individual identified himself as Lee Oswald, who contacted the Soviet Embassy in Mexico City inquiring as to any messages. Special Agents of this Bureau, who have conversed with Oswald in Dallas, Texas, have observed photographs of the individual referred to above, and have listened to a recording of his voice. These special agents are of the opinion that the above-referred-to individual was not Lee Harvey Oswald." Combined with the multiple instances of an "Oswald" popping up conspicuously on shooting ranges and other places in the weeks leading up to the assassination, when he was known to have been somewhere else, this memo demonstrated conclusively that the future alleged assassin was being impersonated by *someone* for nefarious reasons.

The mysterious deaths of those tied in some way to the events in Dallas began almost immediately after the assassination. Edward Grant Stockdale, a friend of JFK's who'd served as his ambassador to Ireland, fell or jumped from his thirteenth floor office in Miami on December 2, 1963. Stockdale had supposedly held a private conversation with Robert and Edward Kennedy on November 26, and afterward told friends "the world was closing in." His attorney, William Frates, recalled that when he saw him last on December 1, "He started talking. It didn't make much sense. He said something about 'those guys' trying to get him. Then about the assassination."

Three people who met in Jack Ruby's apartment with his roommate, George Senator, on November 24, 1963, shortly after Ruby had shot Oswald, were all dead just over a year later. Bill Hunter, a reporter for the *Long Beach California Press Telegram*, was accidently shot in a police station on April 23, 1964. Jim Koethe of the *Dallas Times Herald* was, incredibly enough, killed by a karate chop to the throat on September 21, 1964. Tom Howard, who was Ruby's first lawyer, died of a heart attack at only forty-eight on March 27, 1965. George Senator actually testified before the Warren Commission on the very day Hunter was shot, but claimed not to have remembered the November 24 meeting. Dorothy Kilgallen, well-known journalist and one of the regular panelists on the television game show *What's My Line*, was the only reporter to privately interview Jack Ruby. She supposedly told friends she was going to "blow the case sky high." She vowed, "That story isn't going to die as long as there is a real reporter alive. . . ." (*New York Journal-American*, September 3, 1965). Kilgallen also claimed to have been under surveillance. (*Kilgallen* by Lee Israel, p. 393). On November 8, 1965, Kilgallen was found dead in her Manhattan brownstone. Death was attributed to an overdose of alcohol and barbiturates. There were numerous other unnatural, often bizarre deaths, fraught with conspiratorial overtones, of those connected in some way or other with the death of John F. Kennedy.

Those who have studied this case continue to debate supposedly educated skeptics about absurdities like the single-bullet theory, when the holes in the back of JFK's coat and shirt alone reveal they are clearly too low to have come from a spot six stories above, while exiting from a higher point in the throat area. This location—some 5–6 inches down on JFK's back—is corroborated by where Dr. J. Thornton Boswell "mistakenly" marked the wound on his original autopsy face sheet, and is also the precise location where Admiral Burkley described the back wound on the death certificate. The "magic" bullet, which allegedly caused seven wounds in Kennedy and Connally (including shattering the wrist—one of the body's thickest bones—of the latter), was visibly undamaged, appearing to be identical to the test bullets fired from the same ammunition into cotton wadding. Meanwhile, photos that appeared in the Warren Commission's own volumes of Hearings and Exhibits, revealed that identical bullets fired into a goat carcass or the wrist of a cadaver were severely deformed.

The majority of witnesses who testified declared that at least some shots had come from in front of the limousine, most often in the general vicinity of what came to be called the grassy knoll. In the photos taken immediately after the shooting, spectators and police alike can be seen converging on the grassy knoll area. Very little, if any, attention was paid initially to the Texas School Book Depository building, where "lone nut" Lee Harvey Oswald was supposedly firing from.

A few years after the assassination, someone in a position of authority attempted to actually investigate the murder of JFK. New Orleans District Attorney Jim Garrison theorized that a conspiracy had been born in New Orleans, centered around bizarre pilot David Ferrie, who had intelligence and organized crime connections, and Clay Shaw, the well-respected head of the International Trade Mart. Garrison was intrigued by the fact that Guy Banister, a right wing, ex-FBI official, had an office in the same building with the Fair Play for Cuba Committee, the pro-Castro group run by Alex Hidell, Oswald's supposed alias. Banister died of a heart attack in June 1964, less than a month after his business partner Hugh Ward, who had worked closely with David Ferrie (who was an investigator for Banister and Ward's detective agency), was killed in a plane crash in Mexico. Maurice Brooks Gatlin was an attorney connected to Banister, but he also died unnaturally in 1964, falling from the sixth floor of the Panama Hotel. Banister's secretary, Delphine

Roberts, would admit that Oswald had worked for Banister in the summer of 1963, and claimed to have been present when Banister suggested that Oswald start a local chapter of the Fair Play for Cuba Committee.

On February 22, 1967, less than a week after news of Garrison's investigation was published in the newspapers, his chief suspect, David Ferrie, was found dead in his apartment. Ferrie had complained to Garrison aide Lou Ivon, shortly after the story broke, "From here on, believe me, I'm a dead man." Two typed suicide notes were found at the scene; according to Jim Garrison, Ferrie's *signature was typed* as well. Another important witness in Garrison's investigation was Eladio del Valle, a former influential figure in Cuba who had fled the country, and become a leader of anti-Castro forces in Miami. Twelve hours after Ferrie's body was discovered, del Valle was found murdered in a Miami parking lot. He'd been tortured and shot in the heart, and his head had been split open by an ax.

Garrison's witnesses were dropping like flies, while others were simply not available due to the incredible fact that the governors of the states where they resided (including California's Ronald Reagan and, ironically, John Connally of Texas) would not extradite them, an unprecedented bit of prosecutorial noncooperation. As Garrison described it in his interview with *Playboy* magazine: ". . . the reason we are unable to extradite anyone connected with this case—is that there are powerful forces in Washington who find it imperative to conceal from the American public the truth about the assassination. And as a result, terrific pressure has been brought to bear on the governors of the states involved to prevent them from signing the extradition papers and returning the defendants to stand trial. I'm sorry to say that in every case, these Jell-o-spined governors have caved in and 'played the game' Washington's way."

Garrison was viciously attacked by the mainstream media. One NBC special was so biased that the FCC gave the New Orleans DA an hour of airtime to respond. NBC's lead reporter on the case, Walter Sheridan, was a former aide to Robert Kennedy whose bias against Garrison was appallingly transparent. He actually tried to bribe Garrison's witnesses Perry Russo and Marlene Mancuso, offering them jobs in California and cash if they helped to ruin the DA's investigation. In one of many telling instances, NBC reported that two of Garrison's witnesses had failed polygraph exams. Garrison countered by promising to resign if they could produce any documentation for this claim. They didn't.

Jim Garrison uncovered some amazing information during his investigation. He found that David Ferrie had deposited about $7,000 in his bank account after the assassination, for instance. An unexpectedly fruitful area of research revolved around Oswald's fellow employees at the Reilly Coffee Company, where the future alleged assassin had worked earlier in 1963, shortly before hitting the streets of New Orleans with his pro-Castro pamphlets. When Garrison sent one of his assistants to interview some of the Reilly employees who'd worked with Oswald, he found they were all long gone from the company. That was strange enough, but what was positively impossible to explain away innocently was the fact they'd all gone to work for the same place. Dante Marachini, who started working at Reilly the same day as Oswald, left several weeks after the future lone nut, finding employment at the Chrysler Aerospace Division of NASA. Alfred Claude, who hired Oswald for Reilly, also went on to NASA. Another fellow employee at Reilly, John Branyon, wound up at NASA. Emmett Barbee, Oswald's immediate supervisor at Reilly, went on, as may be easily surmised, to the greener pastures of NASA as well. The NASA connection extended to James Lewallen, David Ferrie's former apartment mate who Garrison found during the course of his investigation, to be living next to Clay Shaw at 1309 Daupine Street in New Orleans. Garrison's investigators discovered that Lewallen was working for Boeing out at NASA. Yet another link was found when Melvin Coffee, who'd accompanied Ferrie to Texas on the eve of JFK's assassination, was tracked down as an employee in the Aerospace division at Cape Canaveral. (*On the Trail of the Assassins*, pp. 134–135). Am I the only one who finds it curious that there should be some sort of natural connection between coffee and NASA?

It was Garrison's contention that Clay Shaw's alias was Clay Bertrand. This was important since the colorful New Orleans lawyer Dean Andrews Jr. had told the Warren Commission that a Clay Bertrand had phoned him while he was in the hospital, after Oswald's arrest but before his murder, and asked him to represent the alleged assassin. Andrews had met Oswald in late June 1963. Andrews told the FBI, in an interview on November 25, 1963, that Oswald appeared at his office "with several individuals who appeared to be homosexuals." Oswald hadn't been able to find work, and he wanted Andrews to open his dishonorable discharge from the Marines as well as check into the immigration status of his wife. Oswald never paid him, or produced the paperwork Andrews requested. Just after Garrison's investigation became public knowledge, in February 1967, Andrews was interviewed by reporter Bob Scott on radio station WNAC in Boston. Here are some pertinent excerpts:

ANDREWS: . . . I just don't want to get involved in it. Besides that, I like to live. If a guy can put a hole in the President, he can just step on me like an ant . . .

SCOTT: Has the government shown any further interest in you?

ANDREWS: Yeah, they watch me. Got a tap on the phone you're talking on now. . . . I just can't see anything will come out of it. What difference does it make? The guy's dead. Start a lot of . . . and, uh, mess up a bunch of people. . . . All I can get out of publicity is a hole in my head. . . . (On Oswald) Oh, he never killed him. All the people know that. He ain't nothing but a decoy. Everybody knows that. . . . You can't win for losing in this game. . . . He's just a patsy.

SCOTT: If we ever open the investigation again on some sort of a nationally recognized or governmental plane, will you testify before a new investigation committee?

ANDREWS: Well, I got the shortest memory in the world. Round about a minute. . . . One day we'll write a book, if you're ever down here, "Who killed Cock Robin?"

(*Oswald in New Orleans* by Harold Weisberg, pp. 140–142).

Andrews would go on to recant everything, and participated in NBC's smear job on Jim Garrison. In a purely coincidental way (yes, there are some coincidences), I became good friends with Andrews's son, Dean Andrews III, about ten years ago. Dean maintains a keen interest in the case, and rejects the official story. He told me that his father became extremely paranoid in the last years of his life (he died in 1981), even to the point of locking the doors of his home obsessively, so that when his youngest son arrived home from school, he couldn't get inside. Andrews was under the impression that "they" were out to get him, and he definitely believed in a conspiracy.

As we know, Clay Shaw was acquitted, and the establishment celebrated another victory over the truth. In my view, Ferrie, Banister, Shaw, and Jack Ruby would have been the conspirators Oswald worked with personally, on the ground level, while far more powerful forces manipulated everything behind the scenes. I share Jim Garrison's theory that Oswald was some kind of intelligence operative who was assigned to infiltrate what he was told was a plot to kill the president, shortly before the actual assassination. At least that's where I think the evidence logically leads.

Garrison was vindicated less than a decade later when former CIA official Victor Marchetti, coauthor of the explosive bestseller *The CIA and the Cult of Intelligence*, revealed that the Agency had worked to assist Clay Shaw during the Garrison investigation. He described how his boss, Richard Helms, would ask in meetings, "Are we giving them all the help they need?" Marchetti also confirmed that David Ferrie had been a CIA operative as well. The agency authored multiple memos about the Garrison investigation and produced the unbelievable "Countering Criticism of the Warren Report" memo on April 1, 1967, which offered strategic advice that seems to have been followed religiously by the mainstream media over the years.

Many critics have speculated that Ruth Hyde Paine and her estranged husband, Michael, were involved, in some way, with "setting up" Oswald as a patsy. Both of the Paines had interesting backgrounds. Ruth's father, William Hyde, had worked for the Agency for International Development, an organization long linked to the CIA. Her mother, Carol Hyde, had been active with the Women's International League for Peace and Freedom, alleged to be a Communist front. Ruth's sister, Sylvia Hoke, started working for the CIA in 1954. Sylvia's mother-in-law, Helen Hoke Watts, was alleged to be a member of the Communist Party. Ruth was very politically active in leftist circles; she'd been the chair of the East-West Contact Committee, which was devoted to bringing about world peace through greater contact with the Russian people. Ruth had a strong desire to master the Russian language, which was the pretense for the odd living arrangement involving Marina Oswald; she would give Lee's wife room and board in exchange for assistance in learning Russian.

Ruth Paine was instrumental in getting Lee Harvey Oswald the job at the Book Depository. Ruth had a 1963 pocket calendar, and written on the March page were the words, "Oct 23," followed by a star and then "LHO purchase of rifle." Ruth freely admitted this was her handwriting, and since, according to the Warren Commission, Oswald's alleged rifle was shipped from Klein's Sporting Goods on March 20, 1963, it certainly seemed significant. In her Warren Commission testimony, Ruth invented a ridiculous explanation, wherein she had written the note after the assassination, but inadvertently wrote "Oct 23" instead of "Nov 23," when she claimed to have learned the information. (*Hearings and Exhibits*, Vol. 9, pp. 358–359). It is important to remember that much of the crucial "evidence" against Oswald, including the preposterous backyard photos, was discovered at the Paines' residence. The strongest indication that the Paines were not merely an average couple who took an interest in the struggling ex-Marine Oswald is a Navy Department document disclosing that Ruth Paine was requesting information about the family of Lee Harvey Oswald in 1957, long before she met the Oswalds. (*Destiny Betrayed* by James DiEugenio, p. 343).

Warren Commission Document 206, p. 66, which was declassified in 1976, recounted a strange telephone conversation between the Paines on November 23, 1963. The FBI had tapped their phones, and at one point Michael Paine was heard to say ". . . he felt sure Lee Harvey Oswald had killed the President but did not feel Oswald was responsible, and further stated, 'We both know who is responsible.'" Michael Paine denied making any such remarks in his appearance before the Warren Commission. Dallas Police Detective Guy Rose told the Warren Commission that, when they first arrived to search the Paine house on November 22, 1963, before Oswald's name had even been mentioned as a suspect, Ruth Paine told them, "I've been expecting you all." (*Hearings and Exhibits*, Vol. 7, p. 229). Critics naturally wondered *why* she would have been expecting them. Fellow detective Richard Stovall backed up Rose's account.

Another bizarre "coincidence" here is the fact that according to his coworker Dave Noel, Michael had discussed "the character of assassins" on November 22, 1963, *before* JFK was assassinated at 12:30 p.m. Central time. Oddly, while Michael claimed he had been at lunch with Noel at the time he heard about the assassination, another coworker, Frank Krystinik, claimed *he* had been eating lunch with him. Krystinik also told the Warren Commission about the strange comments Michael Paine made when they were first discussing the news of the assassination:

> *Mr. Krystinik.* And it wasn't but just a little while later that we heard that Officer Tippit had been shot, and it wasn't very long after that that it came through that the Oswald fellow had been captured, had had a pistol with him, and Michael used some expression, I have forgotten exactly what the expression was, and then he said, "The stupid," something, I have forgotten. It wasn't a complimentary thing. He said, "He is not even supposed to have a gun." And that I can quote, "He is not even supposed to have a gun." Or, "Not even supposed to own a gun," I have forgotten. (*Hearings and Exhibits*, Vol. 9, pp. 472–473).

Michael had done classified work for major Defense Department contractor Bell Helicopter. Michael's father had taken him to Communist Party meetings in New York when he was only thirteen years old. He came from a prestigious background, descended on his mother's side from poet Ralph Waldo Emerson and on his father's side from a signer of the Declaration of Independence. Mary Bancroft, a close friend of Michael Paine's mother, Ruth Forbes, had an affair with future Warren Commissioner Allen Dulles. Talk about six degrees of separation. . . .

Dallas Deputy Buddy Walthers (yet another unnatural death, shot and killed in a motel room shootout on January 10, 1969) supposedly told researcher Eric Tagg that he had participated in the search of the Paine home, and that they had found "six or seven metal filing cabinets full of letters, maps, records and index cards with names of pro-Castro sympathizers." During their late 1970s investigation, the House Assassinations Committee ignored Ruth Paine; in her own words, "They never even called me." When Jim Garrison attempted to look at the tax returns of both Paines, he found they were classified as secret. Other Commission documents relating to the Paines had also been classified on the grounds of national security. (*On the Trail of the Assassins* by Jim Garrison, pp. 71–72).

In the 1990s, researcher Mark Oakes conducted several important interviews with often overlooked witnesses. He was especially interested in the series of photos taken by freelance photographer Jim Murray, as was I. On November 22, 1963, Murray snapped pictures of Buddy Walthers, Deputy J. W. Foster, and an unidentified man picking up what appeared to be a bullet from the grass in Dealey Plaza. Oakes believed the unidentified man, who is seen placing whatever he found in the grass into his coat pocket, was FBI agent Robert M. Barrett. Deputy Al Maddox was Walthers's partner, and he told Oakes that Walthers had shown him the bullet they found. Dorothy Walters, Buddy's widow, sent Oakes a letter in which she stated that her husband had informed her he'd discovered a bullet there. Foster told the Warren Commission that he had "found where one shot had hit the turf there at the location." He also testified to seeing a bullet mark on a manhole cover. (*Hearings and Exhibits*, Vol. 6, pp. 248–253). On November 23, 1963, *The Fort Worth Star-Telegram* reported, with an accompanying photo, that a bullet was found in the grass on Elm Street. The following day (November 24), the *Dallas Times Herald* ran a story quoting Dallas Police Lieutenant J. C. Day as estimating the distance from the sniper's window to "where one of the bullets was recovered" to be one hundred yards. These corresponding reports represent yet another intriguing lead that honest investigators would have pursued. An additional bullet here totally demolishes the official story.

During his sporadic interaction with the press, as he was paraded through the halls of the Dallas Police headquarters, Lee Harvey Oswald seemed to be primarily concerned with two things. First, he was intent upon expressing his innocence publicly. Second, he made several requests for a lawyer to "come forward to give me legal assistance," to quote from the very brief "press conference" held late at night on November 22, 1963. All these pleas for legal representation seem decidedly odd, when juxtaposed against the testimony of Gregory Lee Olds, president of the Dallas Civil Liberties Union, and H. Louis Nichols, president of the Dallas County Bar Association. The president of the Austin affiliate of the American Civil Liberties Union had alerted Olds to Oswald's statements about being denied counsel, and thought his organization needed to check on the situation. Olds never actually got to see Oswald, but he told the Warren Commission that the Dallas police had assured him and a few other representatives from the Dallas Civil Liberties Union that Oswald had declined counsel. (*Hearings and Exhibits*, Vol. 7, pp. 322–325). This was apparently good enough to satisfy him.

H. Louis Nichols, however, did visit Oswald in jail. Oswald supposedly told him he wanted John Abt, a high-profile New York attorney who specialized in defending leftists, to represent him. Abt, eventually tracked down by reporters in Connecticut, stated that he had received no formal request from Oswald or his family, and rather strangely claimed it would have been difficult to represent the accused presidential assassin because of his commitments to other clients. Nichols then stated that Oswald responded to his offer to get him an attorney through the Dallas Bar Association by saying "No, not now." (*Hearings and Exhibits*, Vol. 7, pp. 325–329). All one has to do is listen to Oswald's recorded statements on the subject, and compare them with the testimony of Lee and Nichols, to understand why the rabbit hole is so deep in this case. Remember, at his midnight "press conference," Oswald had complained, ". . . I protested at that time that I was not allowed legal representation during that very short and sweet hearing." It's just impossible to accept that he would, during this same time period, assure the president of the Dallas Bar Association that he wasn't in dire need of a lawyer.

We are ultimately left to play what Donald Sutherland, as Mr. X in Oliver Stone's wonderful movie *JFK*, called a "parlor game." The facts are clear: Kennedy was not protected by those whose job it was to protect him. The Dallas Police, FBI, Secret Service, CIA, Justice Department, and Warren Commission had no interest in investigating the crime and never did, and the official story they fed the public was completely, unequivocally impossible.

I am among those who still find it strange that, while one can see the crowds lined several rows deep all along the motorcade route, up until the minute the limousine made the hairpin turn onto Elm Street, there are only a handful of scattered spectators on either side of the actual kill zone. What happened to all the people? Why didn't more of them attempt to get a fantastic close-up view of the president on Elm Street itself, where there was so much open space on both sides? Whatever this means, it provides food for thought. If law enforcement was restricting access along Elm Street, we've heard nothing about it and there would seem to be no innocent explanation for it.

Why was there almost no professional footage of JFK's motorcade in Dallas, when his entire trip to Texas heretofore had been filmed thoroughly? Oddly, the press bus was assigned a spot far back in the motorcade that day, instead of being located close to the limousine, as was normal protocol. We can only imagine what professional photographers would have caught on camera during the assassination. Vince Palamara, who has studied film of previous Kennedy motorcades more thoroughly than any other researcher, assured me in an email that "the flatbed truck with still and motion photographers (and sometimes even live television feeds) was nearly if not always in front of JFK's motorcades . . . until it was cancelled at the last minute at Love Field."

Without the cooperation of the mainstream media, the public would never have accepted this nonsensical explanation for such a heinous crime. The media, from the beginning, was all too willing to cover up the facts about the Kennedy assassination. Their attitude was exemplified by a December 11, 1963, teletype from the New York office of the FBI to J. Edgar Hoover, reporting that NBC had promised to "televise only those items which are in consonance with bureau report [on the assassination]." ("JFK: How the Media Assassinated the Real Story," *The Village Voice*, March 31, 1992).

Later, CBS News, led by stalwart reporters Walter Cronkite and Dan Rather, would host two different specials about the assassination, each of them painfully transparent apologies for the Warren Report. Cronkite's ridiculous statement in the 1967 CBS documentary on the JFK assassination, wherein he attempted to defend the fact that the network's test had essentially failed to duplicate Oswald's miraculous shooting, was especially memorable: "It seems reasonable to say that an expert could fire that rifle in five seconds. It seems equally reasonable to say that Oswald, under normal circumstances, would take longer. But these were not normal circumstances. Oswald was shooting at a president." It's hard to argue with logic like that. And even though the names of the reporters, directors, and producers change, the passionate desire to bolster the lone-nut story remains. To cite just one example, the 2003 ABC documentary *Beyond Conspiracy*, hosted by Peter Jennings, was beyond awful and no improvement at all on the earlier CBS efforts.

The media continues to distort the truth about the Kennedy assassination. Actor Tom Hanks, having failed in his efforts to produce a miniseries for HBO based on the Vincent Bugliosi Warren Report rewrite *Reclaiming History*, did produce the horrendous 2013 movie *Parkland*, which thankfully bombed at the box office. "We're going to do the American public a service," Hanks told *Time* magazine. "A lot of conspiracy types are going to be upset." Shock jock radio hosts like Howard Stern admonish their impressionable listeners about the absurdity of "conspiracy theories" and consistently maintain that Oswald alone killed Kennedy.

Popular author Stephen King's book *11/22/63* postulates, to no one's surprise, that Oswald did it. King's grasp of the subject matter was such that he told National Public Radio, in November 2011, that Oswald's "mother was a domineering force in his life. Lee slept with her until he was eleven, and until he was thirteen years old a weekly ritual was that he would take off all his clothes so she could look at him and see whether or not he was getting manly yet." There is no known source for this inflammatory statement, although it sounds like the same sort of contrived psychobabble utilized extensively by author Don DeLillo in his novel *Libra*. King would tell Errol Morris in the November 10, 2011, edition of the *New York Times* that he put the probability of Oswald being guilty at "98 percent, maybe even 99" and called him a "dangerous little fame junkie." King admitted being influenced by Thomas Mallon's fanciful novel *Mrs. Paine's Garage*, and clearly accepted as gospel all the dubious testimony of Ruth Paine. And native New Englander King acknowledged that he'd "never loved" Kennedy. In another interview with the Sixth Floor Museum, King labeled Oswald "a little shit, basically."

Virtually every program devoted to the subject that has ever appeared on American television, outside of Nigel Turner's impressive series *The Men Who Killed the President*, trumpets the party line that a lone assassin was responsible for what happened in Dallas. Right wing Fox News star Bill O'Reilly, who in the past expressed his view that there was a conspiracy, wrote yet another Oswald-acted-alone book, *Killing Kennedy*, which was heavily publicized by the reliable mainstream media. Actor James Franco, in a September 9, 2012, piece for the *Huffington Post*, waxed rhapsodic about the Warren Report. In September 2012, Jesse Ventura's article about 9/11 was scheduled to appear in the *Huffington Post*, but it was axed by the high-profile founder. Ariana Huffington is well known to strictly forbid the dissemination of any "conspiracy theories" in the articles she publishes, as she told *We Are Change* stalwart Luke Rudkowski in an interview shortly afterward.

"Leftist" journalists such as Alexander Cockburn and the late Christopher Hitchens regularly denigrated the Kennedy legacy and swallowed the lone-assassin nonsense. Even Seymour Hersh, who has done some important investigative work on other subjects, penned the sensationalist anti-Kennedy book *The Dark Side of Camelot*. In a 1998 letter to a San Francisco bus driver, Hersh wrote, "You're right in believing, if that's what your letter suggested, that there might have been some justice—one reviewer wrote 'rough justice'—in John F. Kennedy's terrible death by assassination. . . ." The Kennedys are nominally thought of as "liberals" by the public, but it's pretty clear that most of the "left" treats them quite differently than they treated Woodrow Wilson, Franklin D. Roosevelt, Harry Truman, and other well-known "liberal" luminaries.

Once Judith Campbell Exner burst upon the scene in the mid-1970s with her dubious allegations regarding JFK's sexual affairs and mob connections, a genuine anti-Kennedy campaign gained momentum in the mainstream media. Exner's story was introduced to the public during a press conference on December 17, 1975. Dramatically donning large sunglasses, Exner initially denied any knowledge of underworld activities, which made her future, ever-changing assertions all the more laughable. Thanks largely to the blind acceptance of her story by the same establishment press that refused to even consider any "conspiracy theory," even those supposedly close to the Kennedys began to blame Robert Kennedy—and ultimately JFK himself—for the assassination. Jim DiEugenio, author of the important books *Destiny Betrayed* and *Reclaiming Parkland*, covered this topic beautifully in an article for *Probe* magazine, titled "The Posthumous Assassination of JFK."

LBJ was the first to publicly postulate this ridiculous theory with his declaration "Kennedy was trying to get Castro, but Castro got to him first" during an interview with journalist Howard K. Smith. Nicholas Katzenbach would tell author David Talbot, "My own feeling was that Bobby was worried that there might be some conspiracy and that it might be his fault. . . . . It might very well have been that he was worried that the investigation would somehow point back to him." (*Brothers* by David Talbot, p. 277). Longtime Democratic Party insider Joseph Califano wrote, "I came to share LBJ's view [that Castro 'got him first']. . . . Over the years I have come to believe that the paroxysms of grief that tormented Robert Kennedy for years after his brother's death arose, at least in part, from a sense that his efforts to eliminate Castro led to his brother's assassination." (*Inside: A Public and Private Life* by Joseph A. Califano Jr., p. 126). Reliable mainstream journalist Evan Thomas, grandson of perennial Socialist presidential candidate Norman Thomas, who wrote a biography of Robert Kennedy, also pushed this "blame Bobby" theme. Thomas would tell ABC News, in an interview, that RFK had "a fear that he had somehow gotten his own brother killed" since the efforts to kill Castro "had backfired in some terrible way."

The notion that RFK or JFK approved of the CIA plots to kill Castro is absurd. RFK assistants Peter Edelman and Adam Walinsky would recount how the former attorney general exploded in rage after reading former OSS agent Jack Anderson's March 7, 1967, newspaper column that first insinuated RFK had been the mastermind behind the plots. "I didn't start it. I stopped it. I found out that some people were going to try an attempt on Castro's life and turned it off," RFK told them. (*Robert Kennedy and His Times* by Arthur Schlesinger Jr., p. 532). There are credible accounts that RFK was extremely angered in May 1962 to discover mobster Sam Giancana (alleged by Judith Exner to be JFK's pal and another of her lovers) had been used in an operation, and summarily ordered the CIA to clear such projects in the future with the Justice Department. Declassified CIA documents revealed that the Agency hadn't briefed the Kennedy brothers on the nefarious use of the Mafia in their Cuban escapades. Researcher Peter Dale Scott has shown how, after March 1963, the Kennedy administration clearly did not sanction such anti-Castro activities. JFK would tell *New York Times* reporter Tad Szulc that he was under "extreme pressure" to approve assassination attempts against Castro, but he agreed with Szulc's assessment that such a plan would be disastrous.

The mainstream media continues to infer that the Kennedys at least approved of the plots to assassinate Castro, and quite possibly were the driving force behind them. A story in the August 5, 2012, *Boston Globe* typified this kind of coverage. The article bore the antagonistic headline "Kennedys Keep Vise-Grip on RFK Papers." Ostensibly about RFK's collected papers archived at the John F. Kennedy Library, buried within the story were these revealing words: ". . . the US government was trying to assassinate Fidel Castro—an effort in which Robert Kennedy was deeply enmeshed." This was not an individual being quoted; it was a declarative statement by the newspaper. In reality, all of "the Kennedys knew" about the attempts to kill Castro allegations invariably can be sourced back to someone connected to intelligence agencies, usually the CIA.

In 2010, an even more reprehensible accusation was lodged. Former Secret Service agent Gerald Blaine produced the profoundly misleading book *The Kennedy Detail*, with the premise that JFK himself was at least partially responsible for his assassination. Despite the fact that researcher Vince Palamara had interviewed several Secret Service agents who told him JFK had never interfered with their work in any way, Blaine boldly declared that Kennedy "banned agents from his car." The rumor that JFK had "ordered" the agents to stay off the back of the limousine was contradicted by the recollections of all the agents Palamara talked to. This didn't stop Blaine from writing, "None of the agents understood why he was willing to be so reckless." (*The Kennedy Detail* by Gerald Blaine and

Lisa McCubbin, p. 184). Even more amazingly, Blaine himself had told Palamara, on February 7, 2004, that JFK "was very cooperative . . . he never interfered with our actions."

Secret Service agent Clint Hill, who wrote the foreword to Blaine's book, had provided some self-serving testimony to the Warren Commission. He told Commission counsel Arlen Specter that he'd been advised by his superior Floyd Boring that President Kennedy had requested the agents to stay off the special "steps" on the back of the limousine during a recent trip to Tampa, clearly inferring that the edict was still in effect in Dallas. Contradicting himself, Hill readily admitted that he'd left the backup car *four* separate times during the motorcade in Dallas to jump onto the rear "step" of the limousine. (*Warren Commission Hearings and Exhibits*, Vol. 2, pp. 132–144). Boring was questioned about this by the Assassination Records and Review Board's (ARRB) Doug Horne, on September 18, 1996. After reviewing Hill's Warren Commission testimony, Boring explained that his statement to Hill was merely an "anecdote about the President's kindness and consideration in Tampa in not wanting agents to have to ride on the rear of the Lincoln limousine when it was not necessary to do so because of a lack of crowds along the street." In no way had Boring issued a change in policy, or told Hill that the agents couldn't ride on the back of the limousine in Dallas. Hill would produce his own inaccurate book, *Mrs. Kennedy and Me* (also cowritten with Lisa McCubbin), in 2012, which repeated the untrue assertion that he and the other agents had been instructed by Boring not to position themselves on the back of the limousine.

No presidential candidate has ever raised the assassination as a campaign issue, not even in 1976, when public interest was at an all-time high, and the House Assassinations Committee was being formed. The only investigative work that has ever been done on the Kennedy assassination was by citizen activists like Mark Lane, Harold Weisberg, Shirley Martin, Vincent Salandria, Penn Jones. Jr., Sylvia Meagher, and many others. The only professional journalists to truly tackle the subject were local Texas reporters Jim Marrs and Earl Golz—and more recently, Jefferson Morley and David Talbot.

We've only scratched the surface here. Huge volumes have been written by dedicated and knowledgeable people, focused on only one particular aspect of this case. I've tried to emphasize what I feel are the most obvious flaws in the official version of events as well as the most overt signs of conspiracy.

The JFK assassination really spurred the growth of what are dismissively referred to as "conspiracy theorists." Speaking personally, once I realized that the president of the United States could be killed in broad daylight, without a single high-ranking public official questioning what really happened, and without any supposed journalist having the slightest curiosity about the subject, I understood that anything was possible. As we shall document in the pages that follow, the JFK assassination was only the tip of the iceberg.

CHAPTER TWO

THE SIXTIES

"The last thing I wanted to do was to be a wartime president."
—Lyndon B. Johnson

Jim Morrison, lead singer of the rock group The Doors, had a father who was a Navy admiral. George S. Morrison wasn't just any admiral, however. He was the commander of American naval forces during the Gulf of Tonkin incident in 1964. While it would later be acknowledged as a fabricated event, in order to sway public support toward escalating the Vietnam conflict, the incident would result in a swift resolution from Congress authorizing President B. Lyndon Johnson to take military "retaliation" against North Vietnam.

On November 26, 1963, President Johnson had signed National Security Action Memorandum, 273, which was in diametrical opposition to JFK's NSAM 263. While Kennedy's body was still warm in his grave when LBJ's signature changed future US direction in Vietnam, NSAM 273 had, incredibly enough, actually been drafted on November 21, 1963, while Kennedy was still alive. The memo was written by National Security Advisor McGeorge Bundy (more on him later). Why would such a memo have been created, when it contradicted JFK's policy and certainly would not have been signed by him? LBJ let it be known early on that he wanted to "win" in Vietnam, and had no intention of following Kennedy's plans to withdraw completely by 1965.

The Gulf of Tonkin wasn't the first "false flag" of the decade. In 1962, the CIA had attempted to convince the Kennedy administration to approve a maniacal plan called Operation Northwoods. The plan proposed that a series of terrorist acts be carried out in the United States that would subsequently be blamed against Cuba. The agency was still reeling from the disastrous Bay of Pigs fiasco the year before. Kennedy took the blame for the failed attempt at ousting Fidel Castro, despite his own strong reservations about it and the fact the entire operation was planned during the Eisenhower administration and totally controlled by the CIA. JFK reacted strongly to the disaster by firing the top three CIA officials at the time, Director Allen Dulles (who would later serve on the Warren Commission "investigating" JFK's assassination), Deputy Director General Charles Cabell (whose brother Earle, in another of those coincidences, was mayor of Dallas when JFK was assassinated in his city), and Deputy Director of Planning Richard Bissell.

Operation Northwoods represented the CIA at its most out-of-control state. By the early Sixties, the CIA had turned into a truly renegade outfit whose activities seemed anything but traditional or patriotic. For instance, one high-ranking official of the "Company" was General Edward Lansdale, who headed the diabolical Operation Mongoose program that tried, comically and unsuccessfully, to assassinate Fidel Castro. A master of "psy ops" (psychological operations), Lansdale once devised a plan to plant a submarine just off the shores of Cuba, where it would perform a fantastic light show in the night skies, creating an illusion of the second coming of Jesus Christ. Thus, suggesting that innocent Americans be killed, planes be hijacked, and bombings be blamed on totally innocent people, as Operation Northwoods did, all in the name of whipping up a war fever against Cuba, was really not far from standard operating procedure for the Agency. Operation Northwoods was approved by every member of the Joint Chiefs of Staff. To his eternal credit, Kennedy vetoed the proposal.

Kennedy loyalists were instantly suspicious of Lyndon Johnson's behavior on November 22, 1963. His insistence on taking the oath of office on Air Force One before leaving Dallas, which he claimed was agreed to by Bobby Kennedy during a phone conversation, irritated many who had worked for JFK. When RFK found out that LBJ had told others he had approved of the unnecessary swearing-in ceremony (LBJ legally became President immediately upon JFK's death under the Constitution), he was livid, and the brewing animosity between them would grow into a legendary feud. The fact that LBJ forced a devastated Jackie Kennedy, still in her blood-stained dress, to stand next to him during the ceremony smacked of the well-known Johnson sadistic streak. It didn't take critics long to notice LBJ's crony, Congressman Albert Thomas, distinctly winking at the new president in one of the photos of the swearing-in, as well as the incongruent pseudo-smile that was all over the face of LBJ's wife, Lady Bird Johnson. The best-selling book *Johnny We Hardly*

Knew Ye, by loyal JFK aides Kenneth O'Donnell and Dave Powers, went into some detail about the resentment most of the Kennedy people felt toward LBJ after the assassination.

President Kennedy's personal secretary, Evelyn Lincoln, who would later become one of the more visible JFK associates to publicly declare there had been a conspiracy, supposedly told researcher Penn Jones Jr. that "Liz Carpenter [Lady Bird Johnson's press secretary] and the others were really whooping it up" inappropriately during the long plane ride back to Washington, D.C., from Dallas. Lincoln was also deeply offended by how quickly LBJ booted her out of her office in the White House and had JFK's things removed. One of LBJ's first official acts, on the morning of November 23, in fact, was to fire Evelyn Lincoln. RFK would find her sobbing in tears outside her old office, where she informed him incredulously that LBJ had told her to move out by 9 a.m. An outraged RFK interceded and got a small concession from Johnson; Lincoln had until noon to pack her things. (*Atlantic*, online excerpt from *The Dark Side of Camelot* by Seymour Hersh).

LBJ was the antithesis of JFK. Symbolically, the transformation from the elegant, intellectual John F. Kennedy to the crude, overbearing hack party politician Lyndon B. Johnson was a significant one. LBJ couldn't hide who he was, no matter how hard he tried. There are voluminous, appalling anecdotes about him, from his habitual practice of conducting meetings and dictating letters while sitting on the toilet to fondling other women in front of his wife to threatening and bullying everyone around him. His cruel nature was captured for posterity when photographers snapped the proud president holding his dogs up by their ears. "It's good for them," he told the astonished reporters. This was apparently nothing new for Johnson; it was alleged by author Barr McClellan (father of George W. Bush press secretary Scott McClellan) that he'd once killed a dog, as well as a mule, in his youth, and he quite possibly may have ordered the murder of his own sister, Josefa. (*Vanity Fair*, June 3, 2008).

LBJ's press secretary, George Reedy, wrote a revealing book about his boss. The portrait he paints of LBJ is remarkably unflattering. "He was notorious for abusing his staff . . . for paying the lowest salaries for the longest hours of work on Capitol Hill, for publicly humiliating his most loyal aides, for keeping his office in a constant state of turmoil by playing games with reigning male and female favorites," Reedy remembered. "There was no sense in which he could be described as a pleasant man." (*Lyndon B. Johnson: A Memoir* by George Reedy, p. x). Reedy explained that his old boss viewed Robert Kennedy as "the focal point for all the forces who sought the downfall of Lyndon Johnson." (Ibid, p. 6). This paranoid notion began when LBJ was still vice president and grew leery that "Bobby Kennedy was directing an anti-LBJ campaign." (Ibid, p. 70).

Kennedy aide Arthur Schlesinger was hardly much kinder in his recollections of Johnson. Schlesinger noted, "Obviously Johnson's actions in the first 24 hours after JFK's death left wounds which will take a long time to heal." Schlesinger described a conversation with RFK, in which he told him, "You know the worst thing Johnson has said? Once he told Pierre Salinger, '. . . Sometimes I think that, when you remember the assassination of Trujillo and the assassination of Diem, what happened to Kennedy may have been divine intervention.'" (*Journals* by Arthur Schlesinger, pp. 227–228). Interestingly, Schlesinger also hinted that RFK was not pleased with the "investigation" into his brother's death. During a discussion of the Warren Report, "RFK wondered how long he could continue to avoid comment on the report. It is evident that he believes it was a poor job and will not endorse it, but that he is unwilling to criticize it and thereby reopen the whole tragic business." (*Journals*, p. 254).

The election that earned Lyndon Johnson the unflattering nickname "Landslide Lyndon" was a race for the US Senate in 1948, when Johnson was eventually declared the winner over Texas Governor Coke Stevenson by eighty-seven votes. In the July 31, 1977, edition of *The Fort Worth Star-Telegram*, local election judge Luis Salas admitted that he'd certified fictitious ballots for Johnson on orders from George Parr, a powerful Texas political boss known as the "Duke of Duval County." Parr, interestingly enough, committed suicide in 1975. Salas stated: "Johnson did not win that election; it was stolen for him." After this tainted election, Texas journalist Bill Mason, who was investigating the incident, was murdered by one Sam Smithwick, a Parr associate who in turn was found hanged in his jail cell after proclaiming a willingness to talk. (*Crossfire* by Jim Marrs, p. 292).

Murders seemed to follow LBJ. For instance, during Johnson's tenure as vice president, an investigation was launched by the Agriculture Department of Billie Sol Estes, a Texas financial bigwig who had allegedly collected millions in illegitimate federal cotton payments. Henry Marshall was an Agriculture Department official who was investigating Estes and his ties to longtime close friend Lyndon Johnson. On June 3, 1961, Marshall was found shot to death, with five bullets in him, in a remote part of his Franklin, Texas, farm just as his investigation was beginning. No autopsy was performed, and a local justice of the peace ruled Marshall's death a suicide. The *Dallas Morning News* (June 1, 1962) would later inform its readers that President

Kennedy had "taken a personal interest in the mysterious death of Henry Marshall" and that Attorney General Robert Kennedy had ordered the FBI to "step up its investigation of the case."

More than twenty years later, Dallas newspapers reported the belated confession of Billie Sol Estes, who charged that then-Vice President Johnson had ordered Marshall killed to prevent him from exposing his connections to LBJ. In 1985, following Estes's contentions, a Texas district judge changed the official cause of Marshall's death from suicide to homicide. (*Fort Worth Star-Telegram*, August 14, 1985; *Dallas Morning News*, March 24, 1984; *Dallas Times Herald*, March 26, 1984). On April 4, 1962, Estes's accountant, George Krutilak, was found dead, an alleged suicide. Estes was indicted, along with three others, the following day on fifty-seven counts of fraud. Two of those three associates, Harold Orr and Coleman Wade, died unnatural deaths. Estes would later claim that Mac Wallace, the same "hit man" and LBJ crony whom he'd stated had killed Marshall, had murdered Orr and Coleman, too. Most interestingly of all, an independent fingerprint expert would identify a single fingerprint lifted from a box found on the sixth floor of the Texas School Book Depository as belonging to Wallace.

Another burgeoning scandal linked to then-Vice President Lyndon Johnson involved his young aide and protégé, Bobby Baker. Former military officer Don B. Reynolds, who claimed to have been a "bag man" delivering kickbacks to Baker and other prominent Democrats, was actually testifying before the US Senate Rules Committee on the day of the Kennedy assassination. One of the foremost mainstream "journalists" of the day, Drew Pearson, was actually planning to meet with LBJ at his ranch on the night of November 22. Predictably, it was not to confront Johnson with anything; on the contrary, Pearson wrote an attack piece on Reynolds instead. Worries over LBJ's connections to both the Estes and Baker scandals had caused President Kennedy to tell his personal secretary, Evelyn Lincoln, during their last conversation together, that he was going to be replaced on the 1964 Democratic ticket.

Robert Kennedy saw through Lyndon Johnson, and the two would battle each other behind the scenes for the remainder of the decade.

FALSE OPPOSITION

As the war in Vietnam began to escalate in the mid-1960s, organized opposition arose all over the country. While the public would become either enamored with or annoyed by radical leaders of the counterculture movement, such as Jerry Rubin and Abbie Hoffman, a truly independent researcher, Chicago's Sherman Skolnick, began to look seriously into their backgrounds. Skolnick would claim, in a later report, that high-profile leaders of the movement—like Rubin, Hoffman, Tom Hayden, and Rennie Davis—had actually been funded by establishment think tanks like the Carnegie Foundation and Institute for Policy Studies, as well as government agencies like the Office of Economic Opportunity. The notion that anti-government radicals were being financed by the government was a real eye-opener. However, Skolnick had a limited following, and the mainstream media, as always, steered clear of subjects like this. Another organization supposedly funding radical activities was the Roger Baldwin Foundation, which Skolnick alleged had members sitting on its Board of Overseers who had connections to the CIA.

Skolnick specifically charged that Tom Hayden, husband of actress Jane Fonda, was a counter-insurgent posing as a radical revolutionary. He maintained that Hayden had one of the highest security clearances in the country. Skolnick also claimed that Rennie Davis had a publicist that had been an executive with the Public Administration Service in Chicago, labeled by Skolnick as an "ultra right-wing, quasi-government organization." He further stated that this publicist was connected to the CIA through the Public Administration Service. The attorney for the "Chicago Seven," as Hoffman, Rubin, and the others were labeled, was well-known leftist William Kunstler. According to Skolnick, Kunstler had formerly been an officer with the OSS, the predecessor of the CIA.

While Kunstler would go on to defend the most objectionable persons imaginable, such as New York subway killer Colin Ferguson, he didn't seem to like the Kennedys. In a 1976 speech at Southern Methodist University in Dallas, Kunstler stated that he was "not entirely upset by the Kennedy assassinations," inasmuch as he believed John and Robert Kennedy were "two of the most dangerous men in the country." Attempting to downplay the remarks in an interview with *People* magazine (February 16, 1976), Kunstler revealed that he was on board with the newly burgeoning, establishment "left's" view of Kennedy: "What I meant to say was that in retrospect, from what I know about the violent excesses of the Kennedy administration—the Bay of Pigs invasion, the foreign assassination plots, the deployment of the first troops in Vietnam—I am glad they are not around. God knows what would have happened if they had stayed in power."

Kunstler's blatant hatred of the Kennedys brings up a curious point about the anti-establishment movement of the Sixties. Why didn't any of those "radicals" talk about the JFK assassination? Why didn't they protest the implausible official findings of the government, or question the legitimacy of the Johnson presidency in light of that? Surely a genuine antiwar movement ought to question the death of the most peace-loving president in the modern era, a death that precipitated the escalation of the war they were supposed to be protesting. There was the Shakespearean parody *MacBird*, but although it accused a thinly disguised LBJ of complicity in the assassination, it painted a picture of both JFK and his brother Robert that was hardly flattering. In a 2006 *Washington Post* interview, *MacBird* author Barbara Garson, asked if she thought Johnson had been responsible for JFK's death, pragmatically stated, "I never took that seriously. I used to say to people, 'If he did, it's the least of his crimes.' It was not what the play was about. The plot was a given."

McGeorge Bundy had been JFK's national security advisor, and he played the same role in the Johnson administration. Bundy has long been suspect in many critics' eyes. As noted earlier, he drafted NSAM 273, which contradicted JFK's expressed policy in Vietnam, the day *before* the assassination. On November 22, 1963, Bundy informed the members of JFK's cabinet, who were in the air at the time of the assassination en route to a meeting in Hawaii, that it had already been established there was no conspiracy in the shooting of the president. Bundy was communicating from the White House Situation Room, only a few hours after the crime had been committed, when very few facts were known and no one could reasonably have been so certain about the situation.

Bundy left LBJ in 1966 to become president of the Ford Foundation, where his goal was to use their substantial resources to "leverage change in America." The Ford Foundation funded the radical Mexican nationalist group La Raza, for example. Congressman Henry Gonzalez of Texas, mentioned elsewhere in these pages, was appalled at this financing, stating that the president of the Mexican American Youth Organization "likes to threaten to 'kill' what he terms 'gringos' if all else fails. . . ." Theodore Roosevelt's sharp-tongued daughter, Alice Roosevelt Longworth, remarked, "The Ford Foundation's support of provocateurs and revolutionaries throughout the nation is raising numerous eyebrows." The Ford Foundation also financed the autobiography of Black Panther Huey Newton. Senator Edward Kennedy showed some understanding of how things worked when he lamented the "Growing use of domestic spies—in schools, in political groups, at public meetings, of informants who sometimes help to foment the very acts they are supposed to be investigating."

Author David Halberstam quoted one of McGeorge Bundy's colleagues as defining Bundy as "a very special type, an elitist, part of a certain breed of men whose continuity is to themselves, a line to each other and not the country." "Bundy was clearly putting Ford money into the pockets of people who described themselves as social activists, progressives and agents of radical change," author Randall G. Holcombe wrote. "The Ford Foundation also supported the National Student Association (NSA), which was not in fact an association of students at all but an interest group that confronted faculty and students in an attempt to change campus policies. Through the NSA, the Ford Foundation financed the campus rebellion that was a visible part of 1960s social activism."

Jeffrey Hart, quoted by Holcombe, described the Ford Foundation as supporting those "who spouted the most extreme rhetoric, who presented the most exotic appearance, who were foundations of anti-white racism. . . ." (*Writing Off Ideas* by Randall G. Holcombe). One of Senator Robert F. Kennedy's least publicized interests was in examining the role of the Ford Foundation and other groups as a conduit to disguise CIA funding. In an unexplained outlay of funds, the Ford Foundation gave $131,069 to eight members of the staff of the late Senator Robert F. Kennedy on November 8, 1968.

What we can see clearly here is a pattern of regulated resistance, what many on both the left and right fringes have labeled as "controlled opposition." Journalist Bob Feldman put it succinctly: "Are the interests of the people being served by 'dissidents' who are being subsidized by the agencies of the ruling class whom they should be exposing?" The far "left" Pacifica Broadcasting, for example, is funded by the Rockefeller Foundation. Just how "radical" can something funded by the Rockefellers be? Powerful billionaire "progressive philanthropist" George Soros has invested at least $100 million in the arms-dealing Carlyle Group, and he owns substantial stock in military contractors Boeing and Lockheed-Martin. He is also a former director of the establishment's inner sanctum, the Council on Foreign Relations.

Katrina vanden Heuvel, editor of the "leftist" magazine *Nation*, is the daughter of William vanden Heuvel, and a member of the CFR. William was a protégé of "Wild Bill" Donovan, founder of the OSS, forerunner to the CIA. He'd served as a board member of the International Rescue Committee, which was financed by the Ford Foundation and allegedly tied to the CIA. He also served at one time as Robert Kennedy's executive assistant. Veteran antiwar activist Charles Shaw, publisher of *Newtopia*, has linked him with the CIA's Operation Mockingbird, a devious plan to insert friendly assets into key positions within the media. This project was so successful that former

CIA Director William Colby would later state, "The CIA owns everyone of any significance in the major media."

Aldous Huxley is known today primarily as the author of the novel *Brave New World*. He was one of the first prominent Americans to publicly endorse the use of psychedelic drugs. Controversial political theorist Lyndon Larourche called Huxley "the high priest for Britain's opium war," and claimed he played a conspicuous role in laying the groundwork for the Sixties counterculture. Huxley's grandfather was Thomas H. Huxley, founder of the Rhodes Roundtable and a longtime collaborator with establishment British historian Arnold Toynbee. Toynbee headed the Research Division of British Intelligence during World War II, and was a briefing officer to Winston Churchill. Aldous Huxley was tutored at Oxford by novelist H. G. Wells, a well-known advocate of world government. Expounding in his "Open Conspiracy: Blue Prints for a World Revolution," Wells wrote, "The Open Conspiracy will appear first, I believe, as a conscious organization of intelligent and quite possibly in some cases, wealthy men, as a movement having distinct social and political aims. . . . In all sorts of ways they will be influencing and controlling the apparatus of the ostensible government." Wells introduced Huxley to the notorious Satanist, Aleister Crowley.

Huxley's brother Julian was a prominent evolutionary biologist and a founding member of the World Wildlife Fund. He was also the first director of UNESCO. Notoriously, he was the president of the British Eugenics Society from 1959–62. Like the rest of his eugenicist peers, Huxley's distaste for the "common" folk could be found in his public utterances. While in charge of UNESCO, he once said that intelligence testing had determined that "only 10–20 percent of the population are capable of profiting by a university course." Like so many of his ilk, he longed for a "single world culture."

Aldous Huxley came to America in the 1930s and worked as a scriptwriter in Hollywood. His "leftist" credentials were epitomized by his comment "That all men are equal is a proposition which, at ordinary times, no sane individual has ever given his assent." Lyndon Larouche alleged that he also formed several cults "devoted to Isis and other cult gods." Later, in 1952, Huxley returned to America, accompanied by his family's private physician, Dr. Humphrey Osmond, who was connected via Allen Dulles to the CIA's notorious MK-Ultra, mind-control program. Huxley, along with Osmond and the University of Chicago's Robert Hutchins, participated in an LSD mescaline project funded by the Ford Foundation. The proposal would later turn into a four-year experiment sponsored by the Rand Corporation, a front for the CIA.

Huxley began using psychedelic drugs recreationally, and drew into his inner circle noted writer Alan Watts and Dr. Gregory Bateson (ex-husband of Margaret Mead, an early advocate of broader sexual morals). Watts would become a Zen Buddhist guru and founded the Pacifica Foundation, which would push cutting-edge rock music and "leftist" ideology throughout the Sixties on their radio stations, at the Rockefellers' expense. Bateson, meanwhile, would experiment with LSD on mental patients, at the Palo Alto (California) VA hospital. One of his recruits from the hospital was Ken Kesey, future author of *One Flew Over the Cuckoo's Nest* and later leader of the radical "Merry Pranksters" group. Kesey and his pranksters would go on to travel about the country, disseminating LSD to mostly unwary targets. In 1965, Kesey invited members of the nefarious Hells Angels gang to a party at his home, where he introduced them to LSD. How much of the LSD came from Allen Dulles's CIA supply is unknown; former classified documents revealed to the public that Dulles had purchased over 100 million doses of LSD for the Agency.

Kesey's cult handed out so much LSD in San Francisco that it was probably directly responsible for transforming the Haight-Asbury District into the epicenter of the "Flower Power" movement. Bateson set up a free clinic in Haight-Asbury, and one of the staffers was Roger Smith, who was the parole officer for street criminal Charles Manson. Another worker at the clinic was Dr. Peter Bourne, who would later become special assistant on drug abuse to President Carter.

Huxley was also associated with Dr. Louis Jolyon West, notorious for killing an elephant by injecting it with LSD-25 under the auspices of the CIA's mind-control MK-Ultra program. An expert in brainwashing, West was supposedly advised by Huxley to hypnotize his subjects prior to giving them LSD, providing the possibility of steering the experience in a particular direction. West would later be asked by the government to examine Jack Ruby, killer of Lee Harvey Oswald. West had a long background working in the mind-control arena, and he allegedly treated Charles Manson, Sirhan Sirhan, and Branch Davidian "cult" leader David Koresh. Renegade former FBI official Ted Gunderson also claimed that West visited Timothy McVeigh in prison on multiple occasions. West was a director of the Cult Awareness Network, which has been associated with the CIA's MK-ULTRA program. West was a protégé of Dr. Ewen Cameron, who performed countless hideous "brainwashing" experiments on patients during the height of the Cold War, financed by the CIA. The fact that Cameron served as president of both the American and Canadian Psychiatric Associations, and was the first president of the World Psychiatric Association, ought to make everyone question the overall credibility of the psychiatric field.

Aldous Huxley, in a bizarre coincidence, died on November 22, 1963, the same day John F. Kennedy was assassinated. In a US State Department-sponsored speech to the Tavistock Group in 1961, Huxley issued this bleak forecast: "There will be in the next generation or so a pharmacological method of making people love their servitude and producing dictatorship without tears so to speak. Producing a kind of painless concentration camp for entire societies so that people will in fact have their liberties taken away from them, but will rather enjoy it, because they will be distracted from any desire to rebel by propaganda, or brainwashing, or brainwashing enhanced by pharmacological methods. And this seems to be the final revolution." The Tavistock group in California shares the same name as England's Tavistock Institute, an outfit long associated with behavior modification and mind control. The Tavistock Institute sponsored a conference on the Dialectics of Liberation in 1967, and two of the American attendees were black radicals Stokely Carmichael and Angela Davis.

The intelligence ties of Sixties drug guru and Harvard professor Timothy Leary, whose credo "Turn on, tune in, drop out" influenced untold numbers of impressionable young people, are well known. In his 1983 autobiography *Flashbacks*, Leary credited CIA official Cord Meyer, who was allegedly responsible for overseeing funding to the so-called counterculture movement, with "helping me to understand my political cultural role more clearly." Cord Meyer's wife, Mary Pinchot Meyer, allegedly had an affair with JFK before being murdered in October 1964. Mary supposedly had a diary containing juicy government secrets, which was rumored to have been burned after her death by legendary CIA spymaster James Jesus Angleton.

Leary's background was decidedly establishment; his father was an Army officer who taught at West Point. Leary described his father Timothy "Tote" Leary celebrating his birth in *Flashbacks*: "Tote poured an illegal recreation drug (Irish whiskey) from a silver pocket flask into the glasses of his friends: Captain Omar Bradley, Captain Geoffrey Prentice and Lieutenant George Patton." Leary also noted that his mother, Abigal, was good friends with Douglas MacArthur, superintendent of West Point and his father's commander. Leary himself attended West Point before dropping out and entering the University of Alabama. Another indication of his powerful family connections is the fact that his mother called upon an old family friend, then-US Senator David Walsh, to help her son when Leary was embroiled in an honor code violation scandal at West Point.

Leary's interest in LSD had been piqued by author Aldous Huxley, whose book *The Doors of Perception* was responsible for inspiring Jim Morrison's famous band's name. According to Leary, while ingesting mushrooms together, Huxley told him, "Your role is quite simple. Become a cheerleader for evolution. That's what I did and my grandfather before me. These braindrugs will bring about vast changes in society. We [must] . . . spread the word. The obstacle to this evolution, Timothy, is the Bible." One of Leary's more surprising followers was actor Cary Grant, who admitted to using LSD "more than 100 times," often under the guidance of Leary. Leary's boastful claim that "My crime is the ancient and familiar one of corrupting the minds of youth" seemed to validate the fears of his critics.

Leary admitted being an admirer of the loathsome Satanist Aleister Crowley, during an appearance on PBS's *Late Night America*: "Well, I've been an admirer of Aleister Crowley. I think I'm carrying on much of the work that he started. . . ." Crowley himself summed up his core beliefs with this flip statement: "I was not content to just believe in Satan, I wanted to be his chief of staff." Crowley began torturing and killing animals as a young boy, and his own mother came to label him "The Great Beast of Revelation," which actually pleased her son. Crowley believed in human sacrifice, and he considered innocent children the perfect victims.

Author Walter Bowart, who wrote the excellent book *Operation Mind Control,* met and spoke at length with Leary during his waning years (Leary died in 1996). Bowart had come across two separate CIA memos, obtained under Freedom of Information lawsuits; one dealt with Aldous Huxley, another with Timothy Leary. Both were vague in nature, and they indicated that a security division chief was concerned about what other CIA divisions might be involved in. In previous correspondence with Bowart, Leary had stated that he didn't find anything wrong with the CIA's experimentation of LSD on unwitting subjects. He also chastised Bowart for promoting conspiracy theories and writing about government corruption. During a rambling, often contradictory taped interview with Bowart, he exclaimed at one point, "I like the CIA!" At other points, he said, "I proceeded as an intelligence asset since 1962. . . . I wanted my side to win the war. . . ." To Bowart's direct question, "Did you ever willingly work for the CIA?" Leary responded, "Yes! I was a willing agent of the CIA. . . ."

Rhodes scholar and former CIA Director Admiral Stansfield Turner was once asked whether or not the CIA supported Timothy Leary financially or had provided him with LSD. He cryptically replied, "The CIA gave it to those who were doing the research."

Another Sixties counterculture icon, feminist leader Gloria Steinem, had a similar establishment background. She was supposedly raised in abject poverty in Ohio, but somehow she managed to attend the elite Smith College (founding mother of feminism Betty Friedan's alma mater). After graduating, Steinem was awarded the Chester Bowles Student Fellowship, to study abroad in India. In a very odd twist, it appears that she was the first and only recipient of this otherwise unheard-of award. In 1958, the CIA's Cord Meyer appeared on the scene, to place her in charge of an activist group called Independent Research Service. The group was a part of Meyer's Congress for Cultural Freedom creation, which sponsored leftist magazines to counter Marxism. Also through Meyer, Steinem would become heavily involved with the Vienna Youth Festivals. When the Agency's connection to the festivals was exposed by *Ramparts* magazine in 1967, Steinem declared that she approved of the CIA's role. Those who attended these festivals included a young Harvard professor named Zbigniew Brzezinski, future national security advisor to President Jimmy Carter, and Alice Walker, author of many bestselling books, including *The Color Purple*. CIA asset Clay Felker, then an editor at *Esquire* magazine, began publishing articles by Steinem in the early 1960s, promoting her as a leading voice of feminism.

Steinem's personal relationships also contradict her radical image. She spent nine years with Stanley Pottinger, an assistant attorney general to presidents Nixon and Ford who was instrumental in stalling inquiries into the assassination of Martin Luther King Jr. Later, in the 1980s, she would actually date Henry Kissinger. When she was confronted by *New York Times* reporters with the documentation of her CIA connections, Steinem contended that she'd been caught because the CIA wasn't clever enough to hide their tracks. "The CIA's big mistake was not supplanting itself with private funds fast enough," Steinem stated. Steinem's feminist magazine *Ms.* also benefited from substantial CIA funding.

David McGowan has done extensive research on the rock stars and young actors who began congregating together in one particular part of Southern California, beginning in the mid-1960s. His book *Weird Scenes Inside the Canyon: Laurel Canyon, Covert Ops & the Dark Heart of the Hippie Dream* reveals how nearly all of these popular performers came from families with military intelligence backgrounds. Of special interest are all the unnatural deaths connected in some way to these famous entertainers.

"Extremist" groups on both ends of the political spectrum have long been infiltrated by agent provocateurs, under the auspices of the FBI's COINTELPRO and similar programs. In 1965, a group of four calling themselves the Black Liberation Front was arrested for trying to blow up the Statue of Liberty. Three of the members were arrested; the fourth was an undercover cop who drew up the plans and used police funds to pay for the dynamite. (*New York Times*, February 16, 1965). Thirteen Black Panthers charged with plotting to bomb public places reportedly obtained sixty sticks of dynamite from an FBI informant. (*New York Times*, May 8, 1970). A New York detective, in fact, had been in charge of the Bronx office of the Black Panthers and served with them longer than any of those he eventually testified against at trial. (*New York Times*, February 3, 1971). Malcolm X's personal bodyguard, who tried to resuscitate him after he was shot, was a New York detective who'd been working undercover for seven years. (*New York Post*, December 2, 1970). Fred Hampton, the Black Panther who was also shot and killed (by the Chicago Police and the FBI), had a paid FBI informer, who was also head of security for the Panthers, as his personal bodyguard, too. (*New York Times*, February 13, 1974).

Viola Liuzzo was a civil rights worker who was murdered by the Ku Klux Klan following the 1965 marches from Selma to Montgomery, Alabama. One of the "Klan" members riding in the car from which the shots were fired was FBI informant Gary Rowe. In the 1990s, the Imperial Wizard of the True Knights of the Ku Klux Klan in Texas was Robert Leslie Spence Jr. He was also a longtime informant for the FBI and other agencies. (*Texas Monthly*, January 1998). Documents released in 2009 revealed that in the early 1990s the FBI had an undercover sting operation called PATCON, which included setting up its own fictional "white supremacist" group. This was classified as a Group 1 undercover operation, which by definition may involve "activity by an undercover employee that is proscribed by federal, state, or local law as a felony or that is otherwise a serious crime" as well as "activities that present a significant risk of violence, risk of financial loss, or a realistic potential for significant claims against the United States."

George Demerle was the ultimate FBI informant. He admitted that he'd helped assemble bombs during the course of his work. An ex-member of the John Birch Society, Demerle infiltrated, at various points, the Progressive Labor Party, the Revolutionary Contingent, the US Committee to Aid the National Liberation Front of South Vietnam, the Yippies, the Crazies, and the New York Young Patriots (*New York Post*, May 23, 1970).

So we can see that some of the most celebrated leaders of the counterculture movement had discernable links to the establishment they were supposedly trying to undermine. Conversely, it appears that other high-profile leftists actually were connected to the Soviet Union, as far right wingers often alleged. According to former KGB General Oleg Kalugin, in a 1992 speech made in London, celebrated Sixties radical journalist I. F. Stone was indeed a communist. Kalugin claimed that Stone threatened to cut off his ties to the Soviet Union after the invasion of Hungary in 1956, but was talked into remaining a paid agent until he quit in 1968 after Czechoslovakia was crushed by Soviet tanks. (*The Spotlight*, September 7, 1992, p. 3). *The Spotlight* was a courageous weekly newspaper, often unfairly smeared as anti-Semitic.

Certainly no other periodical, in the days before the Internet, covered these kinds of stories. In its April 6, 1992, issue, they revealed the fact that Gus Hall, longtime head of the Communist Party USA, had received $21 million from the Soviet Union over the years in clear violation of US law. In retaliation for this exposé, the Federal Election Commission (FEC) brought an inexplicable $1 million suit against *The Spotlight*, accusing them of "election violations." According to Alexander Drosdov, editor of the newspaper *Rossiya*, Communist Party records reveal that Gus Hall regularly received $2 million a year from the Kremlin until 1991. (*The Spotlight*, January 6 and 13, p. 2).

THE REAL IMPACT OF THE SIXTIES

While those leading the Cultural Revolution frequently had concrete ties to the establishment they were battling, in some important respects very real changes occurred in American culture during the Sixties. In 1920, the number of single women giving birth stood at 3 percent of the population, approximately where it had been throughout the history of the United States. By 1952, the number had doubled, but was still just 6 percent. Thanks largely to the sexual revolution of the 1960s, by 1990 it had grown to 30 percent. (*The Bell Curve* by Richard J. Herrnstein and Charles Murray, pp. 178–179). By 2007, four in ten American births were to unmarried women. (*New York Times*, May 13, 2009).

Divorce rates similarly skyrocketed. Up until World War II, only about eight out of every thousand females experienced a divorce. After a leap upward during the 1940s, the statistics fell back almost to the same point, so that even in 1964 the rate was still only ten of every thousand women. By the 1990s, despite a mild downward trend from the peak figures of the late 1970s, still about half of all marriages ended in divorce. (*The Bell Curve*, pp. 172–173). If anyone wants to know when we developed into the "Welfare State," the statistics are pretty clear here, too. Although Aid to Families with Dependent Children (AFDC) was created in the mid-1930s, with the original intent of assisting widows with children, when John F. Kennedy took office in

1961, less than 2 percent of American families were receiving welfare. From 1966 to 1975, however, the number of families on welfare nearly tripled. (Ibid, pp. 192–193).

While we have seen that many high-profile "leftists" were often aligned with the kind of establishment institutions they were supposedly trying to dismantle, one of the era's allegedly "conservative" politicians had a misleading record as well. Richard Nixon issued the dangerous Executive Order 11490, which provided for the following to take place, in the event of a "national emergency," whatever that is, being declared: the takeover of the communications media; the takeover of all electric power, petroleum, gas and other fuels and minerals; the takeover of all modes of transportation, control of highways, seaports, etc.; the mobilization of all civilians into governmental work brigades, or less politely—slave labor; authorizes the postmaster general to operate a national registration of all persons; provides for the Housing and Finance Authority to relocate communities, abandon designated areas and establish new locations for populations; provides for the confiscation of private property; dismantles the Third Amendment by permitting foreign troops to be housed in private homes. Hardly the kind of thing one would expect from a "small government" conservative like Nixon. Nixon's favorite President, inexplicably, was the very liberal Democrat Woodrow Wilson.

In October 1967, just prior to achieving the presidency in one of history's greatest political comebacks, Nixon wrote an article for *Foreign Affairs*, the official periodical of the Council on Foreign Relations, in which he spoke of evolving to "a new world order." While delivering a toast to China's premier during his 1972 visit, the "anti-communist" Nixon expressed "the hope that each of us has to build a new world order." Jimmy Carter, against all odds, made things even worse with his EO 12148, which incorporated all the unconstitutional garbage from Nixon's EO and created a new onerous federal entity, the Federal Emergency Management Agency, which greatly centralized power and would even permit the new agency to assume the duties of the president. (*The Spotlight*, Supplement to the May 25, 1992, issue, pp. B-2–B-3).

Besides being the first American leader to be wined and dined by his alleged sworn enemies in Communist China, "Tricky Dick" also agreed, in 1972, to accept $722 million from his alleged sworn enemies in the Soviet Union to settle the old, unpaid billions in debt from the World War II Lend-Lease era. The settlement allowed the Soviets to take their time and complete their payments by the year 2001. Completely in character, the Communists paid the United States about $48 million during the 1970s and then simply stopped making payments. (*The Spotlight,* November 20, 1989, pp. 18–19). In addition to his "enemies list" and other assorted unconstitutional domestic crusades, Nixon was the first president to impose wage and price controls. He strung the Vietnam fiasco out in search of "the light at the end of the tunnel" and "peace with honor" and inaugurated detente with not only the Red Chinese but our dreaded foes in the Soviet Union as well. Sounding like a liberal Democrat, the aging, supposedly racist Nixon assessed the field of Democratic Party presidential contenders in 1988 and called Jesse Jackson the "best of the bunch." (*The Spotlight,* April 18, 1988, p. 1).

Plenty of activists who came to public prominence in the Sixties were legitimate. Consumer crusader Ralph Nader, for instance, had no powerful connections and has lived frugally without scandal for decades. It's hard to question the sincerity of someone who doesn't own a car or any real estate and uses public transportation. Abbie Hoffman seemed a legitimate thorn in the sides of the establishment, and he was personally involved in protests against the CIA recruiting on college campuses. He asked quite legitimate questions, like why the government would call an outfit supposedly devoted to stopping drug usage the Drug *Enforcement* Agency. I'm sure the debates he had in later years with Jerry Rubin, who'd grown enamored with "wealth creation," cleverly called "Yippie vs. Yuppie," were entertaining. You have to like anyone who wrote something called *Steal This Book,* but I can't help but wonder how Hoffman got into the prestigious prep school Worcester Academy after being kicked out of his public high school for fighting a teacher.

The radicals were certainly right to protest against American imperialism, and the hypocritical nature of our postwar society. Too many of them, however, lauded repugnant figures like Mao Tse Tung, who is believed to have been responsible for an estimated 50 million Chinese deaths. As another honest Sixties radical, ex-Beatle John Lennon, put it, "But if you go carrying pictures of Chairman Mao, you ain't gonna make it with anyone anyhow."

ASSASSINATION OF MARTIN LUTHER KING JR.

The murders of Malcolm X (shot at a meeting in Harlem on February 21, 1965) and Black Panther Fred Hampton (killed during a joint police-FBI raid of his apartment on December 4, 1969) were significant political events that left many unanswered questions. Malcolm X was yet another radical leftist who clearly had little love for the Kennedys. Malcolm issued the following reprehensible remark following the assassination of JFK: "Being an old farm boy myself, chickens coming home to roost never did make me sad, they've always made me glad." However, the assassination of civil rights leader Martin Luther King Jr. had a tremendous impact across the country. King had become especially dangerous to the establishment after extending his vision beyond equal rights for blacks and questioning the class structure itself. He also spoke out boldly against the Vietnam War. There is no question that the scheduled Poor Peoples March on Washington, D.C., would have been a far more memorable historical event if he had been alive to lead it.

Lifelong petty criminal James Earl Ray was the designated patsy in the King assassination. Ray was talked into confessing as the only way to avoid the death penalty by his attorney Percy Foreman, but he recanted three days later and thereafter consistently maintained his innocence until his death in 1998. Just to cite one example of what can happen to a witness who gets in the way of the establishment, consider the fate of Grace Walden. The only person who claimed to see Ray at the scene of the shooting was her common-law husband, Charles Stephens. Charles stated he saw Ray running from the boarding house's bathroom (where the authorities reported the shot came from) with a bundle in his hand at the time of the shooting. Grace declared that Charles had been drunk at the time and wasn't wearing his glasses. Despite the fact that a taxi driver visited Charles's room that evening and found him too drunk to even get up off the floor, the authorities chose to accept his identification of Ray. Grace had seen a man running from the bathroom, too, but she was positive that it was someone other than James Earl Ray. Because of her adherence to this story, Grace spent over ten years in a mental institution.

The authorities had found a comically convenient bundle of "evidence," designed to incriminate James Earl Ray, incomprehensibly left in a doorway near the assassination scene. It contained a rifle, ammunition, a pair of binoculars, and other items. It took officials two months to apprehend Ray after King's murder, as he had seemingly fled to Canada and adopted a series of sophisticated aliases. The lone slug removed from King's body could not be matched with Ray's alleged rifle. Witnesses who were at the scene of King's murder differed on the source of the shot, with some pointing to the bushes below the balcony of the motel where he was slain.

The mainstream media-anointed "black leader," Jesse Jackson, first gained prominence after King's assassination. Jackson claimed to have cradled King's head in his hands as he lay dying, and he showed up on NBC's *Today* show the next day wearing what he stated was the same turtleneck, still stained with the civil rights leader's blood. In reality, Jackson was not even on the balcony where King was shot, let alone in a position to be the last person to hold him. MLK aide Hosea Williams would state, "I knew Jesse was lying, and I had a feeling about what Jesse was trying to pull." On April 18, 1988, the *New York Times* ran a story quoting then-New York Mayor Ed Koch as saying Jackson had used the MLK assassination "in a way that was false and to feather his own nest."

Ray would maintain his innocence over the years, and he repeatedly told researchers about a mysterious "Raoul," whom had evidently guided his actions with the ultimate intention of framing him. Ray was a typical Southerner of his time, but he appeared to harbor no strong political beliefs. Although he'd committed armed robbery in his criminal past, there was no evidence Ray was a good shot, and he'd never physically harmed anyone. The FBI, under J. Edgar Hoover, had written a letter to Martin Luther King in 1964 that appeared to be a thinly veiled instruction to take his own life; at one point, it states, "King, there is only one thing left for you to do. You know what it is." It would seem to any reasonable person that the FBI had a much stronger motive to kill King than James Earl Ray did. To their everlasting credit, King's widow, Coretta Scott King, and her son Dexter worked tirelessly to help Ray get a new trial in the late 1990s, but Ray died before he could be vindicated.

THE RFK ASSASSINATION

"I hope that someone shoots and kills the son of a bitch."
—Clyde Tolson, lifelong friend and roommate of J. Edgar Hoover

King was assassinated on April 4, 1968, and almost exactly two months later, on June 5, 1968, JFK's younger brother Robert F. Kennedy was gunned down at the Ambassador Hotel in Los Angeles. After LBJ unexpectedly announced he would not seek reelection, and Eugene McCarthy paved the way for him, RFK had finally decided to enter the race. RFK's presidential campaign captured the imaginations of young people, who were inspired by his ties to the John F. Kennedy administration and his antiwar platform. After giving a victory speech following his win in the crucial California primary, RFK, originally scheduled to greet campaign workers by walking through the ballroom, was escorted back through the hotel's kitchen and pantry, in a last-minute change by his handlers.

Unlike Lee Harvey Oswald, who was a patsy who didn't fire any shots at JFK, the alleged "lone nut" in the RFK assassination, Sirhan Sirhan, undoubtedly fired shots in the Ambassador's pantry before being subdued. The problem is, while all witnesses placed Sirhan in front of RFK, and never closer than a foot away from him, the autopsy report showed that the fatal shot entered RFK's head from behind, and the powder burns left behind indicated that the shots were fired from at most one and a half inches from him. There was the infamous "magic" bullet in the JFK assassination, and there appears to have been magic bullets flying all over the panty the night RFK was shot.

DeWayne A. Wolfer, chief criminalist of the LAPD's Scientific Investigation Division (SID), was responsible for overseeing the search of the RFK assassination crime scene. Wolfer's reconstruction of the shooting had bullet number one entering Kennedy's head behind the right ear; bullet two passing through RFK's right shoulder pad without hitting his body and traveling *upward* to strike Paul Schrade in the forehead; bullet three entering Kennedy's right shoulder from the rear seven inches down from the top of the shoulder; bullet four entering Kennedy's right back from the rear only an inch away from where bullet three entered, then traveling upward—the bullet exiting the right front chest and continuing up through the ceiling tile, striking a second plaster ceiling and eventually becoming lost in the ceiling interspace; bullet five striking Ira Goldstein in the left rear buttock; bullet six passing through Goldstein's left pants leg without entering his body, then striking the cement floor and ricocheting into Irwin Stroll's left leg; bullet seven striking William Weisel in the left abdomen; bullet eight penetrating the ceiling tile, going on to strike the plaster ceiling, ricocheting down through another tile, and entering Elizabeth Evans's head.

The last shot's remarkable journey is contradicted by the official medical report of Evans's wound, which describes the bullet as entering her head on an upward trajectory. Of course, defenders of the official story could then maintain that the bullet bounced once again, off the floor and then into Evans's forehead, with enough power to lodge itself there. The Evans's bullet is the most "magical" one of all, and shares with the infamous CE399 from the JFK assassination the unique distinction of entering and exiting all over the place but retaining a substantial amount of its original mass. The hollow-point bullet might reasonably have been expected to mushroom and fragment upon initial impact, but this bullet impacted on several hard surfaces and still had enough velocity to lodge in a human forehead, yet it retained three-quarters of its original mass and weight when recovered and examined.

Shooting victim Paul Schrade, a longtime critic of the lone-assassin theory, found it hard to believe the police's reconstruction of the shot that hit him.

According to this, the bullet that passed through RFK's shoulder pad had to have traveled nearly straight up, at approximately an eighty-degree angle, to have struck him. Schrade, who was standing only four or five feet away from Kennedy at the time he was shot, stated: "The only way I could've been hit by that bullet was if I was nine feet tall or had my head on Kennedy's shoulder." An even more disturbing question about this shot is how Schrade, who was walking *behind* Kennedy at the time of the shooting, could have been hit by a bullet that passed through the back of Kennedy's jacket. Interestingly, Schrade presented LAPD chief Daryl Gates with a copy of Wolfer's diagram of the shots and conflicting photos from the reconstruction during a public meeting of the Los Angeles Police Commission in March 1986. He asked for a legitimate explanation for the shot that struck him in the head, but neither Gates nor any of the other police officials were willing to answer him. Later, Schrade requested the return of his photographs, but the police denied all knowledge of the incident, despite the fact there was an official transcript of the hearing and it had occurred in a crowded auditorium with numerous television cameras. (*The Killing of Robert F. Kennedy* by Dan E. Moldea, pp. 86–87).

Evidence that there were other bullet holes in the pantry, which cannot be accounted for by the eight shots Sirhan's gun could discharge, is really impressive and consistent. The controversy began in earnest with the publication of an article, "Truth Committee Releases Conspiracy Evidence," in the May 23, 1969, edition of the *Los Angeles Free Press* by researchers Lillian Castellano and Floyd B. Nelson. The authors published a photograph of what appeared to be bullet holes in the center divider between the two swinging doors at the west end of the Ambassador's kitchen pantry. The photo was taken by amateur John R. Clemente, and the article included an affidavit from his companion that night, John Shirley. "In the wooden jamb of the center divider were two bullet holes surrounded by inked circles which contained some numbers and letters. . . . It appeared that an attempt had been made to dig the bullets out from the surface . . . ," Shirley stated. Castellano and Nelson located CBS Radio reporter Bob Ferris, who had reported seeing the same circled holes in the divider on June 8, 1968. The article also mentioned an Associated Press wire photo with the headline "Bullet Found near Kennedy Shooting Scene," and the June 5, 1968, caption said: "A police technician inspects a bullet hole discovered in a door frame in a kitchen corridor of the Ambassador Hotel in Los Angeles near where Senator Robert F. Kennedy was shot and critically wounded early today. Bullet is still in the wood."

During the relatively small publicity the article engendered, television reporter Robert Dornan (soon to become fiery right wing US Congressman "B-1 Bob") questioned District Attorney Evelle Younger about the "ten bullets out of an eight [-shot] revolver." Younger responded with typical disinformation about the "tons of information over at the LAPD that's going to be made available" and how "not once was there any evidence to indicate that there was more than one person involved in this thing." Dornan, preparing well for his future role as an elected representative, meekly accepted this nonsense. The LAPD, of course, never explained why they ever bothered to place the two wooden pieces from the divider into evidence if there were no bullet holes in them. What other significance could they have had?

Any chance of ever examining this supposed non-evidence vanished when the wood was destroyed, along with the ceiling insulation that contained confirmed bullet holes, supposedly because the department had no room for it. Police Chief Gates, in response to questions about the destruction of this evidence, said that they "proved absolutely nothing." He acknowledged that the LAPD had made x-rays of the door frames before they were destroyed, but added, "The records of the x-rays and the x-rays themselves are not in existence." Now *that* sounds believable, and anyone who thinks otherwise is a paranoid "wacko."

As a result of Paul Schrade's 1975 civil suit to open up the LAPD's files on the RFK case, several LAPD photos were released revealing that the police had photographed the same apparent bullet holes in the pantry divider that Clemente and AP had. In one LAPD photo, coroner Thomas Noguchi is pictured pointing to apparent bullet holes in the center divider. Noguchi stated, in a December 1, 1975, affidavit, that "I asked Mr. Wolfer where he had found bullet holes at the scene. I forget what he said, but when I asked him this question, he pointed, as I recall, to one hole in a ceiling panel above, and an indentation in the cement ceiling. He also pointed to several holes in the door frames of the [west] swinging doors leading into the pantry. I directed that photographs be taken of me pointing to these holes. . . . I got the distinct impression from him that he suspected that the holes may have been caused by bullets."

Vincent Bugliosi, famed for prosecuting Charles Manson and later to unfortunately turn coat and write a massive defense of the Warren Report, provided invaluable assistance to Paul Schrade in this area. Bugliosi was able to find the two unidentified LAPD officers pointing to the alleged bullet holes in the pantry door. LAPD Sergeant Robert Rozzi stated in a November 15, 1975, affidavit: "Sometime during the evening when we were looking for evidence, someone discovered what appeared to be a bullet a foot and a half or so from the bottom of the floor in a door jamb on the door behind the stage. I also personally observed what I believed to be a bullet in the place just mentioned."

The other LAPD officer was Sergeant Charles Wright, and Bugliosi himself filed an affidavit on November 17, 1975, in which he described how Wright had originally, in a phone conversation on November 16, 1975, been certain that he had seen a bullet hole. Bugliosi quoted Wright as saying, when told that Rozzi had stated he was pretty sure that a bullet had been removed from the hole: "There is no pretty sure about it. It definitely was removed from the hole, but I don't know who did it." Bugliosi reported that he set up a meeting with Wright for the following day, but evidently Sergeant Phil Sartuche moved quickly to intervene, and when Bugliosi met with Wright, Wright told him he had been instructed by Deputy City Attorney Larry Nagen not to give a statement. After discussing the subject with Wright for a few minutes, Bugliosi discovered how suddenly uncertain Wright was about everything and realized that taking his statement would serve little purpose.

On December 1, 1975, Bugliosi took a statement from Angelo DiPierro, the Ambassador Hotel's maitre d' at the time of the assassination. DiPierro stated that after the shooting he noticed "a small caliber bullet lodged about a quarter of an inch into the wood on the center divider of the two swinging doors." DiPierro was certain of this: "I am quite familiar with guns and bullets, having been in the Infantry for 3 1/2 years. There is no question in my mind that this was a bullet and not a nail or any other object." In a December 12, 1975, affidavit, Ambassador Hotel waiter Martin Patrusky reported that at the crime scene reconstruction attended by Noguchi, "One of the officers pointed to two circled holes on the center divider of the swinging doors and told us that they dug two bullets out of the center divider. . . . I am absolutely sure that the police told us that two bullets were dug out of these holes."

On September 18, 1975, Judge Robert A. Wenke ordered a refiring of Sirhan's gun, as well as a reexamination of all bullet evidence by a seven-member panel of firearms experts. In their conclusions, none of the panel members could confirm DeWayne Wolfer's sworn testimony that three of the bullets recovered from the victims, including the one supposedly taken from Kennedy's neck, could be matched with Sirhan's gun. The panel could not match the bullets they fired from Sirhan's Iver Johnson H53725 or any of the victims' bullets with any of the original test bullets allegedly fired on June 6, 1968, by LAPD's SID. The panel also examined the bullets found in Sirhan's car on June 5, 1968, which contained traces of wood. They concluded that these bullets had the same general characteristics as the others they analyzed. Sirhan reportedly told author Moldea, "Why would I do that?" in response to a question as to why he would leave spent slugs in his car. (Moldea, p. 176).

Some have been bold enough to suggest that the bullets were actually those removed from the door frames in the pantry and then planted in Sirhan's car in a further effort to implicate him. Inexplicably, the panel concluded that they could find no conclusive proof of a second gunman. That's all that anybody in the major media heard. The *Los Angeles Times*, a bastion of inaccuracy in the RFK case, stated in an editorial on October 8, 1975: "Seven experts, all conducting separate studies of the ballistics evidence, have come up with an identical conclusion: There was no second gun in the assassination of Sen. Robert F. Kennedy. . . ." In reply to the countless equally misleading reports in the press, one of the panel members, Lowell Bradford, was compelled to issue a statement on October 7, 1975, which read, in part: "The findings of the firearms examiners [are] being improperly interpreted by the news media: 1.The examiners found that the Sirhan gun *cannot* be identified with the bullets from the crime scene. . . ."

What do we make of the FBI report dated August 19, 1968, which consists of an interview with William F. Gardner? Gardner disclosed that on the night of the California primary, some unidentified Ambassador Hotel employees had informed him that ". . . bumper stickers were being passed out in the front lobby and in front of the Embassy Room which bore lettering about killing Kennedy. The persons reportedly passing out these bumper stickers were described as being young people, 'hippie type.'" Gardner was given one of the bumper stickers by a hotel employee and described it as being orange with black lettering. Gardner couldn't recall what it said, but declared that its message approved the assassination of JFK and didn't appear to pertain to Robert Kennedy. The FBI report stated that Gardner showed the bumper sticker to Ace Security guard Elmer M. Boomhower, who also told the FBI about it. *New York Post* reporter Jimmy Breslin reported that two people were passing out bumper stickers that, he believed, read "Expose the Kennedy Death Hoax." (Moldea, p. 208).

Author Dan Moldea interviewed other law enforcement personnel who provided further support that there were bullets in the pantry center divider. LAPD Lieutenant Albin S. Hegge told Moldea, when asked if any bullets were recovered from the crime scene, "I know there were some, because they took out the panels. . . . And they took them down to the lab so that they could examine the bullets." LAPD Inspector Robert F. Rock told Moldea, when questioned about bullet damage in the pantry, "Yeah, in fact, I think they took a whole door frame to preserve it, as whatever evidence would be required." He also confirmed that, "in the final analysis," bullets had been removed from the door frame. Sergeant Raymond Rolon reported to Moldea that during the SID's crime scene investigation, "One of the investigators pointed to a hole in a door frame and said, 'We just pulled a bullet out of here.'" (Moldea, p. 237). LAPD photographer Charles Collier told Moldea that he had taken ". . . lots of pictures of bullet holes. I would estimate six or seven." When asked the location of these holes, Collier replied, "In the walls in the pantry of the kitchen and in the doors, too." He maintained that he was directly ordered to take some of the pictures of these holes by DeWayne Wolfer. Collier was adamant as to these all being bullet holes, declaring, "A bullet hole looks like a bullet hole—if you've photographed enough of them."

When shown photographs of the pantry divider with the circled holes in them, Collier positively identified them as being bullet holes. He also reported that these holes were known to be from bullets by SID investigators and that he had witnessed them posing for pictures while pointing at them. Collier provided even more detail: "They ran strings from the bullet hole to [Sirhan's location to] determine the angle. And they would know where the gunman was standing. . . . They wait for the pictures to be taken. And then dig them [the bullets] out." Collier also supported the contention of LAPD Officer Kenneth Vogl, who told Moldea of finding bullet fragments on the pantry floor. (Moldea, pp. 248–249).

SID officer David Butler told Moldea, in great detail, how DeWayne Wolfer removed bullets from the pantry divider. Butler also reported his knowledge of bullet fragments being discovered at the scene. According to the official LAPD story, no bullet fragments were recovered from the scene. Butler was ignorant of the dynamics of the case, and was in fact completely loyal to the official story, so when Moldea interviewed him a second time, and he realized how damaging to the LAPD his first interview had been, he attempted to back off from his previous assertions. (Moldea, pp. 259–261).

When FBI files on the RFK case were released through a Freedom of Information Act request by researcher Greg Stone in 1976, Stone was astonished to find apparent confirmation by the FBI that at least twelve bullets had been fired in the pantry. There were a series of photographs of the pantry door frame, and an FBI special agent had written, in describing them, such things as: "In lower right corner the photo shows two bullet holes [in the left door frame] which are circled. The portion of the panel missing also reportedly contained a bullet" and "Close-up view of two bullet holes which [are] located in center door frame inside kitchen serving area. . . ." The reports that Stone reviewed were based, in part, on a June 7, 1968, search of the kitchen by FBI Special Agent Alfred Greiner, who wrote the report, and photographer Richard Fernandez, who was an FBI employee. Fernandez wouldn't talk to Moldea, and Greiner went so far, when Moldea finally cornered him in his driveway, to order him off his property. (Moldea, pp. 265–266).

William Bailey had been a special agent for the FBI at the time of the RFK murder. He stated, in a November 1976 affidavit obtained by Vincent Bugliosi: "I was assigned to interview witnesses present at the time of the shooting. I was also charged with the responsibility of recreating the circumstances under which same took place. This necessitated a careful examination of the entire room and its contents. At one point during these observations I (and several other agents) noted at least two (2) small caliber bullet holes in the center post of the two doors leading from the preparation room (the pantry). There was no question in any of our minds as to the fact that they were bullet holes and were not caused by food carts or other equipment in the preparation room." Later, Bailey confirmed his story to author Moldea, saying, "I will go to my grave, knowing that they were two bullet holes. There were clearly two bullet holes lodged in that center divider." (Moldea, pp. 268–269).

The *Chicago Tribune* reported, in a front-page story written by Robert Wiedrich on June 6, 1968, headlined "'Felt Him Fire Gun,' Hotel Worker Says": "On a low table lay an 8 foot strip of molding, torn by police from the center post of the double doors leading from the ballroom. These were the doors thru which Senator Kennedy had walked, smiling in his moment of victory. Now the molding bore the scars of a crime scene laboratory technician's probe as it had removed two .22 caliber bullets that had gone wild."

There seems to be, to any reasonable person, overwhelming evidence of bullets in the pantry center divider, and thus more bullets than Sirhan could have fired, with or without the imaginary magic of Lee Harvey Oswald.

Detective Mike Rothmiller, who worked in the LAPD's Organized Crime Intelligence Division (OCID) from 1978–83, reported in his book *L.A. Secret Police: Inside the LAPD Elite Spy Network* that he had "read the detailed file on Bobby Kennedy. Investigators accounted for ten spent .22 caliber slugs in the kitchen of the Ambassador Hotel where RFK was shot dead. Sirhan Sirhan's revolver held eight bullets. Nowhere did the file draw any conclusion about the discrepancy." (*L.A. Secret Police: Inside the LAPD Elite Spy Network* by Mike Rothmiller, p. 106).

Witnesses to the assassination of RFK had much the same experience at the hands of authorities as did their predecessors in the JFK case. For instance, Larry Arnot was the individual who allegedly sold Sirhan the ammunition used in the assassination. Arnot was working behind the counter of the Lock, Stock 'n' Barrel on June 1, 1968, and he told police that three individuals had come in that afternoon, including one he subsequently identified as Sirhan Sirhan, and bought the .22 caliber ammunition. The authorities, although there was not necessarily any reason to assume the two persons with Sirhan had been accomplices in the ensuing assassination, nevertheless had a clear disposition to dispose of them and put Sirhan alone in the gun shop.

At the "trial," prosecutor David Fitts questioned Arnot sharply about the two individuals he'd seen with Sirhan. He then asked him to recall "a conversation with Lieutenant Enrique Hernandez of the Los Angeles Police Department" as well as his polygraph test. Hernandez subsequently had explained to him that he'd been "confused" about the incident. The owners of the gun shop, Ben and Donna Herrick, were angered by the treatment accorded Arnot at the hands of the prosecution (he was, after all, supposed to be a prosecution witness), but neither was called to testify. "They didn't want her to testify, because she wouldn't change her story," Ben Herrick declared after the trial in Ted Charach's film documentary *The Second Gun*. "The sales slip definitely proves the fact that he was telling the truth and then they say the lie detector says he was telling a lie and they throw him off the witness stand. It just discredited the man's testimony and made a fool out of him. . . ." Donna Herrick filed statements with both the police and the FBI to the effect that she had seen Sirhan in the store previously with two companions.

Charach had been in the Ambassador Hotel pantry the night RFK was shot. His film was nominated for a Golden Globe documentary award, and shortly thereafter Warner Brothers purchased the rights to it. Much like *Life* magazine, which had bought Abraham Zapruder's home movie of the JFK assassination and then suppressed it, the media mega-corporation refused to show *The Second Gun*. Charach was the recipient of the usual threats; he had a copy of the film stolen from him at gunpoint, with the thief telling him, "You aren't going to show that film anymore." During a scheduled showing before a panel of the Academy of Forensic Sciences, someone poured oil on the film. When Charach returned to his hotel room afterward, he received a phone call warning, "This time it was the film, next time it's you." Oddly, a NARA (National Archives and Records Administration) document available via the invaluable Mary Ferrell online archives indicates that in July 1968, Charach offered to work as a "spy" for the LAPD, infiltrating the Jim Garrison investigation.

Donald Schulman was a runner for L.A. television station KNXT. Right after the shooting, Schulman was grabbed by Jeff Brent of Continental

News Service for a radio interview. In the interview, Schulman stated, "Okay. I was . . . ah . . . standing behind . . . ah . . . Kennedy as he was taking his assigned route into the kitchen. A Caucasian gentleman stepped out and fired three times . . . the security guard . . . hitting Kennedy all three times. Mr. Kennedy slumped to the floor . . . they carried him away . . . the security guards fired back. . . . As I saw . . . they shot the . . . ah, man who shot Kennedy . . . in the leg. . . ." Brent then asks another question, ending with "Now . . . is this the security guard firing back?" Schulman reiterates that a security guard had indeed fired back at presumably Sirhan and hit him. (*Shadow Play* by William Klaber and Philip H. Melanson, p. 118). Ace security guard Thane Eugene Cesar has been thought by some researchers to have fired the "second gun" in the pantry that night.

One of the most fascinating aspects of the RFK case is the mysterious girl in the polka-dot dress. Several witnesses, unconnected to each other, described an individual who was obviously the same person. When the LAFD finally released their witness interrogation tapes, a clearer picture of this girl emerged. Then college student Thomas Vincent DiPierro, a part-time waiter at the Ambassador Hotel and son of the aforementioned maitre d' Angelo DiPierro, was one of the closest eyewitnesses to the shooting. He told the police that he had seen Sirhan with an attractive woman who had a "pudgy" nose, dressed in "a white dress with black or purple polka dots." When asked repeatedly by the clearly skeptical police questioner why he felt they were together, DiPierro said it was obvious. "Well she was following him . . . and she—like—it looked like she was almost holding him."

Sandra Serrano, cochair of the Pasadena-Altadena chapter of the Youth for Kennedy Committee, was sitting on an exit stairway, trying to cool off from the heat in the crowded ballroom, when an identical woman, accompanied by two men (one of whom she would identify later as Sirhan), brushed by her on the way up the stairs. About a half hour later, after encountering no one else in the meantime, Serrano claimed to see two of the three people rush back down the stairs, with the woman shouting, "We shot him! We shot him!" When Serrano questioned her as to who they had shot, she said, "Senator Kennedy." Serrano ran inside and related her encounter to her friend Irene Chavez and found out Kennedy had indeed been shot. Serrano was interviewed by NBC reporter Sander Vanocur not long afterward and described the girl: "She was Caucasian. She had on a white dress with polka dots. She was light skinned, dark hair. She had on black shoes, and she had a funny nose." (*Shadow Play*, pp. 13–15).

Albert LeBeau was the night manager for Robbie's Restaurant in Pomona, California, who claimed he saw Sirhan at an RFK fund-raising luncheon at the restaurant on May 20, 1968. The man he identified as Sirhan after seeing the suspect on television had been accompanied by a woman whom he described as having a "nice shape, built proportionately." William Schneid, a Pomona police officer on duty at the restaurant, corroborated the story, telling the FBI he saw the couple trying to cross over a brick casing, just as LeBeau had reported. He also stated that he'd seen LeBeau stop the couple. While Schneid told the FBI that the man he'd seen bore a likeness to Sirhan, the FBI summary reported the opposite, stating, "He did not feel the man observed by him would have been Sirhan Sirhan." Schneid described the Latin or Mexican man with dark curly hair, five foot six or five foot seven inches tall, as being in the company of an "attractive" woman with a "proportionate" figure. Schneid was not taken to a lineup to try and identify Sirhan and wasn't interviewed by the LAPD. On June 12, 1968, LeBeau identified Sirhan, for the FBI, from a mug shot as "closely resembling" the man he'd seen in the restaurant. LeBeau also was never asked to try and identify Sirhan in a police lineup.

No tape recording or official report of LeBeau's June 26 interview by the LAPD is in the police files, but an interesting summary of that interview did survive. The summary refers to an earlier LAPD interview of LeBeau, by an "Officer Thompson," that also isn't in the files. The summary states that LeBeau failed to pick out Sirhan from a Racing Commission ID photograph and is liberally laced with direct quotes from the interview. The final sentence states: "Just before the conclusion of the interview LeBeau was asked, 'Could you swear under oath that Sirhan is the man involved in the incident on May the 20th?' LeBeau hung his head and stared at the floor for several long moments and replied, 'No.'" The LAPD's 1,500-page *Summary Report* of their "investigation" was not released to the public until 1986. Warren Report-style, the report dismisses Albert LeBeau by saying he had "initially stated the man was Sirhan, but later admitted he lied." There is nothing in the extant record to indicate that LeBeau ever said anything like this. (*Shadow Play*, pp. 122–124).

As in the JFK case, witnesses reported being threatened. Laverne Botting, a volunteer in RFK's Azusa, California, campaign headquarters, had encountered two men and a woman in the office on May 30, 1968. The woman was described as having an "excellent figure." She was questioned by LAPD Officer C. B. Thompson and picked out Sirhan from a group of photos, but wasn't asked to identify him in person, although she had specifically told the

FBI she felt she could do that. Officer Thompson, in his summary report of the interview, stated that Botting had claimed to have received a phone call in which the anonymous caller told her, "I hear you think you saw Sirhan" and "You had better be sure of what you are saying." Thompson, in spite of Botting's description of the man, which closely resembled Sirhan by any reasonable standards, concluded irrationally, "Witness has obviously made an honest mistake." There is no transcript or recording of this interview either in the files.

Like LeBeau, Botting had corroboration for her story. Ethel Creehan, another volunteer at the Azusa headquarters, called the LAPD on June 7, 1968, and reported seeing the same group. She said she was "fairly certain" one of the men was Sirhan, but didn't want to testify to this without seeing him in person. She too was not given the opportunity to do this. Interviewed by Officer Thompson a month later, she picked Sirhan out from a photograph and also described his female companion, like other witnesses did, as having a "prominent" nose. Officer Thompson, on the basis of the fact Creehan reported "Sirhan's" height as five foot eight, concluded, "It is doubtful if the person she observed was Sirhan." (*Shadow Play*, pp. 124–126).

One witness who obviously felt pressured to change his story was Evan Freed, then a part-time photographer covering the RFK campaign. Freed reported, in a 1992 petition to the L.A. County Grand Jury, that he'd seen another man with Sirhan in the pantry prior to the shooting who was "very similar in appearance." They seemed to know each other and he thought they might have been brothers. Freed stated he was only "about 4 feet away" from Kennedy at the time of the shooting and said "I saw the 2nd man (wearing darker clothing) who had been in the pantry with Sirhan during the speech pointing a gun in an upward angle at the Senator. Based on the sound I heard, I believe the first shot came from this man's gun."

Once Sirhan started firing, everyone seemed to ignore the other man. Freed saw the second man fleeing, pursued by another man yelling, "Stop that guy, stop him!" Freed also reported the police asked him if he heard the man running after Sirhan's companion yelling "Get an ambulance" or "Get a doctor" and that "I told them that was not correct, but they insisted that I had been incorrect in what I heard." Freed gave a description of the man he'd seen pursuing the second man and yelling, but he was not asked to identify him in any way or even to have a sketch drawn. The summary from Freed's first LAPD interview, on June 14, reports that he had seen two men and a woman, who was "possibly wearing a polka dot dress." In a follow-up interview on August 1, no mention is made of this trio, and in a September 11 FBI interview, we learn that "Sirhan was the only person Freed saw shooting."

By 1996, Freed, a deputy city attorney for the city of Los Angeles, reconsidered his previous support for a reexamination of the RFK affair, the purpose of which he stated in his initial affidavit to the Grand Jury was ". . . to help insure that a fair investigation is conducted in this case. I declare under the penalty of perjury that the foregoing is true and correct." When Freed was approached in 1996 by lawyers for Scott Enyart, the then-teenager who'd had his film of the assassination confiscated by authorities and never returned, to support his claim of damages against the LAPD, Freed responded by sending Enyart's attorneys a copy of a letter dated May 15, 1992 (two days after the date of his original affidavit, which was submitted to the Grand Jury), to attorney Marilyn Barrett. Barrett was representing the petitioners, and the letter she received from Freed was a self-proclaimed "corrected copy" of the original affidavit, which was now termed a "letter." Freed instructed Barrett to "discard" the original affidavit because it contained "factual errors." Freed claimed to have sent the original affidavit inadvertently "without reading it first." Barrett reported that she'd never received any such letter or other affidavit from Freed and the original one was submitted to the Grand Jury. (*Shadow Play*, pp. 128–130).

Dr. Marcus McBroom told researcher Greg Stone in a 1986 interview that ". . . a woman in a polka dot dress ran out of the kitchen shouting 'We got him' or 'We shot him.' . . . Immediately after she ran out, a man with a gun under a newspaper ran out in a very menacing way and myself and a man by the name of Sam Strain and the man running the ABC camera we drew back instinctively when we saw the gun." McBroom reported the woman in the polka-dot dress as fairly attractive and "proportionate." The menacing man with the gun was described as an "Arab looking person," and McBroom picked out one of Sirhan's brothers from a series of mug shots as being similar in appearance. Real estate salesman George Green reported to the FBI that he'd seen a man he subsequently identified as Sirhan standing at the edge of the crowd in the pantry, at around 11:15 to 11:30 on the night of the assassination, near a tall, thin man and a Caucasian woman with a "good figure" wearing a white dress with black polka-dots. He saw the woman in the polka-dot dress and a man rush out of the pantry after the shots began. Jack J. Merrit, a uniformed security guard with the Ace Guard Service, told the LAPD and the FBI that he had seen two men and a woman, who "seemed to be smiling," leaving the kitchen after the shots were fired. The woman was wearing a polka-dot dress. Richard Houston stated to the LAPD that he'd seen a woman in a polka-dot dress run out of the pantry shortly after shots were fired. He heard her say, "We killed him." Darnell Johnson saw a "well built" woman in a polka-dot dress, standing along with three men near Sirhan. After the shooting, Johnson saw the woman and the three men leave the pantry.

This woman was seen by many witnesses before the shooting and described by RFK volunteer Susan Locke as seeming "somewhat out of place" in the Embassy Room prior to Kennedy's last speech, with an "expressionless" appearance amid the celebrants. Locke noticed that the woman, who she stated was "well proportioned" and clad in a white dress with blue polka-dots, was not wearing the yellow badge required for admittance to the Embassy Room. Locke pointed this out to Carol Breshears, who was in charge of the "Kennedy Girls" support organization, who then alerted a security guard. It is not known what, if any, action the security guard took. Junior high school student Jeanette Prudhomme told the police she'd seen Sirhan with another man and a woman and that the woman was "wearing a white dress with black polka dots. . . ." (*Shadow Play*, pp. 131–132). All this makes laughable the assertion by Chief Prosecutor Lynn Compton, during Sirhan's trial, that the "FBI and the Los Angeles Police Department have interviewed literally thousands of people running out every suggestion, lead or possibility, and they have failed to find any connection between Sirhan and anyone else." (*New York Times*, February 28, 1969, p. 14).

In most all the witness reports of the polka-dot woman and/or Sirhan accomplices, the LAPD would either ignore or distort their testimony. George Green's initial statement to the FBI about the polka-dot woman wasn't a part of his subsequent LAPD interview. Both Lonny Worthy, who'd also reported seeing the woman in the polka-dot dress to the FBI, and Susan Locke, saw this part of their story disappear when they were interviewed by the LAPD. Jeanette Prudhomme's testimony was discounted in the LAPD *Summary Report* with a snide "She was shown photographs of Sirhan, but was unable to make an identification." Richard Houston's account was left out of the summary report as well as the testimony of Judith Groves, who also initially claimed to have seen the girl in the polka-dot dress. Darrell Johnson's story is discredited, a la Warren Report style, with the comment "Note: Investigators believe Johnson's statements unreliable and contrary to fact."

Like the Warren Report, the *Summary Report* didn't feel the need to provide any specific examples of such unreliability. The report mentions witness McBroom describing Sirhan as seeming "out of place" and then declares, "All additional statements made by McBroom were later retracted and not reported here." McBroom denied that he made any such retractions. Witness Booker Griffin's story of seeing a man and a woman running from the pantry was transformed into Griffin's confession that it was "a total fabrication on his part." When shown this part of the summary report in 1987 by authors Klaber and Melanson, Griffin reacted angrily and said, "This is totally untrue." (*Shadow Play*, pp. 133–135).

LAPD Sergeant Paul Scharaga got into trouble when he filed an APB at 12:30 a.m. on the morning of June 5, 1968, for a woman who'd been seen in the company of suspect Sirhan Sirhan wearing a "white voile dress . . . with small black polka dots." After hearing about the shooting on his patrol car radio, while stationed one block from the Ambassador Hotel, Scharaga drove to the parking lot behind the hotel. There he encountered a distraught older couple he could remember only as the "Bernsteins," who reported seeing a young man and a woman with a polka-dot dress running from the hotel laughing and shouting, "We shot him! We shot him!"

Police communication tapes, released from the LAPD files, reveal that at 1:41 a.m., in response to a patrol car's request for clarification of the APB, the dispatcher said, "Disregard that broadcast. We got Rafer Johnson and Jesse Unruh who were right next to him [Kennedy], and they only have one man and don't want them to get anything started on a big conspiracy." Scharaga would later say, in an angry response to a summary report of an alleged interview with him by two Special Unit Senator detectives, "That report is phony." In a 1988 interview from his Missouri home, he declared, "No one ever interviewed me, and I never retracted my statement from 'We shot him' to 'They shot him.' This is just how things were done. If they couldn't get you to change your story, they'd ignore you. If they couldn't ignore you, they'd discredit you, and if they couldn't do that, they'd just make something up." (*Shadow Play*, pp. 140–142).

The most well-known of all the polka-dot girl witnesses is the aforementioned Sandra Serrano. Serrano had lots of corroboration. Besides her national television interview only an hour or so after the shooting, she told her account to a guard, a close friend, and then John Ambrose, a Los Angeles assistant district attorney, who helped calm Serrano down. Ambrose filed a report with the FBI about his encounter with Serrano, describing the girl she'd seen as "wearing a white dress with black polka dots and heels, with a good figure." Ambrose assessed Serrano thusly: "Serrano impressed me as a sincere girl who was a dedicated Kennedy fan, not interested in publicity." The police waged an intense campaign to impugn Serrano's credibility, despite the consistent and early nature of her story, as well as all those she'd told it to. While Serrano originally had stated she'd heard "backfires" just prior to seeing the fleeing couple, the LAPD transformed that into "gunfire" and used it to destroy her credibility. They brought her in to the Ambassador Hotel and fired a .22 handgun in the pantry, recording with a tape recorder on the steps outside where Serrano had been sitting when the man and woman ran by. The audiotape of this LAPD experiment reserved for posterity Serrano's vain cries that it "sounded like backfires of a car, and I never heard a gun. I don't know what a gun sounds like." This didn't matter to the LAPD, the FBI, or the SUS (Special Unit Senator). Serrano was branded with having heard shots she couldn't possibly have heard, and the rest of her story was therefore easier to discredit.

All this culminated in the incredible polygraph examination/mental torture session inflicted upon Serrano by the LAPD's master of conspiracy bashers, Sergeant Enrique Hernandez. After treating her to an SUS paid-for steak dinner, Hernandez tried repeatedly to get her to change her story. The excerpts from the audio tape, which somehow survived when so many others didn't, are reminiscent of Jack Ruby's Warren Commission testimony for their different but just as obvious conspiratorial overtones.

"Nobody told you," Hernandez berates Serrano, "'We have shot Kennedy.'" Serrano steadfastly maintains her story as Hernandez says ridiculous things like "One of these days, you're gonna be a mother. You're gonna be a mother, you're gonna have kids, and you know that you can't live a life of shame, knowing what you're doing right now is wrong" and "Please, in the name of Kennedy . . . don't shame his death" and "The Kennedys have had nothing but tragedy. . . . And I'm sure—you mark my words—that one of these days, if you're woman enough, you will get a letter from Ethel Kennedy—personal—thanking you for at least letting her rest on this aspect of this investigation." After, a broken, frustrated Serrano exclaims, "Damn cops, why don't you just leave me alone?" Hernandez responds, "The only time you will be left alone is when you tell me the truth about what happened outside on the staircase." After finally breaking down her will and getting her to admit that she was "messed up," Hernandez helpfully offers: "The facts that you saw were apparently misquoted, or misprinted, or mistelevised to the actual true facts." Orwell couldn't have dreamed of anything more absurd than that. Hernandez was much commended for his efforts and was promoted to lieutenant several weeks after this disgraceful performance. (*Shadow Play*, pp. 142–149).

Interestingly, when Hernandez conducted the same kind of ludicrous polygraph exam/interview with another inconvenient witness, waiter

Vincent DiPierro, who broke down under his relentless badgering more easily than Serrano had, he ultimately got DiPierro to answer "Yes, sir, I did" to the question: "But I think what you have told me, is that you probably got this idea about a girl in a black-and-white polka-dot after you talked to Miss Sandra Serrano." There is a disturbing problem with this, for ten days earlier he had forced Serrano to "admit" she had stolen the girl in the polka-dot dress story from DiPierro. (*Shadow Play*, pp. 150–151).

DiPierro, at the "trial" of Sirhan, would attempt to juggle the uncontestable truth of what he'd seen and reported with the desire of the authorities for him to deny that reality. He stated that he'd first noticed Sirhan because of the pretty girl, dressed in a polka-dot dress, standing "not definitely by him, in the area of him." When confronted with his denial of having seen such a girl to Hernandez, under cross-examination by defense attorney Grant Cooper, DiPierro didn't blink in agreeing that denial was correct and then, under redirect from prosecutor David Fitts, testified there had indeed been a girl in a polka-dot dress standing near Sirhan at the time of the shooting, who'd attracted his attention with her good looks.

Fitts tried to salvage things by maintaining the girl DiPierro had seen was Kennedy worker Valerie Schulte. Schulte, when she appeared in court the next day on the witness stand, had one leg in a brace and was using a crutch due to a skiing accident that had occurred before the assassination. The whole contention was absurd because Schulte had not been standing anywhere near Sirhan at any time, and the dress she showed the court and testified she was wearing that night was dark green with large yellow lemon shapes on it. Another question the authorities should be asked is, if DiPierro had "admitted" getting the story of the woman near Sirhan from Serrano (and conversely, if she "admitted" getting it from him), then how does it translate that DiPierro saw Valerie Schulte in her "polka-dot" dress? (*Shadow Play*, pp. 152–155).

DiPierro's story continued when just over a month after Sirhan's trial ended, he wrote a letter to local radio reporter (KHJ) Art Kevin, who was doing a series about the unanswered questions in the RFK case. DiPierro termed Kevin's segment on the girl in the polka-dot dress "the first 'real true' report," and he lauded the reporter for "the extensive research and brilliant job of reporting a factual story." Art Kevin drove out to the DiPierro home a few days later and the door was answered by his father, Ambassador maitre d' Angelo DiPierro. Kevin could see both men "looked all shook up." While Vincent stood nearby, Angelo informed Kevin that the FBI had visited them and explained how hard the police had worked reconstructing what had happened in the pantry that night. After Angelo hinted at some threat to his son's life, he told Kevin to forget the whole thing and shut the door. In 1988, Vincent DiPierro praised the work of the police in an interview with authors Klaber and Melanson and maintained they'd protected him when his "life was in danger." If Sirhan was in custody and had acted alone, who would have been threatening his life, one wonders? (*Shadow Play*, p. 156).

Ramsey Clark, LBJ's attorney general, would assert, in a Justice Department press conference the day after the assassination, that there was "no evidence of conspiracy." Clark also issued a far-too-premature public statement that there had been "no conspiracy" to kill Martin Luther King Jr., either. Oddly, Clark would later become somewhat of an establishment loose cannon, severely criticizing the government's actions at Waco and offering legal defense to the likes of Slobodan Milosevic and Saddam Hussein.

The theory that Sirhan killed RFK because he was enraged at his support of the sale of jet bombers to Israel has nothing credible to back it up. Sirhan's ballyhooed "diary," which was really just a bunch of rambling papers in a notebook, contains nothing about Kennedy's policies toward Israel. It does, however, strangely mention the Illuminati and alleged Boston Strangler Albert DeSalvo and repeats the line "Pay to the order of Sirhan Sirhan" numerous times. No witnesses ever stepped forward to claim they knew of an animosity by Sirhan toward RFK because of this, or any other issue. Sirhan even maintained that up until the time just before the assassination, he was an admirer, even a supporter, of Kennedy, much as Oswald had admired JFK. (*Shadow Play*, pp. 160–161).

Again, as in the JFK "investigation," witness reports were clearly altered by the authorities. Nina Rhodes, who was in the Ambassador Hotel with her husband celebrating RFK's victory that night, supported a petition to the Los Angeles Grand Jury in 1992 to investigate the LAPD's performance in the RFK case. Rhodes stated, ". . . I heard 12–14 shots, some originating in the vicinity of the Senator not from where I saw Sirhan. . . ." This is interesting, because the summary of her July 9, 1968, FBI interview reports, "She later recalled hearing eight distinct shots." When shown the FBI summary of her interview in 1992, Rhodes found fifteen inaccurate items and most importantly said, "From the moment the tragedy began I knew that there was at least 10–14 shots and that there had to be more than one assailant." Nina Rhodes is not even on the LAPD's list of witnesses who were in the pantry that night. (*Shadow Play*, pp. 26–128).

On April 30, 2012, CNN and other mainstream media outlets ran a report on this long-overlooked witness. Now known as Nina Rhodes-Hughes, she'd been standing only a few feet away from RFK when he was shot, and remained certain there were two guns fired that night. "What has to come out is that there was another shooter to my right," Rhodes-Hughes recounted in an exclusive interview with CNN. "The truth has got to be told. No more cover-ups." In an all too familiar complaint, Rhodes-Hughes noted the fifteen "errors" in her FBI statement. "I never said eight shots. I never, never said it," Rhodes-Hughes declared. "When they say only eight shots, the anger within me is so great that I practically—I get very emotional because it is so untrue. It is so untrue." Sirhan's lead attorney William Pepper called the FBI's alterations "deplorable" and said it "mirrored the experience of other witnesses."

As can be easily seen, there are numerous holes in the official story of Bobby Kennedy's death. Whether Sirhan was some kind of Manchurian Candidate, as has long been suspected by many, it can't be denied that there were strong indications he was not acting alone that night. Sadly, the authorities failed to investigate any of these promising leads, much as they had failed to investigate any promising leads in Dallas five years earlier. Sirhan has consistently maintained that, while admitting he was in the Ambassador Hotel Room pantry the night RFK was shot, he doesn't remember anything about what happened there. Although he seems to have been a different sort of "patsy" than Oswald or James Earl Ray was, logic compels the assumption that greater forces than this lone young Palestinian were behind the assassination of a US senator who was on the verge of being elected president.

There is disagreement among researchers about whether RFK actually said something like "the secrets of my brother's death will only be revealed with the powers of the presidency," in a speech a few days before his death at San Fernando State College, as has been alleged. I listened to the only archived speech at that location available to review online, and nothing like that is to be found there. On the contrary, RFK told disappointed students he would not reopen the "Warren Report investigation" if elected president. However, as David Talbot showed in his essential book *Brothers*, there is little question that, while maintaining a public posture of supporting the Warren Report's conclusions, behind the scenes JFK's younger brother was working to find out the truth. Talbot quoted former RFK campaign worker Richard Lubic, who reported RFK told him, "Subject to me getting elected, I would like to reopen the Warren Commission." RFK press spokesman Frank Mankiewicz claimed that Kennedy had answered "yes" when asked whether he'd reopen the investigation into the death of his brother, at a campaign appearance days before his assassination. In my view, both Kennedy assassinations were connected and were the result of powerful conspiracies.

I first became really interested in the RFK assassination after watching ex-Congressman Allard K. Lowenstein on Tom Snyder's *Tomorrow* television show in 1974. Lowenstein had become an active critic of the official version of Bobby Kennedy's assassination, and I found his arguments very persuasive. Like too many counterculture leaders of the 1960s, however, Lowenstein turned out to have apparent connections to American intelligence. Published in 1985, *The Piped Piper: Allard K. Lowenstein and the Liberal Dream* by Richard Cummings provided documentation that the purportedly radical Lowenstein was tied to the CIA. Said to have been an inspiration to future career politicians like Barney Frank and John Kerry, Lowenstein was assassinated in his Manhattan office on March 14, 1980, by a demented admirer, Dennis Sweeney.

Lowenstein was also deeply involved in Eugene McCarthy's 1968 presidential campaign, although he would later maintain his "heart had been with Kennedy."

Another interesting figure in McCarthy's campaign was James Woolsey, chairman of the Yale Citizens for Eugene McCarthy in 1967–68. Woolsey would later become director of the CIA under President Bill Clinton. This leader of the "antiwar" movement would develop into a substantial foreign policy "hawk," culminating in his endorsement of war aficionado supreme John McCain for president. Thomas Finney spent seventeen years with the CIA before resigning in 1968 to become a "top aide" to candidate McCarthy. Another longtime CIA official, Thomas McCoy, who "held top Agency posts at Rome and Madrid," went on to retire "in the spring of 1968 to become a top campaign aide to peace candidate Eugene McCarthy." (*OSS: The Secret History of America's First Central Intelligence Agency* by R. Harris Smith, p. 381). Finney had ties to mainstream Democratic favorite Hubert Humphrey, and there were allegations of substantial funds from Humphrey arriving with him in McCarthy's campaign. This fueled suspicions that Humphrey and McCarthy were combining forces to stop Kennedy. Finney's insertion as "campaign boss" drove some of McCarthy's staff to resign in protest. (*Brothers* by David Talbot, p. 360). As Talbot noted, "But McCarthy himself was surprisingly popular in CIA circles, where Kennedy was reviled. . . ." An extremely unlikely McCarthy fan was CIA honcho Richard Helms; he and the "peace candidate" would be occasional lunch partners over the years.

Like so many others on the "left," Eugene McCarthy had little love for the Kennedys. According to author Dominic Sandbrook, quoted in his book

Eugene McCarthy: The Rise and Fall of Postwar American Liberalism, McCarthy chastised the RFK campaign for "shooting the wounded and declaring victory when the battle was won." He also issued the following caustic comment after RFK's assassination: "He brought it on himself, demagoguing to the last."

CHAPPAQUIDDICK

"There has to be more to it."
—Edward Kennedy, referring to his brothers' assassinations

There was still one Kennedy brother left, however, and there was some talk of attempting to draft Senator Edward Kennedy as the nominee at the contentious 1968 Democratic convention. While Teddy resisted the overtures in 1968, his future political prospects seemed brighter than ever after the tragic deaths of his older brothers. The events at Chappaquiddick, however, on July 19, 1969, changed all that.

There are two schools of thought about Chappaquiddick: liberals generally tend to ignore the subject and resent any mention of it, and conservatives believe that Teddy was directly responsible for the death of Mary Jo Kopechne and lied about it, and the "liberal" media helped to cover up his crime. The facts suggest a third alternative: Chappaquiddick represented the political assassination of Edward Kennedy, orchestrated by the same forces responsible for the deaths of John and Robert Kennedy.

There are a number of troubling questions about Chappaquiddick. Clearly, the official story, related by Edward Kennedy, is highly implausible. Kennedy was a big man, with a bad back, and it simply isn't feasible that he was able to exit an upside-down car lying on the bottom of a pond, with strongly swirling waters all about him (not to mention then swimming across the entire channel). This becomes especially unlikely due to the fact that the other passenger in the car, former RFK campaign worker Mary Jo Kopechne, was not able to free herself despite being younger and in much better shape. Kennedy's lame excuse that he made a wrong turn, when he knew the area extremely well, failed to convince many people and fueled theories that he was not only having an affair with the young girl, but had impregnated her.

Researcher R. B. Cutler's impressive work *In Re: Chappaquiddick* provided a scenario that makes the most sense, in my view. He analyzed the marks on the bridge where the car veered off and into the pond, and revealed that they showed it had stopped and then suddenly accelerated at a high speed over the edge, which contradicted Kennedy's account. Some of the damage to the car appeared to have been inflicted before it entered the water. All witnesses testified that Kopechne never drank and had not been drinking that night, but there was alcohol found in her blood, leading to speculation she'd been drugged. Teddy had wounds on the back of his skull, including a huge bump on top, lending credence to theories that he was knocked out and not even in the car, let alone driving it, when it went off the bridge and into Poucha Pond.

Kennedy appeared perfectly calm and normal, according to Ross Richards and Stan Moore, friends of the senator who met him in the hotel lobby early the next morning. Then Kennedy's cousin Joe Gargan arrived, along with US Attorney Paul Markham. According to Richards, Gargan and Markham were "soaking wet." During his conversation with these two men, Kennedy became visibly upset. Several people, including Deputy Sheriff Christopher Look, testified that they'd seen Kennedy's car shortly before the time of the accident, and that there were three people inside. However, despite the nagging questions, no autopsy was performed on Mary Jo Kopechne, and as a result of the ridiculous cover story Kennedy told, his presidential aspirations were forever ruined.

Nixon White House spy Anthony Ulasewicz would maintain he'd been ordered to fly immediately to Chappaquiddick to "dig up dirt" on Ted Kennedy. As author Richard E. Sprague (not to be confused with the first counsel to the House Assassinations Committee) pointed out, in his excellent book *The Taking of America, 1-2-3*, "The only problem Tony has is that, according to his testimony, he arrived early on the morning of the 'accident,' before the whole incident had been made public." This brings to mind an overlooked remark from the Senate Watergate hearings, when CIA spy E. Howard Hunt mentioned going to Hyannis Port to obtain information for possible use against Kennedy in the 1972 campaign. Hunt was disguised in his legendary red wig, and was intent upon inquiring about the events at Chappaquiddick. Critics have wondered if he was returning to the scene of the crime.

There was one of those curious connections here, and another unnatural death as well. In the early 1960s, Mary Jo Kopechne had worked as a secretary to US Senator George Smathers (D-FL), one of JFK's closest friends in the Senate. During this time, she lived in Washington, D.C., with Nancy Carole Tyler, secretary to Bobby Baker, the LBJ crony embroiled in scandal, in a home owned by Baker. Tyler was even profiled in *Time* magazine (November 6, 1963, issue), in which she was described as a "shapely" former Miss Loudon County who had become Baker's well-paid private secretary. Penn Jones Jr. would claim that Tyler was the one who first leaked the story that JFK was going to replace Johnson on the 1964 ticket with George Smathers. Tyler died in a plane crash near Ocean City, Maryland, on May 10, 1965.

Chappaquiddick destroyed Ted Kennedy's chances of ever being elected president, as surely as if he'd been slain by another "lone nut." It was Teddy who really ignited the fatalistic notion that the Kennedys were "cursed" when he said, during his televised statement following the events at Chappaquiddick, that he had contemplated "whether some awful curse did actually hang over all the Kennedys." Not only have Kennedys been dying unnatural deaths since Joseph Kennedy Jr.'s airplane exploded in 1944, those connected to the Kennedys have also shown a propensity to die unnaturally. There was even a very odd unnatural death associated with Joe Jr., albeit decades later; a woman he was engaged to at one time, Althalia Ponsell Lindsley, was brutally hacked to death on the front steps of her Florida home with a machete, on January 23, 1974. Even stranger, Lindsley's friend and neighbor Francis Bernis was found dead with a crushed skull in a vacant lot only days later. Bernis was a professional journalist rumored to be working on a book about her friend's death. Neither murder was ever solved. (*St. Augustine Record*, January 30, 2007).

It is not generally known that RFK's wife, Ethel Skakel Kennedy, lost both her parents in a 1955 plane crash. The Skakels were involved in other unnatural deaths. Ethel's brother George Skakel Jr. died in a 1966 plane crash, and nine months later his wife choked to death on a piece of food, leaving behind four children. Francis Michael Medaille, son of Ethel's first cousin, pushed a seven-year-old girl to her death from a New York apartment building on February 11, 1958. Another Skakel girl was driving a convertible on Thanksgiving, 1966, when a six-year-old flew out of the car and died weeks later. And in 2002, Michael Skakel was convicted of the 1975 murder of Martha Moxley.

In 1973, future congressman Joseph P. Kennedy II, eldest son of RFK, was driving a car that crashed, leaving a passenger permanently paralyzed. Another son of RFK, David Kennedy, died of an apparent drug overdose on April 25, 1984. David was extremely close to his father and seems never to have gotten over the assassination. *The Continuing Inquiry*, Penn Jones Jr.'s delightful, off-the-wall little periodical (my first published work appeared there), speculated that there were unanswered questions involved in this case as well. Still one more son of RFK, aspiring politician Michael Kennedy, died on December 31, 1997, in a bizarre skiing accident. Jackie Kennedy remarried five years after the JFK assassination to the much older Aristotle Onassis, a Greek shipping magnate. Both of Onassis's children died young and unnaturally; his son was killed at age twenty-four in a 1973 plane crash, and his thirty-seven-year-old daughter died in 1988, apparently as a side effect from diet or sleeping pills.

Consider that between them, Robert and Ethel Kennedy had a mother and father, four siblings, and a nephew go down in separate plane crashes. All but Ted Kennedy were killed in those crashes. *Six* unconnected plane crashes for one family? It's remarkable that any member of the Kennedy family is still willing to fly.

Whatever all this means, it certainly is unusual to have that many accidents and unnatural deaths connected in some way to one particular family.

CHAPTER THREE

THE SEVENTIES

"From Watergate we learned what generations before us have
known; our Constitution works."

—Leon Jaworski, special prosecutor,
former Texas liaison to the Warren Commission

After the assassination of Robert Kennedy, and the turmoil that followed at
the Democratic National Convention in Chicago, the presidential election
of 1968 was both boring and anticlimactic. Richard Nixon, JFK's old nemesis
who had lost to him in the 1960's historically close contest, won a narrow
victory over LBJ's lame vice president Hubert Humphrey, and became the
poster child for the counterculture movement's old-school opposition.

As the new decade began, another outfit exemplifying the concept of
"loyal opposition" was established. Referred to as the "people's lobby" by
its proponents, Common Cause was created with the intention of advocating
for more open government. The organization was, in reality, completely
controlled by those associated with the institutions it was allegedly supposed
to monitor. Founded by establishment stalwart John Gardner (whose
important posts included a stint with the OSS, twenty years with the Carnegie
Corporation, secretary of HEW under LBJ, president of the Urban Coalition,
and a trustee of the Rockefeller Brothers Fund), it was bankrolled from the
beginning by the elite of American society. Although Gardner stated that
his organization would lobby on behalf of "the people" against "the power
of the special interests," and that "Now somebody besides big companies
and special-interest groups is in on the act," the "people" who financed his
project were pretty "big" and "special" themselves. Assorted Rockefellers,

led by John D. Rockefeller III's $25,000, donated funds to Gardner's group, as did Arthur Sulzberger, head of the *New York Times* (which gave Common Cause invaluable favorable publicity), the Ford Motor Co. gave $10,000, Wall Street tycoon Andre Meyer found $10,000 to surrender to "the people's lobby," and Sol Linowitz, Xerox bigwig and later mastermind of the Panama Canal giveaway, gave away $500. That's quite a brand of "grass" in Common Cause's "roots." It's no wonder that the organization invariably has favored the establishment position on key issues, such as consistently supporting pay raises for members of Congress. (*The Spotlight*, December 4, 1989, pp. 4, 5, and 14).

Another present-day leftist institution, *Mother Jones* magazine, began publication in 1976. The magazine was named for "Mother" Mary Jones Harris, a radical labor union organizer. Mother Jones, like many leftists, was predisposed in favor of war, however. She broke with many of her fellow socialists, supporting President Woodrow Wilson and US involvement in World War I. In her delicate, tender words: ". . . . when we get into a fight I am one of those who intend to clean hell out of the other fellow, and we have to clean the Kaiser up . . . the grafter, the burglar, the thief, the murderer." (*The Populist Persuasion* by Michael Kazin, p. 69). *Mother Jones* has faithfully towed the party line on the truly important issues, like the JFK assassination, supported the dreadful 9/11 Commission, and dismissed notions of voting fraud in the 2000 and 2004 elections. If Rush Limbaugh represents an example of a false alternative to the "liberal" media, *Mother Jones*, on a much smaller level, is one of the "leftist" versions of "loyal opposition."

By the 1990s, there were four major "progressive" news outlets in the mainstream media: *The Nation, The Progressive, In These Times,* and *Mother Jones.* The previously mentioned Bob Feldman exposed the questionable financing of these groups in his "Reports from the Field: Left Media and Left Think Tanks—Foundation Managed Protest." They were financed to a great degree by grants and contributions; in 2010, *The Nation* alone received more than $2 million and *Mother Jones's* Foundation for National Progress took in more than $4.7 million. Former LBJ aide Bill Moyers, who would adopt the persona of a "renegade" journalist in later years, became president of the Schumann Center for Media and Democracy, which funded The Nation Institute (representing *The Nation*) and the newer online "leftist" outlet *Truthout.* Moyers's conglomerate brought in more than $3 million in 2010 and had reported assets in excess of $33 million.

The Schumanns themselves had typical establishment pedigrees; Ms. Schumann was the daughter of one of IBM's founders, and her husband had made his fortune establishing several banks and served as president of the General Motors Acceptance Corporation. And yet they chose to finance primarily ostensible "anti-capitalist" outfits. While funding radical environmentalist groups, the Schumann Center heavily invests in companies that are categorized as environmentally unfriendly. The watchdog website undueinfluence.com characterizes such common business practices as "using capitalist investments to destroy capitalist society." As might be expected, these groups enjoy tax-exempt status and are not required to list *any* of the sources of their funding.

WATERGATE

The seminal event of Nixon's administration—the Watergate scandal—has been analyzed ad nauseam by the court historians. On the surface, it was a farcical effort to increase Nixon's chances of winning reelection by breaking into Democratic National Committee headquarters. For perhaps the first and only time in modern history, the mainstream press—led by *The Washington Post*—appeared to do its job, exposing official wrongdoing with true journalistic zeal. Reporters Bob Woodward and Carl Bernstein became celebrities through their stories on the scandal, and the resultant Senate Watergate Committee's nationally televised hearings made the likes of Senator Sam Ervin, Senator Howard Baker, Senator Lowell Weicker, future actor Fred Thompson, former Nixon aide John Dean, and his attractive young wife, Maureen, household names.

The details of the scandal were somewhat confusing, and the political significance paled in comparison to the assassinations of the Sixties, which had huge ramifications for the world. There were, however, a lot of unnatural deaths associated with the Watergate affair, but few of them were covered by the media in the same way as the supposedly important work of "Deep Throat" was, for example.

Mae Brussell, a controversial researcher who also wrote extensively about the JFK assassination and related issues, came up with a list of thirty mysterious deaths of those who were associated with the Watergate scandal in some way, similar to the string of unexplained deaths of JFK assassination witnesses, that feisty Texan Penn Jones Jr. had reported—and was still reporting at that time in his Midlothian, Texas, newspaper. Among the more interesting deaths was that of forty-two-year-old Beverly Kaye, who died of a "stroke" in a White House elevator in December 1973. Kaye had been involved with storing and preserving the notorious White House tapes, recorded by Nixon himself. Brussell claimed that Kaye had been talking to her friends and knew everything that was on those tapes, including the missing eighteen minutes that had been mysteriously erased.

Longtime Nixon friend Murray Chotiner was killed on January 23, 1974, when his car was struck by a government truck. Congressman William Mills allegedly committed suicide on May 24, 1973, a few days after it was reported that he'd failed to report a $25,000 campaign contribution from Nixon's reelection committee. There were supposedly seven suicide notes found at the scene. Oddly, two of Mills's campaign aides had been killed in a car accident in February 1972, one of whom was alleged to have accepted delivery of the $25,000 contribution.

Dorothy Hunt, wife of White House "plumber" E. Howard Hunt, was killed in a plane crash on December 8, 1972. In another strange twist, the name of Dr. Gary Morris, a Washington, D.C., psychiatrist, was found written on a slip of paper in Dorothy's wallet when her body was discovered after the crash. Morris and his wife had been in the Caribbean when their boat disappeared in March 1972. Brussell claimed that Morris had been a specialist in hypnosis. Louise Boyer, Nelson Rockefeller's longtime assistant, fell to her death from a New York apartment building on July 3, 1974. The just as controversial Sherman Skolnick would identify her as Louise Auchincloss Boyer (Jackie Kennedy's stepfather was Hugh Auchincloss, although no blood relation is alleged here), as other online references do, and added that she was Rockefeller's "Girl Friday." Rockefeller would go on to become an unelected vice president of the United States (and die a murky death himself, apparently while having sex with his much younger mistress), upon the ascension to the presidency of the unelected Gerald Ford, ex-member of the Warren Commission.

The wife of Andrew Topping was found dead on April 6, 1972, only two weeks after the Watergate break-in. Her death was ruled a suicide, and her husband would later be arrested, in August 1972, of plotting to kill President Nixon. And there was Martha Mitchell, colorful and talkative wife of Attorney General John Mitchell, who died of cancer in 1976. She made numerous allegations against Nixon, her husband, and others; claimed to have been held against her will at one point; and ended up abandoned by most of her family. Nixon himself told interviewer David Frost in 1977, "If it hadn't been for Martha Mitchell, there'd have been no Watergate."

While Nixon was a typically ambitious, corruptible politician, there seems little doubt that *someone* powerful wanted him removed from office. On the surface, Watergate was child's play compared to dozens of more serious scandals that had been ignored and covered up by the same kept press. After Watergate, the journalists who had seemed so diligent and civic minded returned to their previous dull and disinterested state. If they thought a rather pointless break-in was a matter serious enough to warrant the first impeachment of a president in over a hundred years, why did these same folks sneer and snicker at notions of conspiracy in the Kennedy assassinations?

Nixon feared one politician above all others during his presidency: Senator Edward Kennedy, the sole remaining brother of JFK. Nixon instructed his aides to talk to Secret Service agents to try and get them to expose the senator's well-known womanizing. Nixon removed the Secret Service protection granted to Teddy in wake of the George Wallace shooting, after the 1972 election. "If he gets shot, it's too damn bad," Nixon declared. White House tape recordings revealed that Nixon had a pervasive obsession with Ted Kennedy. He had Teddy followed on a Hawaiian vacation and during his trips to Martha's Vineyard. Nixon was clearly disappointed when aide John Ehrlichman told him the report from Hawaii indicated that, "No, no, he's very clean. . . . He was just as nice as he could be the whole time." Nixon tried to get his aides H. R. Haldeman and Charles Colson to plant a fake news story, linking Arthur Bremer, accused assailant of George Wallace, with Ted Kennedy. And then there was the cryptic comment Nixon aide John Dean made about Chappaquiddick, recorded on the March 3, 1973, White House tape: "If Kennedy knew the bear trap he was walking into. . . ."

Richard Nixon continued to feel bitterness over the close loss he suffered in 1960 to John F. Kennedy. Years later, he was still steadfastly attempting to tarnish the Kennedy legacy. In 1971, the Nixon White House requested that CIA spymaster E. Howard Hunt forge "some [diplomatic] cables in order to blame John F. Kennedy for the death of the leader of South Vietnam [Ngo Dinh Diem] . . . for the purpose of publishing them in *Time* and *Life*." (*New York Times*, September 25, 1973).

THE SHOOTING OF GEORGE WALLACE

Once again bullets, not ballots, may have helped influence a presidential election. On May 15, 1972, presidential candidate George Wallace was shot by "lone nut" Arthur Bremer at a campaign rally in Laurel, Maryland. Whether Wallace could have garnered enough votes away from Nixon, assuming he ran another third-party campaign, to swing the election to huge underdog Democrat George McGovern is highly questionable. Regardless, the shooting and Wallace's withdrawal from the race did impact the electoral process. CIA spymaster E. Howard Hunt would maintain that Nixon aide Charles Colson had asked him to break into Bremer's apartment after the shooting in an attempt to find material that might link him to George McGovern, but then subsequently called it off.

When two FBI agents entered Bremer's apartment only hours after Wallace was shot, they discovered that the Secret Service was already there, having been ordered to break into the residence by James Rowley, who'd been the chief of the Secret Service since before the JFK assassination. The Secret Service apparently removed some unknown documents from the apartment. Neither the FBI nor the Secret Service locked the door to Bremer's residence, and it is known that reporters entered and left freely for some time afterward, even taking some documents themselves. A typical "lone" assassin's diary was found, allegedly written by Bremer, but Gore Vidal would later speculate that E. Howard Hunt was the true author. Martha Mitchell would tell George Wallace that her husband had admitted to her that Charles Colson had met with Bremer four days prior to the assassination attempt.

On October 16, 1972, a plane carrying Congressman and former Warren Commission member Hale Boggs of Louisiana vanished in Alaska. In a perfect example of what some conspiracy researchers call a "cosmic coincidence," Boggs was driven to the airport for the first leg of his trip by young future president Bill Clinton. Boggs, along with Senator Richard Russell, had been the closest thing the Warren Commission had to a dissident. An unnamed aide was cited in Bernard Fensterwald's *Coincidence or Conspiracy* (p. 96) as claiming Boggs told him, "Hoover lied his eyes out to the Commission—on Oswald, on Ruby, on their friends, the bullets, the guns, you name it. . . ." Boggs's wife, Lindy, was also quoted, saying, "He wished he had never been on it [the Warren Commission] and wished he'd never signed it [the Warren Report]." A further interesting connection here is the fact that Congressman Nick Begich, who was on board the plane with Boggs, had a son, Nick Jr., who has become notable for researching the frightening new weather technology known as HAARP, and has appeared on the television show *Conspiracy Theory with Jesse Ventura*.

CONGRESS FINALLY LOOKS AT THE CIA

Following Nixon's resignation from office, and new President Gerald Ford's subsequent full pardon of him (not to mention the ascension to an unelected vice presidency by establishment figurehead Nelson Rockefeller), the Democrats saw large gains in both houses of Congress during the 1974 elections. With a mandate for reform, Congress overrode President Ford's veto and strengthened the Freedom of Information Act, but otherwise limited their efforts to changing campaign finance, disclosure, and ethics laws. However, under the leadership of Senator Frank Church (D-ID), the Senate did look closely at the activities of the CIA and other intelligence agencies for the very first time. Texas Republican John Tower, who years later met his demise in a plane crash, would serve as vice chairman of the committee. The House established a similar committee, chaired by New York Democrat Otis Pike.

Beginning in 1975, the Church Committee held hearings that disclosed to the public the CIA's attempts to assassinate Cuba's Fidel Castro, the Congo's Patrice Lumumba, Rafael Trujilo of the Dominican Republic, and the Diems of Vietnam, among others. President Ford would sign an executive order explicitly forbidding the assassination of foreign leaders in response to these revelations. When we consider that President Barack Obama would publicly boast of assassinating an American citizen who had never been tried or convicted of any crime, only thirty-five years later, it is sobering to reflect upon how far we've gone in the wrong direction. Senator Church would issue some prescient remarks about the intelligence gathering capabilities of the National Security Agency (NSA), warning that it could be "turned around on the American people, and no American would have any privacy left." Sounding like no present-day American politician, Church declared, "I know the capacity that is there to make tyranny total in America, and we must see to it that this agency and all agencies that possess this technology operate within the law and under proper supervision. . . ." (James Bamford, "The Agency That Could Be Big Brother," *New York Times*, December 25, 2005). Church ran for the Democratic presidential nomination in 1976, winning several primaries before eventually dropping out. He was defeated for reelection in 1980, and he died at only fifty-nine four years later.

The Church Committee also touched upon the performance of the intelligence agencies in relation to the JFK assassination, which was the first step in paving the way for a congressional investigation of the crime. They investigated the FBI's COINTELPRO efforts against American citizens, usually those labeled as "radicals." One of their most important achievements was exposing the poisonous MKULTRA program of the CIA, which, in the words of the committee, involved "the research and development of chemical and biological agents." They also shone the light on the abuses of the CIA's Operation Phoenix program in Vietnam. James Schlesinger and William Colby became the first two directors of the CIA who made attempts to reform the Agency and work more openly with Congress. This new era didn't last long, however, as President Ford fired both CIA Director Colby and Schlesinger, who'd become secretary of defense, on November 4, 1975, in what was called the "Halloween Massacre." Colby was replaced by future president George H. W. Bush, and Schlesinger was supplanted by establishment stalwart Donald Rumsfeld.

The presidential campaign of 1976, on the heels of the big Democratic gains in Congress, the Bicentennial celebration, and a post-Watergate national consensus for openness and reform, should have been exciting. Frank Church was the only presidential candidate who reflected the views of the more radical members of Congress. Many speculated that the time was perfect for Edward Kennedy to make a run for the White House. Polls showed him far ahead of any other candidate. Much as he had in 1972, Teddy once again declined to run, for what he deemed family reasons. Eventually, little-known Georgia governor Jimmy Carter emerged as the "front-runner," a term the media would grow quite fond of hoisting upon its particular favorites in years to come. Carter was a very active member of David Rockefeller's Trilateral Commission, which was a newer version of the tried and true globalist outfit, the Council on Foreign Relations. Virtually every member of Carter's administration would be fellow Trilateralists.

One of the most influential men around Carter was Rockefeller's cofounder of the Trilateral Commission, Zbigniew Brzezinski. Brzezinski's 1970 book, *Between Two Ages*, was chock-full of nefarious passages. He wrote of "magnetic and attractive personalities" and their ability to "manipulate emotions and control reason." He wrote, "The technocratic era involves the gradual appearance of a more controlled society. Such a society would be dominated by an elite, unrestrained by traditional values [of liberty]. Soon it will be possible to assert almost continuous surveillance over every citizen and maintain up-to-date complete files containing even the most personal information about the citizen. . . ." As National Security advisor, Brzezinski would play the same role for Carter that Henry Kissinger had played for Nixon and Ford. "

Carter beat Gerald Ford in a narrow race, and he immediately established a folksy, populist image by walking instead of riding in a car during his inauguration. He also banned the playing of *Hail to the Chief* during his appearances, and he brought back FDR-style "fireside chats." He tried to appoint former JFK speechwriter Ted Sorensen as director of the CIA, which would have virtually guaranteed significant changes in the Agency, but the nomination was quickly rejected by Congress. While Carter's administration was probably the most scandal-free since JFK's, he did create the odious monstrosity known as FEMA (Federal Emergency Management Agency) and established the Office of Special Investigations, which would go on to spend American taxpayer money persecuting elderly Ukranians, Estonians,

Croatians, and others who'd been forced to choose between Nazis and Communists during World War II. Zbigniew Brzezinski was instrumental in steering the Carter administration toward a normalization of relations with the brutal Communist regime in China.

On March 6, 1975, the long-suppressed Zapruder film, the home movie of the JFK assassination taken by Dallas dress manufacturer Abraham Zapruder, was finally shown to the American public, on Geraldo Rivera's television program *Good Night America*. As a result of the reform-minded Congress, and the information unearthed during the Church Committee hearings, public sentiment for a new inquiry into the assassination was at a fever pitch. After the nation had seen the Zapruder film, with JFK's head being driven back so forcefully, sharply contradicting the official story that Oswald was firing from behind, an overwhelming majority of Americans believed they weren't being told the full truth about the matter.

THE HOUSE SELECT COMMITTEE ON ASSASSINATIONS

Later in 1975, I joined well-known Warren Report critic Mark Lane's nation-wide research and lobbying group the Citizens' Committee of Inquiry (CCI). I was co-chairman of the local chapter in my area. We attempted to lobby Congress and speak to journalists about reopening the investigations into the deaths of the Kennedys and Martin Luther King. Virginia Democrat Thomas Downing had been trying to get the House of Representatives to reopen the Kennedy case, while the previously mentioned Henry Gonzalez of Texas had proposed a bill to reinvestigate the JFK, MLK, and RFK assassinations. Eventually, a bill was passed that struck a compromise between the two proposals by agreeing to look into the JFK and Martin Luther King murders.

Because of my affiliation with CCI, in early 1976 I was able to schedule a private screening of the Zapruder film in the National Archives. I was also able to hold the Mannlicher-Carcano supposedly used to assassinate JFK, as well as CE399—the infamous "magic bullet"—in my hands. The staff at the Archives was gracious and very accommodating. It was a heady experience for a nineteen-year-old who was thoroughly obsessed with the subject.

One afternoon in late 1976, I was thrilled to meet Mark Lane at his Washington, D.C., office. Lane related to me and another young volunteer how he'd just received a lengthy long-distance call from Freddie Prinze, at the time one of the top young comedians in the country. According to Lane, Prinze was absolutely obsessed with the JFK assassination, watching his own personal bootleg copy of the Zapruder film over and over again. He told

Lane that he was trying to drum up support in Hollywood for a national telethon, to raise funds for a new congressional investigation. In light of the consistently bad press the newly formed House Select Committee on Assassinations (HSCA) was receiving, that would have gone a long way toward deflecting one of the main thrusts of the criticism—that the inquiry was an expensive, unnecessary waste of taxpayer funds. Prinze, however, reported he was finding it difficult to find any celebrities who would be willing to appear on such a telethon.

A few months later, Freddie Prinze allegedly killed himself. If I hadn't been in Mark Lane's office that day, I would never have known anything about his interest in the JFK assassination, and thus would not have connected his death at the tragically young age of twenty-two to it. However, well aware of all the unnatural deaths associated with the Kennedy assassination, I wasn't surprised at all. When one of those predictable television movies about the "last days" of Freddie Prinze was broadcast a year later, there was not a single mention of the JFK assassination, or Prinze's keen interest in it at that time.

The new House Committee started off promisingly. The lead counsel was Richard A. Sprague, a veteran prosecutor who promised to leave no stones unturned in his quest for the truth. However, HSCA Chairman Henry Gonzalez (recall that Governor John Connally's clothing had mysteriously been found in his office after the JFK assassination) became mired in a confusing feud with Sprague, probably fueled by the predictable series of slanderous attacks in the mainstream media. Eventually, Gonzalez tried to replace Sprague as lead counsel, but after he was met with opposition from other committee members, he resigned himself. When Ohio's Louis Stokes took the reins as HSCA chairman, Sprague unfortunately agreed to resign as well. Stokes didn't have the interest Gonzalez had in the subject, and he became a yes man for new lead counsel G. Robert Blakey.

Blakey led the HSCA in an entirely different direction: limiting the inquiry, agreeing to a shameful secrecy agreement with the CIA, and backing up every one of the Warren Commission's untenable and long-discredited conclusions. Along with virtually every other American with a strong passion for the subject, I was extremely disappointed in the performance of the HSCA and grew disillusioned with politics in general afterward. The fact that a last-second introduction of some questionable acoustics evidence caused the HSCA to conclude that the assassination was "probably the result of a conspiracy" was little consolation to most of us.

Some elements in the establishment press reacted in an even more ridiculous fashion than usual to this unexpected, unwelcome conclusion.

The HSCA declared that one shot had almost certainly come from the grassy knoll area, but that this shot had missed. Thus, it was left for our vaunted mainstream media to reason that, just because there was someone shooting from the grassy knoll at the same time Oswald was shooting from the sixth floor window, it didn't mean there had to have been a conspiracy. Yes, some actually suggested that two unassociated "lone nuts" happened, by the most remarkable of coincidences, to show up in Dealey Plaza on November 22 with the same idea.

One of the more interesting items found in the HSCA's records was the 1978 interview staff counsel Lee Matthews conducted with Dr. Charles Laburda, the psychiatrist with the Veterans Administration Hospital in Bonham, Texas, who'd been treating former Dallas Deputy Seymour Weitzman since 1974. Laburda informed Matthews that Weitzman "told me once that he believes positively that there were two people shooting. That he saw some men crouching behind some bushes." Laburda also claimed that Weitzman had disclosed that he'd "found a spent cartridge at that time, and it was from a Mauser rifle 7.65. He said he found it in that area." Recall that Weitzman was one of the two officers who initially discovered the alleged murder weapon on the sixth floor of the Texas School Book Depository Building, and that both of them "mistakenly" identified it as a 7.65 German Mauser. Laburda described Weitzman's condition thusly: ". . . fear of persecution, or fear for his life, and that is very much based on, I think, on his experiences because of the death of the former President Kennedy. . . . He mentioned that exactly other people that are somehow witnesses of the situation, or part of the investigation, died mysteriously. . . . His hands tremor; it is obviously very upsetting for him."

A woman purporting to be Weitzman's niece exchanged emails with a JFK assassination researcher, and excerpts were posted on JFK assassination Internet forums as early as 2002. She claimed that in private Weitzman told everyone that he hadn't been mistaken; the gun he discovered on the sixth floor of the TSBD had indeed been a Mauser. She also stated that Weitzman had saved a piece of JFK's skull, which he'd supposedly found at the scene of the murder and given to a "Secret Service" agent. Weitzman was busy on November 22, 1963; he was also one of those witnesses who reported meeting "Secret Service" agents on the grassy knoll, complete with official credentials, when it was known that all the agents had proceeded on with the motorcade to Parkland Hospital. Author Michael Canfield, who cowrote *Coup D'etat in America* with A. J. Weberman, had interviewed Weitzman in Dallas in 1975. Weitzman, who had suffered a nervous breakdown in 1972, told Canfield about "two Cubans" breaking into his house and waiting for him; he chased them away with his revolver. "I feared for my life," he stated.

In November 2013, I tracked down Seymour Weitzman's nephew, Larry Weitzman, still living in Texas. We had a phone conversation that consisted primarily of him saying "I don't know anything" over and over again. He did acknowledge he'd "heard" a few things from family members, including the belief that Weitzman's efforts to do his job that day in Dallas were what eventually led him to be institutionalized. He told me that "they're all dead now," meaning Seymour and his wife (they had no children), and when I asked about his sister (whom I presumed was the person who'd exchanged emails with the JFK researcher), he said he hadn't talked to her "in years" and didn't even know her married name. I detected a clear reluctance to talk in his voice, perhaps even fear about the general subject of Seymour Weitzman.

Another fascinating tidbit from the HSCA files was the March 18, 1977, memorandum from original committee chief Richard A. Sprague. In the memorandum, Sprague disclosed, "William F. Illig, an attorney from Erie, Pa., contacted me in Philadelphia this date, advising me that he represents Dr. George G. Burkley, Vice Admiral, US Navy retired, who had been the personal physician for presidents Kennedy and Johnson. . . . Dr. Burkley advised him that although he, Burkley, had signed the death certificate of President Kennedy in Dallas, he had never been interviewed and that he has information on the Kennedy assassination indicating that others besides Oswald must have participated." Sprague also stated, "Illig was calling me with his client's consent and that his client would talk to me in Washington." Unfortunately, this was only a few days before Sprague was forced from his position, and the HSCA never questioned Burkley, who provided them instead with a comparatively worthless affidavit. Author Henry Hurt claimed that Burkley told him that he believed the assassination was the result of a conspiracy, during a 1982 telephone conversation. (*Reasonable Doubt* by Henry Hurt, p. 49).

Admiral Burkley was perhaps the most important witness that was inexcusably ignored by the Warren Commission. During a 1967 oral history he provided for the JFK Library, Burkley was asked if he agreed with the Warren Commission about the number of shots. "I would not care to be quoted on that," was the admiral's enigmatic reply. In the mid-1990s, Burkley's daughter Nancy Denlea at first agreed to sign an attorney client waiver for the ARRB's Doug Horne, to release her father's files, but abruptly changed her mind a few days later. Researcher Frankie Vegas contacted the Illig law firm in 2011, inquiring about any files left by Admiral Burkley. She received a letter indicating that any files left by either William Illig or Burkley had been "destroyed over 20 years ago."

While many connected to the JFK assassination had met unnatural deaths in the first few years after the event, at the time the HSCA was being formed, a slew of important witnesses met sudden demises. Mobsters Sam Giancana and John Roselli were murdered in 1976. The CIA's William Harvey, who'd coordinated joint mob-CIA efforts, also died in 1976. William Pawley, an ex-ambassador connected to anti-Castro Cubans, committed suicide in January 1977. The enigmatic George DeMohrenschildt, tied closely to Oswald via one of history's most mismatched friendships, who knew Jackie Kennedy's family well and had powerful intelligence connections, allegedly committed suicide in March 1977. That same month, another scheduled HSCA witness, Carlos Prio Socarras, former Cuban president and active anti-Castro figure, also died from a gunshot. If it can be believed, a *third* witness, mobster Charles Nicoletti, scheduled to testify before the HSCA died, again from a gunshot, on March 29, 1977.

What are the odds of *three* people from a witness pool dying unnaturally in the same month? William Sullivan, former number three man in the FBI who headed the Bureau's domestic intelligence division, was killed in a hunting accident in November 1977 when he was mistaken for a deer. In an August 20, 2007, interview, journalist Robert Novak, hardly a "conspiracy theorist," recounted that Sullivan ". . . told me the last time I saw him . . . he had lunch at my house . . . he had been fired by Hoover and was going into retirement . . . he said that, 'Someday you will read that I have been killed in an accident, but don't believe it, I've been murdered. . . .'"

Three other FBI officials scheduled to testify before the HSCA died as well. In June 1977, Louis Nicholas, former number three man in the Bureau, special assistant to J. Edgar Hoover, who worked on the JFK assassination investigation, died of a heart attack. In August 1977, Alan H. Belmont, Hoover's special assistant who had testified before the Warren Commission, succumbed to a long illness. That same month, FBI document expert James Cadigan, who'd also been a Warren Commission witness, died from a fall at his home. In October 1977, two other scheduled HSCA witnesses, FBI fingerprint expert Donald Kaylor and the former head of the FBI's Forensic Science Lab, J. M. English, died of heart attacks. Kaylor had examined prints at the assassination scene, and English was in charge of the lab where Oswald's alleged rifle and pistol were tested. While these deaths were seemingly all "natural," the sheer volume of related demises is certainly curious. In a possibly related, but definitely unnatural death, JFK's former chief Air Force One steward, Joseph Ayres, was killed in a shooting accident in August 1977.

On September 26, 1978, CIA veteran John Paisley's body was found in the Patuxent River in Maryland. Weights were tied to his body and he'd been shot in the head. It was an unfortunately fitting way for a man who'd organized sex parties for important figures in Washington, D.C., and been tied to everyone from Lee Harvey Oswald to CIA legend James Jesus Angleton, to end his life. Incredibly, the official cause of death was suicide. Is there anything one can say in response to that? While not directly connected to the JFK assassination, Paisley's gangster-style murder seemed to spread a fitting coat of bitter frosting on the cake, as it were.

The HSCA fiasco left the JFK assassination research community fractured and rudderless.

BREWING RIGHT WING ANGER

The country began to take a sharp philosophical turn to the right at the end of the decade. Fueled by economic woes during the Carter administration, which featured long gas lines and record-high interest rates, many Americans became convinced that government was incapable of providing the solutions to problems. In the heartland of the country, a brand-new type of radical was being formed.

John Singer, a Utah man fed up with the public education offered his children, was probably the founding father of the now thriving home school movement. His groundbreaking efforts brought him harassment from all levels of government and eventually, on January 19, 1979, he was shot and killed by law enforcement officers on his own property, evidently as he opened his mailbox. (*The Spotlight*, February 19, 1979, p. 8). In an almost incomprehensible twist of fate, one of Singer's primary opponents turned out to be the father of a boy whose life Singer had saved five years earlier, in an incident that resulted in the drowning death of Singer's own son. This was a shocking, naked show of state power. A citizen's life had been terminated exclusively because he didn't want his children to participate in any government educational program. The police's contention that Singer was shot while they attempted to serve a warrant on him was contradicted by the fact that the bullet entry wound was in his back. Singer's widow attempted to seek legal restitution, but the Circuit Court of Appeals rejected her lawsuit and in March 1985 the US Supreme Court refused to hear the case.

An earlier incident took the life of Bill Smiley, who died of a single gunshot wound at his home in Salem, Virginia, on March 4, 1976, just minutes after being approached by two IRS agents. Smiley's death was officially ruled a "suicide," although at least one Roanoke County, Virginia, law enforcement official, Donald Jones (who was first on the scene), disputed that finding. The body of Mr. Smiley, according to Jones, appeared to be "propped" in an unlikely position, and the gun that fired the fatal shot was on the opposite end of the trailer in which Smiley died. Also, the bullet that killed Smiley was never found, although it didn't leave the camper. The police told Smiley's wife that an autopsy would be performed, but one never was. Attempts by *The Spotlight* to interview the two IRS agents who shared Smiley's last minutes alive were repeatedly denied by the IRS. (*The Spotlight*, July 3, 1989, p. 14). Smiley's death represented one of the first battles between the government and tax rebels.

Finally, in 1980, when his supporters least expected it, Senator Edward Kennedy decided to run for president. It was a curious move; while he had dodged attempts to recruit him in 1972 and 1976, when his odds of winning were substantially better, now Kennedy suddenly decided to challenge incumbent Jimmy Carter for the Democratic nomination. Presumably, the safety concerns for his family still existed, but perhaps he felt an irresistible historical pull as the heir to Camelot.

There was no love lost between Kennedy and Carter; Carter declared he wouldn't raise Chappaquiddick as an issue, but instead used subtle code words to mention the topic while assuring everyone he wouldn't mention it. *The Free Lance Star* (October 3, 1979) and *Evening Independent* (October 3, 1979) would criticize Carter over this, with the latter running an article headlined "Carter Sanctimonious on Chappaquiddick." At one point during the campaign, Carter responded to Kennedy's criticism that he wasn't being specific on issues by saying, "I don't have to kiss his ass." While polls at the end of 1979 showed Kennedy crushing Carter, the hostage crisis in Iran permitted the party establishment to rally around Carter and stave off the Kennedy challenge.

Ted Kennedy would undoubtedly have run a more effective campaign if longtime Kennedy insider and campaign strategist Kenny O'Donnell hadn't passed away far too soon, at the age of fifty-three, on September 9, 1977. O'Donnell had suffered from alcoholism for years, and he was said to have irrationally blamed himself for JFK's assassination. O'Donnell had been riding in the Secret Service follow-up car in Dallas, directly behind the presidential limousine, and he was among those who criticized driver

William Greer and the other Secret Service agents. In the bestseller he wrote with fellow Kennedy insider Dave Powers, *Johnny, We Hardly Knew Ye*, O'Donnell wondered, "If the Secret Service men in the front had reacted quicker to the first two shots . . . if the driver had stepped on the gas before instead of after the fatal third shot was fired, would President Kennedy be alive today?" O'Donnell would tell House Speaker Tip O'Neill years later that he had heard shots coming from the front, but the FBI pressured him into saying they came from the rear, stating, ". . . they said it couldn't have happened that way and that I must have been imagining things. . . . I just didn't want to stir up any more pain and trouble for the family."

The 1980 campaign was thoroughly disorganized, unlike the previous campaigns of John and Robert Kennedy. The mainstream media, which had largely ignored Chappaquiddick over the years, suddenly treated the subject as an important issue. Teddy's memorable stuttering and inept responses about it to CBS reporter Roger Mudd (which the network kindly left intact for the viewers to enjoy), during a November 4, 1979, television special aired three days before Kennedy's official announcement that he was running, helped to derail his campaign before it began.

Ted Kennedy enjoyed the longest political career of any Kennedy. His immediate family experienced the standard share of Kennedy tragedy; his son Teddy Jr. lost a leg to cancer as a teenager, and his lone daughter, Kara, died suddenly at only fifty-one after her daily gym workout in 2011, two years after Ted Kennedy lost his own battle with cancer. Ironically, Ted's finest oratorical moment probably came in defeat, when he delivered the stirring "the dream will never die" defense of liberalism at the 1980 Democratic national convention.

CHAPTER FOUR

THE REAGAN YEARS: TRICKLE-DOWN TREACHERY

"Unemployment insurance is a pre-paid vacation for freeloaders."
—Ronald Reagan

Ronald Reagan, riding a new wave of popular unrest against the era of "big government," demolished President Jimmy Carter in the 1980 presidential election. He garnered more electoral votes than any non-incumbent in history, leaving him with a powerful mandate from the people.

Despite an unimpressive first term in office, which featured huge tax cuts for the wealthiest Americans and tax increases for everyone else, Reagan was reelected in 1984 in an unprecedented landslide, winning forty-nine of the fifty states against hapless Democrat Walter Mondale. While he has become the patron saint of all Republicans, especially those who revel in wearing the "conservative" mantle, Reagan's record is far, far removed from his rhetoric. Despite this, the collective delusion of his supporters is best exemplified by noted Republican speechwriter Peggy Noonan's claims, regarding his 1980 campaign promises, that they were "Done, done, done, done, done, done and done. Every bit of it."

REAGAN ASSASSINATION ATTEMPT

By the time Reagan was elected president, most Americans were quite familiar with the so-called "Zero-Year Curse." Supposedly, an Indian had put a curse on William Henry Harrison, who was elected in 1840, and all future presidents who attained the presidency in a year ending in zero. Every such president since Harrison had died in office, and with Reagan being the oldest man ever elected as president, it seemed a pretty good bet that the curse would continue. Only a few months into his administration, Reagan was shot in an assassination attempt on March 30, 1981. The alleged "lone nut," like Sirhan Sirhan, was on the scene firing a weapon, but again there were those who questioned if he truly acted alone. John Hinckley was said to have acted in order to "impress" actress Jodie Foster. This seemed to be an odd motivation even for a disturbed mind, but such nonsensical explanations are routinely given for political events in the United States.

While only reported sporadically in the mainstream media, it appeared that the family of Vice President George H. W. Bush was associated with John Hinckley's family. In fact, Neil Bush, son of the vice president and brother of future president George W. Bush, was scheduled to have dinner with Scott Hinckley, the alleged assassin's brother, the day after the shooting. Neil Bush's reaction to these early stories was curious. "I don't recognize any pictures of him," he was reported as saying. "I just wish I could see a better picture of him." The Associated Press reported that George W. Bush was unsure if he had met John Hinckley. "I don't recognize his face from the brief, kind of distorted thing they had on TV and the name doesn't ring any bells," Dubya stated. "I know he wasn't on our staff. . . ." The Hinckleys were rumored to have been large financial contributors to George H. W. Bush's unsuccessful 1980 presidential campaign.

There were "magic" bullets in this assassination attempt, too. The nearly fatal shot had supposedly ricocheted off the presidential limo in a most unlikely manner, through a space of an inch or less between the open passenger door. NBC's Judy Woodruff declared, in early news accounts of the shooting, that at least one shot came from somewhere above. It was alleged that Hinckley had shown up armed at a couple of campaign events for Jimmy Carter. Texas Governor Bill Clements criticized the press for publicizing the fact that Hinckley was from Texas, like Lee Harvey Oswald and Mark David Chapman, who had shot and killed former Beatle John Lennon on December 8, 1980. There have been numerous questions raised about the Lennon killing, and the "lone nut" involved shared a common affiliation with Hinckley in World Vision, an international Christian relief and advocacy organization. Mark David Chapman was also obsessed with the novel *Catcher in the Rye*, sitting down calmly and reading it until police arrived, after firing the shots at Lennon.

Incomprehensibly, John Hinckley has never been interviewed on television. Shouldn't some news program have devoted a segment to this subject during the last thirty years? A story in the October 1, 1989, *Los Angeles Times* reported that Hinckley had been petitioning a federal court to "allow" him to talk to reporters. The article stated that journalists such as Barbara Walters wanted to interview him. The story raised an interesting point: Why had Charles Manson been the subject of so many televised interviews, and serial killers such as John Wayne Gacy permitted to talk to the media, but not Hinckley?

Ironically, well-known JFK assassination researcher David Lifton has stated on a public forum that Reagan was keenly interested in the JFK assassination and kept a slew of books about the subject on his bedside table. In an email to me, Lifton described the source for this contention as someone who "worked for Reagan, in a significant capacity. . . ." In his book *Friends in High Places*, Bill Clinton's associate attorney general, Webb Hubbell, claimed that Clinton asked him to find out the truth about two things—the JFK assassination and UFOs. History records that neither of these leaders of the free world used their power to do anything to uncover the facts about the Kennedy assassination. Clinton, in fact, would publicly declare his belief that JFK was killed by Lee Harvey Oswald.

REAGAN'S DISTORTED RECORD

While Reagan campaigned against "gubmint" in general, in reality federal spending increased by an incredible 64 percent during his first term. This was especially unbelievable considering that the supposedly spendthrift Jimmy Carter had increased spending by a comparatively paltry 22.5 percent. In a similarly astounding statistic from the US Office of Personnel Management, the number of nonmilitary government workers increased by 238,000 during the Reagan years, while they had actually *decreased* by eight thousand under President Jimmy Carter. Reagan not only failed to even attempt to eliminate newer federal agencies like the Department of Education and the Department of Energy, he actually added a new cabinet level department—the Department of Veterans Affairs. Perhaps the most telling statistic of all is the oft-quoted one denoting that Reagan spent more money than all the presidents before him combined. The Grace Commission, tasked to find ways to reduce waste in government, delivered a report to Reagan in 1984, concluding that an astonishing one-third of all tax dollars were frittered away on waste and inefficiency. Reagan never tried to institute the solid recommendations of the Grace Commission, and Congress ignored it.

Even foreign aid, which was tremendously unpopular with the vast majority of Americans, went up steadily. Every year of his two terms in office, Reagan asked for more foreign aid than even Congress wanted to spend. Reagan raised gasoline taxes, increased Social Security tax rates, and raised payroll taxes. As even friendly mainstream conservative Republican senator Alan Simpson would admit, to National Public Radio, "Ronald Reagan raised taxes eleven times in his administration—I was there."

As President, Reagan attacked small nations like Grenada and Libya, and unwisely committed Marine forces to Lebanon, where more than two hundred of them subsequently were killed. Reagan also ousted Ferdinand Marcos from the Philippines, at the behest of the bankers who were miffed at the president of that country for his establishment of a chain of "People's Banks." These were banks from which the common people could borrow up to $5,000 at interest rates of 2 to 3 percent. Marcos was vilified in the controlled press until he was pressured into calling an unscheduled election. Although thousands of observers, including a large contingent of US State Department personnel, witnessed the proceedings, Marcos was reelected.

Despite his closely monitored, untainted electoral victory, Marcos was practically abducted by US government personnel and transported to Hawaii. As soon as he reached Hawaii, Marcos received a phone call from President Reagan, who welcomed him warmly to the United States and assured him he would be treated as an honored guest. Shortly after the phone call ended, Marcos was stripped of all his possessions by US customs officers and placed under house arrest, without being charged with any crime. US puppet Cory Aquino, a member of a wealthy oligarchical family, was installed as president, and she complied with the wishes of her masters by borrowing billions and perpetually enslaving her people. (*The Spotlight*, October 23, 1989, pp. 4, 5, and 10). The only establishment journalist to delve into this story, Britain's Derek Swanepool, made numerous visits to the Philippines during 1992, gathering evidence on reported payoffs received by US officials and CIA agents who had helped overthrow Ferdinand Marcos in 1986. In February 1993, in the customary manner of those investigating this sort of thing, he was found shot to death in his hotel room. (*The Spotlight*, May 31, 1993, p. 3).

Reagan ushered in a new style of foreign interventionism. Much smaller nations, representing no discernible threat to the United States, became fair game. The neoconservative movement was born during the Reagan years. These "neocons" were often former liberals, supposedly disenchanted with all that big government "leftism" had wrought. In reality, they were more often than not strident Zionists who helped to divert American foreign policy in a direction that mirrored the interests of Israel.

The Searle drug company (later to be bought by Monsanto, anathema to health food enthusiasts due to its "genetically engineered" seed) had developed aspartame in the 1960s. In October 1980, a Public Board of Inquiry impaneled by the FDA to evaluate aspartame found that the chemical caused an unacceptable level of brain tumors in animal tests. They advised against approving aspartame for public consumption. When Reagan was elected president a month later, he brought Donald Rumsfeld, who'd been president of Searle since 1977, onto his transition team. In January 1981, Rumsfeld allegedly promised Searle that aspartame would be approved by the end of the year. On the day after Reagan's inauguration, the FDA commissioner's authority was suspended, and the following month Dr. Arthur Hull Hayes became the new commissioner. Hayes, a former Rhodes scholar and Defense Department researcher, overrode the objections of FDA advisors and approved aspartame for use in dry foods in July 1981. In November 1983, the FDA approved the dangerous substance for usage in soft drinks, and Hayes, who'd been under fire for accepting corporate gifts, left immediately afterward to join Searle's public relations firm as senior medical advisor.

While the government was approving these kinds of deadly chemicals as "safe" for Americans to consume, the FDA was all but outlawing laetrile, a naturally occurring substance found in the kernels of apricots, peaches, and almonds. Several studies by alternative health researchers, performed in the 1970s, suggested that laetrile was effective in treating and preventing cancer. The most notable of these was probably Dr. John A. Richardson, who shared his research in the 1975 book *Laetrile Case Histories: The Richardson Cancer Clinic Experience*. Richardson was persecuted by the authorities and had to endure three expensive trials in California, each of which resulted in a dismissal of charges. The medical establishment was obviously threatened by Richardson, and he was eventually convicted in a federal court, fined $30,000, and had his medical license revoked.

Another laetrile researcher, Ernst T. Krebs, had his car windshield shot out following a lecture on alternative treatments for cancer in California. When his tailgate was shot the following night, Krebs went to the police. Their response was to advise him, "Maybe someone is trying to tell you something." Krebs's partner, Dr. Arthur Harris, was threatened with assassination by two men, if he continued his laetrile research.

President Ronald Reagan, who underwent surgery for colon cancer while in office in 1985 (*New York Times*, July 16, 1985), was given laetrile daily by IV to treat the disease, according to Senator Mark Hatfield. Another advocate of laetrile was Congressman Larry McDonald, who was also a urologist and the most notable victim of Korean Air Lines Flight 007 in 1983. Following two bogus 1980 "studies" into laetrile conducted by the National Cancer Institute, the substance was effectively banned in the United States (unless you were someone like Ronald Reagan), although it is still a popular way to treat the disease in Mexican clinics. The FDA launched what *Natural Products Insider* called a "witch hunt," with a series of armed raids on natural health-care clinics and health food stores in the 1980s.

Two especially odious pieces of legislation were produced under Reagan's watch. First, there was the Tax Reform Act of 1986, called in true Orwellian doublethink the "Tax Simplification Act." Instead of addressing the myriad of problems with the Internal Revenue Service and the absurdly complex tax code, it managed to make a horrible situation even worse. Deductions for interest on all consumer loans except mortgages were eliminated. Deductions for local sales taxes were eliminated. The new act made it extremely difficult to deduct medical expenses. The negative impact from the changes fell disproportionately on the poor and middle class.

Also in 1986, we saw the passage of the Immigration Reform Act. Illegal immigration, primarily from Mexico, had become an issue of growing concern among Americans. However, again, this legislation managed to not only make a bad situation worse, it signaled a virtual surrender to a problem that any rational sovereign nation would address logically. The general amnesty provisions of the law resulted in an explosion of illegal immigrants over the next few decades. The legislation was the culmination of heavy lobbying by two disparate forces—liberal groups anxious to curry favor with the conveniently created "Hispanic" bloc of voters, and unprincipled conservative business groups desirous of expanding upon a cheap source of labor. The immigration issue is a prime example of the fallacy of "Left" and "Right" labels; in reality, both ends of the political spectrum come together whenever the issue is important enough to the powerful forces controlling them.

The deindustrialization of America began in earnest under Reagan. What Walter Mondale had vainly decried as a burgeoning "rust bowl" was only the tip of the iceberg. A new age of greed was born in the 1980s. Influential movers and shakers smitten with the selfish credo of author Ayn Rand, and a good many Americans impressed by the bestseller *Looking Out for Number One* by Robert Ringer, helped develop a pervasive, collective mindset that would culminate in the birth of the "me" generation. Profits became the sole concern of powerful business executives, who started being referred to in a more impressive way, as CEOs. Incomprehensibly large bonuses for upper management, frequently accompanied by massive layoffs of workers in the same company, became all too commonplace. The 1982 recession was perhaps the beginning of the humongous gap in wealth we see today, as untold numbers of formerly well-paid factory workers, many of them once protected by viable unions, were laid off and forced to find lower-paying jobs.

The gradual transformation from an industrial to a service economy was based on typical shortsightedness by business leaders and the usual timidity on the part of our elected representatives. Honest critics from both ends of the ideological spectrum, from Pat Buchanan to Ralph Nader, warned against the dangers of deindustrializing America. Still, as always, the leaders of both "competing" major political parties agreed completely on the substantive issues that permitted this disastrous change in our economic base to occur. A country that doesn't manufacture anything will obviously be entirely dependent on those that do. But, hey, Walmart provides us with all those cheap products, so why should we worry about it if they're being made with slave labor?

The decline of unions also began under Reagan. After he fired more than elven thousand members of the Professional Air Traffic Controllers Organization on August 5, 1981, the power of organized labor was never the same. Despite the mob-fueled corruption rife in so many unions, it is undeniable that the presence of strong unions lifted the wages and improved the benefits of nonunion workers as well. By January 2013, it was reported that only 11.3 percent of Americans belonged to a union, a ninety-seven-year low. (*Time*, January 29, 2013).

In 1928, just before the onset of the Great Depression, the consolidation of wealth in America was such that the top 10 percent of the population earned almost 50 percent of all income in the country. More telling, the top 1 percent possessed 23.9 percent of all income. After the most difficult years of the Depression, the income gap narrowed, so that from the period of 1942–82, the top 10 percent made about 33.5 percent of all income, while the take for the top 1 percent was down to less than 9 percent by 1976. These figures corresponded directly to the changing tax rates for the wealthiest Americans. For the forty years when income disparity was at its least, for instance, the highest tax rate was always at least 70 percent.

Reagan's first income tax cut, in 1981, lowered the top rate dramatically, from 70 percent to 50 percent. Reagan's 1986 Tax Reform Act lowered the top tax rate from 50 percent to 28 percent and raised the bottom rate from 11 percent to 15 percent. Following these massive tax breaks for the wealthiest Americans, the disparity in income began to increase again. The inequity in wealth grew steadily through the 1990s, and by 2007 the top 10 percent were once again controlling some 50 percent of the income, mirroring the late 1920s, and the top 1 percent had climbed back to earning 23.5 percent of all American income. Put another way, official Congressional Budget Office data reveals that after-tax income for the top 1 percent grew 281 percent from 1979 to 2007, and the top 20 percent increased 95 percent. Before the Reagan tax cuts, the wealthiest 1 percent of Americans saw an average yearly increase in income (unadjusted for inflation) of about 7 percent in the period from 1942–1982. With higher tax rates for the wealthy, the 99 percent below them saw even larger income increases, with those at the bottom making the most progress. However, the disparity had grown so much by the year 2000 that the richest American households saw an increase in inflation-adjusted income of 22.2 percent in the period from 2000–06, while the bottom 90 percent of Americans collectively saw their income decrease by 4 percent.

Ronald Reagan is often credited with "ending the Cold War." Supposedly, his hardline, anti-Communist zealotry caused the Soviet system to ultimately collapse. There is no denying that his administration gave unlimited financial resources to the military-industrial complex during his eight years in office. However, when Korean Airlines 007 was "accidentally" shot down over Soviet airspace, on August 31, 1983, with the aforementioned right wing ideologue (and fervent anti-Communist) congressman Larry P. McDonald onboard, Reagan did absolutely nothing in response. While McDonald was connected to organizations like The John Birch Society, he was one of the few members of Congress to speak out about the Federal Reserve and the unchecked power of banks in general.

McDonald was also a diehard "conspiracy theorist," as his following comment illustrates: "The drive of the Rockefeller family and their allies is to create a one-world government, combining super-capitalism and Communism under the same tent, all under their control. . . . Do I mean conspiracy? Yes I do. I am convinced there is such a plot, international in scope, generations old in planning, and incredibly evil in intent." Representative Ron Paul called McDonald "the most principled man in Congress." "Liberal" journalist Jack Anderson issued a despicable comment after the crash, which caused no furor in the mainstream media—or Congress. "While I feel a great deal of sympathy for any man who dies prematurely," Anderson stated, "if any single member of Congress had to die in that crash, they certainly picked the right one." (*The Spotlight*, October 7, 1985, p. 18).

OCTOBER SURPRISE AND IRAN-CONTRA

The two most well-known scandals of the Reagan years were interconnected. The first was dubbed "October Surprise." Lyndon Larouche was among the first to accuse President-Elect Reagan of conspiring with the leaders of Iran to stall the release of the American hostages until after the 1980 election, thereby denying incumbent Jimmy Carter an inevitable boost in public support. The "conspiracy theory" that the release of the hostages was delayed in return for the promise of arms to Iran was initially published in Larouche's *Executive Intelligence Review*, December 2, 1980. However, when the second major scandal, the Iran-Contra affair, broke in 1986, the fact that it seemed to reinforce the American part of the alleged bargain brought renewed public attention to both issues.

Barbara Honegger had worked for the Reagan administration in the White House Office of Policy Development, but she ultimately resigned as a matter of conscience. Her book *October Surprise* was published in 1989. Honegger pointed out that then-Vice President George Bush had been a director of the CIA, and thus had plenty of covert connections and knowledge, to aid him in implementing the secret deal between the Reagan team and Iran. Many in the CIA held an animosity toward Jimmy Carter over his attempts to downsize the Agency, and they were eager for revenge. Honegger was careful to consistently refer to the October Surprise story as "alleged." Honegger questioned why the many witnesses who had claimed the allegations were true hadn't been given the opportunity to tell their stories to the American people. Honegger wrote: "As an independent journalist, I believe profoundly in the right of the American public to hear from all parties who claim to have information on charges as serious as that an arms-for-hostage-delay deal was made between the Reagan-Bush campaign and Iran."

Honegger touched on some darker forces in her book as well, including the Propaganda Due, or P-2, connection. P-2 is an exclusive, Masonic lodge founded in Italy by powerful financier Licio Gelli in 1966. Honegger noted that Alexander Haig, later to become the secretary of state under Ronald Reagan, had been made an "honorary" (non-Italian) member of P-2 sometime prior to 1980. Honegger further stated that Licio Gelli, finance wizard Michele Sindona, Haig, and CIA Director William Casey "were also reportedly members of the Vatican's military order, the Knights of Malta, whose initiates must take an oath of allegiance to the Pope." P-2 has also been linked to the Mafia.

As Honegger described it: "A number of press reports, taken together, suggest that there may have been a P-2 and Gambino Mafia connection to the release of the fifty-two American hostages from the US embassy in Tehran." In June 1982, "God's banker" Roberto Calvi's body was found hanging beneath Blackfriars Bridge in London. Calvi was chairman of Italy's second-largest bank, Banco Ambrosiano, and had been a member of P2. Because P2 Masons often called each other "black friars," some were quick to grasp the symbolism and connect his death to the secretive order. It took many years, but finally in 2005 Gelli was accused of having ordered Calvi's death as punishment for embezzling money from the Bank of Italy. Inexplicably, Gelli avoided indictment and five underlings were prosecuted instead. Two years later, all charges were dropped due to "insufficient evidence." The Italian Court of Appeals agreed with the judge's decision in 2010.

The courageous Harry V. Martin, publisher of the *Napa Sentinel*, ran articles in his newspaper detailing the testimony of Gunther Russbacher, a US Navy captain who claimed to have been the pilot of a BAC 111 aircraft that flew to Paris on October 19, 1980. Russbacher stated that also on board were soon to be CIA Director William Casey and future vice president and president George H. W. Bush. Bush, however, claimed he was at Andrews Air Force Base at the time. Russbacher would be charged with misappropriation of government properties and sent to Terminal Island (nice name, huh?) federal prison. Russbacher had also worked with the Office of Naval Intelligence and the CIA. Russbacher told the *Napa Sentinel*, in an exclusive interview, that this was the first of a series of flights, after which an agreement was struck between Bush, Casey, and Iranian officials to delay the release of American hostages until after the November election.

Former CIA operative and international arms dealer Richard Brenneke would back up Russbacher's claims in federal court, declaring that he was on the Paris flight himself. The government charged Brenneke with perjury in retaliation, but he was acquitted by a jury. The congressional investigation into the matter, chaired by dependable establishment figure Representative Lee Hamilton (D-IN), was delayed until 1992. Predictably, the entire affair was a whitewash. Hamilton, in fact, refused to investigate the roles of Reagan or Bush, stating that it would not be "good for the country." Russbacher, somewhat surprisingly, lived on until succumbing to cancer in 2005.

National Security Council staff member Oliver North would first garner public attention when it was disclosed that he was in charge of diverting funds from arm sales to Iran to the Contra rebels in Nicaragua. North would be fired by President Reagan in November 1986 after the weapons sales were reported publically. He became a familiar figure to Americans after he testified before the joint congressional committee investigating Iran-Contra in the summer of 1987. North would somehow bounce back from all this to become a semi-respectable talking head on television by the mid-1990s.

Author Terry Reed exposed the real story of Iran-Contra in his invaluable book *Compromised: Clinton, Bush and the CIA*. Reed described the "conservative" North playing a prominent role in the drug trade, under the alias John Cathey, working hand in hand with then Arkansas Governor Bill Clinton, his supposed "liberal" enemy, as well as CIA drug transport pilot Barry Seal and Panama's General Noriega. FBI Special Agent Richard M. Taus, attempting to investigate these complex tentacles connecting the CIA to drug trafficking, was set up and railroaded into prison. Seal, at the time under investigation by the DEA, was killed in February 1986, allegedly by Columbian hit men. Shortly after his death, President Reagan revealed one of the photos Seal had taken earlier, purporting to show Nicaraguan Sandinista leaders making a deal with members of the notorious Columbian Meddelin Cartel, in an effort to garner congressional support for the Contras. Much of the activities described in Reed's book took place at Mena Airport, in Mena, Arkansas. Mena would subsequently be at the center of some of the numerous scandals attached to President Bill Clinton. Another related death occurred in October 1994, when Seal's bookkeeper, Florence Martin, was found in her bed, shot three times through a pillow. Nothing in the home was taken, including her nearby wallet, and there were no indications of robbery.

Former Israeli prime minister Yitzhak Shamir probably summed it up best, when he was asked in May 1993 if there had been an October Surprise. Shamir responded, "of course, it was."

THE INSLAW SCANDAL

One of the forgotten scandals of the Reagan years involved a privately owned company called Inslaw. Bill and Nancy Hamilton, the owners of Inslaw, alleged that the Reagan Justice Department, in 1983, stole the new PROMIS software from their company. Journalist Danny Casolaro probably lost his life because of his investigation into this scandal. Casolaro was found dead in a Martinsburg, West Virginia, hotel on August 10, 1991, allegedly a suicide. He was working on what he called the "Octopus" conspiracy, which tied together the Inslaw case with Iran Contra, the October Surprise, and other scandals of the 1980s. Among many mysterious aspects of his death was the fact the medical examiner allowed the body to be embalmed before the Casolaro family had even been notified of Danny's death. Danny's brother, Dr. Anthony Casolaro, was very vocal in expressing his opinion that his brother could not have committed suicide. The official story was that Danny had slit his wrists and was found in a bathtub filled with blood. Dr. Casolaro maintained that his brother was so scared of the sight of blood that he wouldn't allow samples to be drawn for medical purposes. Thus, it seemed highly unlikely that he would choose the method of suicide that he allegedly did. Danny was, by all accounts, an extremely happy person, and he had just told friends he was going to Martinsburg to "bring back the head of the octopus."

The Hamiltons did receive some publicity from their fight against the government, mainly because former attorney general Elliot Richardson agreed to serve as their counsel. (*The Spotlight*, March 1, 1993, pp. 14–17). Interestingly enough, Elliot Richardson was quoted as saying, in regards to the "suicide" of Danny Casolaro, "It's hard to come up with any reason for this death, other than he was deliberately murdered because he was so close to uncovering sinister elements in what he called 'The Octopus.'"

Two different federal bankruptcy courts found that the Justice Department had stolen the PROMIS software from Inslaw. An investigation by the House Judiciary Committee confirmed the findings of theft on the part of the Justice Department. The Committee recommended that then-Attorney General Richard Thornburgh compensate Inslaw, but Thornburgh ignored them. In 1993, an investigation under the lead of Special Counsel Nicholas J. Bua exonerated the Justice Department of any wrongdoing. Showing some of that good ol' reliable bipartisanship again, Bill Clinton's attorney general, Janet Reno, issued a lengthy review in 1995, concluding there was no credible evidence of conspiracy on the part of the government to steal Inslaw's software, and that the company was not entitled to any remuneration.

Maverick editor Harry V. Martin, in a series of exposés in his *Napa Sentinel* (California) newspaper, extensively investigated Inslaw, as well as other scandals. He reported additional deaths, besides Cassolaro's, of witnesses connected to the case. For instance, Alan D. Standorf, suspected of being one of Cassolaro's key sources, was found dead on the rear floor of his car at Washington's National Airport, in September 1991. The cause of death was determined to be a blow to the head, and investigators believed he'd been killed weeks earlier at another site. Earlier in 1991, Barry R. Kumnick, an ingenious computer engineer who'd invented a new artificial intelligence to dramatically enhance Inslaw's PROMIS software, simply disappeared. By September 1991, no member of his family had heard from him in six months, and they were told by Kumnick's known business partner that he'd never heard of him. (*The Spotlight*, September 30, 1991, p. 7). Attorney Dennis Eisman, who was reputed to have "information" on Inslaw, was found shot to death on April 5, 1991. Ian Spiro was associated with the grand jury proceedings on the Inslaw case. His wife and three children were found murdered in their home on November 1, 1992. Spiro's dead body was found a few days later in a parked car in the desert.

Michael Riconosciuto was a brilliant computer programmer, described by his cousin, talk show host Anita Langley, as a "Tesla type." Riconosciuto claimed to have programmed Inslaw's PROMIS software with a secret "back door" that would permit clandestine tracking of individuals. Riconosciuto stated that PROMIS was some kind of "reward" to his associate Earl Brian, a longtime Reagan aide, for the October Surprise operation. He alleged that Earl Brian used the proceeds from the illegal sale of PROMIS to foreign governments to finance the manufacture of weapons at the remote Cabazon Indian Reservation in Indio, California. He would also claim that he'd been threatened by a Justice Department official. One week after he swore out the March 21, 1991, affidavit about Inslaw, Riconosciuto was arrested on drug charges. He was given a thirty-year prison sentence, unheard of for a first-time drug offender (although the drug offense was clearly bogus). Earl Brian sued Elliot Richardson for libel, but the case was dismissed. In 1996, Brian was convicted of falsifying company finances. He was sentenced to prison and released in 2002.

As for the courageous Harry V. Martin, he and his wife were eventually forced to live in a homeless shelter after his tabloid newspaper published its last issue in May 2011. He suffered a series of strokes at the shelter a few months later. Undeterred, the seventy-two-year-old Martin and his wife left the shelter in November 2011 to live in Sacramento. A group of his admirers donated $6,000 to subsidize their rent with the new landlord. (*Napa Valley Register*, November 4, 2011).

BO GRITZ AND THE DRUG TRADE

A perfect illustration of how our "free" press reacts to real, significant news occurred when Lieutenant Colonel James "Bo" Gritz, upon whom the Rambo character in Hollywood was based, attempted to expose the international drug trade. Gritz, along with his colleague Scott Weekly, was sent to Burma in 1986, at the request of Vice President George Bush, to look for prisoners of war. They found no POWs, but they did uncover strong indications of US governmental involvement in drug trafficking. Gritz brought back a video-taped interview with General Khun Sa, the "overlord" of the infamous Golden Triangle of heroin. Khun Sa requested that the videotapes be sent directly to President Reagan, and in the interview he declared that he would stop the tons of opiates intended for delivery into the United States from the Golden Triangle. He also promised to expose the names of every prominent US official that "has been my best customer for the last 20 years" if Reagan would help him legitimize his economy. Gritz turned the tapes over to the White House, but there was absolutely no interest in them. Gritz then went back to Burma in 1987 and returned with the names of American government officials whom Khun Sa claimed had been dealing heroin and trading for arms for more than twenty years.

The top-ranking official accused was Richard Armitage, who would be appointed assistant secretary of defense by President George H. W. Bush. Instead of Armitage facing any legal scrutiny, Gritz comrade Scott Weekly was sent to prison on totally fabricated charges for fourteen months until an honest judge finally threw the case out of court. Loose cannon billionaire and future presidential candidate Ross Perot found out about the story, went to then-FBI Director William Webster, and was later seen carrying a pile of documents into the White House. Yet, according to *Time* magazine, in its May 4, 1988, issue (p. 18), "The Reagan administration has given him no help." Secretary of Defense Frank Carlucci supposedly instructed Perot to stop pursuing his underling Armitage. The most astounding part of this entire story is the fact that Gritz, who was a well-known figure in governmental circles, called a press conference in Los Angeles and revealed his information, documenting it with the videotapes, before representatives of the national television networks, all local television stations, the *Los Angeles Times*, the *Daily News*, and the Associated Press. Despite the explosive nature of Gritz's charges, the only voice in the press to report what he said was *The Spotlight*. (*The Spotlight*, August 8, 1988, pp. 13–20).

REAGAN BODY COUNT

A truly bizarre death was that of CIA agent Kevin Mulcahy, forty, whose body was found on October 26, 1982, lying crumpled between the screen and front doors of a motel cabin, with his pants pulled down, in rural Shenandoah County, Virginia. Mulcahy had blown the whistle on his fellow agent Edwin Wilson's dubious dealings with Libya. Foul play was predictably ruled out by Northern Virginia Deputy Chief Medical Examiner James Beyer (later to be involved in the Vince Foster case), who attributed Mulcahy's death to bronchopneumonia. Mulcahy was scheduled to be one of the prosecution's chief witnesses at Wilson's trial. Wilson's dealings with Libya were coordinated through the Nugan Hand Bank, a CIA front. A few years earlier, on January 27, 1980, Frank Nugan, one of the bank's founders, was found shot to death in his Mercedes-Benz. Also discovered in the car was a Bible, with a piece of paper in it, on which the names "Bob Wilson" and "Bill Colby" had been written. Wilson was a veteran US congressman and Colby was a former director of the CIA who'd served as the bank's legal counsel. Michael Hand, his partner, disappeared shortly afterward and was never seen again.

THE DEATH OF R. BUDD DWYER

Another disturbing incident, which epitomized the way the establishment news media distorts the truth about important events, involved Pennsylvania State Treasurer R. Budd Dwyer. Dwyer drew the ire of then-Pennsylvania Governor (and future Bush attorney general) Richard Thornburgh when he refused to pay a travel voucher for the governor's wife, Ginny, following a trip to Europe. Mrs. Thornburgh wanted the taxpayers to reimburse her for a personal trip, and Dwyer refused. Following this, Dwyer claimed, Thornburgh told a number of people that he was going to "get" Dwyer, whom he referred to indelicately as "the fat-ass." Shortly thereafter, Dwyer upset the governor again when he learned from a *Philadelphia Inquirer* reporter that Thornburgh was using a state police security detail to chauffer his sons back and forth from a private school in New England. Dwyer questioned this expense of taxpayer funds, too. As a result, Dwyer was hounded by Thornburgh, and eventually the governor was able, after launching an "investigation," to charge the honest state treasurer with bribery.

On Thursday, January 22, 1987, the day before he was scheduled to be sentenced, Dwyer called a press conference and read a detailed, twenty-two-page statement, proclaiming his innocence—as he had done from the beginning—and charged that Thornburgh had engineered his conviction for political reasons. In his statement, Dwyer chastised the major media for failing to "expose the close connection between Thornburgh and acting US attorney James West," who had prosecuted Dwyer. Despite all the details of political skullduggery in the long statement Dwyer read to reporters, the establishment press concentrated on the sensational end to the press conference, when Dwyer placed a .357 magnum in his mouth and pulled the trigger.

The *Washington Post* acted typically, in that it called Dwyer's statement "rambling," and never mentioned any of the serious allegations that the treasurer made. It did, however, true to form, publish a series of gruesome photos of Dwyer shooting himself. *The Spotlight* obtained a full copy of Dwyer's final statement and interviewed JoAnn Dwyer, his widow. Mrs. Dwyer later credited *The Spotlight* with being the only paper to expose the truth behind the political intrigue that resulted in her husband's unfortunate actions. (*The Spotlight*, September 5, 1988, p. 26). In late 2010, a documentary titled *Honest Man: The Life of R. Budd Dwyer* was released. Dwyer's children attended the premiere and took questions from the audience afterward. The film included William Smith, the witness whose testimony had led to Dwyer's conviction, admitting on film that he had lied under oath and that the charges against Dwyer were false.

REX 84

Under the auspices of Jimmy Carter's nightmarish creation FEMA (Federal Emergency Management Agency), the Reagan administration devised a diabolical plan called Readiness Exercise 1984, or Rex 84. Using a problem solely created and enabled by the same corrupt authorities, illegal immigration, as a pretext, under Rex 84 an undisclosed number of concentration camps were set up throughout the United States. The ostensible purpose was to round up illegal aliens and detain them in these FEMA-run camps. The existence of the Rex 84 plan was first revealed during the 1987 Iran-Contra hearings, and subsequently reported on in the July 5, 1987, *Miami Herald*. The newspaper acknowledged that the plan permitted FEMA to declare martial law with the mere signature of a president. Rex 84 also allowed the conversion of numerous military bases into prisons.

Rex 84 was cowritten by Lieutenant Colonel Oliver North. During his 1987 Iran-Contra testimony, North was asked by Representative Jack Brooks of Texas about his work on "plans for the continuity of government in the event of a major disaster." As North's attorney visibly winced at this veiled reference to Rex 84, the committee chairman, Senator Daniel Inouye of Hawaii, interceded with, "I believe that question touches upon a highly sensitive and classified area, so may I request that you not touch upon that?" Brooks tried again, declaring that he'd heard such a plan existed, that "would suspend the American Constitution," in the event of a declared emergency. Inouye again requested the matter not be broached, and promised that if need be the subject could be explored in an executive session.

On a 2010 episode of his controversial television show *Conspiracy Theory with Jesse Ventura*, the ex-Minnesota governor touched on this delicate issue. Ventura examined the proliferation of so-called "Fusion Centers" all over the country. These bizarre law enforcement centers serve an unclear purpose; in one memorable scene, Ventura's cameras panned to a swing set in the playground outside one such "center." Exactly what kind of "criminals" are the authorities anticipating at these "centers?"

THE TAXPAYER REBELLION

The Reagan years also saw the real beginnings of a taxpayer revolt movement, which was ironic in light of the president's reputation as a "tax cutter." The most notorious of these tax rebels was North Dakota rancher Gordon Kahl. Kahl, a respected, decorated WWII veteran, had already served a year in prison for tax evasion, when on February 13, 1983, after attending a meeting of his extremist group Posse Comitatus with his wife Joan, son Yorie, and a few friends, he ran into a roadblock conducted by the FBI and other law enforcement personnel. According to Yorie and Joan, one of the marshals fired the first shot, which struck Yorie. Gordon Kahl then returned the gunfire, killing two marshals and wounding two others. The next day, a military force, including an armored personnel carrier, firebombed and wrecked Kahl's modest home, but he and an associate escaped.

After the FBI conducted a nationwide search, it discovered Kahl's hideout in Annieville, Arkansas, and on June 3, 1983, five heavily armed officers broke into the home occupied by the fugitive. A great deal of dispute follows about what happened next, but the house was burned and Kahl was either shot or perished in the flames. Even the establishment press had to admit what was obvious to everyone who knew Gordon Kahl. To quote Tom Fitzpatrick, in the June 10, 1983, *Arizona Republic*, Kahl was one of the kindest, most generous individuals imaginable, and was "completely law abiding in all respects, except in regard to the federal income tax and related matters." Afterward, the surviving Kahls were subjected to more punishment. Joan was acquitted on charges of murder, but was left penniless when the IRS seized her farm. Yorie was convicted of second-degree murder and given two life sentences. Later, juror Maryls Klimek signed an affidavit that alleged US marshals had unduly influenced jurors to obtain a guilty verdict. Yorie continues to languish in prison, the victim, according to his mother, of exceptionally bad treatment by the prison authorities. (*The Spotlight*, August 1, 1983, pp. 16–17).

On June 18, 1985, a federally funded SWAT team under the direction of the Cass County, North Dakota, sheriff descended on the North Dakota family farm of Ron Brakke. Evidently for the express purpose of seizing a tractor, the brave lawmen beat Brakke, his aunt, his invalid wife, and their three children. Brakke's wife eventually died as a result of her injuries. (*The Spotlight*, April 9, 1990, pp. 14–15). Arthur Kirk, a Nebraska farmer whose only crime appears to have been a stubborn unwillingness to relinquish the farm that had been in his family for generations, was executed by a Nebraska State Patrol SWAT team a year after Kahl was murdered. It is impossible to determine exactly what took place at the Kirk farm on the day he was killed, as his attackers were the only witnesses. (*The Spotlight*, November 12, 1984). Interestingly, Kirk's widow later became engaged to another beleaguered farmer, Lawrence Keiswetter, who was railroaded into prison in 1989 and died shortly thereafter under mysterious circumstances. (*The Spotlight*, December 18, 1989, pp. 10, 11, and 18).

Less than a month after the death of Arthur Kirk, on December 8, 1984, at the end of a thirty-five-hour siege, an assault force of nearly one hundred US marshals, FBI, Secret Service, and Treasury agents bombarded a small house near Seattle with a barrage of gunfire, killing the lone man barricaded inside. Then, with no firefighting equipment on the scene, the government agents fired incendiary missiles at the house and burned it to the ground, destroying everything—including the body of the victim. The victim was thirty-one-year-old Robert Jay Mathews, leader of the White Nationalist group The Order, who was wanted by federal authorities on a fugitive warrant, issued as a result of an earlier confrontation in which an FBI agent was wounded. (*The Spotlight*, January 7 and 14, 1985, pp. 31 and 38).

Proving that radical black organizations weren't immune from overzealous law enforcement either, on May 13, 1985, Philadelphia's MOVE group, which didn't trust modern technology and lived a back-to-nature lifestyle, engaged police in an armed standoff from their commune. Police eventually dropped a bomb from a helicopter, burning down more than sixty houses and resulting in the deaths of eleven group members.

On July 3, 1988, Iran Air Flight 655 was shot down over the Strait of Hormuz by US missiles, killing all 290 people aboard. Early on, American officials actually floated out the absurd possibility that the Iranians had loaded the plane with corpses or dummies, and had incited the attack to make the United States look bad. Even establishment publications such as *Newsweek* criticized the US military of recklessness. Military officials would belatedly acknowledge that the US Navy cruiser *Vincennes* had indeed been in Iranian waters at the time, something they'd previously denied. While the American government expressed "regret" over the loss of life, it never apologized to the Iranians, or admitted any wrongdoing. In 1996, the United States reached a settlement with Iran at the International Court of Justice.

The burgeoning AIDS epidemic throughout the 1980s created a few "conspiracy theories." The most notable one was that the virus was manmade, created for diabolical purposes. On June 6, 1969, Pentagon spokesman Dr. Donald MacArthur told Congress: "Within the next five to ten years, it would probably be possible to make a new infective microorganism which could differ in certain important aspects from any known disease-causing organism. Most important of these is that it might be refractory to the immunological and therapeutic processes upon which we depend to maintain our relative freedom from infectious disease. A research program to explore the feasibility of this could be completed in approximately five years at a total cost of $10 million." The HIV virus certainly fit that definition. Critics alleged that scientists working at Fort Detrick in Maryland had been responsible for developing the virus in the biowarfare lab there.

The fact that the New York Blood Center in Manhattan had specifically requested actively gay men to test their Hepatitis-B vaccine in 1978–79 certainly provides some food for thought. Similar vaccine programs would be carried out in Los Angeles, San Francisco, Denver, and other cities the following year. There is no recognizable correlation between sexual orientation and vaccination. Feeding the paranoia was the fact that two of the leading voices advocating a biowarfare theory behind AIDS died unnaturally within a month of each other. Ted Strecker allegedly shot himself on August 11, 1988, leaving behind no suicide note. On September 22, 1988, Illinois State Representative Douglas Huff, who had promoted Strecker's research, died from a supposed drug overdose. Strecker had claimed the AIDS virus was in fact developed by the National Cancer Institute, in conjunction with the World Health Organization, at Fort Detrick, Maryland.

REAGAN THE FAMILY MAN

If Ronald Reagan's political record was distorted, so was his personal image. While he received tremendous support from "family values" types of groups, Reagan's own family was dysfunctional. Reagan was the first man elected to the presidency who had been divorced. Reagan's youngest daughter, Patti

Davis, would accuse her mother, Nancy, of abuse, writing in her memoir, *The Way I See It,* "I first remember my mother hitting me when I was eight. It escalated as I got older. . . . The last time it happened was when I was in my second year of college." Ron Reagan Jr. backed up his sister Patti's claims that Nancy had abused her. His closeness to his parents was best expressed when he married without even telling them about it.

Michael Reagan, Ronald's adopted son from his first marriage, felt so strongly about Nancy that he wrote, regarding his delight as a teenager at seeing her car roll downhill and become totaled: "I laughed and was only sorry she wasn't in it." Michael would become one of the strongest defenders of his father's legacy, but he issued bitter public complaints during the early years of Reagan's presidency that his father hadn't even seen his grandchild yet. Nancy, in contradiction to any "traditional" values, relied heavily on astrology to guide her everyday actions. Her influence over her malleable husband was such that he had his own personal astrologer, Joan Quigley. Reagan aide Donald Regan would maintain that "virtually every move and decision the Reagans made" had to be cleared first with the astrologer from San Francisco.

When Reagan's personal diary was published in 2007, observers were most astonished by the absence of any expressions of affection for his four children. This was especially perplexing because Reagan did mention Nancy repeatedly in heartfelt, emotional terms. All of his children were estranged from him to varying degrees. There is little doubt that he was a rather cold and distant father.

Like Bill Clinton and George W. Bush, Reagan was also accused of rape. In a little-noticed and quickly buried story, *People* magazine interviewed Selene Walters for its April 29, 1991, issue. Walters claimed that the then-forty-two-year-old Reagan had raped her in her apartment in 1952, when she was nineteen years old. Other than *Slate*'s March 5, 1999, article titled "Gipper the Ripper," her serious allegation seems to have been forgotten. Sensationalist author Kitty Kelley, in her book *Nancy Reagan: The Unauthorized Biography,* would highlight Walters's claim, and call it "date rape," while additionally reporting that Nancy Reagan—then-actress Nancy Davis—was renowned for her ability to perform oral sex (which actor and onetime JFK brother-in-law Peter Lawford also supposedly attested to). Kelley even wrote that Nancy serviced her longtime pal Frank Sinatra in the Oval Office during the Reagan years.

Despite having the overwhelming support of fundamentalist Christians, Reagan himself rarely attended church. While exemplifying the American work ethic, he probably worked less than any president in recent memory, regularly taking afternoon naps and spending an inordinate amount of time at his ranch in California. The Reagans were close friends with Alfred and Betsy Bloomingdale. Alfred, heir to the department store fortune, garnered lurid headlines when news of his longtime affair with model Vicki Morgan, thirty-six years younger than him, broke shortly after his death in 1982. Morgan attempted to lodge a palimony lawsuit against Bloomingdale's estate, but it was thrown out of court. She was also supposedly in the process of writing a tell-all book about Alfred, and the other powerful acquaintances who participated in their sadistic sexual rituals, when she was brutally murdered, allegedly by her roommate, on July 7, 1983. The roommate, Marvin Pancoast, confessed to her murder but then recanted in prison, dying shortly thereafter of AIDS. Morgan's attorney, Robert Steinberg, claimed to have been given graphic videotapes of Bloomingdale and Morgan engaging in orgies, which also included two members of Reagan's administration and a congressman. Steinberg said he offered to give the tapes to President Reagan, but then reported they'd been stolen.

Ronald Reagan left office with a final slap at the American people by accepting a $2 million thank-you from the Japanese for his trade policies, which helped to destroy our industrial base.

CHAPTER FIVE

BUSH THE ELDER

"I will never apologize for the United States—I don't care what the facts are."

—George Herbert Walker Bush

After eight years as Reagan's very influential vice president, George Herbert Walker Bush was elected president in 1988. While he had, during his unsuccessful 1980 presidential campaign, attacked Reagan's ideas as "voodoo economics," Bush would continue the disastrous trade policies and the "trickle-down" theories that began under Reagan and widened the gap between rich and poor to new, unimaginably sinful dimensions. Bush would brag about hating broccoli, had no idea about the price of everyday items such as milk, and most importantly would speak glowingly of the "New World Order."

George Bush came from a truly blue-blood, upper-class background. His father, Prescott Bush, was a banker who served eleven years in the US Senate. Prescott's father, the president's grandfather, was the president of a steel company, and during World War I coordinated government contracts with weapons dealers. His father, the president's great-grandfather, was a graduate of Yale, establishing a family tradition. Another great-grandfather was an Ohio State Supreme Court judge. Bush had ancestors who were on the *Mayflower*.

Despite this patrician's background, Bush had some surprisingly shady friends. For instance, there was speedboat designer and builder Don Aronow. Aronow had other powerful contacts, and he built speedboats for the Shah of Iran, Lyndon B. Johnson, Malcolm Forbes, and George H. W. Bush himself. Aronow was also supposedly close friends with powerful mobster Meyer

Lansky. In his controversial book *George Bush, The Unauthorized Biography*, author Webster Tarpley claimed there was "compelling evidence to conclude that Aronow was a drug smuggler and suspected drug-money launderer," citing information gleaned from *Blue Thunder* by Thomas Burdick and Charlene Mitchell, p. 229. Aronow was shot to death by an unknown person or persons on February 3, 1987. In the days before his death, he was said to have made numerous personal calls to George H. W. Bush.

OPERATION WATCH TOWER

George Bush the elder was our first, and to date only, president who'd previously been a director of the CIA. A fifteen-page affidavit from Army Special Forces Colonel Edward P. Cutolo, who in 1976 was the commander of "Operation Watch Tower," a secret operation that trafficked drugs from Colombia into the United States, indicated that then-CIA Director Bush was aware of the whole thing. The smuggling originated in Colombia, went through Panama, and entered the United States, and it involved a team of high-level CIA and Israeli Mossad agents. Colonel Cutolo prepared the affidavit with instructions that it be used to expose the clandestine CIA operation in the event he was killed. According to Cutolo, future US enemy Manuel Noriega, then a Panama Defense Force officer, met the planes in Panama, along with other fellow officers.

The list of deaths that Cutolo recounts in his affidavit is frightening. Sergeant John Newby, who was one of the soldiers who'd participated in Watch Tower operations, told Cutolo of receiving threats that, Cutolo states, were "just prior to the parachuting accident that claimed his life in October 1978." On March 5, 1980, Cutolo sought assistance from former POW Colonel James "Nick" Rowe (mentioned later in this book as one of those "thanked" by the author of a dubious book on the POW-MIA issue), and asked him to determine if Operation Watch Tower was an authentic US government operation. Evidently, Cutolo naively believed the Agency's "cover" version of the operation. Colonel Rowe's investigation produced an Israeli link in the person of one David Kimche. Chillingly, Cutolo reported that he had first been shown a photo of Kimche in 1977 by his friend, Colonel Robert Bayard, "just prior to his murder in Atlanta, Georgia, in 1977." Another Israeli, notorious Mossad hit man Michael Harari, was reportedly involved as well, and Cutolo declares in his affidavit: "I was told from Pentagon contacts, off the record, that (then) CIA Director Stansfield Turner and former CIA Director George Bush are among the VIPs that shield Harari from public scrutiny."

In July 1987, Colonel Rowe had attempted to get *60 Minutes* to look into Operation Watch Tower, but CBS turned him down. Neri concluded his letter thusly: "I have not contacted you prior to now because I am very ill and wanted my final days free of intrigue. . . . I have left this letter, the affidavit and instructions with a co-worker. This person will find you, if you are still alive, when I die." Neri died on April 29, 1990. (*The Spotlight,* May 13, 1991, pp. 1, 14–15).

While Americans would never learn about such things on mainstream news broadcasts, the US Congress heard testimony that indicated the CIA was indeed involved in drug trafficking. Ex-CIA pilot Michael Tolliver appeared before a Senate subcommittee in May 1988 and testified that his routine duties for the Agency were to fly ". . . about 28,000 pounds of military supplies—guns, ammunition, things like that" from Florida to Honduras and to return with "pot—some 25,000 pounds of it. I mean marijuana. . . . We brought the marijuana back to Florida in the same plane."

OPERATION DESERT STORM

George H. W. Bush may have been thinking of Noriega's role during past misdeeds, in conjunction with US intelligence, when as president he authorized a mission to literally abduct the Panamanian leader, dubbed Operation Just Cause, in December 1989. Certainly there was no rational or justifiable reason to forcibly remove a foreign leader from power, and lose twenty-six Americans as well as an estimated two thousand Panamanian civilians in the process.

On January 16, 1991, Bush topped that fiasco with Operation Desert Storm, in which five hundred thousand of America's finest were deployed to "liberate" a tiny, corrupt oligarchy. There is ample evidence that the American ambassador to Iraq, April Glaspie, assured Saddam Hussein, prior to the "war," that America did not care about Iraq's border dispute with Kuwait and would not become involved. Hussein, following his army's invasion of Kuwait, suddenly became the devil incarnate, after years of favor that saw Iraq receive billions in aid from America in its decade-long war with Iran. The "Gulf War," which was in reality tantamount to a heavyweight champion fighting a toddler, killed an estimated two hundred thousand civilians, destroyed priceless historical artifacts, and left the dreaded Saddam in power. Americans were conditioned, by the mass media, to vilify Hussein, whom probably 99 percent of them couldn't have identified prior to the invasion of Kuwait, utilizing the usual war propaganda horror stories alleging "rape" and "pillage" that were disseminated constantly.

The most famous testimony to the "rape" of Kuwait came from a young lady who told a horrified Congress that Iraqi soldiers had been dumping Kuwaiti babies out of incubators. Later, this young lady was identified as the daughter of the Kuwaiti ambassador to the United States, and everyone was forced to acknowledge that her testimony was wholly fabricated.

Jimmy Carter's former CIA director Stansfield Turner went on CNN to talk about "a bigger objective" than the mere invasion of Iraq. "This is an example," Turner explained, "the situation between the United Nations and Iraq, where the United Nations is deliberately intruding into the sovereignty of a sovereign nation. . . . Now this is a marvelous precedent [to be used in] all countries of the world. . . ."

The American invasion of Iraq was especially hypocritical, considering how the Bush administration had chosen not to confront China after their oppressive government had crushed pro-democracy demonstrations in Tiananmen Square with brutal military power in April 1989. Cables from the US embassy in Beijing reported that several American journalists "were severely beaten by Chinese troops in Tiananmen Square." The embassy also estimated the death totals to be as high as five hundred, with thousands injured. American officials didn't even revoke China's most-favored-nation trade status as a token gesture of outrage.

Desert Storm ushered in the era of techno-warfare, as giddy "journalists" drooled over footage of US bombers striking target after target, and boasted about each new "Coalition" success as if they were competing in a video game. Every network had its own special military general talking head to pontificate even more earnestly about the magnificent results. The notion that the air campaign was pristine and perfect, hitting only their intended military targets, was later belied by the over one hundred thousand civilian deaths that occurred during the bombing. By the end of the war, despite the previous claims of a tremendous success rate, the Pentagon would begrudgingly admit that 70 percent of the bombs had missed their targets. They did manage, however, to hit a factory devoted to making baby formula.

They also, in violation of battlefield traditions, continued to massacre Iraqi troops that were fleeing from them, despite the fact that Iraq was officially seeking a cease-fire. Even establishment media organs such as *Newsday* reported on the shameful brutality of US tanks using plows to bury untold numbers of Iraqi soldiers—many of them still alive—in trenches stretching along some seventy miles. US soldiers who were interviewed indicated how defenseless the Iraqis were, and spoke of the "buried trenches with people's arms and things sticking out of them." There were apparently no US casualties during this grisly episode, and one soldier gleefully declared that he "enjoyed it," while another called the entire "war" against an overmatched and often defenseless foe "a stroll in the park."

Thanks to the power of 24/7 television coverage, Operation Desert Storm was sold more effectively than previous US forays into foreign lands had been. Alleged journalists, fawning over guest commentators such as war hawk extraordinaire Senator John McCain and an endless parade of military "experts," displayed their total worthlessness as sources of accurate information.

But the war against the people of Iraq had barely begun. It is estimated that more than one million Iraqi civilians died over the next decade as a result of the harsh economic sanctions levied by the American government. About half of them were children.

In a June 1992 interview with Sarah McClendon, a Washington veteran and rare breed of independent-minded mainstream reporter, President George Bush provided an appropriate epitaph for his presidency. He stated, in reference to the Iran-Contra scandal: "If the people were to ever find out what we have done, we would be chased down the streets and lynched." The feisty McClendon published this quote in her newsletter. (*The Spotlight*, October 16, 1995, p. 12).

THE POW-MIA COVER-UP

For years, independent researchers had been claiming that there was solid evidence that the American government had left POWs and MIAs behind in Vietnam. In November 1991, the US Senate finally decided to look into the matter. Earlier that year, in June, Colonel Millard A. Peck, one of the Army's most highly decorated heroes of the Vietnam War, had tacked a five-page resignation letter to his office door, vacating his position as the DIA's top POW-MIA officer. Peck blasted not only government officials in his dramatic gesture but also Ann Mills-Griffiths, the executive director of the National League of Families, a group according to Peck that "occupies an interesting and questionable position in the whole [cover-up] process."

Peck charged that Mills-Griffiths ". . . is adamantly opposed to any initiatives to actually get to the heart of the problem, and, more importantly, interferes in or actively sabotages POW-MIA analyses or investigations. She insists on rewriting or editing all significant documents produced by the office. . . . This is then touted as the DIA position. She apparently has access to top-secret, code-word message traffic, for which she is supposedly

143

not cleared. . . . She was brought from the 'outside' into the center of the imbroglio, and then, cloaked in a mantle of sanctimony, routinely impedes real progress and insidiously 'muddles up' the issue. One wonders who she really is and where she came from."

Following Peck's resignation, Mills-Griffiths appeared on CNN to deny his allegations. CNN then interviewed another MIA relative, Judy Taber, in California, who backed up Mills-Griffiths. A severe conflict of interest that went undisclosed to the national audience was the fact that Taber and Mills-Griffiths were sisters! A furious Dolores Alfond, head of the National Alliance of Families, called CNN to find out if they'd been duped or were merely being predictably biased. A CNN official told her he would "take care of it," whatever that meant.

Peck wrote further in his letter of resignation: "I feel very strongly that this issue is being manipulated and controlled at a higher level, not with the goal of resolving it, but more to obfuscate the question of live prisoners and give the illusion of progress through hyperactivity. . . . From my vantage-point, I observed that the principal players were interested primarily in conducting [a] 'damage limitation exercise,' and appeared to knowingly and deliberately generate an endless succession of manufactured crises and 'busywork'. . . . The mind-set to debunk [live sighting reports] is alive and well. It is held at all levels and continues to pervade the POW-MIA Office. . . . Practically all analysis is directed to finding fault with the source. . . . From what I witnessed, it appears that any soldier left in Vietnam, even inadvertently, was, in fact, abandoned years ago. . . ." (*The Spotlight*, June 10, 1991, pp. 20–21).

Anyone who watched the televised hearings before the House Committee on POWs and MIAs a year after Peck's bitter resignation could not help but come away with the feeling that Committee Chairman Senator John Kerry, member Senator John McCain, and others were indeed concentrating their efforts on "debunking" and "finding fault with the source." *The Spotlight* obtained White House documents that indicated the League of Families was actually "set up" by President Nixon to counter real criticism of the abandonment of POWs and MIAs. In light of this, it was certainly understandable why some would suspect that Mills-Griffiths *was* a perfect figurehead to deflect investigations and suppress the truth.

A memorandum, initialed by White House Chief of Staff H. R. Haldeman, written by one of his aides, and sent to Richard Nixon, concerned an April 14, 1971, meeting between Nixon and then-Republican National Committee Chairman Robert Dole. The memo states: "There was also some discussion of the Prisoner of War problem and the Chairman made the point that this is a tender box [sic] that is about to explode as there is a real danger of great numbers of POW wives reversing their support of the president. He suggested, therefore, a fairly major move for cosmetic purposes and the president asked that this possibility be explored." The memo went on to say: "According to Al Haig [General Alexander Haig, at that time aide to National Security Adviser Henry Kissinger and later to become secretary of state under President Ronald Reagan], the next eight weeks are critical and the efforts of the Ad Hoc Coordinating Group on POW/MIA matters will be devoted to keeping the families on the reservation in order to buy this time." (*The Spotlight*, September 2, 1991, pp. 1, 12–13).

Russian President Boris Yeltsin wrote a letter to the US Senate Select Committee on POW and MIA Affairs in 1992, in which he flatly stated that the Soviets had held US prisoners of war dating back to World War II. He added that some could very well still be languishing in prisons and/or psychiatric hospitals throughout the former Soviet republics. White House and Pentagon officials, of course, had consistently denied any Americans were held in Soviet captivity. Yeltsin then reiterated his opinions to newsmen aboard an aircraft en route to Washington for his summit with President Bush. He added, in his comments on board the plane, that American POWs from the Vietnam War were interrogated by Soviet intelligence officials and that they, too, could still be alive somewhere within the vast territories that comprised the shattered Soviet empire. (*The Spotlight*, July 6, 1992, pp. 6–7).

The Senate Select Committee on POWs and MIAs wasn't interested in this or any other real information. Chairman Senator John Kerry (D-MA) clashed bitterly with Senator Robert Smith (R-NH), who seemed genuinely interested in ascertaining the truth about the issue they were tasked to investigate. Two staff members fired by Kerry charged afterward that the committee suppressed documents showing a clear pattern of betrayal and abandonment of POWs by the US government, going back to World War II. The two were Deputy Staff Director Dino Carluccio and former Representative William "Billy" Hendon (R-NC). "I left [the Select Committee staff] because Senator Kerry fired me," Hendon explained at a press conference on the lawn of the Capitol. Hendon called for a special prosecutor to investigate the cover-up by the Defense Intelligence Agency and Congress, calling the suppression of information "despicable treason." Hendon also alleged that documents had been shredded. (*The Spotlight*, July 20, 1992, pp. 1 and 3).

A key investigator for the Senate Committee, John F. McCreary, accused Chairman Kerry and the panel's staff of violating federal law by ordering the destruction of the original copy of a report that indicated that POWs and MIAs were still alive in Southeast Asia as recently as 1989. The accusation was made in a memo to the committee's vice chairman, Senator Robert Smith, dated May 3, 1992. The memo stated, in part: "On April 9, 1992 . . . Sen. McCain produced a copy of the intelligence briefing text, with whose contents he strongly disagreed. He charged that the briefing text had already been leaked to a POW/MIA activist but was reassured by [Kerry] that such was not the case. He replied that he was certain it would be leaked. Whereupon, the chairman assured Sen. McCain there would be no leaks, because all copies would be gathered and destroyed, and he gave orders to that effect. . . . Following the briefing on April 3, the staff director, Ms. Frances Zwenig, restated to the intelligence investigators the order to destroy the intelligence briefing text and took measures to ensure execution of the destruction order. During one telephone conversation with the undersigned [McCreary], she stated that she was 'acting under orders.' The undersigned was also instructed to delete all computer files. . . . In a meeting on April 15, 1992, the staff's chief counsel, J. William Codinha . . . minimized the significance of the documents and of their destruction. He admonished the investigators for 'making a mountain out of a molehill.' When investigators repeated their concern that the order to destroy the documents might lead to criminal charges, Mr. Codinha replied, 'Who's the injured party?' He was told, 'The 2,494 families of the unaccounted—for US servicemen, among others.' Mr. Codinha then said, 'Who's gonna tell them? It's classified.'" (*The Spotlight*, December 20, 1993, p. 10).

Internal Defense Department memos, obtained not only by *The Spotlight* but mainstream press outlets such as the *Washington Times*, revealed that Kerry, along with his loyal staff director, Frances Zwenig, had even coached Defense Department witnesses. The documents reveal this unequivocally. Kerry also, during a ballyhooed trip to Hanoi to show how "cooperative" the Vietnamese were now, actually apologized to the Communist leaders for "inspecting" the Vietnamese military compound, and he referred to the search as "silly." One of Kerry's cohorts, Senator Thomas Daschle (D-SD), answered reporter Mark Mooney of the *New York Post*, who accompanied the delegation and asked if the purpose of the trip was to convince "remaining skeptics in America to close the book on the emotional issue of MIAs," by saying, "You got it, absolutely." (*The Spotlight*, December 14, 1992, pp. 10–11).

The member of the Senate Committee who most rabidly disavowed any notions of a cover-up or conspiracy on the part of the government, however, was Senator John McCain (R-AZ). This was seemingly bizarre, in that

McCain's political career had been primarily built upon his own experiences as a Vietnam prisoner of war. McCain was hostile to every witness called before the committee who was claiming that the government had withheld information about missing soldiers in Vietnam. One would logically have expected him to be a dogged crusader for the truth about this issue, and a strong supporter of all those individuals and groups who were working so hard to expose high-level treachery. However, despite official documents, radio intercepts, witness depositions, satellite photos, electronic messages using individual code numbers belonging to missing airmen, rescue missions aborted by Washington, and admissions from high government officials that "men were left behind," McCain was not convinced there was any reason to delve into the subject.

McCain viciously attacked those, like former POW Eugene "Red" McDaniel, who were actively seeking answers, as frauds who were preying on grieving families. McCain had even bitterly opposed the so-called "Truth Bill," introduced in 1990, which called simply for openness and disclosure of all records and information, including live sightings, pertaining to soldiers missing since World War II. It was certainly a reasonable and noncontroversial measure, but McCain preempted this by introducing his own countermeasure, which permitted the Pentagon to basically control what was released.

One of the committee's first witnesses was Tracy Usry, former chief investigator for the Senate Foreign Relations Committee. Usry testified that the Soviets had interrogated US POWs in Vietnam. This, of course, would be verified by Boris Yeltsin's comments the following year. Senator McCain became incensed at Usry's allegations, interrupting him repeatedly and stoutly declaring, "None of the returned US prisoners of war released by Vietnam were ever interrogated by the Soviets." Colonel Bui Tin, former North Vietnamese Army officer, testified after Usry, and informed the committee that his position in the Communist Party had permitted him access to the most top-secret information in the Politburo. He reported that not only was Usry correct about the Soviets questioning American POWs, but that they'd been badly mistreated as well. As a result of these embarrassing disclosures, Usry and all other members of the minority staff were fired.

In subsequent hearings, McCain would treat Dolores Alfond, head of the National Alliance of Families, so shamefully that, in her words, "I mean he was yelling and screaming at me and had me in tears!" The only committee member who initially attended Ms. Alfond's appearance was Vice Chairman Robert Smith. However, Senator McCain was so angered by her testimony that he burst in at one point and loudly accused her of "making allegations that are patently and totally false. . . ." He shook his fist at her and pointed his index finger in a confrontational manner, and he chastised her for insulting President Bush's emissary to Vietnam. He charged that she was insinuating there was "some conspiracy without proof, and some cover-up." McCain became so out of control that he eventually stalked out of the room, to shouting and boos from those in the audience.

Senator Robert Smith would later say, "Many, many documents were held back for no reason." Some in the POW-MIA community even believed McCain's war record was severely tainted. Following its ridiculous "investigation," the Senate Select Committee was further aided in covering up the massive governmental record of misdeeds in this area by American officials. General Thomas Needham, Navy Commander Dale Hayes, and an unidentified CIA employee virtually took over the US embassy in Bangkok, Thailand, and destroyed POW-MIA case files that filled from "20 to 30 feet" of wall cabinets, during the period of March 25 to March 29, 1993. The documents were invaluable, and had been declassified under executive order by President Bush, but predictably enough the Senate Select Committee failed to pursue them. Once they were shredded by the trio of heroic patriots, there was no chance of the public seeing them. (*The Spotlight*, April 19, 1993, pp. 1 and 3).

After the committee had finished its "honorable" work, the revelations kept flying. In the April 13, 1993, edition of the establishment flagship, the *New York Times*, the findings of researcher Stephen J. Morris—of the Harvard Center for International Affairs and the Russian Research Center at Harvard—were published. The most explosive of all the documents of the former GRU, the Chief Intelligence Directorate of the Soviet Red Army, unearthed by Morris was a report by General Tran Van Quang, deputy chief of staff of the North Vietnamese Army during the war. The report was dated September 12, 1972, and revealed that 1,205 American prisoners of war were being held by the North Vietnamese. At one point in the document, Quang states, in reference to these 1,205 servicemen: "The Government of the USA. knows this well." (*The Spotlight*, April 26, 1993, pp. 10–11).

President George Bush, during a 1992 speech before the annual convention of the National League of POW and MIA families, had a run-in with some vocal protesters. Bush had apparently only agreed to speak before the group because the organization's leader, Ann Mills-Griffiths, had been charged, by Millard Peck and others, with participating in covering up any real efforts to find out the truth about missing servicemen, and he thus was expecting a receptive audience. The president became ruffled when the demonstrators, many of them elderly women, began chanting "no more lies." Flustered, he finally told them to "sit down and shut up." Mills-Griffiths, perfectly in character, defended the president, and Bush's campaign director, the talentless future television talking head Mary Matalin, commented, "I did not think [Bush's] response to those rude people there was inappropriate." Interestingly enough, the woman considered to be the "ringleader" of the protesters, Gloria Bristow of Arlington, Texas, who later claimed she was not the first to stand up during the speech and chant "tell the truth, no more lies," was, just coincidentally of course, fired from her job only a few days after returning home from the convention. (*The Spotlight*, August 17, 1992, pp. 16–17).

President Bush solemnly declared, in an October 23, 1992, Rose Garden ceremony, "Today, finally, I am convinced that we can begin writing the last chapter in the Vietnam War." John McCain was standing at his side.

McCain would continue to clash with POW-MIA activists. Jeannette Jenkins of Atwater, Ohio, claimed—to the total silence of the national establishment press—that the senator shoved her in a hallway outside his Senate office. On June 20, 1996, Jenkins was among a group of about fifteen family members and activists who attempted to hand-deliver letters protesting McCain's bill to amend the Missing Personnel Act. Jenkins was pushing the wheelchair of her aged aunt, Jane Duke Gaylor of Sent, Ohio, whose son, Charles R. Duke, was a civilian MIA missing since May 30, 1970, in South Vietnam. Gaylor was a longtime POW-MIA activist, confined by health problems to a wheelchair. In 1995, she had somehow avoided the headlines when she chained herself to the White House fence in protest of President Clinton's handling of the POW-MIA issue.

Jenkins filed a complaint with the Senate Ethics Committee, wherein she declared: "We were attempting to hand-deliver letters to Senator McCain requesting him to please drop his amendment to the Missing Personnel Act. . . . McCain came out of his office with a young woman [apparently his aide Nancy Ives] and began walking toward our group. As he approached us, Carol Hrdlicka [the wife of a confirmed POW] asked the Senator, 'May we speak with you?' Then John Parsels [a former POW who was returned by the Communists] asked him if he would take the letters. That was when his face changed and he became very angry. He then burst through our group shoving me with unreasonable force in a hostile manner. I was standing next to my aunt, who is in a wheelchair. Senator McCain did not give me a chance to get out of his way. His look was angry and hostile and he shoved me without cause."

Gaylor's letter to the Ethics Committee echoed her niece's story: "Senator McCain . . . shoved my niece hard in a very hostile manner, not caring what harm it could have caused her." Hrdlicka, of Conway Springs, Kansas, a well-known and respected activist, supported the others' testimony. McCain "stated he would not accept the letters and knew nothing of the Missing Personnel Act," Hrdlicka stated. "He then shoved his way through the group, pushing one of the ladies into the wall as he hurried down the hall away from us. . . ." (*The Spotlight*, July 22, 1996, pp. 1 and 3). So here we had a US senator charged, by a number of witnesses, one of them the aged, wheelchair-bound mother of a Vietnam MIA civilian, with an unprovoked physical attack upon a woman in a US Senate hallway. And yet, the mainstream media was not interested in the story. Hrdlicka's attorney, Arnold L. Beizer, was still bitter over the incident in January 2008, when he stated, "Mrs. Gaylor filed a complaint for assault against the Senator but the matter was squelched by the powers that be."

Ted Sampley, a highly decorated Vietnam veteran and publisher of the *U.S. Veteran News and Report*, had earlier, in 1992, reported a very similar experience, albeit not with McCain himself. While dropping off a copy of his newspaper at the Senate office of John McCain, Mark Salter, a top McCain staffer, became belligerent with him and challenged him to a fight. After following Sampley down a flight of stairs, blows were exchanged between the two men. Sampley was charged with assault and hauled away in handcuffs by police to a city lockup, where he was held in solitary confinement for thirty hours and denied the right to make a call to his attorney. Although Sampley claimed the McCain aide struck the first blow, Salter was evidently not charged with anything. (*The Spotlight*, January 11, 1993). Sampley would also become a bitter foe of John Kerry, whom he dubbed "Hanoi John," establishing the website vietnamveteransagainstjohnkerry.org during his 2004 presidential run.

A book was published in 1994, *Prisoners of Hope: Exploiting the POW/ MIA Myth in America* by Susan Katz Keating, a reporter with the *Washington Times*, which towed the new establishment line that there were no POWs left behind, the government didn't cover up anything, and that those who claimed otherwise were perpetrating the "worst crime in American history." Keating's book is filled with errors and undocumented assertions, but it is in her "acknowledgments" at the beginning of the book that she shows her ulterior motives. Among those whom she "thanks" are: "Col. James 'Nick'

Rowe," as previously noted, also connected to the frightening Operation Watchtower program, whom she praises for all the "insights" he gave her. In fact, Rowe was one of the few American POWs to have escaped and had been assassinated several years before Keating's book was written, taking to his grave the firm conviction that American servicemen remained alive and in captivity in Vietnam. Keating also acknowledged the previously mentioned, Delores Alfond, head of the National Alliance of POW-MIA Families, who had no knowledge of contributing anything to Keating, and Albo Lundy III, whose father is listed as MIA and who considers Keating's work an outrage.

Most amazingly of all, Keating described Marion Shelton, wife of Air Force Colonel Charles Shelton, who'd recently been declared dead by the Pentagon after having been listed for years as a POW, as a "victim" of POW-MIA activists, when in reality she was one of the most dedicated and visible of them and grew so despondent over the way her government treated her that she eventually took her own life. Apparently, establishment journalist Lars Erik Nelson, in his laudatory review of Keating's book in *New York Newsday*, didn't even cursorily examine her scholarship, for he termed her work "a courageous new book." (*The Spotlight*, November 28, 1994, p. 3 and 9).

BUSH BODY COUNT

Charles M. McKee, a military attaché for the DIA in Beirut, and Matthew Gannon, CIA deputy station chief in Beirut, were on board Pan Am Flight 103, which exploded over Lockerbie, Scotland, on December 21, 1988. They were part of a counterterrorist team in Beirut investigating how to rescue the nine American hostages being held in Lebanon. They had uncovered evidence that a rogue CIA unit called COREA was doing business with a Syrian arms dealer and drug trafficker, who was part of the covert network run by US Lieutenant Colonel Oliver North. Outraged that the COREA unit was doing business with a Syrian who had close terrorist connections, the McKee team decided to fly back to Virginia unannounced and expose the COREA unit's secret deal. "For three years, I've had a feeling that if Chuck hadn't been on that plane, it wouldn't have been bombed," Beulah McKee, seventy-five, Charles McKee's mother, stated to *Time*. McKee has never been satisfied with the government's version of events in the Lockerbie incident.

Senator John Tower had been appointed by the Reagan administration to chair the bipartisan committee that investigated the Iran/Contra scandal. He oversaw the Tower Report and knew the inside story of Iran/Contra. Senator John Heinz, like President G. W. Bush and his son Dubya, and Democratic Senator John Kerry, who would be Dubya's opposition in the

2004 presidential election, was a member of Yale University's notorious Skull and Bones society. On April 4, 1991, Senator Heinz was killed when his plane collided with a helicopter over a Pennsylvania elementary school. Heinz had frequently clashed with the Republican establishment over the years, from urging President Nixon to normalize relations with Cuba to protesting mightily over President Reagan's attempts to categorize ketchup as a vegetable in his effort to cut funding for school lunch programs. He had also chaired a three-man presidential review board in the Iran/Contra affair. Incredibly, John Tower was killed in a plane crash the following day, on April 5, 1991, in Brunswick, Georgia. What are the odds of a pair of Republican US senators dying in separate plane crashes two days in a row?

While Tower seemed like the ultimate political insider, and had produced a complete whitewash of Bush & Co.'s involvement with the Tower Commission investigation, he had become a bitter man since his nomination for secretary of defense was rejected by the Senate. Allegations of womanizing and alcoholism were said to be behind the rejection, but Tower did not take kindly to being singled out. The *New York Times*, on April 7, 1989, reported some bitter comments from Tower about his colleagues in the Senate. He dubbed Senator John Glenn, "not the brightest guy in Washington," and said another Democratic Senator, Jim Exon, "drinks, and drinks heavily." He called Ernest Hollings "the Senate bully" and declared that the powerful Sam Nunn suffered from blind ambition and cruelty. Tower's tell-all book, *Consequences: A Personal and Political Memoir*, had been published shortly before his death. John Heinz's widow, Theresa, was remarried, to Senator John Kerry, in 1995. Author Rodney Stich, in his book *Defrauding America*, claimed that senators Heinz and Tower were both on board the rumored October 19, 1980, flight to Paris, arranged by then Vice President Bush and CIA Director William Casey, as part of the October Surprise scandal to bribe Iranian officials to retain American hostages until after the 1980 election.

ROSS PEROT'S CAMPAIGN

George Bush's approval ratings hit record highs shortly after the Gulf War, but his popularity quickly waned as the 1992 presidential campaign unfolded. The entrance into the fray of loose-cannon billionaire Ross Perot, who'd drawn the wrath of the Reagan and Bush administrations over his outspoken belief that American POWs had been left behind in Vietnam as well as his opposition to the Gulf War, made it one of the most memorable elections of modern times. Perot supporters established the United We Stand America organization, which drew together people of various ideologies who were dissatisfied with the Democrats and Republicans. When Perot began running ahead of both Bush and Democratic nominee Bill Clinton in most major polls—an unheard-of feat for a third-party candidate—voters who'd waited for such an alternative for many years, such as myself, were overjoyed.

Perot, along with most of the American public, was opposed to the proposed North American Free Trade Agreement (NAFTA), and he memorably referred to the loss of jobs America would suffer because of it as "that giant sucking sound." Naturally, all high-profile politicians from both major parties supported the disastrous proposal. NAFTA and similar globalist trade deals proved to be exactly what Perot and other critics predicted they'd be; on February 14, 2011, *Forbes* magazine reported that the United States had lost an average of 50,000 manufacturing jobs per month since China joined the World Trade Organization in 2001, for example. By 2010, the United States trade deficit was nearly $500 billion. Establishment stalwart Henry Kissinger wrote, in the July 18, 1993, *Los Angeles Times*, that NAFTA represented, "not a conventional trade agreement but the architecture of a new international system . . . a first step toward a new world order."

NAFTA did not create the jobs its proponents promised it would, and illegal immigration continued on unabated (in fact, it increased by some 300 percent). The agreement had a devastating effect on America's industrial base, which had begun to erode under Reagan. Critics estimated that America lost about 20 percent of its manufacturing jobs during the first fourteen years after the passage of NAFTA. Over three hundred thousand American farms were forced out of business after NAFTA was implemented. Jingoist "conservatives" love to taunt their opponents with "Freedom isn't free." Nothing could be more obvious at this point than "Free trade isn't free."

In July 1992, Ross Perot inexplicably dropped out of the race, at first citing the lame rationale that he didn't want to cause the election to be thrown into the House of Representatives. Eventually, he disclosed that he had in fact quit because the Bush campaign had threatened to sabotage his daughter's wedding. As many noted at the time, this made absolutely no sense; exactly how was someone going to "sabotage" the wedding? Buy off the groom? Mess up the flower arrangements? Clearly, there was more to this story. Perot's reputation seemed damaged, but much of the public was still unhappy with the establishment candidates, and he just as mysteriously reentered the race on October 1. Perot still managed to garner 19 percent of the popular vote in the 1992 election, giving him the most votes of any third-party candidate since Teddy Roosevelt ran on the Bull Moose ticket in

1912. Arkansas Democrat Bill Clinton won the three-man race, becoming the youngest president elected since John F. Kennedy.

CHAPTER SIX

THE CLINTON YEARS: CONSPIRACY CENTRAL

"It depends on what the meaning of the word 'is' is."

—Bill Clinton

"The great story here for anybody willing to find it and write about it and explain it is this vast right wing conspiracy that has been conspiring against my husband since the day he announced for president."

—Hillary Clinton

Ross Perot's candidacy has often been cited as the reason for Bill Clinton's election to the presidency. Regardless, Clinton came into office with a background as sordid as any president before him. Clinton's critics alleged he was recruited into the CIA by Cord Meyer while a student at Oxford in the late Sixties. Clinton supposedly came from a modest background, but he was financially able to participate in antiwar peace conferences in Stockholm and Oslo, and he traveled to Leningrad, Moscow, and Prague while at Oxford. As noted earlier, he was also somehow in a position, as a veritable youngster, to be tasked with picking up a distinguished figure like Hale Boggs and driving him to the airport for his 1972 flight into oblivion.

With the birth of the Internet, Clinton's critics began chronicling his scandals—which were entirely ignored by the reliable mainstream press—and even came up with a colorful term to describe the untidy truth that an inordinate number of those connected to Bill or his wife, Hilary Rodham Clinton, had met unnatural deaths—the Clinton Body Count.

Two of the most tragic deaths in the Clinton Body Count took place on August 23, 1987, when Clinton was governor of Arkansas and the Mena airport was allegedly being utilized to transport illegal drugs in and out of the country. Kevin Ives, seventeen, and Don Henry, sixteen, were run over by a train and the authorities quickly ruled the deaths accidental, claiming the boys had smoked an excessive amount of marijuana and fallen asleep on the tracks. A small, "dime"-sized bag of marijuana was found in one of their pockets, but it was practically full.

Said Linda Ives, mother of Kevin, "Their investigation was so thorough that they left my son's foot out there for two days in plain sight." Evidence emerged after the deaths that one of the boys had been stabbed in the back and the other had been bludgeoned with a rifle butt. The engineer who tried desperately to stop the train stated that they were lying on the track in identical (and unnatural) positions, partially covered with a tarpaulin. Police denied a second gun was at the scene (Don Henry's gun was also found there), even though they were captured on video retrieving this weapon. This, along with much other interesting information, can be seen in the video *Obstruction of Justice: The Mena Connection*.

The medical examiner involved in this case, Fahmy Malak, was charged by critics with a number of improprieties. He obliterated Kevin's skull, for instance, making it impossible to determine where the original fractures were. Malak intended to rule that the boys had committed suicide, until he was persuaded by Saline County Sheriff Jim Steed that the cause of death should be ruled accidental. The grieving parents wanted to get a second opinion in the matter, but Malak refused to obey court orders obtained by the parents to turn over testable samples of the materials he had in his possession. Then-Arkansas Governor Bill Clinton publicly supported Malak. In one of the few investigatory pieces about Clinton's shady past to appear in the establishment press, *The Los Angeles Times* would report, in a May 19, 1992, front-page story, about Malak's controversial ties to Clinton's mother, anesthesia nurse Virginia Kelley. The paper noted that a ruling by Malak had helped Kelley avoid legal scrutiny in the death of one patient in 1981, while she was the defendant in a medical malpractice lawsuit involving the death of another patient.

The FBI predictably advised the parents to accept the fact the boys had not been murdered. Malak had a history of incompetence; in one publicized case, he had ruled that a man whose body had been found without his head had died from an ulcer. Malak went on, in bizarre fashion, to speculate that the man's dog had chewed off and eaten his head and stated that he had found bits of bone and human brain matter in the dog's vomit. This was contradicted by the fact that the victim's head was later found intact. There was an outcry against the medical examiner, but loyal Governor Clinton responded by giving Malak a $14,000 raise. Speculation by independent investigators was that the boys had witnessed a shipment of illegal drugs connected to the burgeoning Mena scandal, a classic case of being in the wrong place at the wrong time.

The Ives-Henry murders begat other unnatural deaths. Nineteen-year-old Keith Coney died on May 17, 1988, when his motorcycle collided with a tractor trailer. On November 10, 1988, Keith McCaskle was stabbed to death. McCaskle had expressed fears for his life to others, because of his knowledge of "the railroad track thing." In April 1989, Jeff Rhodes was mutilated and shot, and his burned body was found in a Dumpster. Richard Winters was a suspect in the Ives and Henry murders, and he was killed in July 1989 during a robbery. Greg Collins was found shot to death in the woods on December 2, 1989. Twenty-one-year-old Jordan Ketelson, who was believed to be connected to the McKaskle murder, was shot in the head and killed on June 25, 1990. What are the odds of so many young people, who had been associated with the deaths on the train tracks in some way, meeting such violent ends in the first few years after Ives and Henry's own suspicious deaths?

Most independent researchers believe that Kevin and Don happened upon some kind of drug drop-off that night and saw something they weren't supposed to see. I exchanged a number of emails with Linda Ives, mother of Kevin, starting in June 2009. She confided that she'd never been supported by Don Henry's father, Curtis, in her efforts to find out what really happened to the boys. She received anonymous calls, in which Don's sister Gayla would be mentioned as knowing "what was going on." Curtis Henry was livid about this and managed to whisk Gayla out of town, refusing to let anyone interview her. Curtis would go on to appear as a character witness for Clinton crony Dan Harmon, an attorney connected by researchers to the drug trafficking in Mena, Arkansas, and alleged by his ex-girlfriend, Sharline Wilson, to have been at the Ives and Henry death scene. Wilson paid dearly for this; when drugs were allegedly found in her home, she was sentenced to an incredible thirty years in prison. Wilson finally was released from prison in late 1999. Harmon would later be incarcerated for racketeering, extortion, and his own drug crimes.

In a July 2012 email, Linda Ives was kind enough to add more details regarding the deaths of individuals who were connected in some way to her son and Don Henry. Regarding Jeff Rhodes, she stated that "Jeff had called his father asking for money to leave town because he feared for his life and knew too much about Kevin and Don's deaths." She also clarified the nature of the "robbery" Richard Winters was killed in, characterizing it as a "set-up." She informed me that Greg Collins, "who was shot to death was scheduled to testify before the county grand jury investigating Kevin and Don's deaths." She also added this detail to yet another death: "Jordan Ketelson's death was ruled a suicide but he was cremated before an autopsy could be performed."

Linda Ives reminded me that those who wind up as collateral damage in these crimes are real people: "there is no way to describe the effect that Kevin's murder had on our family." Linda Ives passionately and eloquently stated to me, "It ripped a hole in our hearts and lives that cannot be filled nor mended. In many ways, the cover-up has been just as devastating to us as the murder itself. It shakes you to the very core of your being and causes you to question everything you ever believed in. 'With liberty and justice for all' has become a great hoax—truth and justice? They are just meaningless words on a piece of paper."

Victor Raiser, the Clinton presidential campaign's national finance cochairman, died in a plane crash on July 30, 1992. Paula Grober, Bill Clinton's very attractive speech interpreter for the deaf, was killed in a one-car accident on December 9, 1992. Jim Wilhite, who'd been an associate with Clinton crony Mack McClarty's old Arkansas company, died in a December 21, 1992, skiing accident. He had a close relationship with Bill Clinton, and had talked with him by phone only hours before. Dr. Stanley Heard, a member of Clinton's health-care advisory committee who'd personally treated his mother, stepfather, and brother, was killed in a plane crash on September 10, 1993. Incredibly, shortly before the crash, he was on another small plane that developed problems, which caused him to land and switch to another one. What are the odds of *that?*

Ed Willey, an attorney and Clinton fund-raiser, was found dead in the woods from a gunshot wound on November 30, 1993. Evidently, he'd actually died two days earlier, the same day that his wife, Kathleen Willey, had visited the White House to ask Bill Clinton for a job, and claimed she was sexually assaulted by the president in the process. In January 1994, Gandy Baugh, who was Clinton crony Dan Lassater's lawyer, jumped to his death from a multi-story building on January 8, 1994. He'd been defending Lassater in a financial misconduct case. Years earlier, Lassater had been indicted by a federal grand jury on charges of conspiring with Bill Clinton's brother Roger to distribute cocaine. Lassater entered a plea bargain and was subsequently granted a full pardon by his friend Governor Bill Clinton.

The "Troopergate" scandal, which involved then-Governor Bill Clinton's sexual harassment of Paula Jones, left at least two dead bodies behind. Kathy Ferguson, ex-wife of Arkansas state trooper Danny Ferguson, who became Clinton's codefendant along with other members of his security detail, was found dead on May 11, 1994, only five days after Paula Jones filed her lawsuit against them. She'd been shot in the head, and it was ruled a suicide. The following month, Kathy Ferguson's fiancé, Arkansas state trooper Bill Shelton, was found shot to death at Kathy's gravesite. Shelton had been critical of the official ruling of suicide in his fiancée's death, a feeling shared by many of her friends.

Paul Wilcher's was a suspicious death that crossed over into previous scandals. Wilcher was an attorney investigating both the October Surprise and Mena, Arkansas, cases. He was found dead on his toilet on June 22, 1993, three weeks after delivering a report to Clinton's attorney general, Janet Reno. In his report, Wilcher claimed to be in grave danger and said people could be "silenced in the near future" if the report he was giving her got into the wrong hands. Yet another plane crash took the life of Herschel Friday, Clinton's Finance Committee chairman, on March 1, 1994. Jerry Parks, head of Governor Clinton's security team in Arkansas, was shot and killed while driving on September 26, 1993. Parks had been living in fear for his life ever since Vince Foster's body was discovered. Parks's wife and son claimed he'd assembled a file on Clinton's past misdeeds, which had been stolen a few months before his murder. Parks's son Gary claimed his father had reacted to the initial reports of Foster's death by uttering the words, "I'm a dead man." He also spoke of the Clintons "cleaning house" and that he was "next on the list."

Parks's widow, Lois Jane, would tell writer Ambrose Evans-Pritchard that their home "was swarming with federal agents" the day after Parks was shot. She remembered seeing credentials flashed from the FBI, Secret Service, IRS, and CIA. No federal agency, of course, had any jurisdiction over the crime, and the FBI would deny ever being in the house. In conjunction with the Little Rock Police Department, the FBI confiscated numerous files and records, including some 130 hours of taped phone conversations. "I've asked them to give it all back," Lois Jane stated, "but the police refuse to relinquish anything. They told me there's nothing they can do about the case as long as Bill Clinton is in office."

In a curious footnote, the man Parks's widow, Lois Jane, later married, Dr. David Millstein, was stabbed to death a decade later. In December 2009, Parks's son Gary was arrested for the murder of Millstein. Initial reports indicated that Lois Jane was a suspect as well. As of June 2012, the trial of Gary Parks for capital murder in the case of Millstein had been delayed twice, and it was rumored he was also considered a suspect in the death of his father, Jerry Parks.

RUBY RIDGE

The case of Randy Weaver is one of the most shameful in American history. Weaver was a white racial separatist who wanted nothing but to be left alone, and to raise his family according to the tenets of his old-fashioned Christian faith. Unfortunately, the federal government had a problem with that, for unexplained reasons. On April 21, 1992, Weaver's Ruby Ridge, Idaho, cabin was surrounded by a team of camouflaged federal agents. The road leading up to the mountain cabin had been blocked and was manned by a force of approximately one hundred ATF, FBI, and Idaho State Police officers. Weaver's crime was, unbelievably enough, failing to appear in court on the charge of selling a sawed-off shotgun—which was only a quarter of an inch shorter than the legal limit—to an undercover federal agent.

For this serious offense, Weaver's cabin was surrounded by all those armed government agents, and during the bloodbath that followed, one federal agent, the Weaver family dog, Weaver's fourteen-year-old son, Samuel, and Weaver's wife, Vicki, were shot and killed. The agents shot the boy in the back as he ran from them, and Vicki was killed by a sniper as she cradled her baby in her arms. (*The Spotlight*, May 25, 1992, pp. 1, 3, and 16). Senator Larry Craig (R-Idaho) asked Attorney General Janet Reno at least three times to release the Justice Department's report on the government's handling of the Weaver incident, without success. (*The Spotlight*, September 12, 1994, p. 2).

The Weaver case represented one of the most monumental government overreactions in US history. Weaver had refused persistent attempts to get him to infiltrate the racist Aryan Nations group, and was eventually entrapped into the very minor gun charge through his friendship with an informer. Why were six trained government snipers, wearing ski masks and in camouflage, involved in a dispute over something as minor as that? There were eventually *four hundred* federal agents at the scene in Ruby Ridge, all to force one "extremist" (or "white supremacist," as mainstream journalists invariably referred to him as) to face minor charges he was tricked into. The Weaver's dead dog was left in the road and run over repeatedly by government vehicles. After they'd killed Weaver's wife,

Vicki, the agents supposedly taunted her family by calling out her name, asking if she was there.

For once, our justice system actually performed adequately in this case; a Boise, Idaho, jury found Weaver and the others not guilty of murder and conspiracy charges. The 1995 congressional inquiry into the travesty was full of typical partisanship, with Democrats uniting to defend Clinton's administration and Republicans asking the only pertinent questions. The Weavers filed a wrongful death suit against the government, and later in 1995, without any admission of wrongdoing, Randy Weaver was awarded $100,000 and his three daughters $1 million each.

Randy Weaver's daughter Sarah appeared on William Shatner's television show *Aftermath* in September 2010. Sarah was gracefully magnanimous, saying that she hoped FBI sniper Lon Horouchi, who had fired the shot that blew her mother's head off as she held an infant in her arms, knew she forgave him. Sarah stated she was sure he thought about the incident every day of his life, and that she wished the knowledge she had forgiven him would bring him peace.

THE VINCE FOSTER CASE

The death of Vince Foster was probably the most examined of all the entries in the Clinton Body Count. Despite the massive indications that he'd been murdered, and that a cover-up involving the White House had taken place, the reliably lame mainstream media was content, as always, to dutifully report the official story. On July 20, 1993, the body of Deputy White House Counsel Vince Foster was found lying on the ground in northern Virginia's Fort Marcy Park. Patrick Knowlton happened upon Foster's body a little over an hour before it was officially discovered, when he entered the park to relieve himself. Although he was a bit luckier than the Ives and Henry boys were, he too appears to have been in the wrong place at the wrong time.

Knowlton didn't see Foster's car there, but he did see another vehicle, with Arkansas license plates, and a menacing-looking occupant inside. As a result of this, Knowlton would be regularly harassed for years, with reporters witnessing some of the harassment firsthand. He was followed by cars, FBI agents would gesture threateningly at him on the street, he was telephoned in the middle of the night, and FBI agents knocked on his door at 3 a.m. When he testified before Special Prosecutor Kenneth Starr's grand jury, he was treated in a hostile manner by Clinton's alleged "enemy" Starr, who in reality whitewashed all the real Clinton scandals. The FBI falsified Knowlton's original statement to them, much as they (and the Warren Commission) had altered the testimony of witnesses to the JFK assassination.

There were numerous holes in the official theory of suicide. The first paramedics in Fort Marcy Park noticed a different weapon than the 1913 Colt revolver belonging to Foster, which later appeared after police had taken over the crime scene. The paramedics also reported a neck wound, which the authorities denied existed, claiming that Foster shot himself in the mouth. The photos taken of the body in its original position disappeared.

Kenneth Starr hired a liberal prosecutor, Michael Rodriguez, to lead the grand jury investigation into the Foster death, but they had different agendas. As Rodriguez explained, "I was told what the result was going to be from the get-go." Rodriguez also claimed, "The FBI told me to back off . . ." and "be careful where I tread." Rodriguez resigned in disgust, and he couldn't interest any congressman or the mainstream press in his story. The media was otherwise preoccupied with creating the image of Starr as Clinton's irascible foe, unfairly hounding the flawed but well-meaning president. A recorded interview with Rodriguez is available on the Accuracy in Media website. During that interview, Rodriguez stated, "The whole notion of [previous Special Counsel Robert Fiske and Starr] doing an honest investigation is laughable. . . . The FBI conducted the first investigation along with the Park Police. The FBI reinvestigated Foster's death under Independent Counsel Fiske, then Kenneth Starr used the very same FBI agents in his investigation, . . . The American press misled the American public by reporting that there have been several independent investigations, when, in fact, all of the investigations were done by the FBI. . . ."

London *Sunday Telegraph* reporter Ambrose Evans-Pritchard was one of the few establishment journalists to write critically of President Clinton, and he produced the explosive book *The Secret Life of Bill Clinton: The Unreported Stories*. In the April 9, 1995, *Sunday Telegraph*, Evans-Pritchard reported that White House aide Helen Dickey had telephoned the Arkansas governor's mansion very early, around 7 p.m., on the night Foster's body was discovered. She supposedly told a state trooper, "Vince got off work, went out to his car in the parking lot and shot himself in the head." There was corroboration for this in Secret Service Document 2551, which reported, "On the evening of 7/20/93, unknown time, US Park Police discovered the body of Vincent Foster in his car. The car was parked in the Ft. Marcy area of VA. . . ." As one might expect, *60 Minutes, 20/20,* and other popular news programs were not the least bit interested in this crucial evidence, which wholly contradicted the most basic crime scene information. If a discrepancy over the location of the dead body of a high-ranking executive department official didn't warrant press coverage, then what would?

The witness who originally found Foster's body in Fort Marcy Park was never publicly identified, and still feared for his life years later. Dubbed "CW" for confidential witness, he provided another bombshell in testimony before Congressman Dan Burton: "As sure as I am standing here . . . there was nothing in his hands." Three years later, CW stated the obvious: "The whole thing stinks, he clearly didn't shoot himself there. You can't shoot yourself without a gun. The man had no gun. End of story." The official story, of course, is that a gun was found in Foster's hand. Medical technician Richard Arthur gave testimony that conflicted with the official account in a different way. He swore the gun he saw was an automatic pistol, and not the eighty-year-old revolver the authorities linked to Foster. Five homes were located less than five hundred feet from the spot where Foster's body was found, yet no one reported hearing a shot, and the authorities didn't question them until months later anyway.

X-rays of Foster's skull either weren't taken or have vanished. Autopsy Dr. James Beyer, who would be involved in other controversial cases, told the Park Police that x-rays didn't reveal any fragments in Foster's head, but he later claimed he never took x-rays. Paramedic Corey Ashford listed the cause of death as homicide in his written report. Ashford, like the other paramedics, saw no exit wound in the back of Foster's head, and his white shirt remained clean despite cradling Foster's head against his body. Dr. Julian Orenstein, who certified Foster's death, also saw no rear head wound exit at the morgue. No skull fragments were found at the scene, and the bullet that purportedly exited Foster's skull was never located. There were hairs and carpet fibers found on Foster, including his underwear, which contributed to the rampant speculation that he'd actually died elsewhere and been moved to the park afterward. Medical technician George Gonzalez and other witnesses reported seeing a dark briefcase in the front seat of Foster's Honda, but it disappeared. Foster's pager was found at the scene, but its memory had been erased and, against all standard procedure, the Park Police turned it over to the White House a short time later.

The alleged suicide note from Foster was torn into twenty-eight pieces. All but one piece was found in a briefcase that had been searched twice previously by White House counsel Bernie Nussbaum in the presence of Park Police. The missing piece was where the signature should logically have been. Even more strangely, Foster's fingerprints were not on the note. Three renowned handwriting experts determined the suicide note was a forgery, but when they held a press conference to announce their findings, virtually the entire mainstream media ignored it. Police failed to seal Vince Foster's White House office, and they permitted staffers to enter and leave at will the night his body was found.

In fact, White House aides were seen ransacking the office. Hillary Clinton's chief of staff, Maggie Williams, was observed by a Secret Service agent as she moved files from Foster's office to her own. Foster aide Deborah Gorham would testify that Bernie Nussbaum demanded the combination to Foster's safe after his death, and that several documents and letters known to her to have been in the safe were discovered missing thereafter. Witnesses stated that Patsy Thomasson, director of the White House's Office of Administration, was also anxious to get the combination to the safe. Mack McClarty told reporters, in response to rumors about the late-night opening of the safe, that Foster's office didn't have one.

Park Police officers searched Foster's pockets in Fort Marcy Park and found nothing. Foster's wallet and credit cards were in his car, but his keys could not be located. Later that night, the same officers searched his pockets again at the morgue and discovered two key rings. This occurred shortly after White House aide Craig Livingstone and White House counsel William Kennedy had evidently forced their way into the morgue. Original special prosecutor Robert Fiske, who if anything was even less curious than Starr, never deposed important witnesses such as Maggie Williams, Craig Livingstone, or Helen Dickey. Journalist Ambrose Evans-Pritchard got a taste of the Knowlton treatment himself; his Washington, D.C., apartment was broken into, and his computers were stolen. His car was later vandalized and his briefcase taken.

Fewer high-profile events have featured such clear-cut evidence of conspiracy and cover-up as the Vince Foster case. As a Clinton insider, Assistant Attorney General Web Hubbell, admitted, "Don't believe a word you hear. It was not suicide. It couldn't have been." (*Esquire*, November 1993).

WACO

A few months prior to Foster's mysterious death, perhaps the most shameful incident in Clinton's eight years as president took place. On February 8, 1993, the Waco, Texas, residence (always referred to in the kept media as the more pejorative term "compound") of a theretofore little-known religious sect called the Branch Davidians was assaulted by an overly aggressive, militarized force of ATF agents. The pretense was that they were trying to serve a warrant to "cult leader" David Koresh on charges of "stockpiling" weapons (whatever that meant) and child abuse. What happened initially, and afterward, is a matter of dispute. The authorities claimed Koresh and his followers opened fire on the faithful ATF agents and they were forced to defend themselves; "conspiracy theorists" believed the evidence showed the agents were at fault and started the standoff. The FBI soon joined in on what the reliable mainstream media invariably called a "siege" that lasted for fifty-one days.

The "siege" was a farce. Clinton's attorney general, Janet Reno, while publicly proclaiming that she was carrying out a crusade to save the children in the Branch Davidian "compound" from sexual abuse, abused them herself in several cruel ways. Armored tanks ran over and crushed their go-karts and bicycles that lay just outside the windows of their home. Hideous, highly amplified sounds of rabbits being slaughtered and Tibetan monks chanting were blared nonstop, depriving everyone—including those precious children—of sleep and probably sanity. This was done in conjunction with nightly sessions of blinding, high-intensity lights shining on their bedroom windows. Reno also cut off the children's food, water, electricity, and plumbing. Remember, these were American citizens who, even if one accepts the dubious notion that "cult leader" Koresh was some kind of horrific criminal, were guilty of nothing except belonging to a religious order that the government chose to attack for unclear and illogical reasons.

The dead body of a Davidian killed by government agents in the initial assault was inhumanely left for days, draped over a fence in plain view of all those inside, until vultures reportedly devoured parts of his body. Even without all this lunacy, no sane person can excuse the dramatic, idiotic final assault on the compound, which took place on April 19, 1993. CS gas, banned by the Geneva Convention for usage in warfare, was pumped into the building, tanks battered the place in true Orwellian fashion, and, if one believes the autopsy results, Koresh and other Davidians were shot by government agents, as bullet holes were found in their heads. Nevertheless, in predictable fashion, government officials and their lackeys in the media unfailingly declared that the Davidians had committed mass suicide, setting the fire themselves.

Anyone watching the video of the tanks crashing down the walls of the "compound" understood exactly who was to blame, despite the newspeak offered by the authorities. Afterward, even some establishment journalists, such as Alexander Cockburn, castigated Reno and the government. As Cockburn stated in a *Los Angeles Times* column, "There was compelling evidence, claimed President Clinton's spokesman George Stephanopoulos, that the children were being abused. . . . In fact, the FBI has conceded that *there's no evidence for these chilling claims*" (emphasis original). (*Big Sister Is Watching You* by Texe Marrs, pp. 149–168).

"Cult leader" David Koresh, who quickly became the establishment press's bogeyman of the moment, could have been questioned—if there was any legitimate reason for the authorities to question him—at any time in public, as he was a highly visible member of the local community. Instead of doing this, the ATF, FBI, and other assorted law enforcement officials chose to attack the Davidians' home like a gang of storm troopers. During the "siege," all sorts of wild allegations were circulated in the press, maintaining that Koresh was a fanatical child molester who fathered children by many different brides, most of them underage. President Clinton even directly called Koresh a child abuser at a press conference shortly after his government burned many of those children to death. Even though the Justice Department's own internal report on the Waco matter later admitted there was no evidence that the Branch Davidian children were mistreated in any way, and that there was no hint of sexual misconduct on the part of Koresh, neither Clinton nor Janet Reno saw fit to apologize for their earlier repeated, irresponsible charges. The end result was that eighty-six Americans, including twenty-four children, lost their lives directly because of unnecessary and unconstitutional government intervention. The tragedy at Waco created a huge backlash among those already inclined to distrust the government.

Pressured by the exploding alternative media on the Internet, and films such as *Waco: The Rules of Engagement*, the FBI in 1999 admitted that flammable devices had indeed been used in the assault on the compound. Government critics had been claiming as much for years, but they had been ignored by the press and ridiculed by the Clinton administration as "right wing extremists." The original FBI and ATF investigations had indicated that the fire that burned the complex to the ground was the sole responsibility of Davidian leader David Koresh. FBI officials had adamantly denied using pyrotechnic tear-gas canisters on the final day of the "siege," as well as the firing of any shots at the compound or the participation of Army personnel and equipment. Recently released infrared videotapes demonstrated, however, that shots were fired against the compound and that incendiary devices were used. Photos of FBI agents with military assault weapons, and testimony and evidence that the military's secretive Delta Force was involved, were produced. Janet Reno reacted by blaming the FBI for "misleading" her. Bill Clinton appointed former senator (and future Bush attorney general) John Danforth to conduct a new investigation. To no one's surprise, the establishment stalwart Danforth completely vindicated the FBI, and his only prosecution was against a prosecutor who had granted an independent investigator too much access to evidence.

During the ensuing congressional investigation into the events at Waco, yet another crucial entry was added to the Clinton Body Count. Carlos Ghigliotti, owner of Infrared Technology, had been retained by the House Government Reform Committee and asked to analyze surveillance footage film from Waco using Forward Looking Infrared (FLIR) technology. During his research, Ghigliotti uncovered additional evidence contradicting government claims. After not being seen or heard from for weeks, his badly decomposed body was discovered seated at his desk in his Laurel, Maryland, home lab on April 28, 2000. Ghigliotti was only forty-two years old. In an unintentionally hilarious footnote, a Laurel Police spokesman declared, "So far, it looks like natural causes." Ghigliotti's friend, attorney David Hardy, told WorldNetDaily, "I think he may have known too much. Carlos told me that he had discovered things that were much, much worse than anything that has yet come out."

The February 26, 1993, bombing of the World Trade Center could have easily been prevented by the FBI. They had planted informant Emad Salem inside the group of Muslim extremists who allegedly set the explosion that killed six people and left more than a thousand injured. Salem became so frustrated with the FBI that he attempted to complain to the Bureau's headquarters in Washington, D.C., but was discouraged from doing so by agent John Anticev. (*New York Times*, October 28, 1993). Following the bombing, the FBI promised to pay Salem *a million dollars* if he developed evidence of further terrorist plots. In tape-recorded conversations afterward, Salem lashed out at the Bureau. "You were informed. Everything is ready. The day and the time," Salem told one FBI agent. On another tape, Salem declared, "Do you deny your supervisor is the main reason of bombing the World Trade Center?" Concerned that an actual bombing was going to take place, Salem had offered to replace the deadly explosives with a harmless powder, but the FBI had inexplicably spurned his idea.

In his disjointed English, Salem, in a call to an FBI agent shortly after the bombing, described exactly how this typically idiotic government sting operation was set up: "We was start already building the bomb, which is went off in the World Trade Center. It was built, uh, uh, uh, supervising, supervision from the Bureau [FBI] and the DA [district attorney] and we was all informed about it. And we know that the bomb start to be built. By who? By your confidential informant. What a wonderful great case. And then he, 'the FBI [supervisor],' put his head in the sand and said, oh no, no, no, that's not true, he is a son of a bitch, okay."

Assistant US Attorney Andrew McCarthy had the audacity to brag to a New York jury that the first World Trade Center attack was one of the FBI's finest hours, declaring, "To the rest of the world out there, [the] explosion in all its tragedy was actually a high-water mark for the FBI." FBI Director William Sessions was similarly deluded about his bureau's utter failures, claiming, "Based on what was known to us at the time, we have no reason to believe we could have prevented the bombing of the World Trade Center." The opposite, of course, is the reality here; in all likelihood, the bombing would never have happened without FBI involvement.

THE DEATH OF RON BROWN

While Vince Foster had been the highest-ranking official in Clinton's administration to die, Commerce Secretary Ron Brown did him one better when he was killed in a plane crash on April 3, 1996, in Croatia. Allegations of wrongdoing had long swirled around Brown, who'd previously been chairman of the Democratic National Committee. At the time of his murder, Brown was under investigation for his involvement in several scandals, by the Justice Department, the FBI, the FDIC, and his own Commerce Department, among others. When Janet Reno appointed a special prosecutor for Brown, he became extremely angry, and supposedly told Bill Clinton he wasn't going to "take the rap." Did he also threaten to bring Clinton down with him? "Conspiracy theorists" alleged that a photo showed a bullet hole in Brown's head, a charge that was heatedly (and predictably) refuted by establishment sources. Lieutenant Colonel Steve Cogswell, deputy medical examiner with the Armed Forces Institute of Pathology (AFIP) at Dover Air Force Base, closely investigated the Ron Brown crash.

In an interview with Christopher Ruddy of the *Pittsburgh Tribune-Review*, December 3, 1997, Dr. Cogswell stated his belief that Air Force sergeants Shelley Kelly and Cheryl Turnage, who were flight attendants seated in the rear of the aircraft, were "potential survivors" of the accident. "Depending on who you talked to, Kelly was found near her seat, on the floor of the plane or outside the plane," Cogswell said. Some reports stated she had only cuts and bruises and was able to help herself into the rescue helicopter. However, Kelly was declared dead on arrival at a nearby hospital. Her autopsy at Dover Air Force Base revealed that she died of a broken neck.

Dr. Cogswell contended that evidence indicating Ron Brown was murdered was simply ignored by investigators. Cogswell spoke of the "apparent gunshot wound," a perfectly round hole in the top of Brown's head. Dr. Cogswell had years of experience working with gunshot wounds. Saying, "This whole thing stinks," Cogswell urged Colonel William Gormley, AFIP public affairs officer, to perform an autopsy, but Gormley only conducted an external exam of Brown's body and told Cogswell, "This is a closed case."

Dr. Martin Fackler, former director of the Army's Wound Ballistics Laboratory in San Francisco, studied the photographs of Brown's head wound. "I'm impressed by how very, very round that hole is," he told the *Tribune-Review*." That's unusual except for a gunshot wound. . . ." When he learned Brown was only given an external examination, he replied, "They didn't do an autopsy. My God. It's astounding." "You can't ignore who this person is," Dr. Cogswell told the *Tribune-Review*. "You can't ignore the controversy surrounding him. To stack up the coincidences: one of thirty-six people has got a hole; the hole is in their head; the hole is dead center in the top of their head; and it just happens to be the most important person on that airplane from a political point of view. That's a whole lot of reason to investigate it."

The newspaper went on to report that, as a result of Dr. Cogswell's controversial statements, he'd been placed under "command investigation" by the Air Force, given orders not to speak to the press, and was forced to retrieve case material from his home for the military police. A follow-up story in the December 9, 1997, *Pittsburgh Tribune-Review* quoted US Army Lieutenant Colonel David Hause, who'd been present during the external exam of Ron Brown. "A commotion" erupted, according to Hause, when someone said, "Gee, this looks like a gunshot wound." He stated that it looked like a gunshot wound to him, too. According to both Cogswell and Hause, all of Brown's head x-rays, the photos of the x-rays, and the negatives for the photographs were now missing from his case file.

Once again, there was a related unnatural death. Barbara Wise's partially nude body was found in a locked Commerce Department office on November 29, 1996. Despite the fact there were bruises found all over her body, police said there was no outward sign of death and found no evidence of foul play. Wise worked in the same division of the Commerce Department that had been the focus of investigations involving illegal foreign fund-raising.

JANET RENO

Attorney General Janet Reno probably garnered the most criticism of any member in Clinton's cabinet. Reno was a decidedly odd person. She was said to enjoy stretching out her six-foot-two-inch frame on her backyard trampoline and reciting passages from Coleridge while surrounded by thirty-five peacocks, all named Horace. Even the friendly *Washington Post* reported that she had an extraordinarily bizarre necklace, made out of fossilized alligator droppings. Reno grew up in a house with no modern conveniences, even though her parents were quite affluent.

Reno's record as Dade County, Florida, state attorney was abysmal. She failed to investigate the "Votescam" charges by the intrepid Collier brother journalists, showing no interest in the matter even after a local newspaper publisher was shot in his driveway one evening. The paper had published articles detailing the voting fraud, but Reno never took action in the shooting, and it is still officially categorized as unsolved. After becoming Clinton's attorney general, Reno fired every US attorney, a move unprecedented in our nation's history. She also fired FBI Director William Sessions the day before Vince Foster was found dead. On the rare occasion when one of the special counsels assigned to Clinton's multitude of scandals attempted to actually investigate anything, Reno steadfastly blocked the way.

Reno was widely rumored to be a lesbian, but she would not publicly address the issue. Attorney Jack Thompson, who ran for office against Reno in Florida and lost, carried on an intense personal crusade against her. He claimed to have documented evidence showing Reno was arrested for stealing lingerie at a Jordan March department store in 1981. He publicly stated that five different police officers were willing to testify to anyone who would listen that Reno was pulled over five times in Dade County while driving under the influence of alcohol. He also claimed that he'd once presented evidence to her about a child pornography ring but she failed to investigate. Perhaps this was due to the fact that, according to Thompson, "A Fort Lauderdale police officer found Janet Reno with an underage girl in the back seat of a car at the Galleria Mall. . . ." (*Media Bypass*, February 1999).

MORE CLINTON BODY COUNT

While there was a steady stream of womanizing allegations against Bill Clinton throughout his eight years in office, former Miss Arkansas Sally Perdue's allegations contained a more serious element than most. Other than *The Spotlight*, no representative of the US media published her startling claims, which were detailed in the London *Sunday Telegraph* (January 23, 1994). Perdue described her affair with then-Governor Clinton but made a more frightening charge: she claimed that Democratic Party official Ron Tucker had told her there were people in high places who knew where she jogged every day, and that she could get her legs broken. How was *that* not fit to print? (*The Spotlight*, March 14, 1994, p. 12).

Chief of Naval Operations Admiral Jeremy Boorda was found dead from a gunshot wound to the chest, an alleged suicide, on May 16, 1996. He was allegedly despondent over a forthcoming *Newsweek* story about him not being entitled to the valor medals he was wearing. He left two typed suicide notes, David Ferrie style, without signing either. The autopsy report was never released. (*New York Times* and others, May 16, 1996). Military Corruption.com interviewed a handful of Navy officers who knew Boorda well, and each doubted the official story. "I wouldn't be surprised if he was murdered," Navy petty officer Mark Carter stated. Ironically, Boorda had mentioned the subject of suicide with disdain in a speech just one month prior to his death at the US Naval Academy.

Armed altercations between embittered citizens and government agents continued unabated throughout the Nineties. Maynard Campbell Jr. was one of those nasty "right wing extremists" who gained a certain amount of fame in fringe circles for his live conversation with *Radio Free America* host Tom Valentine on the night of October 16, 1992, as a SWAT team surrounded his property and nearly killed him. Maynard Campbell told the radio audience that the feds wanted to "get him," but he surrendered against his better judgment and was sentenced to an unbelievable thirteen years in prison for the seemingly misdemeanor offense of cutting down trees on federal property. He was inexplicably sent to a high-security prison in Leavenworth, Kansas, which also housed another notable political prisoner, Yorie Kahl, son of tax protester Gordon Kahl. Campbell, dangerous tree-cutter that he was, eventually found his way to a maximum security federal prison in Florence, Colorado, where he was stabbed to death on January 16, 1997. (*The Spotlight*, February 3, 1997, p. 3).

A forty-five-hour siege, lasting from March 31 to April 2, 1995, between fifty-four-year-old John M. Lekan and a force that included four SWAT teams, two hundred firefighters, and three hundred police officers ended in the tragic deaths of Lekan and his nine-year-old son, John Jr. Police ended the standoff by ramming the Lekans' Brunswick, Ohio, home with armored personnel carriers. The incident brought back memories of how the siege at

Waco was ended by the government. Even an establishment paper like the Cleveland *Plain Dealer* criticized the authorities over the incident, in a cartoon in their April 5, 1995, edition.

According to *The Spotlight*, Lekan had been in a dispute with the Medina County Human Services Department over his possession of three *legal* firearms. Lekan was apparently accused of recklessly handling the weapons in the presence of his son, and he was fearful the police would take his son away. Not surprisingly, Lekan had a strong dislike for the government. The police claimed that Lekan killed his son and then himself, and that officers found the bodies in the bathroom. Most of those who were all too familiar with this sort of "siege," always waged against vocal critics of the government (and never, for instance, against reputed Mafia or violent gang kingpins), believed otherwise. (*The Spotlight*, May 1, 1995, pp. 4–5).

THE OKLAHOMA CITY BOMBING

"The haters and extremists didn't go away, but they were on the defensive, and, for the rest of my term, would never quite again regain the position they had enjoyed after Timothy McVeigh took the demonization of government beyond the limits of humanity."
—Bill Clinton

Two years to the day after the tragedy at Waco, on April 19, 1995, the Alfred P. Murrah Federal Building in Oklahoma City, Oklahoma, was blown up, causing the deaths of 168 Americans, including nineteen children from the building's day care center. The designated "lone nut" for the horrific crime was Timothy McVeigh, an ex-soldier who had gravitated into the forbidden zone of political extremism and was said to have been motivated out of a sense of revenge for the government's actions at Ruby Ridge and Waco.

McVeigh had been stopped by a police officer about an hour and a half after the bombing, for driving a car with no license plates. He also had no registration for the vehicle and was found to be carrying a concealed weapon without a permit. He was arrested and taken to the county jail. President Bill Clinton wasted little time in using McVeigh's "extremist" beliefs to demonize the growing Third Party movement in the country, and he particularly took aim at the increasingly popular militia groups. He extended his criticisms to include "right wing" talk radio as well. No one could exploit a tragedy better than Bill Clinton.

The "investigation" of the Oklahoma City bombing, and the mainstream media coverage of it, reflected the "investigations" and press coverage of previous significant political events. In the familiar pattern, a scapegoat was trotted out to take the blame, and no "journalist" questioned the myriad number of flaws in the official explanation. Brigadier General Ben Partin, perhaps the foremost demolition expert in the country, strongly disputed that a giant fertilizer bomb could have caused all the damage to the building. Longtime FBI agent Ted Gunderson was similarly vocal in his disagreements with the official story, but neither of them could get any mainstream media exposure. A multitude of witnesses reported on the presence at the scene of a man dubbed "John Doe #2," but the government didn't want anyone except McVeigh's fellow "extremist" Terry Nichols (against whom there was no credible evidence of involvement) associated with him.

Even Attorney General Janet Reno initially declared publicly that "John Doe #2 remains at large." Among the countless unanswered questions in this case is the curious fact that the FBI paid Terry Nichols's mortgage for him, in the interval between the time he was arrested in conjunction with the Oklahoma City bombing and his eventual conviction. A Justice Department spokesperson acknowledged the payments had been made, but she said she "did not know" the reason why, nor the amount paid. (*Rocky Mountain News*, April 22, 1998).

The trial of Timothy McVeigh was one of the most unfair in American history. Basically a legal lynching, the pathetic, politically unpopular young man was led to his preordained destiny by his incompetent attorney, Stephen Jones, aided and abetted by Judge Richard Matsch and the usual team of hungry prosecutors. Matsch, while permitting those who'd lost loved ones to testify about their ordeal in heart-wrenching (and obviously prejudicial) fashion, when they were witnesses to nothing instrumental to the case and certainly had no bearing on McVeigh's guilt or innocence, refused to permit Jones (when the occasion moved him) to provide much of a defense at all. For instance, former ATF informant Carol Howe was willing to state that the government knew in advance about a conspiracy to blow up the Murrah building and could name those involved in the plot, which didn't include McVeigh. She even knew the target date was April 19, 1995. However, Matsch refused to allow her to testify.

The video *Cover-Up in Oklahoma*, which was suppressed by the establishment media, showed clearly the parallels between Oklahoma City and Dealey Plaza, 1963. During local television footage from the scene on April 19, 1995, there were repeated references throughout from federal authorities to both a second and third bomb found inside the building. There was even an interview with a terrorism "expert," one Randall Heather, in which he commented on the significance of these undetonated bombs and how they would provide authorities with a clue to the identity of the bombers. There were also references to the "sophisticated device" planted by a "sophisticated group."

The Spotlight wasn't the only paper to tell the truth about the Oklahoma City bombing trial. The *Rocky Mountain News*, for instance, reported in its May 28, 1997, edition about Matsch's suppression of Carol Howe's testimony, including nice quotes from her lawyer and Oklahoma State Representative Charles Key, who stated: "The government is shutting this case down fast, and it raises questions in a lot of people's minds." Glen Wilburn, who lost two grandchildren in the blast and had become a vocal critic of the investigation, said: "You bring Carol Howe in, let her tell her story. Well, the federal government doesn't look too good." The *Post* reported that "although the FBI and federal prosecutors repeatedly denied that either Strassmeir (enigmatic German Andreas Strassmeir, an undocumented alien who was thought by many to be an undercover government agent, and was spirited out of the country before McVeigh's defense could utilize him) or Mahon (ex-Tulsa KKK leader Dennis Mahon, along with Strassmeir, named by Howe as the two individuals who spoke of bombing a federal building in Oklahoma City) were suspects in the bombing, documents turned over to the defense prove that they were and that Howe was extensively interviewed by federal agents two days after the bombing." The *Post* directly made the accusation that "the government has refused to talk about Howe." Judge Matsch also ruled out any evidence, as in the tape of local television coverage, that there were creditable reports of unexploded bombs discovered in the building.

Glen Wilburn conducted his own independent investigation into the bombing. His stepdaughter, Edye Smith, was a familiar face on television after the tragedy, as footage of the sons, ages two and three, she lost that day was replayed over and over. Smith's fifteen minutes of fame ended, however, with her unexpected responses during a May 23, 1995, interview with CNN's Gary Tuchman. The theme of the interview, which was conducted just after the remnants of the Murrah building had been demolished by the authorities, was of survivors "moving on" now that this visible reminder was gone. Smith told Tuchman boldly, "There are a lot of questions that have been left unanswered . . . we're being told to keep our mouths shut, not talk about it, don't ask those questions . . . you know, where was ATF? All fifteen or seventeen of their employees survived, and they live—they're on the ninth floor. They were the target of this explosion, and where were they? Did they have a warning sign? I mean, did they think it might be a bad day to go in the office? They had an option to not go to work that day, and my kids didn't get that option, nobody else in the building got that option. . . ." CNN abruptly cut off the interview after Smith's unanticipated outburst. Glen Wilburn died at the young age of forty-six on July 15, 1997.

The Spotlight provided a synopsis of a Radio Free America broadcast on which attorney (and author of The Franklin Cover-Up) John DeCamp appeared on June 1, 1997, where he described how he had filed a motion to prevent the destruction of the Murrah building. DeCamp would have been able to arrange for a top bomb expert to visit the building, but he agreed to defense attorney Stephen Jones's request that he file the motion himself. Jones ended up merely conducting a walkthrough of the bombed-out structure, accompanied by a photographer and an architect, before agreeing that the building could be destroyed and the rubble taken away and buried. Jones was soundly criticized by DeCamp for spending millions of tax dollars and then launching a defense that he closed after four days. The Spotlight also questioned why McVeigh would be accused by the government of asking for directions to the Murrah building on the day of the bombing, when he was supposedly staking it out earlier. (The Spotlight, June 16, 1997, pp. 21–24).

There are countless unanswered questions in this case. Why was the only evidence of the fertilizer bomb residue introduced by the prosecutors found on a small, nine-inch piece of plywood, which allegedly came from the inside of the large Ryder rental truck? What happened to the supposedly indestructible engine (which weighed about a thousand pounds), the drive shaft, transmission frame, doors, wheels, etc., of the Ryder truck? It would seem impossible for a fertilizer bomb to have completely pulverized the hardened steel and rubber these truck parts were constructed of, especially when one considers the piece of plywood that somehow survived the blast. Why did the authorities rush to remove the remnants of the building— vital evidence to any independent investigation of the crime—and then bury them in an unknown location? (The Spotlight, June 23, 1997, p. 5). The plywood was supposedly found by an unidentified civilian, and FBI forensic laboratory scientist Frederick Whitehurst (who had gained headlines with his revelations of FBI lab incompetence and the fact that evidence had been fabricated and altered, including a specific claim that evidence in this case had been inappropriately processed) stated he'd been told by FBI Special Agent David R. Williams that the plywood would not be used because of

JFK-assassination like "chain of custody" questions. (*The Spotlight*, June 16, 1997, pp. 22–23).

While government witnesses claimed explosive residue was found on McVeigh's shirt, in his pants pockets, and on a pair of earplugs found in his possession, they didn't explain the fact that no residue was found on his boots or anywhere on his body, or on his car's steering wheel or elsewhere in the vehicle. *The Spotlight* reporter covering the trial described how the mainstream press, perfectly serious and attentive during the prosecution's presentation, suddenly began talking loudly among themselves (the few reporters there taking their job seriously were actually unable at certain points to follow the proceedings) once the defense began its case, while laughing at and ridiculing many defense witnesses. (*The Spotlight*, June 9, 1997, p. 7).

In a fantastic, mysterious twist, Attorney Martin Keating, the brother of Oklahoma Governor Frank Keating, proved to be an impressive prognosticator. A novel he began in 1986, eventually published in 1996 as *The Final Jihad* by an obscure publisher, with little ensuing sales or publicity, shared some amazing similarities with the future bombing of the Murrah building. The most astounding one is the fact that one of the characters in the novel is named Tom McVay. Also intriguing is the fact that the major suspect is first apprehended by an Oklahoma state police officer for speeding with a flickering taillight. The fictional policeman, like the real one in the actual case, at first doesn't realize that the man he has stopped is anything other than a traffic offender. After the then-unpublished manuscript surfaced in the wake of McVeigh's arrest, the governor jokingly demanded that his brother provide an alibi for the time of the bombing.

Governor Keating had a strange connection to the case himself. Federal investigators originally reported that the governor had been the one who found the rear axle from the Ryder truck (the only sizable piece of the truck recovered in the wake of the blast). Perhaps realizing this was too incredible for the public to swallow, the story was quickly altered to one whereby an FBI agent had discovered the axle, then changed again at McVeigh's trial (without, apparently, the jury finding anything troubling about these discrepancies) to one where a caretaker at a nearby apartment building had found it. (*The Spotlight*, July 21, 1997, pp. 12–13). Governor Keating, after initially declaring on television that unexploded bombs had been found in the Murrah building and taken away for examination, would later angrily tell a reporter, "I don't really care if the bomb was fertilizer or not—it's irrelevant to me!" (*Media Bypass*, July 1999).

One of the most curious aspects of the whole Oklahoma City affair was McVeigh's lack of passion and unwillingness to protest what was clearly one of the all-time great railroad jobs. Belatedly, McVeigh gave a telephone interview with the *Buffalo News* from the Englewood, Colorado, prison where he was then incarcerated, and lashed out at his attorney Stephen Jones. Claiming Jones had lied to him repeatedly, McVeigh was trying desperately to cut his ties and keep Jones off his appeal process. "The truth is this guy only succeeded in getting the death sentence and now he doesn't want to let go." McVeigh also (accurately) stated: "He screwed up badly but I'm not bitter. I only want him off my appeal."

Asked by the paper to be specific about the lies Jones told him, McVeigh was characteristically vague: "It's for Congress, the bar, and the judiciary to investigate and discover. You would not believe some of the things that have occurred in this case. The man has repeatedly lied to me in the past." McVeigh seemed especially bitter about the inexcusable leak of his alleged "confession" to his attorneys earlier in 1997, before his "trial," which the *Dallas Morning News* printed and was widely reported. "It all came down to the *Dallas Morning News* leak. However, when I found out I was stuck with him, I decided to wait until after the trial," McVeigh stated, "and now I find out he won't be gone and I have no say." McVeigh's attitude about waiting until after the trial to go on the record about his attorney's incompetence is unfathomable. But then not testifying in a trial deciding whether you live or die is even more incomprehensible. McVeigh also defended his stoic courtroom demeanor. "I tried to be a total gentleman in the courtroom when people called me a coward," he said. (*Washington Post*, August 14, 1997, p. A6).

The trial of hapless Timothy McVeigh shared many things in common with the "trials" of other scapegoats from the past. Like Bruno Richard Hauptmann, James Earl Ray, and Sirhan Sirhan, McVeigh received inept legal representation. Stephen Jones presented almost no defense, resting after only three and a half days and just twenty-five witnesses. Even establishment talking head attorney Alan Dershowitz would criticize the incompetent defense McVeigh received. As noted, Judge Richard Matsch did his part, denying much of the evidence Jones actually attempted to present. British reporter Ambrose Evans-Pritchard discovered that Carol Howe's FBI debriefing reports revealed that she named members of a neo-Nazi group that had cased the Murrah building in December 1994 with the intention of blowing it up. Just like in the Kennedy assassination, the FBI refused to follow up on her information, and during the "investigation" of the Oklahoma City bombing, it didn't attempt to locate and interview a single one of those she'd named, even though it had time to conduct an incredible 26,000 witness interviews, according to Evans-Pritchard, "most of them irrelevant."

From the very beginning, the government, as it does seemingly all the time, acted as if it had something to hide. The government blew up the remainder of the Murrah building only weeks after the bombing and then buried the rubble. The intrepid *Spotlight* newspaper covered extensively the FBI's standard falsification of reports and coercion of witnesses. Like Oswald over thirty years before, McVeigh was described as doing impossible things. Again like the Kennedy assassination, there was a critical "alias" supposedly involved in the case. The ridiculous "official" theory begins with the illogical scenario that McVeigh and fellow defendant Terry Nichols constructed a fertilizer bomb capable of toppling a nine-story building at a public lake and that McVeigh then transported that device over two hundred miles without blowing himself up. The government claimed that McVeigh rented a Ryder truck from Elliott's Body Shop using the name "Robert Kling," but three employees of the body shop told the FBI that "Kling" was accompanied by another man. Two of the three described a "Kling" that clearly couldn't have been McVeigh.

The defense and government both possessed a videotape of McVeigh at a McDonald's in Junction City, which is a mile and a third away from Elliott's Body Shop. Much as the Warren Commission had wanted everyone to believe Oswald was capable of any and all movements, regardless of time, space, and logic, the government claimed that, despite the fact that the video was recorded between 3:55 and 4:00 p.m., with McVeigh wearing clothes completely different from those "Kling" was described as wearing, he traversed the distance to Elliott's Body Shop in an Oswald-like sub-twenty minutes (which was required to meet the time frame "Kling" was at the body shop), evidently changing clothes along the way. One of the amazing things about the case that defense attorney Jones did manage to point out was that the government wasn't going to call a single witness from Oklahoma City to identify McVeigh. They couldn't do this because every witness there contradicted the official version of events; no one had seen him who also hadn't seen "John Doe #2." What a damning indictment of the jury's guilty verdict; the prosecution presented no evidence placing the defendant at the scene of the crime.

There were many aspects of the case that went unreported by our "free" press. FBI informant Cary James Gagan had tried to tell the authorities about the bombing, of which he had prior knowledge. Gagan claimed, in a lawsuit he filed against the government, that he had told the FBI in September 1994 that he had information about a plot to blow up a federal building, and his life was now in danger. In Gagan's words, "they let it happen." Subsequently, Gagan claimed to have been physically assaulted and sent to a Denver emergency room. Gagan filed a civil suit in Denver, and former FBI chief Ted Gunderson provided his emergency room records to *The Spotlight*.

In October 1995, renegade juror Hoppy Heidelberg was thrown off the Oklahoma City grand jury, which had been formed largely due to the lobbying efforts of aforementioned state representative Charles Key, for asking pertinent questions and actually trying to get to the truth. Heidelberg went on to establish the Oklahomans for Truth Committee, which took Gagan's deposition on March 13, 1999. They also heard the testimony of Jane Graham, who'd worked on the seventh floor of the Murrah building and had heard multiple explosions on the day of the bombing. She also had seen suspicious people around the building in the days before the bombing, and she later attempted unsuccessfully to give her information to the FBI. (*Media Bypass*, July 1999). Graham told *Red Dirt Reporter*, "I am utterly convinced the ATF and the FBI are involved in the bombing of that building." Gagan would be railroaded into federal prison, where researchers claim he has disappeared into the system. There are also online rumors to the effect that his girlfriend disappeared, too, albeit a bit more literally.

Then there were the prerequisite mysterious deaths. Oklahoma City Police Officer Terrance Yeakey "killed himself" in a manner that would have made the Warren Commission blush. The official report of his death maintained that a distraught Yeakey slashed his wrists, arms, and elbows, stabbed himself in both sides of his neck near the jugular vein, then walked one and a half miles to a spot where he proceeded to shoot himself in the side of the head. In JFK assassination style, the bullet entered the upper temple on the right side and exited below the upper jaw bone on the left side, meaning there was a downward trajectory. Police claimed Yeakey left no suicide note, but *The Spotlight* published a letter he sent to a bombing victim who had questioned the official theory of events. The letter reads, in part:

"The man that you and I were talking about in the pictures I have made the mistake of asking too many questions as to his role in the bombing and was told to back off. . . . I was told by several officers he was an ATF agent who was overseeing the bombing plot. . . . Knowing what I know now and understanding fully just what went down that morning makes me ashamed to wear a badge from Oklahoma City's Police Department. I took an oath to uphold the law and to enforce the law to the best of my ability. This is something I cannot honestly do and hold my head up proud any longer if I keep my silence as I am ordered to do. . . . The sad truth of the matter is that they have so many police officers convinced that by covering up the truth about the operation gone wrong, that they are actually doing our citizens a favor. What I want to know is how many other operations have they had that blew up in their faces? Makes you stop and take another look at Waco. . . ."

Another casualty in the aftermath of the bombing was Dr. Howard D. Chumley, who was killed on September 24, 1995, when the plane he was piloting suddenly plunged into a field. Dr. Chumley was asked to falsify injury reports concerning ATF agents shortly after the bombing and flatly refused to do so. When Dr. Chumley discovered that another less scrupulous Oklahoma City doctor had agreed to falsify such reports, he threatened to turn the physician in to the medical authorities. Witness Leah Moore was badly injured in the blast and reported being threatened by the FBI afterward, in an attempt to stop her from talking to the *Los Angeles Times* about the photos she'd taken of the Ryder truck supposedly used to carry the magic fertilizer bomb. The FBI was accused of browbeating other witnesses, who'd seen the infamous "John Doe #2," in conduct reminiscent of what was reported after the JFK assassination.

Another injured victim of the bombing, Larry Martin, was not so fortunate; he allegedly flew his plane into the ground near his church. Researcher Patrick Briley was told by local KWTV reporter Mike Carpenter that he'd better be careful since the FBI was "pissed off" at him after he'd dared to complain that his wife was mistreated by them.

A truly bizarre element of this story involved G.S.A. employee Mike Loudenslager. Loudenslager had become a vocal critic, in the weeks before the bombing, of the amount of explosives being stored in the building, which of course contained a day care center. He even went to the lengths of warning parents to remove their children from this day care center, which a number of them did. At the time of the bombing, Loudenslager was in court, and was shortly thereafter actively involved in the search-and-rescue efforts at the Murrah building. He was supposedly heard engaging in a loud argument with someone at the scene. Incredibly, it would later be officially reported that Loudenslager had been found dead at his desk, a victim of the bombing.

Consider the case of Kenneth Trentadue. Trentadue was found hung in his Oklahoma prison cell on August 21, 1995, allegedly a suicide. Tim McVeigh supposedly reacted to Trentadue's death by saying he thought he'd been killed because he'd been mistaken for Richard Lee Guthrie, who'd been suspected by some of involvement in the bombing and who also died by hanging while in custody. Alden Gillis Baker, who'd been Trentadue's fellow inmate, declared in 1999 that he had witnessed his murder, and he was found hung himself, in his cell a year later. Officials actually attempted to get the permission of Trentadue's family to cremate him at government expense—an unheard-of proposal—but they refused. Brother Jesse and the rest of the family never accepted the suicide theory, a view that was bolstered considerably when Oklahoma City's chief medical examiner, Fred Jordan, said it was "very likely he was murdered." (*Mother Jones*, July 21, 2011). The FBI and the Bureau of Prisons pressured Jordan to rule the death a suicide, and Oklahoma Assistant Attorney General Patrick Crawley charged that they had "destroyed evidence, and otherwise harassed and harangued Dr. Jordan and his staff."

Oklahoma City Police Officer Don Browning was the Roger Craig of this case. Like Craig, he saw things that contradicted the official account and didn't remain silent about it. In a court deposition presented to the grand jury Hoppy Heidelberg was affiliated with, Browning recounted how he and other local officers were immediately ordered to leave the scene of the explosion by federal marshals, who threatened them with arrest, in spite of the fact that there were victims to rescue and evidence to secure.

"That same morning," Browning swore, "I observed men wearing jackets with 'FBI' printed on the back removing the surveillance video cameras from the exterior of the Murrah Federal Building. I thought this was part of the FBI's evidence gathering or 'chain of custody' procedures since those exterior cameras would have shown and recorded delivery of the bomb in a Ryder truck that morning as well as the person or persons who exited that truck. I knew from my training and experience as a police officer that an investigation of the bombing and prosecution of those involved would require not only preserving the videotapes of the event but also require preserving the cameras and tape decks by which those videotapes were made. Nevertheless, I did think it odd that the FBI's removal of those cameras was taking place while many people were still trapped alive in the rubble of the Murrah Federal Building and so many of us were working desperately to find them."

As late as 2011, in response to a Freedom of Information Act lawsuit, a federal court was reported to be "considering" the release of the unedited videotapes from that day. "Someday, somewhere, somebody is going to have the guts to release that stuff," said David Schippers, who was chief investigative counsel for the House Judiciary Committee during the Clinton impeachment hearing. (*The Examiner*, April 12, 2011).

Browning also questioned the "suicide" verdict in Terrence Yeakey's death, complaining quite reasonably that an autopsy should have been performed. Browning, like Yeakey, had pulled several victims from the rubble before being banished from the site. In a December 22, 2011, interview with talk show host Alex Jones, Browning described FBI agents warning him that he and his wife could end up dead if they didn't do what they were told. They also suggested that he was too close to the "militia," which he clearly wasn't, and needed to find new friends. Browning also discussed how suspicious he, Yeakey, and other officers were that the FBI and ATF had arrived on the scene so quickly; the local FBI office was more than five miles away from the bombing site. Renegade juror Hoppy Heidelberg had previously reported receiving very similar threats in an interview with Jones. Heidelberg even named the FBI agent who'd threatened him *with a gun*; it was Jon Hersley, who went on to write a terribly misleading book on the bombing called *Simple Truths*. Hersley has become the "go-to" guy on the Oklahoma City bombing, whenever the subject is raised on the typical kind of inaccurate programs television networks specialize in.

Then there was the amazing report, ignored by the major media, that celebrated O. J. Simpson defense lawyer Johnnie Cochran had been retained by more than three hundred relatives of the bombing victims who were suing the government. Cochran and his cocounsel, John Merritt, claimed the bombing was a bungled sting operation by the FBI and the ATF. In a wrongful-death petition filed in Oklahoma County District Court, Cochran & Co. alleged that federal officials had "detailed prior knowledge of the planned bombing" but "failed to prevent it from taking place." (*The Spotlight*, May 19, 1997, pp. 3–7, p. 17). Predictably, a judge threw the lawsuit out in July 1996.

In yet another parallel to the JFK assassination, there was evidently a mysterious roll of undeveloped film missing from Timothy McVeigh's belongings. This was revealed during the trial testimony of Nobel County Jail employee Deborah June Thompson. Ms. Thompson testified that the film, which was inventoried among McVeigh's personal belongings after his arrest for driving without a rear license plate, had been "picked up by someone else," and thus wasn't among the belongings turned over to the FBI. FBI agent Lou Hupp also testified that the missing roll of film had been "picked up" before he received the bag containing McVeigh's belongings. Hupp, along with seemingly everyone else, was unable to state just who "picked it up" and where it was. *The Spotlight* reported that "speculation out of Denver" held that the film may have contained some pictures of the infamous John Doe #2, or maybe others linked to the bombing.

Interestingly, like Oswald, McVeigh was very careful about not leaving fingerprints. Agent Hupp also testified that the alleged bomber's fingerprints were not found anywhere in Elliott's Body Shop or the Ryder rental truck office, not even on the contract signed by Bob Kling, McVeigh's alleged alias. McVeigh's prints were also not on the storage locker that supposedly held the explosives prior to the bombing, or on the ammunition cans, or anywhere in the Dreamland Motel, where the Ryder rental truck was supposedly parked before the bombing. Curiously, the only place where McVeigh's fingerprints have been found is on a receipt for the fertilizer, a transaction in which he was not even alleged to be involved. Even more curious is the fact that neither of the alleged parties to this transaction, Terry Nichols or the store clerk, left any fingerprints on the contract. Agent Hupp stated, when asked why McVeigh's fingerprints were not found in Nichols's home, that he was ordered not to look for prints there. (*The Spotlight*, June 2, 1997, p. 3).

Bill Clinton and other leading politicians lobbied passionately for strong "anti-terror" legislation in the wake of the Oklahoma City bombing. The book *Oklahoma City: Day One* by Michele Marie Moore, published in 1996, explored the connection between the Oklahoma City bombing and subsequent draconian legislation. Actually, the Omnibus Counterterrorism Bill had been introduced *before* the bombing, on February 10, 1995. The bill was sponsored in the Senate by senators Joseph R. Biden (D-DE, Obama's future vice president) and Arlen Specter (R-PA, ex-counsel for the Warren Commission, author of the single-bullet theory). The bill, a forerunner of the odious Patriot Act, included many dangerously unconstitutional provisions. It granted sweeping powers to the president to designate any group "terrorist," to seize the assets of any such group, and to imprison citizens or deport permanent residents for supporting the *lawful* activities of any organization the president had labeled "terrorist." Such acts could include the mere donation of funds. The president's determination would not be subject to appeal. The bill authorized the suspension of posse comitatus, and it allowed the use of the military in law enforcement activities. It also reversed the time-honored concept of presumption of innocence.

The bill became law under a slightly altered form and a new name, the Antiterrorism and Effective Death Penalty Act of 1996, on April 24, 1996. Reflecting the "bipartisan effort" that the establishment is always able to invoke at important junctures, then-Senate Majority Leader Robert Dole (R-KS) commented: "The families of some of the bombing victims traveled all the way to Washington . . . to let us know that we must take action now to put an end to the endless delays and appeals that have done so much to weaken public confidence in our system of criminal justice. It is gratifying to see that their efforts had such a profound impact here in the Senate."

Timothy McVeigh was put to death by lethal injection on June 11, 2001, an extremely short time, legally speaking, after the crime he was accused of committing. He became the first prisoner executed by the federal government in thirty-eight years. Six days before the execution, the FBI belatedly turned over thousands of documents it had previously withheld from McVeigh's attorneys. Oddly, McVeigh was not interviewed by *60 Minutes* or even Barbara Walters before he was executed. In fact, he issued precious few public statements until the publication of the book *American Terrorist*, by Lou Michel and Dan Herbeck, which was released shortly before the execution. The public was treated to inflammatory excerpts, including blood-curdling quotes from McVeigh in which he described the deaths of the children in the day care center as "collateral damage" and taunted the public with references to a "168–1" scorecard.

McVeigh's sudden talkativeness was in vivid contrast to his prior demeanor since being arrested, where he had remained stoic and said little at all. It was particularly strange that he'd granted an alleged forty-five hours of interviews with the authors when he hadn't even bothered to testify at his own trial. I was among those who found this alleged confession very dubious, and when the establishment press played excerpts of the interviews on the fifteenth anniversary of the bombing, it wasn't surprising that there was no video. Alex Jones's feisty Infowars website deemed the MSNBC production of the interviews, hosted by reliable Rachel Maddow and featuring computer-simulated images of McVeigh to go along with the audiotape, a "fairy tale."

TWA FLIGHT 800

On the evening of July 17, 1996, TWA Flight 800 left New York's JFK Airport bound for Paris, France, with 230 people on board. Just after receiving clearance to climb to cruising altitude, the Boeing 747 exploded, creating a giant fireball that was seen all along the coast of Long Island. Numerous eyewitnesses immediately came forward, telling reporters they'd seen a bright object streaking toward the airliner just prior to the explosion. Pilots who were flying, including an Air Force crew, at the time reported the same thing. The Associated Press ran a July 19, 1996, story that stated, "Radar detected a blip merging with the jet shortly before the explosion, something that could indicate a missile hit."

Witness Lou Desyron appeared on *ABC News World Sunday* on July 21, 1996, and stated, "We saw what appeared to be a flare going straight up. As a matter of fact, we thought it was from a boat. It was a bright reddish-orange color . . . once it went into flames, I knew that wasn't a flare." The July 24, 1996, *Washington Times* told its readers, "Several witnesses . . . saw a bright, flare-like object streaking toward the jumbo jet seconds before it blew up. ABC News said yesterday that the investigators had more than 100 eyewitness accounts supporting the [missile] theory." On September 22, 1996, the *New York Post* described the FBI interviewing 154 "credible" witnesses who testified to seeing a missile heading through the sky just before Flight 800 exploded. As late as March 10, 1997, the Associated Press ran an article in which they referred to a "compelling testimony" indicating that a missile had hit the plane's right side.

Attention instantly was focused on the Navy's Cooperative Engagement Capability system, which had been running tests in the general area at the time of the explosion. While it was eventually acknowledged that there was explosive residue found on the remains of the 747, the authorities (dutifully backed by the mainstream media) tried to attribute it to contamination from a bomb-sniffing dog training exercise. Much as the feds had taken control after the JFK assassination in Dallas, the Navy immediately sent deep-sea salvage vessels to the area and superseded the New York City police, who had legal jurisdiction there. Contradicting their earlier denials, the Navy admitted at length that there were submarines in the area on the night of the explosion.

One of the TWA employees became so disgusted with the ongoing cover-up that he gave James Sanders, author of *The Downing of TWA Flight 800*, two cloth samples from the TWA Flight 800 seats. The samples were covered with a bright red residue that had stained only three rows of seats in the plane. Sanders had one sample tested by an independent lab, and it was found to have elements consistent with the by-products of a military fuel rocket. Sanders gave the other sample to CBS News, which promptly and predictably gave it to the government. The government would conclude that the red residue was from seat glue, despite the fact it was only found on three rows in the entire airliner. Unbelievably, the FBI retaliated against Sanders by charging him with stealing property from the airplane, something James Kallstrom, who headed the investigation into Flight 800 for the Bureau, had done himself by removing a "souvenir."

The government illegally seized Sanders's phone records, on the personal authorization of Attorney General Janet Reno. They threatened Sanders with the prosecution of his wife if he didn't plead guilty. The FBI would handcuff

Elizabeth Sanders, wife of James, with her hands behind her back, as they showcased her before reporters, and handcuffed her the same barbaric way on another occasion as she was paraded through the courthouse. In an astonishing miscarriage of justice, both Sanders and his wife (who was a TWA employee herself) were found guilty, although they were only sentenced to probation. Jim Hall, chairman of the NTSB, sent a letter to the judge requesting stiff sentences for the Sanderses, citing their "traumatizing the families" for "commercial gain."

James Kallstrom was so fearful of the voluminous eyewitness testimony to a missile heading toward the plane that he requested that none of them be permitted to speak at the NTSB (National Transportation Safety Board) public hearings on the case. The Pentagon visited TWA CEO Jeff Erickson for unknown reasons. An anonymous TWA pilot, after viewing the documentary *Silenced: Flight 800 and the Subversion of Justice*, admitted, "90 percent of us believe there was a government cover-up."

Mike Wire, whose testimony was the basis of the CIA's fanciful animation portraying Flight 800 rocketing upward, declared: "The video 'Silenced' presents a factual reenactment of what I saw that night. My part of the video also is what I told the FBI a few days after the incident at an in-depth interview at my residence. As you can see what I saw originated from behind the houses on the beach that is why I at first thought it to be a firework. It most definitely didn't start up in the sky like the FBI/CIA story says. I don't know how they could [come] up with that scenario because it doesn't match what I saw and told the FBI or what other witnesses I have talked to since May of 2000 had reported." This sounded sadly identical to the way witness testimony had been misrepresented by government authorities since the time of the JFK assassination.

Peter Goelz, managing director of the NTSB, asked *Washington Post* reporter Howard Kurtz to run a story in his paper quoting Kelly O'Meara, a former assistant to New York Representative Michael Forbes, who had joined the staff of *Insight* magazine, published by the *Washington Times*, as saying, "She really believes that the United States Navy shot this thing down and there was a fleet of warships." O'Meara's own audiotape of her interview with Goelz revealed that it was the mocking, evasive Goelz who raised the issue of missiles, not O'Meara. O'Meara had been attempting to interview NTSB officials, with what Goelz labeled an "extraordinarily antagonistic" attitude, about radar data belatedly released by the NTSB in 1999, which showed that there were a score of unidentified vessels in a military warning area twenty-five miles from the site of the crash.

In response to Kurtz's August 23, 1999, *Washington Post* article, *Insight* editor Paul Rodriguez would express bitterness about journalists allowing themselves to be used by "government bureaucrats . . . to slime their colleagues." Goelz childishly responded to Rodriguez's comments by declaring, "In the end there were no missiles, no bombs, no mystery fleet . . . no US Navy involvement. . . . Shame on you." Showing an even more immature and vindictive streak, Goelz emailed World Net Daily, regarding their own responsible coverage of the TWA 800 incident, and taunted them for their "garbage" reporting, then took a nasty swipe at James Sanders: "By the way, I just checked on Amazon.com, and Sanders's book is currently rated as the 92,000th most purchased book. Don't start the new pool just yet." I'm sure I'm not the only American taxpayer who is astonished that someone with this kind of personality could be entrusted with such a position of prominence in the government.

An unexpected entrant into the TWA Flight 800 controversy was former JFK Press Secretary Pierre Salinger. On November 8, 1996, during a press conference in France, Salinger publicly stated his belief that a US Navy test missile had inadvertently struck the aircraft. At that point, Salinger had been affiliated with ABC News for a good many years, and was well respected by the establishment. However, once he started treading into these waters, he began to be attacked by all the usual suspects as "gullible" for trusting those dastardly Internet sources. CNN quickly moved to declare definitively that the "proof" Salinger claimed to have was nothing more than "a widely accessible email" that had been circulating about the Internet. James Kallstrom reassured the public that they had exhaustively investigated the "friendly fire" theories and found them wanting. NTSB Chairman Jim Hall called Salinger's allegations "unfortunate and irresponsible." Bob Francis, vice chairman of the NTSB, was more blunt, labeling Salinger "an idiot." Trusty *Chicago Tribune* columnist Mike Royko wrote, "Pierre Salinger has now joined those of us in the news business who have been taken in by something phony from the gossipy world of the Internet."

Salinger was not altogether unfamiliar with the world of "conspiracy theories," having previously suggested that Pan Am Flight 103 had been blown up over Scotland in 1988 due to a US Drug Enforcement sting gone awry, and he was among the many who accused the US government of tricking Saddam Hussein into invading Kuwait in 1990. Pierre Salinger had grown increasingly disillusioned about America, and he'd left the country for good after the election of George W. Bush.

As a result of their efforts to expose the truth, James and Elizabeth Sanders were forced to sell their home, their son had to leave college, and Elizabeth lost her TWA job. On the other hand, CBS News, in a typical lapdog move, would hire James Kallstrom as a commentator on law enforcement issues.

Film director Oliver Stone was scheduled to produce a documentary about TWA Flight 800 called *Declassified*, and one of those working on it was the aforementioned reporter Kelly O'Meara. ABC, however, eventually canceled the program before it aired. "I talked to 30 eyewitnesses and then wrote them letters saying we were sorry," a disappointed O'Meara recalled. "It took a lot for them to agree to come forward." *Washington Post* reporter Howard Kurtz, in the story mentioned earlier that misquoted O'Meara, also referred to O'Meara's previous "incarnations," which included work on an Oliver Stone "docudrama," in an obvious attempt to associate her with the verboten world of conspiracies. Revealing their bias about as clearly as possible, *Time* magazine ran a story titled "The Conspiracy Channel?" on November 9, 1998, bemoaning the upcoming ABC News program produced by Oliver Stone. The article was filled with journalistic gems like "Network honchos won't call the project a documentary, since documentaries employ what fuddy-duddies like to call 'facts.'"

THE STARBUCKS MURDER/KENNETH STARR

Mary Mahoney was a twenty-five-year-old former White House intern who was working as an assistant manager at a Starbucks in Georgetown, Washington, D.C. Mahoney was said to know Monica Lewinsky, and Lewinsky later told Linda Tripp that she didn't want to end up like Mahoney. On July 6, 1997, Mahoney and two coworkers were killed in what police admitted was an "execution style" slaying. The motive clearly wasn't robbery, as depending upon the reports, anywhere from $4,000 to $10,000 was left behind in the store. The evidence indicated two different weapons were used, which would seemingly rule out a lone gunman.

Reporter Michael Isikoff of *Newsweek* had spoken of a former White House intern with the initial "M" who was on the verge of talking about an affair with Clinton, and this led to speculation that Mahoney, not Lewinsky, was the person involved. In a related death, police informant Eric Butera, who was investigating the Starbucks murders, was beaten to death in a crack house and his family was awarded nearly $100 million in damages. Carl Derek Cooper initially confessed to the slayings, but his lawyer protested that his confession had been coerced. Newsmax.com reported on January 23, 2000, that Cooper vigorously denied being the killer, declaring, "I swear on my father's grave and my son's life that I didn't do Starbucks."

Author David M. Hoffman, who conducted an investigation of Mahoney's murder, told *Globe* magazine that the Starbucks killings happened only three days after Monica Lewinsksy had informed the president she was going to let her parents know about their relationship. Clinton had supposedly angrily reacted by saying, "It's a crime to threaten the president." Hoffman reported new details of Mahoney's time as a White House intern and claimed that, although she was an outspoken lesbian (on July 18, 1997, the *Washington Blade* reported that Mahoney had been a founder of the Baltimore Lesbian Avengers), she had been concerned about all the tales she'd heard from others regarding Bill Clinton's sexual advances toward them.

On February 10, 2000, the *Washington Post* reported that Attorney General Janet Reno, in one of the relatively few times she had opted to do so during her time in office, overruled US Attorney Wilma A. Lewis in opting for the death penalty against Carl Derek Cooper in the Starbucks case. In the article, it was stated that, "Two law enforcement sources, speaking on the condition of anonymity, said the consensus at the US attorney's office was that the Starbucks case did not have such a compelling federal interest that it called for the ultimate sanction of death. . . ." "The article went on to speculate about what role Eric Holder, then deputy attorney general and future Obama attorney general, might have played in the deliberations. In a story the next day, covering the weekly Justice Department press briefing, Holder acknowledged that his office had been a part of the decision to seek the death penalty, even though Wilma Lewis had recommended against execution, but wouldn't comment on his role in the matter. As right wing critic Carl Limbacher noted, Reno had taken "an extraordinary step" in seeking the death penalty, in that Washington, D.C. "currently has no capital punishment statute on its books." Amid mounting criticism from the community, federal prosecutors eventually decided to seek a life sentence without possibility of parole.

In another of those strange coincidences, Monica Lewinsky's original lawyer, Francis Carter, wound up being appointed counsel for Carl Derek Cooper. Cooper was charged with an incredible forty-eight counts, as prosecutors gathered together an alleged series of disparate crimes that hardly seemed to reasonably add up to a federal case. Cooper pleaded guilty to killing the three Starbucks employees on April 26, 2000. There is literally no information about him anywhere following his guilty plea. I have been unable to even determine if he is still alive in prison.

Bill Clinton's eight years in office were marred by scandal and corruption, to an extent that had never been seen before in any previous administration.

After ignoring or downplaying Whitewater (an intricate collage of financial and real estate scandals dating back to Clinton's days in Arkansas), Cattlegate (wherein First Lady Hillary Clinton turned $1,000 into $100,000 in an implausibly short time), Travelgate (where the Clintons fired employees of the White House travel office in favor of friends and family), Filegate (the discovery of more than nine hundred illegally obtained FBI files on Republicans in the White House), Chinagate (involving attempts by China to funnel money to the 1996 Clinton campaign), the charges of rape against the president from Juanita Broderick, the curious death of Vincent Foster, and scoffing at the notion of any Body Count, among others, the mainstream media suddenly paid keen attention to the relatively minor allegations that Clinton had been sexually serviced in the White House by young intern Monica Lewinsky and then forced her to lie about it.

For unknown reasons, Kenneth Starr, who had done all he could to not investigate the far more serious charges against Bill Clinton, did investigate the Lewinsky affair. In a strictly partisan effort, House Republicans voted articles of impeachment, on charges of perjury and obstruction of justice, against Clinton on December 19, 1998. The two charges were associated with the Lewinsky affair and the earlier Paula Jones lawsuit. Despite the fact he was only the second president in American history to be impeached, Bill Clinton continued to receive incredibly positive coverage from the mainstream media. In fact, the twenty-one-day Senate impeachment trial— which represented a tremendously rare historical event and should have been "must see TV"—was practically ignored by the television networks. Most talking heads treated the entire thing as a mean-spirited Republican attack on the president, and joked about it regularly. One of the witnesses for President Clinton was Nicholas Katzenbach, assistant attorney general under Robert Kennedy and author of the infamous November 25, 1963, memo to Bill Moyers, urging that "the public must be satisfied that Oswald was the assassin." "Opponents" of Clinton in the Senate, such as future presidential candidate, Rick Santorum concocted a deal whereby the House managers were not permitted to call any witnesses against the president.

While public attention was focused on Monica Lewinsky and her primary antagonist, Linda Tripp, a woman known only as "Jane Doe #5" in Kenneth Starr's report burst into the news. Well, not the mainstream news, which tried to ignore Juanita Broderick and her troubling allegations against Bill Clinton. As was the case during the JFK assassination "investigation" and other high-profile events, Broderick would allege that her original affidavit contained false information. Broderick's shocking charge was that then-Arkansas Attorney General Bill Clinton had brutally raped her in a Little Rock hotel room in 1978. Four witnesses backed her story, claiming Broderick had confided in them at the time, including a nurse, Norma Rogers, who testified to applying ice to her bruised face and swollen lips. Representative Christopher Shays would later reveal that, based on "secret evidence" he and his colleagues reviewed during the impeachment process, he believed Bill Clinton raped Juanita Broderick twice. Nevertheless, Shays voted *against* impeachment. NBC had Broderick's story for a year, but they sat on it instead of broadcasting potentially damaging news on Clinton during the impeachment trial.

Feminist groups embarrassed themselves throughout all of Clinton's various scandals involving women. They treated the women who alleged Clinton had harassed (or, in the case of Broderick, physically raped) them in a far different manner than they would treat a typical victim. They scoffed at them, verbally assaulted them ("liberal" Clinton aide James Carville memorably labeled Paula Jones "trailer park trash"), and refused to consider their claims legitimate. The public, as usual, followed the lead of the establishment press; in 1995, for instance, only 27 percent of those polled thought Paula Jones's story was more true than false, according to Gallup. Paula Jones never got her day in court; her lawsuit against the president was thrown out by Judge Susan Webber Wright, who had been a student of Clinton in college. Eventually, Clinton settled with Jones out of court.

While the media, especially late-night talk show hosts such as Jay Leno and David Letterman, consistently ridiculed Paula Jones (with endless, derivative jokes about her hair), Linda Tripp was perhaps treated even more unfairly. Tripp had been a coworker and confidante of Monica Lewinsky (but they were not the "gal pals" the media portrayed them as—Tripp's children were Lewinsky's age), and after she learned of Lewinsky's sexual dalliances with Clinton, Tripp understandably felt she needed to record their conversations. Tripp told *Newsweek*'s Michael Isikoff that she'd witnessed another Clinton accuser, Kathleen Willey, emerging from the Oval Office "disheveled. Her face red and her lipstick was off." Tripp was eviscerated by the press after she gave her tapes to Ken Starr. She was accused of betraying a friend, in pursuit of a future book deal. As it turned out, Tripp never wrote a book.

Tripp, who was well aware of the Clinton Body Count, said she recorded her conversations with Lewinsky in order to protect herself, and that she feared retaliation. *Saturday Night Live* savaged Tripp, as actor John Goodman impersonated her in several sketches. The same mainstream media that showed zero journalistic zeal in ferreting out the facts about the numerous allegations of impropriety against Bill Clinton managed to uncover Tripp's arrest for theft when she was nineteen years old. The charges had been dismissed before any trial, but that didn't stop the supposedly prestigious *The New Yorker* from publishing the story. In a final gesture of vindictiveness, Linda Tripp was fired from the Pentagon on the last day of the Clinton administration.

I communicated with Linda Tripp during the writing of this book, and she was gracious enough to provide a lengthy statement for me, although she acknowledged that she routinely declines those kinds of requests. Tripp is a real survivor. She leads a contented life, running the year-round Christmas Sleigh store in Middleburg, Virginia. As she stated to me, ". . . 'Vast right wing conspiracy' notwithstanding, I was a registered Independent then, as I still am today." I want to quote the following from her statement in its entirety:

"By the time I was introduced to the world in January 1998 as the villain who exposed the Clinton-Lewinsky 'affair,' I had spent five full years helplessly observing firsthand untold corruption in the Clinton White House. Helpless because as a career civil servant, I knew this information had to be made public in some way, yet I had no earthly clue how to present all of it in a way that could reach voters across the nation. Call a press conference? Write a book? How on earth does one relay events of this magnitude concerning the President and the First Lady of the United States? Would anyone really believe me? I was up against the most talented actors in the history of Hollywood. Oscar worthy. All these years later, they still are. Coupled with their uncanny acting ability was their control of the most well-oiled PR machine in the world. The taxpayer funded White House Communications umbrella with limitless resources was quite simply at their fingertips and ready, willing and able to annihilate anyone who would dare speak out against Bill and Hill. I knew what I would be facing should I dare go public. I knew I would most certainly lose my Federal Civil Service career; a successful career that at that point spanned a period of some 25 years. Ultimately I chose the cowardly route and kept quiet. I also kept my job."

Linda Tripp found herself in the same situation so many other potential whistle-blowers have over the course of history. As Tripp further noted, she was well aware of what the Clintons were capable of, and in reference to Paula Jones, "I believed her story since it was not at all a stretch for those of us who had seen Bill Clinton in daily action over time. I knew with a fair degree of certainty that once they were aware that I knew the sordid details, my life would be in danger.

Because of Lewinsky's increasingly erratic behavior, I knew that hers was as well." Tripp in retrospect admits she naively thought that Clinton's disregard for his office and lack of respect for the victims of his sexual harassment would "incite the masses to riot." Tripp closed out her powerful, poignant statement thusly: "I'm often asked if I would do it again. The answer is a resounding yes. . . . The personal price was astronomical. The price my family paid incalculable. Today, 15 years later, I remain the only one intimately involved in the saga who never exploited my role for personal gain. . . ."

Kathleen Willey was still bitter at the Clintons years later. She wrote an open letter to Democratic presidential candidate Barack Obama, which was published on the conservative website World Net Daily on January 28, 2008. Willey repeated some of the claims she'd made in her book *Target*. She advised Obama to make certain his personal and tax records were secure, and to get a shredder. "Then, of course, there's the Clintons' secret private-investigator army . . . ," Willey wrote. "I know that army's tactics well. They have threatened my children and my friend's children. They've threatened and killed my pets. They've vandalized my car. They've entered my home and stolen my book manuscript. They've destroyed my peace of mind. . . ." Willey didn't fare as well as Tripp; by November 2013, she'd been relegated to asking for donations on a website to help save her home from foreclosure.

Once Clinton dodged being thrown out of office, the mainstream media continued to lavish favorable coverage on him and his administration. The incredible bias of these professional "journalists" was best expressed by *Time* reporter Nina Burleigh's confession that she'd be happy to give Bill Clinton a blow job for "keeping abortion legal." Who can forget black writer Toni Morrison's statement that Clinton was "the first black president?" Morrison went on to unleash a series of offensive stereotypical characteristics to illustrate her point: "After all, Clinton displays almost every trope of blackness: single parent household, born poor, working class, saxophone-playing, McDonald's-and-junk-food-loving-boy from Arkansas." (*The New Yorker*, October 1998). Kenneth Starr, who "hounded" Bill Clinton so relentlessly according to the establishment press, later declared that if he ever encountered Clinton, he would tell him, "I'm sorry that it all happened." (*New York Times*, February 14, 2010).

Meanwhile, the former "antiwar" demonstrator turned president proved to have quite a penchant for utilizing the huge war machine at his disposal. When Serbian "strongman" Slobodan Milosevic became the new international bogeyman, courtesy of the typical damning reports in the mainstream media, Clinton prodded NATO into approving the bombing of Yugoslavia in March 1999. We heard the favorite new catchphrases: "ethnic cleansing," "the

Butcher of Serbia," "war criminal," and others parroted daily by establishment "journalists." The bombing wreaked enormous havoc, creating hundreds of thousands of refugees while there were untold numbers of civilians killed. As has become typical with modern presidents, Congress—which has the sole legal authorization under the Constitution to declare war—was bypassed by the Clinton administration, which also didn't seek the approval of the United Nations Security Council, where China and Russia were almost certain to object. Giving new meaning to party loyalty, only four Democrats in both Houses of Congress protested this unconstitutional and immoral show of force. In an unintentionally hilarious example of Orwellian doublethink, Supreme NATO Commander General Wesley Clark told ABC's *Good Morning America*, "Bombing cannot stop the killing of civilians."

Again we saw the mainstream media playing the role of giddy cheerleader, with breathless reports of the number of "sorties" flown and the "record" number of bombs dropped. The bombing caused a great deal of harm; Clinton belatedly admitted, on May 13, 1999, that there were one hundred thousand people in Kosovo still missing and that six hundred thousand ethnic Albanians were trapped in Kosovo, "lacking shelter, short of food, afraid to go home, or buried in mass graves dug by their executioners." Even as establishment a voice as the *Washington Post* eventually pointed out the farce in its May 24, 1999, edition, stating that Pentagon and NATO briefings had "acquired a propaganda element aimed at demonizing Milosevic and his Belgrade government and imparting a moral imperative to the conflict." Foretelling the kind of unprofessional braggadocio that would become commonplace under Dubya and Obama, Clinton boasted, in a June 11 speech, "Day after day, with remarkable precision, our forces pounded every element of Mr. Milosevic's military machine, from tanks to fuel supply, to antiaircraft weapons, to the military and political support."

A postwar US military investigation disclosed that, as had been the case in the Gulf War, the official damage claims had been wildly exaggerated. While it had been trumpeted that twenty thousand bombs were dropped on Serbian military forces, the Serbs in reality lost only fourteen tanks and eighteen armored personnel carriers. The bombs were very accurate at hitting the cardboard decoy tanks the Serbians erected all over Kosovo, however. NATO forces were accused of using depleted uranium and targeting chemical plants, creating deadly spills of toxic waste into the Danube River. The end result was that the Serbian army was left in good morale but the civilian infrastructure was ruined. NATO bombs didn't hit real tanks very often, but they found women, children, hospitals, churches, and residences all too frequently. Many holy Catholic shrines were destroyed, a number of them after NATO had taken over and installed KLA-affiliated terrorists in positions of power. In a December 8, 1999, press conference, a deluded Clinton would boast again that he was "very, very proud" of what the United States had done in Kosovo.

Milosevic died under questionable circumstances in prison before his war crimes trial, and he was rumored to have been adamant about exposing whom he felt were the true "war criminals." Both Milosevic's son and wife publicly declared that they felt he had been poisoned. Even usually reliable "opponent" Rush Limbaugh half-jokingly suggested that Milosevic was the final entry in the Clinton Body Count, and that Bill Clinton himself might have had to testify at the barely averted war crimes trial.

THE CLINTON BODY COUNT MARCHES ON

Jim Keith was a very prolific writer of books on conspiracy-related topics. *Black Helicopters Over America*, *Biowarfare in America*, and *Mass Control: Engineering Human Consciousness* (his final work) were some of his memorable titles. In August 1999, Keith fell from a stage and broke his knee. On September 7, 1999, he entered the Washoe Medical Center in Nevada for surgery, ominously telling friends, "I have this feeling that if they put me under I'm not coming back." Sure enough, he died shortly after the routine surgery, allegedly from a blood clot, just a few weeks shy of his fiftieth birthday. For the typically unexplained reasons that seem to pop up constantly in these sorts of unnatural deaths, the coroner nevertheless listed the cause of death as "blunt force trauma."

Incredibly, Keith's publisher met a fate just as strange as his a few years later. On April 8, 2001, forty-eight-year-old Ronald Bonds, who had published several of his conspiracy books, inexplicably died. He'd gone out to eat Mexican food with his wife several hours earlier, and after enduring vomiting and diarrhea, he was rushed to Atlanta's Grady Memorial Hospital. His wife was incredulous when the doctors told her the next morning, "Your husband didn't make it." In another Cosmic Coincidence, the very first book Bonds had published, under his IllumiNet Press, was Kerry Thornley's novel *The Idle Warriors*. As noted earlier in this book, Thornley was one of Lee Harvey Oswald's fellow Marines, and unbelievably enough Thornley was prompted to write the book, which was about Oswald, *before* the Kennedy assassination! The official cause of Bonds's bizarre death was an uncommon form of food poisoning.

HIDDEN HISTORY

Clinton's reign in office was a national embarrassment. However, the economy was robust during that time, due in large measure to the "dot com" boom that arrived with the birth of personal computers and the worldwide web. Thus, he will almost certainly wind up ranked much higher than he deserves to be by the court historians, alongside other unworthy "greats" like Lincoln and FDR.

CHAPTER SEVEN

THE DEATH OF JOHN F. KENNEDY JR.

"We are opposed around the world by a monolithic and ruthless conspiracy."
—President John F. Kennedy

One more, highly significant death occurred during the Clinton administration. On July 16, 1999, John F. Kennedy Jr. took off in his Piper Saratoga plane from New Jersey's Essex County Airport, accompanied by his wife, Carolyn Bessette, and her sister, Lauren Bessette. Kennedy, an experienced pilot, was flying to Martha's Vineyard to drop off his sister-in-law before continuing on to the family compound at Hyannis Port to attend the wedding of his cousin Rory, Robert F. Kennedy's youngest child. After his plane failed to arrive in Martha's Vineyard, a massive search was launched, but it wasn't until the night of July 20 that the bodies of JFK Jr., Carolyn, and Lauren were found on the ocean floor.

Rumors started flying across the Internet. Had JFK Jr. been about to announce a bid for a New York Senate seat, potentially conflicting with First Lady Hillary Clinton's political ambitions? Or was he on the verge of seeking an even higher office, the presidency itself? My suspicions were aroused immediately upon hearing that Kennedy's plane was missing. Family patriarch Joseph Kennedy Sr. had lost both a son and a daughter in separate plane crashes—imagine the infinitesimal chances of *that* happening. A third child, Ted Kennedy, had survived yet another plane crash in 1962. Throw in the violent murders of two other sons—John and Robert—as well as the earlier mentioned unnatural deaths of two of RFK's children, and it was impossible to have confidence that John F. Kennedy Jr. would be found alive and well.

Although you wouldn't know it from following the mainstream media, there were several troubling aspects to this story. First of all, why did it take *fifteen* hours to start searching for JFK Jr.'s plane? Even some in the establishment press wondered about this, as reflected by the story that appeared in the July 20, 1999, *Boston Herald*, "Time Gaps in Early Hours of Search Are Beyond Explanation." Unlike most private planes, Kennedy's Piper Saratoga had a black box. The NTSB (National Transportation Safety Board) official report informed us, however, that its battery had been removed, thus making all recorded conversation in the cockpit conveniently unavailable. Since all planes have an Emergency Locator Transmitter (ELT), which sends out a beacon signal when a crash occurs, why did it take five days to locate the wreckage?

Early reports, such as the one that appeared in the *New York Times* on July 17, 1999, indicated that a flight instructor was on the plane. JFK Jr.'s *George* magazine coeditor Richard Blow recounted that Kennedy had told him he was taking a flight instructor with him during their last lunch together. Kennedy was recovering from a foot injury, had his wife and sister-in-law with him, was flying at night, and was accustomed to having a flight instructor with him. JFK Jr.'s flight log was also missing, according to the NTSB report. It would be admitted that one of the plane's seats could not be found amid the wreckage. Online speculation ran rampant that this missing seat was related to a possible fourth, unacknowledged passenger.

Early news accounts of JFK Jr.'s missing plane featured repeated references to a literal last-minute, 9:39 p.m. phone contact from Kennedy. This was critically important, since the official story would be that the plane went into a death spiral at nearly the same time, which would seem impossible since JFK Jr. had mentioned no problems in his last contact only moments earlier. Originally reported by UPI, ABC News, and WCVB-Boston, among others, the official Coast Guard account of the conversation between JFK Jr. and the FAA can be accessed online. Here it is in full:

> BOSTON—The Coast Guard is actively searching for a Piper 32 Saratoga aircraft overdue on a flight from Caldwell, N.J. to Martha's Vineyard, Mass. John F. Kennedy Jr. was on board the single-engine aircraft with his wife and a third unidentified person. The aircraft took off from Caldwell at 8:38 p.m.
>
> The FAA reported that last contact with the aircraft was at 9:39 p.m. as the aircraft was making its final approach to Martha's Vineyard. The Coast Guard assumed coordination for the waterside search at 8:25 a.m.

today. The shore side search is being coordinated by the Air Force Rescue Coordination Center at Langley Air Force Base in Norfolk, Va.

The aircraft was due to arrive in Martha's Vineyard around 10 p.m., and was later expected to fly to Hyannisport for a family wedding.

The Coast Guard is using all available vessels and aircraft to search the waters west of Martha's Vineyard. An Air National Guard C-130 aircraft from the Suffolk Air National Guard Base is also in the air and actively searching.

Note that the Coast Guard acknowledges it didn't start coordinating the search until 8:25 a.m., and in fact it wasn't actually at the scene until 1 p.m., even though the ELT should have notified the FAA within moments of that last 9:39 p.m. contact that the plane had gone down.

Researcher Scott Myers was kind enough to send me videotape of live news coverage of the search for JFK Jr.'s plane that he recorded from local television station WCVB. Anchor Chet Curtis and others mentioned the 9:39 p.m. phone contact between JFK Jr. and the FAA numerous times during their first two days of reporting on the story. They even interviewed Coast Guard Petty Officer Todd Burgun about the conversation. Burgun was the public information officer for the Boston Coast Guard station. The original UPI article made clear that this was a routine contact, and no problems existed at that time: "At 9:39 p.m. Friday, Kennedy radioed the airport and said he was thirteen miles from the airport and ten miles from the coast, according to WCVB-TV news in Boston. He reportedly said he was making his final approach."

Only a moment later, FAA radar showed the plane going into a dive, dropping twelve hundred feet in just twelve seconds, according to ABC News. "In his final approach message, WCVB-TV said Kennedy told controllers at the airport that he planned to drop off his wife's sister and then take off again between 11 p.m. and 11:30 p.m. for Hyannis Airport," the article continued.

When researchers later obtained archive copies of WCVB-TV's local coverage of the story from Corporate Media Services of Auburn, New Hampshire, reporter Susan Wornick's interview with Coast Guard Petty Officer Todd Burgun was cut off after his initial reply of "All I know at this time is that it was at 9:39 p.m., and it was with the FAA and it was on approach." On the uncut tape, Burgun went on to delineate all the points from the UPI's article: Kennedy was calm, on approach to the airport, had provided his position and trajectory, and had even made a comment about dropping Lauren Bessette off at the airport. Some five hours of coverage was edited out, starting with Burgun's interview. Also edited out were several references to the enigmatic reporter from the *Martha's Vineyard Gazette* who saw an airborne explosion at the time of the crash.

An anonymous poster on an Internet forum shared an email he sent on September 9, 2009, to the Coast Guard, inquiring about the status of and contact information for Petty Officer Todd Burgun. An Angethlor Wimberly of the Coast Guard responded thusly to the poster's inquiry: "I do not show a Mr. Todd Burgun in the USCG." I emailed the Boston Coast Guard myself about Burgun. Not surprisingly, they never replied. I also emailed reporter Susan Wornick three times, to ask her about the interview with Burgun, but she didn't respond. I was able to find Todd Burgun's telephone number, and left a message on his voicemail, but he never called back.

There is simply *no way* the FAA and Coast Guard could have been "mistaken" about such an integral fact to this degree, but that is what we were asked to swallow, since the FAA would subsequently deny they'd received any phone contact from Kennedy. Remember, they sent an information officer out to give a television interview on the subject! There was also a strange, unexplained mention about an emergency beacon signal in that original UPI story: "An emergency beacon thought to belong to the plane was activated and heard by the Coast Guard in Long Island, N.Y., at 3:40 a.m. But as the search went on, authorities seemed to discount the relevance of the beacon signal." The location the signal was coming from was far from the spot where Kennedy's plane was ultimately found, so did another plane go down that night?

Friends of Lauren Bessette had gathered at Martha's Vineyard Airport to greet the party, and when the plane didn't land as scheduled (around 10 p.m.), they became alarmed and notified airport employee Adam Budd, who in turn contacted the FAA in Bridgeport, Connecticut. When the FAA failed to respond, Senator Edward Kennedy himself phoned them at 11 p.m. to report that his nephew's plane was missing. When the FAA still hadn't done anything, the Coast Guard was contacted directly at 2 a.m. At 7 a.m. a frustrated Senator Kennedy called Clinton's chief of staff, John Podesta, who contacted Clinton directly. President Clinton then demanded that the Air Force begin searching within fifteen minutes. The Air Force oddly ordered the Coast Guard to begin the search far from the most logical spot, which would be the area of approach to Martha's Vineyard.

Lieutenant Colonel Richard Stanley of the Civil Air Patrol would report seeing what he thought were Coast Guard helicopters around the crash site at about 7 a.m., hours before the Coast Guard or anyone else arrived. Who, then, was flying those helicopters? A still unidentified reporter with the *Martha's Vineyard Gazette*, who was out walking on Martha's Vineyard's Philbin Beach that night, told WCVB television about seeing "a big white flash in the sky" at around the time Kennedy's plane supposedly crashed. Researcher John DiNardo attempted to track down this elusive reporter. When he asked the *Martha's Vineyard Gazette* about one of their reporters seeing an explosion around the time of the crash, he was told, "Oh, that story was completely bogus. What really happened was that someone was shooting off fireworks on Falmouth." When he asked to speak to the reporter in question, he was told, "Oh, no. We can't do that." When DiNardo expressed surprise at this, the woman he was speaking with said, "We can't permit that." "Can you at least give me his name?" DiNardo asked. "No, we can't do that, either," she replied, then explained, "He no longer works for us." The woman went on to claim that the reporter "went back to school."

Pennsylvania lawyer Victor Pribanic heard an explosion at almost the exact moment Kennedy's plane allegedly went down. "I heard a loud impact like a bomb," Pribanic told conspiracy researcher Anthony J. Hilder. Pribanic contacted local officials the next day, and he gave his information to Hank Myer of the West Tilsbury Police Department. Myer accompanied Pribanic to the site where he'd allegedly heard the explosion. The location turned out to be, Pribanic would tell the *Martha's Vineyard Times*, precisely where JFK Jr. had indicated his position was (about ten miles from shore) in the 9:39 p.m. communication. Hilder asked Pribanic if he thought it was possible that JFK Jr. and his passengers had been murdered. "It's certainly in the realm of possibility," he replied. A third person who'd reportedly seen an explosion was an unnamed guest at the Rory Kennedy wedding, referenced several times by reporter Shepherd Smith during the early coverage on Fox News.

The Pentagon mysteriously took command of the situation, which made no sense since Kennedy had never been in the military and was not flying a military aircraft. Once the Pentagon came on board, the cover story began to take shape. They dutifully informed the meek representatives of the mainstream press that there had not been a flight instructor on board the plane. Contradicting a myriad of previous reports to the contrary, the public was assured that JFK Jr. had not contacted the FAA or anyone else during his flight. We learned that Kennedy had not filed a flight plan with the FAA, something he had done on all his previous flights along that route. Most notably, they claimed the plane had not been reported missing until 2 a.m., in spite of the fact friends and family had started notifying the authorities as early as 10 p.m. Stories were leaked from anonymous sources, painting a picture of JFK Jr. as a reckless pilot who clearly was not qualified to make such a flight, particularly in what was deemed to be extremely bad weather. Intrepid souls on the Internet examined and posted real weather radar images from that night, revealing that flying conditions were actually excellent, with virtually none of the much talked about "haze" registering at all on the radar. The radar data for the exact moment the plane went down, however, was strangely unavailable.

FAA Flight Specialist Edward Meyer prepared the FAA's special report on weather conditions the night JFK Jr.'s plane went down. Meyer grew so disturbed by erroneous press accounts stressing how "poor" the visibility was that night that he took the unusual step of releasing a public statement about the issue. In this statement, Meyer declared, "Nothing of what I have heard on mainstream media makes any sense to me. . . . The weather along his flight was just fine. A little haze over eastern Connecticut. . . . Any mention of 'daring' or 'inexperience' is absolute nonsense. I don't know why the airplane crashed, but what I heard on the media was nothing but garbage."

Even the official NTSB report quoted an anonymous pilot who flew that night along the same route as being told by a flight service station that there were "No adverse conditions. Have a great weekend." He was also assured there was no fog and "good visibility." The Martha's Vineyard tower manager told the NTSB, "The visibility, present weather, and sky condition at the approximate time of the accident was probably a little better than what was being reported. I say this because I remember aircraft on visual approaches saying they had the airport in sight between 10 and 12 miles out. I do recall being able to see those aircraft and I do remember seeing the stars out that night."

I exchanged emails with Edward Meyer during the writing of this book. He remained adamant about what he'd said in an August 3, 2012, email. "My argument was with the ENTIRE mainstream media," Meyer told me. "Every report I saw, read or heard said that the visibility was too low for JFK Jr. to make his approach, but he wasn't making an approach at the time." Meyer explained that the NTSB report contradicted "EVERYTHING that was said by the media. . . . He was fully licensed to fly that night and there were no weather reports that contradicted the VFR flight conditions that the plane was flying in."

And yet, there were quotes from other pilots and various "experts" who questioned the "inexperienced" Kennedy for choosing to fly in such "bad" conditions. One such pilot, Kyle Bailey, was widely reported to have watched JFK Jr. take off and then ruefully told his family, "I can't believe he's going up in that weather." In the August 1, 1999, issue of *Newsweek*, the reliable Evan Thomas would describe it as "an exceptionally hazy summer night." In the same *Newsweek* article, NBC News medical correspondent Dr. Bob Arnot was reported to have flown the same route as Kennedy fifteen minutes earlier, and he stated it was "murky black" and that he could see "no land, no lights and no horizon." Why these gloomy proclamations, when all indications were the weather was actually good? Perhaps sensing that some would question the cremation of the Roman Catholic Kennedy, Thomas also helpfully explained, "Spreading his ashes over the ocean had another virtue: there would be no grave to be defaced by the inevitable ghouls or turned into a maudlin spectacle. . . ." This was a ludicrous notion; no "ghouls" had ever desecrated the graves of JFK or RFK.

An unidentified friend of JFK Jr. told investigative reporter Wayne Madsen that he had been informed by both an FBI agent and a Secret Service agent that Kennedy's death was initially treated as a possible murder. The source told Madsen that FBI agents "fanned out across convenience and other stores in the Caldwell, New Jersey area and asked if anyone had recently purchased epoxy." (*Wayne Madsen Report*, August 12, 2009). Madsen felt this buttressed a report in the French magazine *France Dimanche* that a pilot at the airport had heard a "weird noise" emanating from JFK Jr.'s plane as it took off. Madsen also mentioned that the FBI found some "suspicious boating activity" in the vicinity where JFK Jr.'s plane was headed for its final approach to Martha's Vineyard Airport. They discovered an unusual number of batteries in the fishermen's boat, and were left unsatisfied by their explanation that they were fishing for striped bass, because other local fishermen informed them that there were no striped bass in that area.

Madsen closed his report with a blockbuster disclosure; he claimed that JFK Jr. had inquired, through a colleague with *The Village Voice*, about hiring him as an investigative journalist to look into a number of cases, the most significant being the assassination of his father, President John F. Kennedy. Madsen clarified this in an email to me on August 2, 2012. "I didn't speak to John but had an interview with him scheduled 2 weeks after he died," Madsen wrote. "My friend had already recommended me as one of 4 or 5 journalists for the revised *George* mag. John's first task was to find out who killed his father." He also elaborated on the Connolly and Salinger references: "I had a chance to speak with Connolly at the Gulf America conference in Houston in 1988. He told me there was more than one shooter. In 1993 I met Salinger at Burson Marsteller and he looked at his desk calendar and said it was hard to believe it was 30 years since THEY killed Jack." It was only then that Madsen realized the day he met Salinger was November 22, 1993.

The FAA three-dimensional radar graph, tracking JFK Jr.'s flight, was available on the Internet, and filmmaker John Hankey made great use of it in his excellent documentary *The Assassination of JFK Jr*. The graph showed a completely normal horizontal flight, then an abrupt vertical nosedive. The graph alone would have shown the FAA exactly where the plane went down, yet after delaying the search for many hours, the Air Force conducted a "search and rescue" mission that seemed to concentrate on every other area but the crash site. Lieutenant Colonel Steve Roark, in a press conference, explained that the Air Force had "nothing that pinpoints one area rather than another."

ABC's Martha Raddatz actually mentioned the radar information, indicating the plane went down eighteen miles west of Martha's Vineyard, and Roark replied that "the radar position is just a last possible position." Another reporter timidly suggested, "It didn't look like a normal descent," to which Roark retorted, "It didn't look like anything unusual." Yes, it wasn't "unusual" for a perfectly normal flight to suddenly plunge 1,100 feet in fourteen seconds. In a July 21, 1999, story from *AFP*, flight instructor and former senior crash investigator C. O. Miller was quoted as saying, "To get an airplane like that to descend at 4,700 feet a minute, you would almost have to point it straight at the ground."

The inferences that Kennedy was "reckless" as a pilot were contradicted by all his flight instructors, who invariably described him as prudent and careful. John McColgan, JFK Jr.'s federal licensing instructor from Vero Beach, Florida, belied the claims bandied about in the media that he wasn't capable of flying that night. McColgan stated that JFK Jr. had eighteen years of flight experience, dating back to 1981, and had logged more than 700 hours total flight time. He also reported that Kennedy had completed his written test for instrument flight rating and had finished his training for the in-flight instrument rating test several months earlier, but hadn't taken it yet. McColgan noted that JFK Jr. was basically qualified to fly on instruments alone, not that he would have needed to that night, and described him as an excellent pilot. (*Orlando Sentinel*, July 18, 1999). McColgan reiterated his statements to Seattle talk show host Mike Webb a week later, although Webb the Newshawk website's John Quinn, who did invaluable early work on this case, that he'd been "very reluctant" to talk at first and seemed suspicious or paranoid in his initial responses. Still, these misleading reports continued, and the impression exists to this day that JFK Jr. simply didn't have the "experience."

Experienced pilot Edward Gacio, who had come to know JFK Jr. pretty well, told the *Hartford Courant* (August 1, 1999 edition), "If the weather was questionable, Kennedy would cancel a flight. He didn't appear to be a risk-taker." But the prevailing view in the mainstream media, and even among the general public, was epitomized by veteran right wing journalist William Safire's proclamation that JFK Jr.'s death was the result of his "bad judgment." Former Air Force mechanic Craig Henne reacted typically to the death of JFK Jr.: "He was an arrogant brat and he killed people," Henne announced on America Online. Later, in a phone interview with the *Washington Post*, Henne stated, "He was reckless. I read he had a cast on his leg, too—it's crazy. If you want to risk your life, that's one thing, but don't take two people with you."

KTRS (St. Louis) radio show host Paul Harris lambasted the Kennedys as "rich people who engage in reckless behavior and end up dying and having tragedy befall them." Another radio host, Al Rantel of KABC in Los Angeles, declared, "It was probably a very bad decision for JFK to choose to fly. I have seen those foggy, hazy nights along the water, and I can tell you it's scary weather." (*Washington Post*, July 20, 1999). The press was no kinder in England. "Insanity," read the headline in *The Mirror*. According to the *Daily Mail*, JFK Jr. "had a death wish."

And trusty "liberal" Chris Matthews, an alleged Kennedy family fan, was immediately there, on July 22, 1999, to assure the public that JFK Jr. was only a publisher, and had no plans to ever enter politics. The establishment press doesn't even attempt to cover up their sloppiness; the record showed only days before JFK Jr.'s death that Matthews had declared, on his own *Hardball* television program, that Hillary Clinton had thwarted Kennedy's attempts to run for senator from New York.

Writer C. David Heymann, an ex-Mossad agent who had previously penned the poisonous anti-Kennedy books *A Woman Named Jackie* and *R.F.K.: A Candid Biography of Robert F. Kennedy*, claimed to have spoken to JFK Jr. only nine days before he died. Heymann said that JFK Jr. had complained about having to drop his wife's sister off on Martha's Vineyard, but he felt forced to because his wife was insisting on it. The *New York Post* ran a story on July 19, 1999, written by Heymann, with the sensationalist headline "He Did Not Want to Fly," based on this alleged conversation.

There were obvious reasons to doubt Heymann's story. First, it was extremely unlikely that JFK Jr. would have been speaking so candidly to someone who'd painted such an ugly portrait of his close family members in his previous works. Second, sources at *George* magazine stated they did not know JFK Jr. was acquainted with Heymann at all, let alone his close confidant. Another source told *The Observer* that Lauren Bessette did not ask Kennedy for a ride to Martha's Vineyard until July 12—some five days after JFK Jr. supposedly complained to Heymann about the subject. Heymann's fellow *New York Post* columnist, Neil Travis, was dubious of his story, and was quoted in *The Observer* as saying, "I can't believe John Kennedy would have done anything more than punch out an author who claimed that his mother fucked his uncle." Well-known gossip columnist Cindy Adams, who originally believed Heymann's story, wrote an article in the July 29, 1999 *New York Post* expressing her doubts based on her talks with various Kennedy sources, including JFK Jr.'s appointment secretary, who'd never set up a meeting with Heymann.

In contrast to the early reports indicating a flight instructor was on board the plane, one of Kennedy's flight instructors, Robert Merena, told the NTSB, some six months after the crash, that JFK Jr. had turned down his request to fly with him by saying he wanted to "do it alone." These dramatic, ironic words were reported widely in the establishment press and solidified the image of JFK Jr. as an irresponsible daredevil. Merena's own lawyer would deny he'd ever made such a statement, and the memorandum produced by the NTSB regarding it was suspiciously irregular, with no date, location, or signature on it. Most crucially, Merena had been interviewed five days after the crash by the NTSB, and he never mentioned anything about this, which would certainly seem to have been a pertinent fact. Merena did tell the NTSB in this early interview, however, that he'd never seen JFK Jr. fly without an instructor.

Researcher John Hankey contacted Merena and confronted him with the fact that his lawyer said he'd never mentioned the conversation, to which Merena replied, "Whatever I told the NTSB, that's what happened," then hung up the phone. David Muzio, the NTSB investigator who prepared the report, refused to talk about the subject to Hankey and referred him to his supervisor, who ignored all his phone calls, letters, and emails.

WCVB-TV aired a very strange report, during their early coverage of the search for JFK Jr.'s plane, that featured the following statement, ". . . According to what the family has told us, it is believed that Kennedy was the pilot of the plane and that in fact he was the only pilot on board. There had been earlier reports that perhaps there had been a fourth passenger, a flight instructor. . . . The family is also saying they are not sure that JFK Jr. had the proper license to pilot the plane last night. . . ." Who is "the family"? Why would any family member release a statement at that point in time questioning whether JFK Jr. had the "proper license" to fly the plane?

In a strange twist, JFK Jr.'s closest cousin, Anthony Radziwill, died less than a month after him, on August 10, 1999, from cancer, which he'd been battling for years. Radziwill had been JFK Jr.'s best man, and his wife, ABC journalist Carole Radziwill (often incorrectly identified as "Ratowell" in stories about this case) had been one of those frantically trying to prod the authorities into action the night Kennedy's plane disappeared, making the 2 a.m. call to the Coast Guard. I sent a message to Carole on Facebook (we were Facebook friends before she later deleted her account), asking about this issue, but she never replied.

In 2006, I emailed Steve Sbraccia, who'd been one of the reporters covering the JFK Jr. story for WCVB-TV in 1999. Sbraccia, no longer with the station, responded to me on July 15, 2006. While I'd simply asked for his overall impressions, without detailing any of my own doubts about the official version of events, Sbraccia volunteered his own. Sbraccia wasn't even on duty that day, but he wound up being the first reporter on the island. As he told me, "I had no notepad, no photographer or anything else. . . ." He had to use his cell phone exclusively, which explains why he wasn't able to get the name of the *Martha's Vineyard Gazette* reporter who saw an explosion in the sky, since he was doing his coverage "on the fly," to use his term.

Sbraccia then made this shocking, unsolicited statement: "Perhaps it's the cynic in me—but I've always felt there was something 'wrong' about that crash . . . from the way the police swept through that beach forcing everyone off—to the way they kept the wreck site closely guarded until they pulled up every bit of debris on the ocean floor. . . ." Sbraccia continued, "JFK Jr. was no government official—yet they devoted so many resources to 'security and recovery' that it just didn't add up . . . over the years I've looked at the various 'conspiracy' web sites—and I understand the puzzlement they express about [the] situation." Regarding the anonymous *Vineyard Gazette* reporter, Sbraccia stated, "I can assure you that the reporter I spoke with was a REAL person. . . . He was sure about what he saw. Very sure. . . ."

In a follow-up email a year later, on July 17, 2007, Sbraccia elaborated on his previous comments thusly: "As I said—I had a nagging gut feeling that it may not have been as it was seen—but—that's as far as it went. I've learned over the years that many things are not as they appear on the surface. That's not to say it WAS a conspiracy—but that—a story should be looked at 3 dimensionally—rather than 1-dimensionally. . . ."

I followed up with Sbraccia, and in an August 1, 2012, email, he reaffirmed what he'd said previously. Concerning the *Martha's Vineyard Gazette* reporter, he stated, ". . . I can swear in court that man was real—and I reported exactly what he told me he saw." Sbraccia described this elusive figure as ". . . an older, stocky man about 5'8" with thinning salt and pepper hair in a sort of comb-over. . . ." Needless to say, this firsthand description of the reporter hardly sounds like the person who "went back to school," as a representative of the paper had told researcher John DiNardo.

I also contacted WCVB's Chet Curtis, who had anchored most of the station's coverage of the JFK Jr. plane crash. I'd watched the videotape Scott Myers had sent me numerous times, and Curtis had impressed me as being skeptical of the gradually emerging consensus that JFK Jr. had been "reckless" to fly that night. Curtis had also noted that the weather conditions that night were not bad at all. He personally had reported the 9:39 p.m. communication from JFK Jr. many times on that videotape alone, so I asked him about that, and admitted my own doubts about what really happened. Curtis, while extremely cordial in his email of January 23, 2007, gave a thoroughly predictable response. "I have no reason to believe there was anything 'wrong' about the official story," he stated. "I have no recollection of the last communication and the interview with Coast Guard spokesman Todd Burgun. . . . As for the *Hyannis Port Gazette* reporter and the alleged 'mid-air' explosion . . . I have absolutely no recollection of ever hearing that report . . ." Contradicting the attitude he'd expressed during his coverage of the event in progress, Curtis declared, "I can understand how a private pilot with limited experience and no instrument rating, could easily become disoriented when he loses sight of the horizon on a dark night. . . ."

I emailed the *Martha's Vineyard Gazette* during the writing of this book, asking if they could identify the reporter who'd seen an explosion that night. Editor Julia Wells, who stated she had covered the plane crash for the paper (as well as for Reuters) that weekend, claimed not to have heard anything about such a report. She responded to my follow-up with: "I'll ask around but I think you are mistaken because we did not have any reporters at the scene that day save myself, a photographer and a lot of citizen journalists. I was the senior writer at the paper and we had a small staff of four plus an editor. I'll look up who was on staff at the time. But if there was a credible account of an explosion in the sky that was seen by anyone, especially one of our reporters, I am certain we would have reported it."

I found it hard to believe that a reporter for the paper wouldn't have heard about this dynamic story, witnessed by her coworker at the *Gazette*, but I politely replied with more details of the anonymous reporter's account. She never responded to that email. I emailed her again, in November 2013, asking her if there was another small newspaper in the area that the reporter might have worked for, and been mistakenly connected to hers, but she never replied to that email either.

According to the NTSB report, the fuel selector valve on JFK Jr.'s plane was found in the "off" position. This was an exceedingly curious fact; the valve could not be turned off accidentally during the flight, so someone had to have made the calculated decision to do so during the flight. If the plane had caught fire, there would be a legitimate purpose in turning the valve off, which would cause the fire to burn out, and the plane was capable of gliding for five miles or so to a safe landing. Since there was no evidence found of fire or any other emergency situation on board the plane, and the plane took a sudden vertical dive almost instantly after JFK Jr. had made the now denied 9:39 p.m. communication, it appears as if someone simply grabbed control of the plane and pointed it straight downward. It's implausible to imagine that JFK Jr. or one of the Bessettes decided to commit suicide and take the others along to their deaths, so what explains the abrupt transformation from normal flight path to high-speed plunge into the ocean? And most curiously, what situation could possibly explain the fuel selector valve being turned off?

There were still more unanswered questions. Reports on the Internet quoted unnamed witnesses who'd seen JFK Jr., Carolyn, and Lauren Besette waiting in the Essex County, New Jersey, airport for quite some time before taking off, despite the fact it was growing darker by the minute. Did this indicate they were waiting for the flight instructor who was originally reported as being with them on the plane? Did Newsweek really have a story planned for its July 26, 1999, issue about JFK Jr.'s long-awaited entry into politics? Did Catherine Crier's television show The Crier Report really run an item about JFK Jr. meeting with high-ranking Israeli and Mossad officials to discuss his ongoing investigation into the Rabin assassination?

George magazine had indeed published a bold article questioning the official story of Rabin's death, which featured an interview with the mother of the alleged assassin. More impressively, the October 1998 issue of George featured an article titled "Our Counterfeit History" by conspiracy aficionado and noted film director Oliver Stone. JFK Jr. had also brought a surprising guest to the May 1999 White House Correspondents Dinner—Larry Flynt, notorious publisher of Hustler magazine. Flynt had not only published naked pictures of JFK Jr.'s mother years before, he had also been involved in researching the JFK assassination, once offering a million dollars for information leading to the real killers of the president. The February 17, 1978, National Enquirer had run a story about Flynt and his offer, with a nice photo of Flynt standing with critic Robert Groden and President Jimmy Carter's sister, Ruth Carter Stapleton. Coincidentally or not, Flynt was shot shortly afterward, on March 6, 1978, which left him paralyzed from the waist down.

Despite the rationale quoted earlier from Evan Thomas, many wondered why JFK Jr. and the Bessette sisters were cremated and their ashes quickly disposed of at sea. Catholics don't normally get cremated, and there is no evidence any previous member of the Kennedy family had been cremated. The *Boston Globe* acknowledged the rarity of this event, in a July 23, 1999, story. "The cremated remains of John F. Kennedy Jr., his wife, and her sister were cast from a warship to the ocean currents in a manner not favored by the Catholic Church and in a ceremony that occurred only after the intercession of Pentagon brass," the report began. "The Roman Catholic Church prefers the presence of a body at its funeral rites. And the Defense Department rarely accords the honor of burial at sea to civilians."

The autopsy was completed in less than four hours, and done at night. The *Boston Globe* once again emphasized the unusual nature of this, in a July 23, 1999, story headlined "JFK Autopsy Rushed." Robert Kirschner, former deputy chief medical examiner for Cook County, Illinois, was quoted in the article as believing, "The haste (of the autopsies) in this case could lead to questions about the investigation's thoroughness." Kirschner thought the timing of the investigation made it unlikely that autopsies had been performed on Carolyn or Lauren Bessette. "You can't possibly do three investigations in four hours," he was quoted as saying.

What was behind the reports—which appeared in the *Boston Globe*, ABC News, and other mainstream media outlets—about friction between the Kennedy family and the NTSB? Supposedly, it became so pronounced that the White House arranged for a mediator. Unnamed sources told the *Globe* that the family felt the NTSB hadn't kept them updated sufficiently on the search and investigation. Witness Shoeb Panjwani saw JFK Jr. engaging in a last-minute conversation on his cell phone at the airport. The official NTSB report cited a single cell phone call, an outgoing one at 8:25 p.m., about fifteen minutes before the plane took off. There were no details in the report regarding which of the three occupants made the call, or to whom the call was placed. Who was he talking to? Wouldn't the person who spoke with JFK Jr. just prior to his taking off for the last time, and the details of their conversation, be significant?

The security videotapes from Essex County Airport might shed light on these matters, but if they ever existed, no researcher has seen them. The *National Enquirer* reported on February 20, 2001, that a "cover up" of the case, which was being "dictated by Washington," caused videotapes of the plane on the bottom of the Atlantic Ocean to be destroyed. The *Enquirer* would later publish a suitably sensationalistic little magazine entitled *Secrets of JFK Jr.'s Life and Death*, which made the intriguing claim that "every bulb, including that in the emergency flashlight, had been blown out on the plane and every circuit board, including those in the engine sensors and other electronic equipment, had been literally melted. . . . FBI agents on the scene preliminarily concluded that 'a massive electromagnetic event' caused Kennedy's plane to crash."

ABC News unsuccessfully attempted to obtain a recording of the last known publicly uttered words of JFK Jr., a meaningless exchange with an air traffic controller at Essex County Airport. In a February 7, 2007, story reporting that the government had declined their request, predictably attributing it to the "privacy concerns of the Kennedy family," ABC included the following unexplained tidbit: "A search for recordings between Kennedy and controllers at a second airport closer to the crash site turned up nothing, according to the government's letter." This is a clear reference to the "nonexistent" 9:39 p.m. communication.

An interesting audio clip, between the previously mentioned Martha's Vineyard Airport employee Adam Budd and an FAA dispatcher, was released eight years after the plane crash, following a Freedom of Information Act request. Portions of the clip were played on Boston's WXFT-TV. Budd was oddly described in press accounts as "speaking in a hush tone, his voice slightly quaking" during the brief conversation. This call was recorded at 10:05 p.m., which was only five minutes later than JFK Jr.'s scheduled arrival time. Incredibly, the FAA had no interest in Budd's report that "Kennedy Jr.'s on board. He's uh, they want to know, uh, where he is." They reacted to his request to track the flight by merely informing him, "We don't give this information out to people over the phone." As a prescient poster on an Internet forum observed, "Somebody needs to ask Mr. Adam Budd about the people who wanted to locate JFK Jr. before he was reported missing."

The mainstream media, as usual, completely misinformed the public about this call, reporting, "The government granted ABC News' request for post-crash conversations between an intern at the Martha's Vineyard airport and a Federal Aviation Administration employee discussing JFK Jr.'s, missing plane, hours after it was expected to land." How could a 10:05 p.m. conversation be construed as being *hours* after a 9:45–10:00 p.m. expected landing? At any rate, Budd seems to have taken on an unusually big role here, as he is described variously in news accounts as either a college student interning at the airport, a ramp attendant, or a baggage handler.

I tried contacting Adam Budd in April 2014, and I was able to talk with his mother. She acknowledged my reference to Adam being at the center of things on the night of the crash by saying "he certainly was." She hesitated about giving me his number, so I told her to tell him to call me if he was interested. She told me that night was "interesting," and seemed to be about to go further into the subject before stopping herself. I sensed the same kind of edge in her voice that I had grown accustomed to; those associated with these events seem to have a hesitation in their tone that is noticeable. If these incidents can be innocently explained, and there are no shadowy conspirators to fear, then why are those who were caught up in a moment of history reluctant to talk about it? She was, at least, able to clarify a minor point of confusion, telling me that her son had been a college student interning at the airport. Adam Budd never did phone me back.

The mainstream media would trumpet the official finding that JFK Jr.'s plane crashed because of "pilot error." This despite the fact that even the NTSB report would acknowledge the Piper Saratoga had autopilot, which would have been able to guide the plane to within a hundred feet of the airport, no matter how "disoriented" the "reckless" young Kennedy had become. Once again, the public was treated to homilies about the Kennedy "curse," as if that were a valid explanation for all the unnatural deaths among members of this rich and fascinating family.

John F. Kennedy Jr., unlike his sister, Caroline, and other members of the Kennedy clan, was willing to venture into forbidden political waters, as witnessed by the publication in his magazine of an article by Oliver Stone, director of *JFK*. In 2007, his high school girlfriend Meg Azzoni self-published a book called *11 Letters and a Poem: John F. Kennedy Jr. to Meg Azzoni*. Azzoni provided anecdotal evidence that JFK Jr. was overtly interested in who killed his father, and knew the official story was bogus. "His heartfelt quest," she wrote, "was to expose and bring to trial who killed his father and who covered it up." Azzoni described *George* as "a presidential platform magazine." Meg also claimed that Jackie Kennedy had said, in her presence, that she "did not like or trust Lyndon Johnson." According to Meg, John Jr. had a cat he named Ruby. That certainly struck me as odd; one would imagine that name would conjure up dark memories for him.

Meg Azzoni and I traded a series of emails and letters while I researched the JFK Jr. case. I had questions about a number of things in her book, but I am still not certain that most of my questions were ever clarified. For whatever reason, Meg was reluctant to talk about JFK Jr. online, preferring instead to communicate by snail mail. Maybe it was my innate paranoia, but

I sensed some fear in her. I was able to verify, through a member of JFK Jr's inner circle, who strongly desired to remain anonymous, that he was keenly interested in and knowledgeable about his father's assassination and often talked about it privately.

There is no question that, if John F. Kennedy Jr. had lived, he would have been a formidable political candidate. But his premature death prevented us from ever knowing if he indeed would have publicly confronted the deaths of his father and uncle, and other related issues.

CHAPTER EIGHT

DUBYA

"There ought to be limits to freedom."

—George W. Bush, 1999

The controversial 2000 presidential election will always be remembered for the voting irregularities in Florida, and the eventual declaration by the Supreme Court that awarded the presidency to George W. Bush, son of former president George H. W. Bush. Democratic nominee Al Gore, who'd been Bill Clinton's vice president for both terms, actually received more popular votes than Bush, but under the archaic and illogical Electoral College system, he ended up losing the electoral vote, 271 to 266, after Florida's hotly contested twenty-five votes were awarded to Bush. Terms such as "hanging chads" became briefly familiar to most Americans. As the late Collier brothers had proven conclusively in their blockbuster book *Votescam*, this was hardly an isolated incident—for Florida or the country's electoral process in general.

VOTESCAM AND VOTING FRAUD

Ken and Jim Collier were a couple of ex-hippies whose investigation into voting fraud begin in 1970. Ken Collier decided to run for Congress in Dade County, Florida, against the seemingly untouchable "Father of Social Security," longtime representative Claude Pepper. The Colliers were curious about the way the television networks ran "projections" that seemed to always come out uncannily accurate. They also paid close attention to their own vote totals, and they were dismayed to lose 15 percentage points after the computers "went down" for a period of time. The Colliers' research into the "official" election results—for the September primary, the October run-off, and the final election in November, obtained from the Secretary of State's office—produced an amazing statistic. In both the Florida Senate race and the governor's race, an identical number of votes were listed as having been cast in each of the three separate elections. One doesn't need to be a professional statistician to realize that this was a mathematical impossibility.

The Colliers then compared the "official" vote totals with the "projections" by the television networks on the night of the final election and found that one local network had predicted with near perfection the results of forty different races, involving 250 candidates, only *four* minutes after the polls closed. Another station did even better, "projecting" the final vote total *precisely* at 96,499. The networks declared that their unbelievably accurate projections were derived by running the results from a single Dade County voting machine, through a computer program. Elton Davis, the programmer responsible for the formula that converted one machine's vote totals into nearly perfect total projected totals, worked at the University of Miami. When the Colliers confronted him in his office about the subject, Davis curtly informed them, "You'll never prove it, now get out." Is that one of the all-time great conspiratorial lines, or what?

The networks also reported that members of the League of Women Voters were calling in vote totals to local television channels on election night. The Colliers contacted Joyce Deiffenderfer, the head of the League, who admitted there were no League members out in the field that night. Breaking down in tears, she told them, "I don't want to get caught up in this thing."

The printout of the television networks' "projections" on election night proved they had not actually received any voting results at any time during their coverage, but had instead been devising their own projections. Their earlier claim that the courthouse computer had malfunctioned, causing them to lose access to the "official" vote for some time (during which Ken Collier lost fifteen percentage points), was proven false when the Dade County data processing chief acknowledged that the county computer had never been down, or even been running slow.

The Colliers stayed on top of the issue. In the early 1980s, they decided to try to collect an advertised reward, offered by the Republican Party, to anyone who could prove vote fraud. The Colliers videotaped embarrassed volunteers "sorting" through already punched ballots at the Dade County, Florida, elections' computer facility. They even caught one worker running the same stack of punch cards through the old-fashioned tabulating computer again and again. Jim Collier was able to obtain an armload of blank election tally sheets, along with confessions from precinct officials who admitted to signing the blank sheets days or even weeks before the election. The Colliers complained to the Dade County state attorney, who at the time was none other than future Clinton attorney general Janet Reno. Reno, in typical fashion, did not respond by investigating the obvious irregularities in the electoral process, but instead had Jim Collier arrested for stealing blank tally sheets. (*The Spotlight*, November 14, 1994, p. 16).

Supreme Court Justice Antonin Scalia, then a federal appeals judge, stopped what could have been a historic lawsuit by the Colliers against Justice Department lawyer Craig Donsanto by filing what the Colliers called a "killer memo" that supported prosecutorial discretion and dismissal. Even more ironically, he went against his future Supreme Court colleague Ruth Bader Ginsburg, who had ruled that their case should move forward. Donsanto had refused to prosecute the League of Women Voters' members who had been videotaped by the Colliers tampering with ballots during a closed-door "counting" session. The women could be seen illegally punching holes in ballots that had already been cast. When confronted by the Colliers, the women had claimed they were simply trying to remove hanging chads, after which the brothers were bodily removed from the building.

The Colliers were the first to shine any light upon the theretofore sacrosanct League of Women Voters. I had long wondered myself why this mysterious political club was permitted to play such a prominent role in our elections. The Colliers clearly demonstrated that the League had an agenda and destroyed the false myth that it is a reliable Election Day watchdog. It was hardly surprising, therefore, that the League of Women Voters was a staunch supporter of touchscreen, electronic voting machines. In 1980, the Colliers would unearth a CIA report on the US electoral process that contained the following admission: "The responsibility for the administration of elections and certification of winners in the United States national election rests with a consortium of private entities, including 111,000 members of the national League of Women Voters."

The Colliers confronted voting fraud collusion at every level of the American political system. Everyone who wasn't involved seemed afraid. The Colliers' lives were threatened, and they were vilified by the mainstream press. Dell Publishing had originally agreed on a book deal with them, but they canceled the contract. For some twenty-five years, the Colliers obtained a wealth of documented evidence proving that elections in the United States were controlled by a few powerful, corrupt people. "Now we understand why things have gone so terribly wrong in this country," the Colliers wrote.

The brothers led efforts to stop computerized voting machines and return to using paper ballots.

In August 1964, the shadowy News Election Service (NES), a consortium of the major television networks and other stalwart mainstream outlets such as the Associated Press and *Washington Post*, was created to compile computer voting results and feed them to the rest of the establishment media. Perhaps the most important contribution the Colliers made was to question the NES, something no one had ever done before. The same 1980 CIA memo mentioned earlier was refreshingly candid in evaluating the NES: "The formal structure of election administration in the United States is not capable of providing the major TV networks with timely results of the presidential and congressional elections. In the case of counting actual ballots on national election night, public officials have abdicated responsibility of aggregation of election night vote totals to a private organization, News Election Service of New York (NES). . . This private organization performs without a contract: without supervision by public officials. It makes decisions concerning its duties according to its own criteria." NES, which eventually came to be known by its present name, Voter News Service (VNS), again in the words of the CIA, "uses the vast membership of the network-subsidized League of Women Voters as field personnel whose exclusive job is to phone in unofficial vote totals to NES on election night."

The Colliers' book *Votescam: The Stealing of America* was published in 1992 and immediately banned by the major bookstore chains. These chains actively worked to prevent the sale of the book and would dishonestly list it as "out of print." Thanks largely to the influence of the Internet, *Votescam* was widely read and appreciated throughout the 2000 electoral travesty. Jim and Ken Collier both died relatively young in the 1990s.

In May 2000, Jim's daughter Victoria Collier decided to try and contact someone at the super-secretive Voter News Service (VNS), formerly known as NES. She explained how VNS worked thusly: "All of the precinct vote results aggregated and tabulated in each county, mainly by privately owned and serviced computers, are transferred to VNS where they are *again* aggregated and tabulated, and finally the totals are disseminated to the individual media networks, and then to the public, who accepts them without question." The votes are processed using secretly programmed software, and there is no oversight permitted. The software is not open to public scrutiny. It is hard to imagine a more undemocratic system. VNS is so secretive that Victoria Collier was unable to enter their offices as a youngster, when she pretended to be the sick child of a VNS employee. The VNS guards refused her entrance, and instead offered to call her an ambulance.

On May 18, 2000, a reporter with the *Ashville Global Report* managed to speak by phone with Lee C. Shapiro, press secretary for VNS. When the reporter asked if there was a citizen watchdog group to oversee VNS on election nights, Shapiro sharply retorted that she was "not going to get into this with you," and hung up. Victoria Collier, who was then affiliated with the *Global Report* as well, contacted VNS on May 20, requesting that any available information about VNS be mailed to her, and after being put on hold for a lengthy time, the executive director of VNS, Bill Headline, came on the phone. Headline was clearly nervous, and claimed they had no literature, only a "fax sheet we're in the process of putting together but it's not ready for distribution." He admitted that VNS had no website and no volunteers. According to Headline, they hired "people around the country" to do their exit polling. Headline stated, "we've never been out of sync with the official results," acknowledging the reality that the vote projections of VNS always tally precisely with the official vote totals.

Headline and Collier discussed the needlessly confusing, arcane electoral process VNS is at the center of, with at one point Headline disclosing that the New York City "Police Department" was the "official vote counters in New York." Collier made Headline look foolish when she mentioned the concerns of Pat Buchanan's supporters, who'd alleged fraud in the 1996 Iowa caucuses; Headline seemed only "vaguely familiar" with the subject, but later steadfastly maintained "there was no basis in fact" to the Buchanan supporters' allegations.

Victoria Collier's interview with Headline revealed the VNS's secretive mindset. They certainly *seemed* to be hiding something, with their strong desire for privacy over a matter that should be as public as possible. The unnecessary complexity of it all, like the ever-changing but never disclosed location of the VNS National Input Center (Headline simply would not tell Collier where it was going to be that year), certainly doesn't inspire public confidence. In a follow-up conversation on June 12, things ended abruptly when Collier declared that she didn't trust the major media and worked with the alternative press, wherein Headline said, "That changes the nature of this entire conversation, and I don't want to talk to you anymore. . . ."

I exchanged a series of emails with Victoria Collier in November 2013. She was ashamed of the fact that *Votescam* first appeared in print courtesy of a series of articles in *The Spotlight*. She strongly feels that the newspaper was anti-Semitic and doesn't want her father's work associated with it in any way. I attempted to defend *The Spotlight*, pointing out that not only did they break a great many important stories that no other media outlet was covering, they first exposed readers like me to the extensive fraud in America's electoral process.

In 2003, VNS was disbanded and an identical organization, National Election Pool (NEP) took its place. Most Americans don't even know that the NEP exists. Why are we satisfied with a voting process that is dominated by a mysterious private corporation? There must be a simpler, more trustworthy way of tallying the vote. Veteran journalist Ronnie Dugger wrote one of the few critical pieces on the voting process to ever appear in the establishment press, in an article titled *How They Could Steal the Election This Time*, which appeared in the August 16, 2004, issue of *The Nation*. "Some 98 million citizens, five out of every six of the roughly 115 million who will go to the polls," Dugger wrote, "will consign their votes into computers that unidentified computer programmers, working in the main for four private corporations and the officials of 10,500 election jurisdictions, could program to invisibly falsify the outcomes. . . ." Dugger went on to declare, "The four major election corporations count votes with voting-system source codes. These are kept strictly secret by contract with the local jurisdictions and states using the machines. That secrecy makes it next to impossible for a candidate to examine the source code used to tabulate his or her own contest."

The 2012 Republican primaries and caucuses, which were rife with clear, transparent fraud, revealed how unsuccessful the Colliers and others were in wresting control away from undemocratic usurpers who have thwarted our electoral process. No country can be considered free if their electoral process is tainted. You'd have to be extremely naive at this point to believe America's isn't.

THE BUSH BODY COUNT, PART TWO

The deaths that would quickly be dubbed the Bush Body Count began piling up even before Dubya entered office. Steve Kangas, whose website, Liberalism Resurgent, concentrated on the misdoings of the resurgent forces of the right, such as billionaire publisher Richard Melon Scaife, was found in a bathroom outside of Scaife's offices at One Oxford Centre in Pittsburgh, an apparent suicide on February 8, 1999. The prolific Kangas left no suicide note. After his death, his computer was sold and its hard drive wiped clean. Everything in his apartment was thrown away.

Heinz Prechler, who had been a loyal contributor to Bush the Elder and Dubya, hung himself on July 6, 2001. James (J. D.) Hatfield, author of the controversial book *Fortunate Son*, which detailed Dubya's cocaine usage among other things, was found dead in a motel room of an apparent suicide on July 18, 2001. During the documentary *Horns and Halos*, which detailed the difficult process of getting his book published, Hatfield looked into the camera at one point and said, "If anything happens to me, get it out to the press." Bob Stevens, a photo editor with American Media, which owns the *National Enquirer*, was one of those who died during the anthrax scare in October 2001. The Bush family had been extremely embarrassed by the photos of daughter Jenna Bush, intoxicated and holding a cigarette, as she danced with another drunken female, published by the *Enquirer*.

The body of James Daniel Watkins, a consultant for Arthur Andersen, the accounting firm for Enron Corporation, was discovered in Colorado's Pike National Forest on December 1, 2001. Officials ruled his death a suicide. Clifford Baxter, former vice chairman of Enron Corporation, who had resigned in May 2001, was found dead of an apparent suicide on January 25, 2002. Baxter had clashed with Enron's CEO Jeffrey Skilling over questionable business practices, and he had agreed to testify before Congress, which was investigating the Enron scandal. An unsigned suicide note was found in his wife's car. Enron-related deaths can be traced back to April 1989, when a plane carrying Gulf Power Vice President Jake Horton, who knew about Enron's dubious accounting practices and had offered to come clean with state officials, exploded shortly after takeoff. Dan Rocco, executive vice president of Choice Point, the company that had supplied a questionable list of "felons" to Florida Secretary of State Katherine Harris during the 2000 election debacle, died in a plane crash on April 1, 2002.

THE DEATH OF LORI KLAUSUTIS

A mysterious, severely underreported death occurred on July 20, 2001. The body of twenty-eight-year-old Lori Klausutis, an aide to then-Republican Congressman Joe Scarborough, was discovered behind a desk in his Fort Walton Beach, Florida, office. There were no witnesses and no logical cause of death for the attractive young woman. There was a head wound, but the official conclusion would be that an undetected heart condition made her collapse and hit her head on the desk. Michael Berkland, who performed the autopsy, would acknowledge there was "a scratch and a bruise" on her head, but declared "the last thing we wanted was 40 questions about a head injury." Berkland had a sketchy background, as his medical license in Missouri had been revoked in 1998 and suspended in Florida in 1999. Repeated requests to the Florida Medical Examiners Commission failed to establish that Berkland's suspension had ever been lifted. (*American Politics Journal*, August 8, 2001).

Klausutis was known to be a regular jogger, and was in great physical shape, thus it seemed strange that Scarborough's press secretary Miguel Serrano went on local television stations within a few hours of her body being found and noted that she had a (nonexistent) history of health problems. Another Scarborough aide, Tiffany Bates, was evidently the last person to speak to Klausutis, and she claimed Lori had told her she wasn't feeling well. Dr. Berkland backed these unsubstantiated claims by saying, "She had a past medical history that was significant. . . ." The Klausutis family angrily refuted this, and they responded to the rumors of suicide by writing to the editor of the *Northwest Florida Daily News*, declaring, "For those who knew Lori, the thought of suicide, as your published reports suggested, is absolutely unthinkable. Suicide was contrary to her faith and being. She did not suffer from seizures, nor did she have a history of medical problems."

Oddly, Klausutis's published obituary mentioned a great deal about her life but nothing about her work for Joe Scarborough. *The Northwest Florida Daily News* ran an article on August 29, 2001, with the headline, "Klausutis Head Injury More Severe Than Previously Reported," and demanded the release of the records relating to her case, which were being withheld by the police.

The *American Politics Journal* followed this case closely. Reporter R. S. Miller questioned Miguel Serrano, and the latter wound up becoming angry, telling her, "Isn't there anything else you could be doing?" A Sergeant Pond of the Fort Walton Beach Police actually hung up on Miller, informing her that Klausutis's death was "nobody's business." Pond's superior, Captain Bishop, refused to talk to Miller, and the chief of police was just as unhelpful. Tom McLaughlin, the *Northwest Florida Daily News* reporter who covered the case, was no more interested in the truth than the police were, telling another *Journal* associate, "Suffice to say that I like Dr. Berkland very much as a person and greatly respect his work as medical examiner." When asked to comment on the numerous discrepancies in the story, McLaughlin sarcastically retorted, "Comment on what? You're [sic] ability to cut and paste?" (*American Politics Journal*, 2001 online Special Report).

What should have been a compelling story—young, attractive aide found dead from unknown causes in congressman's office—received almost no coverage in the mainstream media. There were numerous questions in this case that went unasked. Klausutis was supposedly found by a couple, Andreas and Juanita Bergmann, who were scheduled to meet with Representative Scarborough about facilitating Andreas's application for a green card. However, Scarborough was in Washington at the time, and he only flew back to Florida later that day in response to the news of his aide's death. So who would arrange an appointment at a time when Scarborough was known to be out of town? Curiously, Juanita Bergmann, a former nurse, would offer an unsolicited guess that Klausutis had suffered an epileptic seizure.

Why did Dr. Berkland's medical report contain no description of the death scene, or diagram of the body location? When there was no apparent cause of death, and some kind of head wound, why did the authorities so quickly discount any evidence of foul play? The *Pensacola News Journal* was among those who wondered if the questions of marital infidelity had been responsible for Scarborough's unusual resignation from Congress only six months after his reelection. Why did the Emerald Coast Young Republicans remove all information about Klausutis from their website, when she'd been their president at the time of her death? Wouldn't they at least have some sort of memorial to her? Why did the *Pensacola News Journal* seemingly delete her name from their search mechanism? Why the efforts on the part of Scarborough's office to intimate that the decidedly fit Klausutis had health issues? Would they even have access to her medical records, and wouldn't such records be private in any case?

In Scarborough's May 29, 2003, appearance on Don Imus's radio program, Imus joked, "You said that you had sex with the intern and then you had to kill her," to which Scarborough laughed and replied, "Yeah, well, what are you gonna do?" Scarborough resigned from Congress in the middle of his term, two months after Klausutis's death (and only five days before 9/11), and would go on to become a highly visible figure on television, hosting programs such as *Morning Joe* on MSNBC. In 2004, leftist filmmaker Michael Moore, in the midst of a public spat with the conservative Scarborough, registered the domain name joeScarboroughkilledhisintern.com. The website ceased to exist long ago, and I could find no further indications that Moore investigated the case. I emailed Moore twice to ask him about this, but I never received a response.

CHAPTER NINE

9/11

"Our enemies have made the mistake that America's enemies
always make. They saw liberty and thought they saw weakness.
And now, they see defeat."

—President George W. Bush

George W. Bush's legacy will always be defined by the events of September
11, 2001, which provided him with something of a delayed mandate.
Without 9/11, there would have been no unconstitutional Patriot Act, no
Homeland Security Department, no decade-long occupation of Iraq and
Afghanistan, and no open-ended "war on terror." As such, it is important to
look closely at exactly what really happened on 9/11/2001.

The official story is that nineteen radical Muslims of Arabic backgrounds
hijacked four commercial airliners in the boldest act of terrorism imaginable.
The first two, American Airlines Flight 11 and United Airlines Flight 175,
departed from Boston's Logan International Airport at 7:59 a.m. and 8:14
a.m., respectively. At 8:19 a.m., flight attendant Betty Ong used an air phone
to notify American Airlines that the flight was being hijacked, and that two
flight attendants had been stabbed. By 8:20 a.m., FAA flight controllers in
Boston established that Flight 11 had "probably" been hijacked. At the same
time (8:20 a.m.), American Airlines Flight 77 took off from Washington D.C.'s
Dulles International Airport. At 8:24 a.m., air traffic controllers supposedly
heard alleged hijacker Mohamed Atta warn passengers against "making any
moves," and also assuring them the plane was returning to the airport. At
8:37 a.m., NORAD was first notified of the situation regarding Flight 11,
and the Boston Center controller requested military assistance to intercept

the airliner. At 8:42 a.m., United Airlines Flight 93 departed Newark International Airport.

The official conspiracy theory (and yes, it is unquestionably a conspiracy theory) has as many holes in it as the Warren Commission's Report. Flight 11 crashed into the North Tower of the World Trade Center (WTC) at 8:46 a.m., or some twenty-six minutes after flight controllers had already determined it had "probably" been hijacked. NORAD was advised at 8:50 a.m. about the airliner hitting the WTC, thirteen minutes after a plea for military assistance had first been requested. Well-known radio personality Howard Stern talked on air about the situation a few minutes later, and instantly labeled it a terrorist attack. At 9:03 a.m., Flight 175 struck the South Tower of the WTC, about twenty-six minutes after NORAD was first contacted for help.

By 9:17 a.m., CBS News was reporting that Osama Bin Laden was a prime suspect behind the hijackings, according to the "intelligence community." Shortly thereafter, CNN dutifully informed us that Bin Laden had been "determined" to attack the United States. Only moments after that, former Federal Reserve chairman Alan Greenspan's longtime wife, NBC reporter Andrea Mitchell, disclosed to her audience that Bin Laden may have been involved. At 9:24 a.m., the FAA and NORAD began discussing the situation with Flight 77, which had also obviously been hijacked. Almost fifteen minutes later, at 9:37 a.m., Flight 77 crashed into the western side of the Pentagon. The South Tower of the WTC collapsed at 9:59 a.m., oddly about a half hour *before* the North Tower, which was struck seventeen minutes earlier. The North Tower didn't collapse until 10:28 a.m., which means it took the same magical jet fuel about forty-six minutes longer to cause an identical, pancake-style destruction. At 10:06 a.m., Flight 93 crashed in Somerset County, Pennsylvania, according to the authorities, after a heroic band of passengers, shouting out "let's roll," brought the plane down in a selfless act of patriotism.

From first realizing there was a problem of some sorts, at 8:19 a.m., officials had well over an hour to respond before Flight 77 crashed into the Pentagon at 9:37 a.m. If the FAA or NORAD took any reasonable action during that time, it went undetected and unreported. Critics quickly would latch onto this curious inactivity on the part of our government. Here we had the very heart of our military under potential assault; they knew a plane that had been reported as hijacked was flying around in the airspace over Washington, D.C., and yet they did not engage fighter jets to try and intercept it. By contrast, when golfer Payne Stewart's Learjet had encountered difficulties in October 1999, a local fighter pilot was rapidly diverted from a training routine and then two F-16s took over the chase. (ABC News, October 25, 1999). On October 26, 1999, CNN would recount that "officers on the Joint Chiefs were monitoring the [Payne Stewart] Learjet on radar screens inside the Pentagon's National Military Command Center." Reports on exactly how long it took for authorities to react in the Stewart case vary greatly, but the consensus seems to be that they responded quicker than they did on 9/11.

A 1994 report from the General Accounting Office stated that, during the previous four years, NORAD's alert fighters had been assigned to intercept aircraft 1,518 times. Another 1998 document warned pilots that any airplanes persisting in unusual behavior "will likely find two [jet fighters] on their tail within 10 or so minutes." (*The War on Freedom* by Nafeez Ahmed, p. 148). On August 12, 2002, the Associated Press reported that NORAD had scrambled sixty-seven fighter planes from September 2000 to June 2001. The September 15, 2001, *Boston Globe* quoted Marine Corps Major Mike Snyder as saying that its fighters "routinely intercept aircraft." How, then, did all that time elapse on 9/11, with a far more serious problem obvious to everyone, without aircraft being scrambled anywhere? American taxpayers had spent untold trillions on defense over the years, and here we had a plane that was known to be acting suspiciously for quite some time, plowing into the Pentagon itself, with absolutely no retaliatory response whatsoever.

There are a myriad of perplexing questions that have caused an ever-increasing number of Americans to become what are popularly (and derogatorily) referred to as 9/11 "truthers" over the years. Mohammed Atta, the alleged ringleader of the hijackers, owned the only two pieces of luggage left behind at the airport by the eighty-one passengers on board Flight 11. One of them contained a convenient, "paradise" suit, which officials quickly identified as Atta's "wedding" attire for what he trusted would be his impending wedding in heaven. For good measure, a gold-painted Koran was found as well. A five-page incriminating letter attesting to his upcoming nuptials with the "women of paradise" was located in the other piece of luggage. The rest of the five-page letter contained a virtual confession to his actions, and nicely delineated his motives. There was even a flight-operating manual for the Boeing 757, if anyone doubted he had intended to take over as pilot.

Coincidentally, of course, on September 11, 2001, NORAD happened to be in the midst of a weeklong exercise called "Vigilant Guardian." Although it might be expected that the lackadaisical response on the part of officials that day could be attributed to personnel believing the "hijackings" were part of the exercise, the 9/11 Commission actually concluded, against all logic, that the response was "if anything, expedited by the increased number of staff at the sectors and at NORAD because of the scheduled exercise. . . ." If that's the case, one can only wonder how ineffectual the response would have been if there *hadn't* been a scheduled exercise. In contradiction to every known fact, General Ralph Eberhart told the 9/11 Commission that because of the exercise, the military was "postured for wartime conditions" on September 11, and that NORAD had "responded immediately" with appropriate measures. This testimony would indicate that it was officially considered appropriate to do exactly nothing for the nearly hour-and-a-half time period between the first plane being identified as hijacked and the third airliner crashing into the Pentagon.

Bringing to mind memories of President Reagan's alleged would-be assassin John Hinckley's brother having a scheduled dinner engagement with then-Vice President George H. W. Bush's brother the day after Reagan was shot, former President George H. W. Bush met with Shafig Bin Laden, brother of purported 9/11 mastermind Osama Bin Laden, on September 10, 2001, at a meeting hosted by powerful defense contractor The Carlyle Group. How likely is it that all five of the alleged hijackers of Flight 77 would be staying in a hotel located just outside the gates of the National Security Agency (NSA)? Why did the Bureau of Transportation Statistics show no stats regarding the takeoff of Flight 77 on September 11?

It is curious that the pilot of Flight 77, Charles Burlingame, had once worked on antiterrorism issues in the same area of the Pentagon that was hit that day. Another prestigious passenger on Flight 77 was Navy Rear Admiral Wilson "Bud" Flagg, who'd held important posts in the Pentagon in the past. Finally, also on board was Barbara Olson, wife of Solicitor General Ted Olson, who frequently appeared as a talking head on various news programs and had authored the book *Hell to Pay: The Unfolding Story of Hillary Rodham Clinton*. She was working on another anti-Clinton book, *The Final Days: The Last, Desperate Abuses of Power by the Clinton White House*, which was published the month after her death. Can she also be included in the Clinton Body Count?

President George W. Bush was at Emma E. Booker Elementary School in Sarasota, Florida, that morning. He was there to read the book *My Pet Goat* with the students in teacher Kay Daniels's second grade classroom. At a town hall meeting, aired December 4, 2001 by CNN and other major networks, Bush would claim he "saw" the first plane crash into the WTC while sitting outside in the hallway, waiting to go into the classroom. Bush said, "The TV was obviously on, and I used to fly myself, and I said to myself, 'There's one terrible pilot.'" Of course, there was no live broadcast of this event, so why would he say something like that? Bush repeated this ridiculous story in a town hall forum on January 5, 2002. At any rate, the timeline wouldn't permit this either, as the first plane had already hit the WTC before the president even arrived at the school. Bush's chief of staff, Andrew Card, would walk up to the president later, as he sat reading with the children in the classroom, and whisper in his ear that a second plane had hit the towers, adding the dramatic words, "America's under attack." Video taken of the scene captured Bush's rather befuddled expression upon hearing this dire news, but he didn't appear interested in more details, and he stayed nearly the entire scheduled twenty minutes with the students.

The Secret Service curiously didn't whisk the president away to a secure location. In fact, Bush remained inexplicably inside the building long enough to issue a brief statement in the school library. The 9/11 Commission would report that, during this critical time, "as far as we could determine, no one with the President was in contact with the Pentagon." (*The 9/11 Commission Report*, pp. 39–41). Meanwhile, Vice President Dick Cheney was being physically carried out of his office and transported to an underground White House bunker. When Bush was at last rushed out of the elementary school, he had trouble getting a secure phone line to Vice President Cheney established, and had to borrow a cell phone, which also didn't work. The communication problems persisted on Air Force One, despite the advanced, top-of-the-line equipment it possessed. Never was Bush's dimwittedness more apparent than during his January 5, 2002, speech, when he summed up the tragic events of 9/11 by declaring, "Anyway, it was an interesting day."

On February 16, 2004, the Family Steering Committee, a group consisting of family members who'd lost loved ones on 9/11, expressed some of their concerns in a series of questions publicly submitted to President Bush. One of their questions was, "What defensive action did you personally order to protect our nation during the crisis on September 11th?" Another was, "In your opinion, why was our nation so utterly unprepared for an attack on our own soil?" Yet another pointed out a glaring inconsistency from that day: "Is it normal procedure for the Director of the White House Situation Room to travel with you? If so, please cite any prior examples of when this occurred. If not normal procedure, please explain the circumstances that led to the Director of the White House Situation Room being asked to accompany you to Florida during the week of September 11th."

They also questioned all his curious actions at the school that day, particularly his failure to leave immediately upon learning that a second plane had struck the WTC. They brought up the fact that Bin Laden family members in the United States—including the brother Dubya had met with the day before 9/11—were permitted to fly out of the country even after all commercial flights had been grounded, and demanded to know why they were granted this special privilege. Summing up the entire mess nicely, the grieving family members inquired, "Please explain why no one in any level of our government has yet been held accountable for the countless failures leading up to and on 9/11?"

They sought any proof that Al-Qaeda was connected to Iraqi dictator Saddam Hussein. Another pertinent question was: "Please explain your 14 month opposition to the creation of an independent commission to investigate 9/11 and your request to Senator Daschle to quash such an investigation." It's a shame that the woeful 9/11 Commission, tasked to "investigate" the tragic events that day, didn't have any of the zeal these family members had. Their questions were all important, and they have all remained unanswered.

The establishment closed ranks quickly after the "terrorist" attack, and as usual on such occasions, the "left" and "right," "liberal" and "conservative" designations were meaningless. At a Council on Foreign Relations meeting on September 12, the day after the attacks, "leftist" Senator Gary Hart declared, "There is a chance for the president of the United States to use this disaster to carry out what his father—a phrase his father used I think only once, and it hasn't been used since—and that is a new world order."

Critics would soon look closely at the think tank Project for a New American Century, cofounded by highly visible neoconservative William Kristol, son of Irving Kristol, who was affiliated with the far-left Congress for Cultural Freedom, later exposed by *Ramparts* magazine as being a CIA front, and who went on to transform himself into "the godfather of neo-conservatism." In their publication *Rebuilding America's Defenses*, published in September 2000, exactly a year before the attacks, was this eerie declaration: "Further, the process of transformation, even if it brings revolutionary change, is likely to be a long one, absent some catastrophic and catalyzing event—like a new Pearl Harbor."

Paul Wolfowitz, a leading neocon and Bush's deputy secretary of defense, echoed his ideological "enemy" Gary Hart's sentiments. On September 13, he called for "ending states who sponsor terrorism." The reliable mainstream media chimed in as well, with Tom Brokaw telling viewers, on October 11, 2001, that we were now in "a new world order."

Hani Hanjour, who is generally credited with piloting Flight 77 into the Pentagon, managed to achieve this feat (executing in the process what the *Washington Post* quoted a top aviation source calling "a nice, coordinated turn") in spite of failing a chaperoned test flight at Maryland's Freeway Airport only three weeks before 9/11. Hanjor was attempting to *rent* a Cessna there and was so lacking in basic proficiency that he was considered unqualified to do so. Earlier in 2001, the Arizona flight school he'd attended had voiced some of the same concerns about Hanjor, even going so far as to contact the FAA, because they felt his piloting skills and his grasp of English were so shoddy that they questioned the legitimacy of his pilot's license. One instructor was quoted as saying, "He could not fly at all." (*New York Times*, May 4, 2002).

But Hanjor wasn't the only subpar pilot among the alleged terrorists. Rick Garza, a flight instructor with California's Sorbi's Flying Club, provided a similar critique of two other would-be pilots in the group, Khalid Almihdar and Nawaq al-Hamzi: "It was like Dumb and Dumber. I mean, they were clueless. It was clear they were never going to make it as pilots." The mainstream press handled these extremely disturbing facts in their customary fashion. On September 30, 2001, the *Washington Post* addressed the obvious inadequacies of the alleged pilots by calling the preparations of the nineteen hijackers "imperfect." With unintentional humor, the *Post* wrote, "Some were kicked out of pilot schools. . . . Two were late for the Boston flight that would be the first to slam into the World Trade Center. But inexact as it was, their plot succeeded in claiming more than 6000 lives." Later, of course, the official death tally from 9/11 would be reported as about half of that. The *Post* story also quotes Garza again, in relation to Alhazmi and Almihdhar, as having sat them down after only two flights, to explain, "This is not going to work out."

The official story was that these nineteen hijackers managed to take control of four airliners by threatening the passengers and crew with . . . *box cutters*. Is it credible that eight experienced pilots, not to mention all those passengers, could be subdued with such "weapons"? Wouldn't one expect some red-blooded male passengers—like the boys on Flight 93 who yelled out "Let's roll" before forcing the plane down in Pennsylvania—to have at least attempted to overpower the small group of hijackers, who weren't exactly the textbook definition of armed and dangerous?

Well, they also had another deadly weapon. Attorney General John Ashcroft explained to ABC News on September 15, 2001, that "investigators believed that each of the commandeered planes had been hijacked by groups of three to six men armed with box cutters and plastic knives." The next day, Secretary of Defense Donald Rumsfeld, presumably with a straight face, told Fox News that the hijackers had used a "distinctly different" sort of weapon—plastic knives. On October 9, Rumsfeld appeared to have forgotten about the box cutters, telling CBS's Dan Rather that "plastic knives and the use of a US airliner filled with American people as a missile [were used] to destroy a World Trade Center." Yes, forcing a large group of people to submit using plastic knives was certainly a "distinctly different" strategy.

Perhaps a semi-reasonable argument can be made that a large group of people could be frozen into fear by box cutters, but *plastic knives*? Realizing that this is part of the official explanation of events, how can we take any other part of it seriously? There were a few other reports of weapons on board the planes. Flight attendant Betty Ong claimed to have seen four hijackers kill one passenger and utilize what she called "some sort of spray" that made it hard to breathe and her eyes burn. Todd Beamer, leader of the heroic efforts to thwart the hijacking of Flight 93, talked about a "terrorist with a bomb" during a cell phone call.

There have been numerous impressive studies of the photographic evidence from the North and South Towers of the WTC, demonstrating that the official story is impossible. I recall watching the towers collapse, in what appeared to be a perfect implosion, and thinking instantly that it looked like the buildings had been purposefully demolished. The official story was that jet fuel from the planes burned so intensely that it eventually caused two hundred thousand tons of steel supports to melt, creating a ripple effect that brought the structures crashing down. According to every known scientific source, steel cannot melt until it reaches a temperature of 1535 degrees Celsius. In spite of this, mainstream media outlets like the BBC News, on September 13, 2001, confidently explained that the fires in the WTC had reached temperatures of 800 degrees Celsius—"hot enough to melt steel floor supports."

Establishment "experts" rushed to the forefront to support the ridiculous official story. MIT engineering professor Eduardo Kausel told a panel of Boston-area structural engineers: "I believe that the intense heat softened or melted the structural elements—floor trusses and columns—so that they became like chewing gum, and that was enough to trigger the collapse." Various "experts" on the television networks assured the public that the joints, trusses, and/or columns within the structures had melted, causing each floor to collapse onto the one below. Enterprising non-mainstream researchers on the Internet have examined the visual evidence from September 11 and presented a powerful case that the fires can be seen dying down and even burning out, not intensifying, before the implosion-like fall of the buildings.

Explosives placed in the buildings, causing a controlled demolition, were suspected early on. The *Albuquerque Journal*, on September 11, 2001, quoted explosives expert Van Romero as saying, "My opinion is, based on the videotapes, that after the airplanes hit the World Trade Center there were some explosive devices inside the buildings that caused the towers to collapse." Ten days later, however, Romero predictably retracted his remarks with, "Certainly the fire is what caused the building to fail. . . ." On September 12, 2001, demolition expert Mark Taylor told *New Scientist*, "It cascaded down like an implosion." High-ranking Danish military officer Jens Claus Hansen declared, "Additional bombs must have been placed inside the WTC towers—otherwise they would not have collapsed as they actually did."

Besides the perfect, pancake freefall of the buildings, the fact that the remnants were pulverized into dust indicated a demolition rather than some other sort of progressive collapse. The symmetrical nature of the fall, with the debris falling only into the structure's footprints, again indicated an implosion by demolition. During a September 8, 2002, broadcast, Colonel John O'Dowd of the US Army Corps of Engineers told The History Channel that he'd never seen anything like the remains from the twin towers. "It seemed like everything was pulverized," he said. The Associated Press reported, on January 15, 2002, that Dr. Charles Hirsch, New York City's chief medical examiner, believed many of the bodies had been "vaporized."

While the twin towers and everything in them were turned to dust, including the nearly indestructible black boxes from the planes, one of the alleged hijacker's passports somehow managed to miraculously survive intact, and was recovered a few blocks away from the WTC. In a story headlined "Uncle Sam's Lucky Finds," the March 19, 2002, *Guardian* expressed the widespread skepticism that greeted this discovery, stating "the idea that Atta's passport had escaped from that inferno unsinged [tests] the credulity of the staunchest supporter of the FBI's crackdown on terrorism."

William Rodriguez was a maintenance worker who'd been employed at the WTC for twenty years. He was in the sub-basement of the North Tower when it was hit by Flight 11. Rodriquez was with at least fourteen other people in an office, and he testified to hearing an explosion, which caused his feet to vibrate and the walls to start "cracking and everything started shaking." Rodriguez then said, "I hear another explosion from way above." Rodriguez went on to become a genuine hero that day, helping great numbers of people in the North Tower. However, his experience contradicted the official version of events; how could the impact of a plane over eighty stories above him cause damage to the sub-basement of the building? Rodriguez would come to question the established story, but his attempts to talk to the 9/11 Commission or other officials were ignored. Engineer Mike Pecoraro would also testify to the damage inflicted in an area far removed from the point of impact, as he witnessed a machine shop and a parking garage in the sub-basement completely gone, turned to rubble. Philip Morelli described being thrown to the ground by two explosions while he was in the fourth sub-basement of the North Tower.

A documentary film by French brothers Jules and Gedeon Naudet was aired in March 2002 by CBS. During their filming, they happened to capture the only live video of Flight 11 crashing into the North Tower, by a startling coincidence. Jules Naudet claimed that when he entered the North Tower's lobby, moments after the airliner had struck it, he found victims on fire, which he felt was too traumatic an image to film. The logical question is, of course, how could an aircraft striking the building over eighty stories above the lobby cause people to catch fire there? The New York City firefighters they were filming also reported finding widespread damage throughout the North Tower's lobby area. The firefighters expressed their amazement over this, saying it "looked like the plane hit the lobby." New York City firefighters weren't exactly helping the official story with some of their comments. Louie Cacchioli, who rescued people from the South Tower, stated in the September 12, 2001, issue of *People* magazine, "We think there was bombs set in the building."

An NBC documentary about the 9/11 tapes, aired on June 17, 2002, contained several references to explosions by NYC firefighters. Firefighter Edward Cachia was one of those later quoted in the *New York Times*. He stated, "We thought there was like an internal detonation, explosives. . . ." Assistant Fire Commissioner Stephen Gregory testified to seeing "low level flashes" on Tower 2 before it came down: "You know like when they demolish a building, how when they blow up a building. . . ." He stated that a Lieutenant Evangelista had independently observed the same thing. Firemen Lieutenant Paul Isaac Jr. boldly declared, "Many other firemen know there were bombs in the buildings, but they're afraid for their jobs to admit it because the 'higher-ups' forbid discussion of this fact."

Isaac even alleged that ex-CIA director Robert Woolsey, serving as the fire department's antiterrorism consultant, had issued a gag order throughout the ranks. Scott Forbes, who worked in the World Trade Center, had September 11 off, but he claimed that his coworkers who were trapped in the South Tower told family members, during cell phone calls, about hearing "bomb like explosions" throughout the building. Several other employees referred to hearing explosions. BBC reporter Steve Evans, who was inside the towers, described hearing "huge explosions." Even CBS's Dan Rather noted that the fall of the towers resembled the cases where "a building was deliberately destroyed by well-placed dynamite to knock it down."

There were some curious anomalies at the World Trade Center in the weeks before 9/11. Financial analyst Ben Fountain, who worked in the South Tower, told *People* that there were numerous unusual drills in the weeks leading up to September 11, where both towers and Building 7 were evacuated for "security reasons." The previously mentioned Scott Forbes reported that his company was notified three weeks in advance that there would be a power outage in the South Tower on floors forty-eight and above on the weekend prior to 9/11, to install new computer cables. Forbes stated that such a power outage had never occurred before that time. Because the power was out for some thirty-six hours that weekend, the security cameras on the upper floors were left conveniently nonoperational. Forbes also noted that the video cameras atop the World Trade Center were inexplicably not working on the morning of 9/11, and he reported that another employee had told him how amazed he was at the number of FBI agents who were already at the site of the complex immediately after the first airliner struck.

Forbes also described hearing strange, loud noises a month or so before 9/11, coming from the ninety-eighth floor, above his office. He knew the office was vacant, yet he heard heavy machinery work going on there. Curious, he went and checked but the entire office space was empty. Oddly, William Rodriguez had recounted an eerily similar experience. As he was climbing the stairs in the North Tower, helping people on 9/11, he "heard strange noises on the 34th floor." It sounded like heavy equipment being moved. Rodriguez knew there was no one on the floor, and that you couldn't even access it without a special key. Forbes expressed frustration in being rebuffed by the 9/11 Commission and others in his attempts to contact them with his information.

I spoke with Scott Forbes in April 2014. He had been living in the UK for several years. It was obvious to me that he's still haunted by the events of September 11, 2001. I asked him to summarize his feelings for this book. In Scott Forbes's words:

"My name is Scott Forbes and I am a 9/11 survivor. I worked on the 97th floor of the South Tower and I survived because I had the day off work on that infamous Tuesday. I had the day off as I'd worked over the previous weekend, September the 8th and 9th, so in effect I survived as I worked the weekend. I work in Technology for a financial institution (still do work for them) and on the weekend prior to 9/11 I worked with several of my colleagues on a 'power down' condition. We had been informed by the Port Authority of NY and NJ that there would be a power outage for a 24 hour period as a re-cabling project was being completed. As our Data

Center was on the 97th floor we had a legal obligation to secure our data, bring down all systems and communications, and then restart them fully when the re-cabling work was completed. Then 9/11 happened and 89 of my friends and colleagues were killed. My gripe is that no one in authority will acknowledge that the power down took place nor investigate it. I contacted the 9/11 Commission but they did not respond to my testimony. And now the PANYNJ deny that the power down and re-cabling work took place at all, even though my testimony is supported by my many colleagues. I witnessed the outage. There was a 24 hour period when there was no electronic security or monitoring in the top half of the South Tower, and when many 'engineers' were on site working on the exercise. Surely this should be investigated and explained, if only to be then filed away. I feel like I am shouting and no one can hear me. My second gripe concerns the response to my testimony. I registered my information on a blog site in 2003, hoping to garner interest and help in getting to the truth. I am not a conspiracy theorist nor do I have an agenda. I was inundated with hundreds of emails, some supportive, many abusive. I was told I did not exist, did not work for my company, that I was a liar. On the other side I was informed I was a Patriot and a Hero. It's laughable. More frustratingly many of the supporting 'Truther' community were only interested in using me and my testimony for their own ends, just like Politicians. So where do I go now? I have key information that questions the official Disney 9/11 story . . . but I am powerless to take it anywhere and I am cynical about the truth and those who seek it. Here is the irony. Had I died on 9/11 I would have been honored as a Hero. Instead I am alive and in Purgatory."

Like Linda Haydon Ives and Linda Tripp had, Scott Forbes reminded me once again that there are real people connected to these important events, who suffer real consequences because of that connection.

A significant find was a previously lost audiotape, discovered on August 2, 2002, which revealed that firefighters had reached the actual crash site on the seventy-eighth floor of the South Tower. The tapes reveal them to be confident they had controlled the situation there. How could a fire so intense it caused one of the world's most massive structures to collapse permit firefighters to work comfortably at the point of impact? Witnesses like Brian Clark, a vice president with Euro Brokers, reported few problems dealing with the heat on the floors near the impact.

Some people appear to have been given advance notice that it was dangerous to fly on September 11, 2001. San Francisco Mayor Willie Brown was advised, about eight hours prior to the first airliner being hijacked, to "be cautious about" traveling by air. This warning came from what Brown curiously called "my security people at the airport." (*San Francisco Chronicle*, September 12, 2001). On May 17, 2002, Pacifica Radio would report that it was actually Secretary of State Condoleezza Rice, not any mystical "airport security people," who advised Brown to stay away from planes on 9/11. Even though the initial report had appeared in the mainstream media, Willie Brown would react to questions from the Philly 9/11 Truth Squad, on February 12, 2008, by claiming, "Some jerk on the Internet started that nonsense. . . ." Brown became agitated at the group and warned them to "drop it." Brown then urged them to go to the library and "read the damn report," referring to the 9/11 Commission Report, which contained nothing about him being advised not to fly.

Newsweek magazine noted that, on September 10, 2001, "a group of top Pentagon officials suddenly canceled travel plans for the next morning, apparently because of security concerns." Attorney General John Ashcroft had stopped flying commercial in July 2001, due to what the Justice Department told CBS News was a "threat assessment." (CBS News, July 26, 2001). The *Washington Post* even spoke of a July 5, 2001, meeting at the White House at which officials from a dozen federal agencies were warned, "Something really spectacular is going to happen here, and it's going to happen soon," by Richard Clarke, the government's top counterterrorism expert. Author Salman Rushdie claimed that US authorities "banned him from taking internal flights a week before the terrorist attacks." (*The* [London] *Times*, September 27, 2001).

A group of powerful business leaders, who normally would have been at work in the World Trade Center on September 11, were instead meeting that morning with Warren Buffett, at an Air Force base in Omaha, Nebraska. (*San Francisco Business Times*, February 1, 2002). President Bush's cousin, Jim Pierce, managing director of AON Corporations, had arranged a conference on the 105th floor of the South Tower that day, but the group turned out to be too large, so they moved it across the street to the Millennium Hotel. (*Ananova*, September 18, 2001).

As in the Waco and Oklahoma City tragedies, authorities moved quickly to get rid of the evidence left behind. An editorial in the January 4, 2002, *Fire Engineering* magazine dubbed the official investigation a "half baked farce." They noted that destruction of evidence was illegal, in reference to the removal of the remnants of the WTC that had been rapidly recycled almost immediately after 9/11. New York Congressman Sherwood Boehlert bemoaned the fact that the investigation had been "shrouded in secrecy," and "valuable evidence has been lost irretrievably. . . ." Even before that, New York Mayor Rudy Giuliani had issued a baffling order making it illegal to take photos around the complex.

Three months prior to 9/11, Silverstein Properties and Westfield America signed a new lease for the World Trade Center. Terms of the contract enabled the new owners to walk away from the deal in the event of "an act of terrorism." Larry Silverstein was the sole beneficiary of the more than $7 billion insurance policy. A federal jury would later determine that Silverstein's filing of separate claims, since there were two attacks, entitled him to collect up to $4.6 billion. (*Forbes*, December 6, 2004).

Silverstein has long been the focus of 9/11 truthers for his comment that a decision was made to "pull" WTC Building 7 on 9/11. "Pull" is a term commonly used to describe the planned demolition of a building. Building 7 was crucial to critics of the official story, because its collapse could not be attributed to a magical jet fuel cocktail, since no plane or debris ever struck it. Silverstein made his notorious remarks in the PBS 2002 documentary *America Rebuilds*. Lest someone doubt what "pull" meant, in the same program a cleanup worker says, "We're getting ready to pull Building 6," which was admittedly brought down by explosives. In spite of the impossibility of such a claim, FEMA would conclude, after a "thorough investigation," that the collapse of Building 7 was the result of fires from the debris of WTC Building 1, which caused it to supposedly burn for seven hours. Photos showed, on the other hand, only limited fires in isolated sections of Building 7. Building 7 was not struck by aircraft. It did not suffer any damage from debris from the collapsing twin towers, since both of them fell almost perfectly into their own footprints. Film records reveal no raging inferno, and it was thought that steel was impervious to fire. As many have noted, the key to understanding 9/11 is Building 7.

Before September 11, 2001, there was not a single documented historical instance of a steel building collapsing from fire. On 9/11, there were three huge steel buildings that we are told collapsed from fire. Since September 11, 2001, there has not been another such case. As Bill Manning of *Fire Engineering* magazine would state, "Fire has never caused a steel building to collapse." A 1991 fire at the Meridian Plaza in Philadelphia had burned for nineteen hours, without the building even cracking. On February 13, 2005, a fire reported to be the worst in Madrid's history burned for two days and gutted the Windsor building. While some upper floors collapsed onto lower ones, the overall structure, which was far weaker than the WTC's, remained intact. In April 2012, Moscow's Federation Tower, still under construction but set to be a mammoth ninety-three stories high, burned for several hours.

Not only didn't it collapse, helicopters were used to help extinguish the fire on the upper floors. Many have questioned, of course, why authorities didn't fly helicopters with water jets near the impacted floors of the Twin Towers on 9/11. It's certainly hard to understand why this wasn't at least attempted.

On a related note, I have often pondered why so many people, presumably none of them previously suicidal, decided to plunge willingly to their deaths from the Twin Towers on that awful day. Most official accounts reported that at least *two hundred* people jumped out of the World Trade Center on 9/11. That amounts to some 7 to 8 percent of all those in the buildings. Wouldn't they have clung to the hope that perhaps helicopters *would* be sent to extinguish the fires, if not initiate rescue procedures? Was there any reason for them to logically expect the entire massive structure to collapse? It was reported that *ninety* bodies of those who jumped were found intact afterward. That just seems to be an awfully large figure to me. Not to be ghoulish about it, but doesn't it seem unlikely that all those bodies would have remained intact, after falling from such tremendous heights?

Some of the more "extreme" Internet researchers analyzed the rather limited number of images of these 9/11 jumpers in detail and purported to find some disquieting anomalies in them. One photo analysis I was particularly impressed with scrutinized a falling body that appeared to be way too far from the building. It would seemingly be impossible for a physical body to catapult itself fifty feet or so out into space. In many of the pictures portraying people gathered in windows, who subsequently jumped, there is no fire visible around them. The networks stopped showing the falling bodies early on, and it's still a sensitive subject all around. *Esquire* magazine, as late as September 8, 2009, would quote the New York Medical Examiner's Office as saying, "We don't like to say they jumped. Nobody jumped. They were forced out, or blown out."

There are numerous questions about the official story of Flight 77 hitting the Pentagon as well. During CNN's nonstop coverage on the afternoon of September 11, 2001, reporter Jamie McIntyre declared, "From my close-up inspection, there is no evidence of a plane having crashed anywhere near the Pentagon." He went on to observe that there were no traces of wings, fuselage, or any other large part of the Boeing 757 to be seen. Needless to say, he would not be the last to wonder about that. Critics noticed that the opening in the Pentagon's wall, where the huge aircraft had supposedly entered, was far too small for a 757. There were no impact marks from the wings, and no trace of them left behind outside the structure, so where did the wings go? I tried emailing Jamie McIntyre about his initial report, but he never replied.

239

While the public could watch the planes hitting the WTC towers over and over again, on all the television networks, there were oddly no films, or even a single photo, of the Boeing 757 crashing into the Pentagon. With security cameras by that time becoming a standard feature inside and outside most large buildings, it was beyond belief that the heart of our national security apparatus would have failed to capture the plane on any of its multitude of cameras. We supposedly have the most powerful military industrial complex the world has ever known, but on 9/11, a plane was allowed to meander about in highly protected airspace for more than forty minutes, without being challenged by fighter jets, and then crashed into the epicenter of our defense system, without being captured on film?

The FBI moved quickly to confiscate two videotapes that most definitely did exist—one from the Doubletree Hotel and another from a Citgo gas station located across the street from the Pentagon. The Citgo tape would be belatedly released in September 2006, due to a Freedom of Information Act (FOIA) request and lawsuit from Judicial Watch, but it seemed to have missed the actual crash. A month later, due to the same lawsuit, the video from the Doubletree Hotel was released as well, but although it showed an explosion, again it somehow missed capturing the plane. In May 2006, the Pentagon had released some unimpressive footage of the strike, which didn't show *what* had hit the building but captured a giant fireball afterward. The mainstream press reacted as if the plane was indeed shown on the footage, which it most definitely was not. At this point, there is still no extant film of the plane, missile, or whatever it was that struck the Pentagon on 9/11. There is also the question of the mysterious, never-explained "exit hole" in the Pentagon's inner ring, some 310 feet away from the point of impact. Since everything supposedly disintegrated after the crash, what was left to exit?

Dr. Thomas Olmstead, a psychiatrist and ex-naval officer from New Orleans, examined the medical evidence from the Pentagon crash and wrote an explosive article about it: "Autopsy: No Arabs on Flight 77." Olmstead filed FOIA requests for a passenger list from Flight 77, as well as a list of those who were autopsied afterward by the Armed Forces Institute of Pathologies. Olmstead reported, "So I figured that the government would want to quickly dispel any rumors. It seemed simple: produce the names of all the bodies identified by the AFIP and compare it with the publicized list of passengers. . . . Fourteen months later . . . I finally get the list. Believe me that they weren't a bit happy to give it up. . . . No Arabs wound up on the morgue slab; however, three additional people not listed by American Airlines sneaked in. I have seen no explanation for these extras. I did give American the opportunity to 'revise' their original list, but they have not responded. . . . "

Olmstead was quite critical of the fact that the AFIP had claimed to be able to identify nearly all bodies by November 16, 2001, and wondered how they were able to distinguish the bodies of hijackers from victims. The AFIP suggested there were sixty-four passengers on Flight 77. American Airlines originally declared there were fifty-six passengers, but the list obtained by Olmstead recorded fifty-eight. There were no explanations for the discrepancies. Olmstead had previously exposed the sensational news that there were no Arabic names on the official Flight 77 passenger list. Where was Hani Hanjour, the alleged pilot who'd been unable to fly a plane well enough to rent one just a few weeks before 9/11? Olmstead studied the backgrounds of those on the official passenger list, and delineated their connections to the defense and intelligence industries. Further research produced a more startling fact; none of the purported nineteen hijackers appear on the passenger flight lists for any of the airliners in question.

The questions are endless. Why were there so few passengers on each of the four hijacked airliners? The four planes could have seated a total of 762 people, but the official lists reported by CNN (although the numbers do vary) showed only 229 passengers, which amounts to an incredibly low 30 percent of capacity. The airlines regularly shift passengers going to the same destination to other flights if the number on board is too low to justify the flight. Another question: How did the authorities obtain any DNA from passengers on Flight 77 when they explained the absence of wreckage by declaring the intense heat from the Pentagon crash vaporized the engines and fuselage? It would take temperatures of 11,000 degrees Fahrenheit to vaporize aluminum, while human DNA is destroyed at only a few hundred degrees. How were all but one of the passengers on Flight 77 identified by DNA, when there were no traces of even the largest parts of the aircraft? How did a plane that was 125 feet wide and 155 feet long fit into a hole that was only sixty feet across (at the Pentagon)?

Was it a mere slip of the tongue when Secretary of Defense Donald Rumsfeld said a missile had hit the Pentagon? Why does the time stamp on the video footage from the Pentagon, finally released in 2006, say September 12, 2001? Why does the Bureau of Traffic Statistics (BTS) database show no departure times for two of the flights on 9/11, Flights 11 and 77? Airports are notoriously meticulous about recording BTS data for every flight. Are there really indications that Flight 93 out of Newark was boarded twice? Why are the airport surveillance tapes for the four doomed flights strangely unavailable? Why was there only a single person—an amateur photographer—in the Twin Towers that day who took any pictures? Is it feasible that no one else—including any professionals—thought that this might be worth capturing on film?

Some researchers went deeper into the rabbit hole, looking closely at the passengers themselves. What are we to make of the heart-wrenching story, exploited for maximum emotional impact by the mainstream media, about lifelong friends Ruth McCourt and Paige Hackel? Supposedly they had always flown together, but they were unable to get tickets on the same flight on 9/11, so they ended up with one going on Flight 11 and the other on Flight 175. How could this be possible, when both flights were filled with empty seats? Their tale was recounted in the September 12, 2001, edition of *USA Today*. Some have wondered how the details were discovered and published so quickly. There were other fantastic elements to this story; five years after the tragedy, in September 2006, Ruth McCourt's husband, David, was given his wife's wedding ring by the New York City Police. It somehow had survived the inferno that obliterated nearly everything. As if this "miracle" wasn't enough, it was casually mentioned, as if this was an everyday occurrence, that Ruth and David had been married in 1994 at the *Vatican*.

What about Waleed Ishkandar, reported as a passenger on Flight 11 in newspaper accounts and Internet memorials? Ishkandar was not listed as a passenger on the original manifest or the official list provided by American Airlines. And what about the curious fact that so few relatives of those lost on the crashed flights stepped forward to collect the significant amount of money offered by the 9-11 Victims Compensation Fund? Critics examined the 9-11 Compensation Fund list and discovered that only eleven relatives from the 266 collective passengers had applied for compensation. Human nature being what it is, it's simply not believable that family members would bypass financial compensation like that. Researchers also found that only about a quarter of the victims from that day were in the Social Security Death Index, even though they boast an accuracy rate of 83 percent.

Most bizarre of all, some on the Internet began to scrutinize the available photos of the three thousand-plus victims of 9/11. There are scores of examples of really awful, blurry photographs—some in black and white—that were presumably given to the media by grieving family members to display in remembrance of their lost loved ones. I was impressed with the argument that this made no sense; wouldn't anyone want their deceased relative to be represented by a quality picture? In fact, wouldn't we all want to pick out the best one we could find? While some had already suggested the planes that hit the WTC were drones, or even something more esoteric, a few began postulating that at least some of the passengers were contrived, and not real human beings. Some on Internet forums examined the photo provided by the family of American Airlines Flight 11 Captain John Ogonowski, for instance, and quite reasonably wondered why they would choose an outdated picture of him dressed in his First Officer uniform. Certainly, he would have been proudly photographed at some point after being promoted to captain. Letsrollforums.com, in particular, had extensive threads devoted to this subject, which made the outlandish but intriguing claim that the entire Ogonowski family was either in on the hoax or didn't exist. I have to admit that even I wondered at the odd name of one passenger, Yeshavant Moreshewar Tembe, and the fact one can so easily find the message YES MORE WAR within it.

There was at least one certified phony in that rabbit hole. Tania Head claimed to have been a survivor of the attacks on September 11, 2001, and became president of the World Trade Center Survivors' Network. Her harrowing tale of escaping from the seventy-eighth floor of the South Tower, where she was said to have been one of only nineteen people above the point of impact to survive, captivated Americans and earned her a highly publicized kiss from Mayor Rudy Giuliani. In 2007, her story was exposed as fraudulent in a front-page story in the *New York Times* and throughout the mainstream media. Her real name was Alicia Esteve Head, and she had not even been near the Twin Towers on 9/11 (she had actually been in Spain and belonged to one of Barcelona's wealthiest families). She had, in fact, not even visited the United States until 2003. After her hoax was revealed, Head vanished from sight, only to reappear in 2010 at a White Plains, New York, memorial, this time assuming the name of Ester DiNardo, mother of a supposed victim.

The phone calls allegedly made from the hijacked planes, from distraught passengers describing their nightmarish situation, were analyzed by critics early on. While some calls were supposedly made with air phones installed on the planes, others were said to have come from the user's personal cell phone. Was it even possible, in 2001, to make such phone calls? In 2004, American Airlines announced the development of a new wireless technology "which will at some future date allow airline passengers using their cell phones to contact family and friends from a commercial aircraft. . . . Travelers could be talking on their personal cell phones as early as 2006."

The best available information would indicate that cell phone calls were just not possible in September 2001, once an airplane reached a certain altitude. The first phone call from Flight 175 came at 8:52 a.m., when the plane would have been at cruising altitude (thirty-one thousand feet), far too high to permit cell phone transmissions (the cutoff was generally said to be eight thousand feet). Another call a moment later reiterated the same dire information; someone had been stabbed and both pilots killed. One wonders, of course, how the hijackers could have killed anyone with their box cutters and plastic knives. At 9:00 a.m., passenger Peter Hanson, who'd made the first 8:52 a.m. call, phoned his dad Lee again. He seemed strangely resigned to being killed and even mentioned, "I think they intend to go to Chicago or someplace and fly into a building."

The Flight 77 phone calls began well after the plane had reached cruising altitude. At some point between 9:16 and 9:26 a.m., Barbara Olson called her husband, Solicitor General Ted Olson. FBI reports on the alleged phone calls from the hijacked planes, released for the 2006 trial of Zacarias Moussaoui, the so-called "twentieth hijacker," recorded that Barbara Olson's only call was "unconnected" and lasted "0 seconds." Ted Olson would claim that his wife called two times from the plane, and he reportedly told the FBI he didn't know if she was using a cell phone or an air phone. A year later, mainstream sources like CNN were still reporting Barbara Olson had used a cell phone. Olson spoke of hijackers armed with knives and box cutters and said they'd all been herded to the back of the plane. She also told her husband that nobody seemed in charge and asked what she should tell the pilot to do.

Doesn't that sound a bit odd? Pilots are normally confident people; why would she think her bureaucrat husband could instruct him on what to do? If Captain Burlingame hadn't been killed (with box cutters or plastic knives, somehow), why would he even permit himself to be herded to the back of the plane? For the record, American Airlines apparently did not have functioning on-flight telephones in September 2001. American Airlines would later tell Pilots for 9/11 Truth, "That is correct; we do not have phones on our Boeing 757. The passengers on flight 77 used their own personal cellular phones to make out calls during the terrorist attack."

Ted Olson understood how the game was played. Olson told the Supreme Court on March 20, 2002, as he defended the government in a lawsuit lodged by a widow who alleged a CIA informant had been involved in her Guatemalan leader husband's torture and murder, "It is easy to imagine an infinite number of situations . . . where government officials might quite legitimately have reasons to give false information out. It's an unfortunate reality that the issuance of incomplete information and even misinformation by government may sometimes be perceived as necessary to protect vital interests."

One of the oddest, most scrutinized of the alleged 9/11 phone conversations is the one that began with the line "Mom, this is your son Mark Bingham" and included the curious remark "You believe me, don't you?" Bingham, on board Flight 93, contacted his mother, Alice Hoglan (variously spelled as Hoagland), at his Uncle Vaughn Hoglan's house. Strangely, he knew she was there, but she claimed not to know he was flying that day. His mother initially thought him using his entire name was suspicious, but then later claimed that was how he always introduced himself to her. Mrs. Hoglan participated in a rather bizarre interview with ABC's Peter Jennings, on September 11, during which she appeared to be *laughing*.

Mark Bingham was supposedly the owner of the Bingham Group, and even that has been analyzed on Internet forums, where intriguing questions about the company have been raised. Mark Bingham, who was reported to be gay, was a huge strapping fellow—a rugby player who had run with the bulls in Pamplona. This powerful, young gay man had struck a blow for political correctness and shattered stereotypes by participating in the heroic efforts to bring down Flight 93. Bingham was one of those purported to have overwhelmed the hijackers, along with Todd Beamer and others. Beamer's thirteen-minute phone call to Lisa Jefferson, customer service supervisor at GTE Airfone's Chicago call center, was also suspicious. At one point, he refused Jefferson's request to put him through to his wife. In that situation, who would prefer to ramble on to a complete stranger instead of their spouse?

Flight 93 was allowed to fly freely for nearly two hours after the first airliner was known to have been hijacked. The best available evidence suggests that the government did react once that day, when it shot down Flight 93. According to reports, an incredible twenty-three out of the forty-four passengers on board Flight 93 were not supposed to be on the flight that day. But there is some doubt that Flight 93 ever crashed, or was shot down. Local Cleveland news reports on September 11, 2001, quoted Mayor Michael R. White as saying a Boeing 767 out of Boston had made an emergency landing at Cleveland Hopkins International Airport, due to concerns it may have had a bomb on board. United identified it as Flight 93, and Mayor White went on to report that the airliner had been evacuated and moved to a secure area in the airport. The local news based the story on an Associated Press dispatch. Subsequently, it would be claimed that these reports were in error, and that the plane in question was really Delta Flight 1989.

An anonymous female whistle-blower, who was stationed at Fort Meade, would come forward and claim she personally heard military commanders give the orders to shoot down Flight 93. She said she heard no talk of hijackers, and the plane was shot down strictly because they'd lost all contact with it and the protocol was to intercept and destroy. The alleged crash site in Shanksville, Pennsylvania, was exceedingly weird; small pieces of wreckage strewn for miles all around, with a huge crater in the midst of it. The crater, like the hole in the Pentagon, seemed too small for the large aircraft.

Officially, most of the plane was said to have been imbedded underground, where the black boxes were supposedly found. The FBI would claim it had recovered 95 percent of the plane by September 24, but the public never saw pictures of it. Several witnesses would report seeing a second plane, flying low and erratically in the vicinity of the alleged location of the crash. Wallace Miller, coroner of Somerset County, issued some provocative comments about the crash scene: ". . . Usually you see much debris, wreckage, and much noise and commotion. This crash was different. There was no wreckage, no bodies, and no noise. . . . It appeared as though there were no passengers or crew on this plane." He also declared, "It was as if the plane had stopped and let the passengers off before it crashed." (*Pittsburgh Post-Gazette*, October 15, 2001).

As always, there were the associated unnatural deaths afterward. Prasanna Kalahasthi, the twenty-five-year-old wife of alleged Flight 11 passenger Pendyala Vamsikrishna, killed herself in her Los Angeles apartment a month after 9/11 (October 19, 2001). Vamsikrishna was one of those passengers who was not listed on the original Flight 11 manifest, and only appeared later on a couple of contradictory unofficial lists. Kenny Johannemann was a part-time janitor working in the North Tower on 9/11 who became a hero when he pulled a burning man from the building. He also reported hearing explosions in both towers. Johannemann shot and killed himself at age forty-three, on August 31, 2008, twelve days before the seventh anniversary of the day that had allegedly deeply depressed him and caused him to drink heavily.

Barry Jennings was the deputy director of the Emergency Services Department of the New York City Housing Authority. Jennings claimed to have seen and heard explosions in Building 7 before the twin towers fell on 9/11, Jennings shared his experience with a reporter on the day of the tragedy, and he gave an interview to researcher Dylan Avery (director of the sensational *Loose Change* film) in 2007. After the interview, he was threatened with the loss of his job, and he requested it not be included on the new *Loose Change Final Cut*. When Jennings went on to refute what he'd told Avery on the BBC's *Third Tower*, Avery felt obligated to release the full interview in response. A month after the BBC interview, Jennings died on August 19, 2008, age fifty-three, and the circumstances surrounding his death remain curiously unclear. Avery hired a private detective to look into Jennings's death, but she quit the investigation and told him, "Never contact me again." Avery visited Jennings's family's home and found it vacant and for sale. I asked Dylan Avery on Facebook if there were any updates on the Jennings story, but his only reply was a cryptic, "Find his kid and talk to him."

Explosives expert Danny Jowenko was vocal about his fervent belief that Building 7 had been brought down by demolition. Jowenko was killed in a car accident on July 16, 2011. Beverly Eckert, who lost her husband on 9/11, knew the official story was bogus and became a member of the Family Steering Committee for the 9/11 Independent Commission. She wrote a piece for *Salon* called "My Silence Cannot Be Bought." Eckert was among those who met with President Barack Obama in the White House on February 6, 2009, to discuss the fight against terrorism. Incredibly, one week later, Eckert died in a plane crash. David Wherley, a commander working at Andrews Air Force base on 9/11, was killed in a Metro train crash on June 22, 2009.

Christopher Landis, an employee with the Virginia Department of Transportation and one of those interviewed by the makers of the film *The Pentacon*, committed suicide on November 16, 2006. As the Citizen Investigation Team noted on their website: "In an extremely strange and suspicious twist that we can only pray is a coincidence, about a week after we had obtained the CITGO witnesses testimony on film, Christopher Landis committed suicide. . . . So this happened about 2.5 months after we met him and he gave us the images. . . . Coincidence? We can only hope so but he was a very young man with 4 young children (2 boys and 2 girls) and a great job. We definitely thought he was noticeably nervous when we talked with him."

New York City firefighter Salvatore Princiotta was murdered on May 23, 2007. Michael Tuohey, a US Air employee who checked in alleged hijacker Mohammed Atta on 9/11, mentioned during a September 11, 2005, appearance on Oprah Winfrey's show that the American Airlines ticket agent who checked in Atta at the Boston airport had committed suicide. No name or date was provided. Oprah's producer supposedly received a message from the anonymous woman's husband, who wanted Tuohey to understand it wasn't his fault. Tuohey never mentioned this subject in any of the other stories about him in the press, and no further information about it is available on the Internet.

Phillip Marshall, a former airline pilot who became a notable 9/11 "truther," and wrote the books *False Flag 9/11* and *The Big Bamboozle: 9/11 and the War on Terror*, allegedly shot and killed his two teenage children and then turned the gun on himself on February 6, 2013. For good measure, he also shot the family dog. According to the *Santa Barbara View*, Marshall had expressed some paranoia during the editing and pre-marketing process prior to his book's publication. (*Daily Mail UK*, February 7, 2013).

There were at least ten phone calls reported coming from Flight 93, the first of which came shortly after 9:32 a.m., four minutes after the plane was reported to have reached an altitude of thirty-five thousand feet. From these passengers, we learned that, as on the other flights, someone had been stabbed, and possibly the captain and first officer had been killed. One caller suggested that the hijackers might have "a gun." Another passenger saw no trace of guns, and no remnants of weapons were found at the crash scene in Pennsylvania. What, then, did they use to stab and kill people? Plastic knives? The 9/11 Commission Report related that one of the hijackers could be heard yelling, in Hollywoodish fashion, "Allah is the greatest!" on the cockpit voice recorder as the plane was going down. Authorities had been alerted earlier when passenger Edward Felt contacted an "emergency official," Glenn Cramer, in Pennsylvania. How he got Cramer's number and managed to reach him is unknown. A year later, the *Daily Mirror* would report that Cramer was subsequently gagged by the FBI.

Scientific American columnist A. K. Dewdney conducted experiments in 2003 that showed that most, if not all, of the reported cell phone calls from the hijacked airliners would have been impossible. At even twenty thousand feet of altitude, he found, the chance that one cell phone call would succeed was one in a hundred; the chance of two such calls succeeding was less than one in ten thousand. In response to the independent research on the phone calls, the FBI would later attempt to claim that all but two of the calls had been made with air phones. However, there were numerous references from those who'd received the calls to "cell phones" specifically, and there was testimony from recipients about recognizing their loved ones' cell phone number on their caller IDs.

The 9/11 Commission Report did little to quell the reservations critics had about the official version of events. One of the Commission's members, Senator Max Cleland, resigned in December 2003 and told the *Boston Globe* (November 13, 2003), "If this decision stands [to limit 9/11 Commission access to White House documents], I, as a member of the commission, cannot look any American in the eye, especially family members of victims, and say the commission had full access. This investigation is now compromised." He would go on to label the Commission's performance "a national scandal."

Former Senator Mike Gravel called for a new investigation into 9/11 in a speech to the United Nations on September 11, 2007. He noted that the 9/11 Commission did not have subpoena power, and demanded that George

W. Bush be forced to testify alone. Three years later, he would refer to the 9/11 Commission developing "a storyline of what happened to be fed to the American people. . . ." On August 28, 2005, Representative Curt Weldon, during an appearance on Fox News, asked, "What's the 9/11 Commission got to hide?" Scott Ritter, chief weapons inspector for the United Nations Special Commission in Iraq, stated, "I, like the others, am frustrated by the 9/11 Commission Report. . . ."

Barbara Honegger, mentioned earlier as the author of a book on the October Surprise scandal and a former Reagan administration official, expressed the following bold doubts about the official story: "The US military, not al Qaeda, had the sustained access weeks before 9/11 to also plant controlled demolition charges throughout the superstructures of WTC1 and WTC2, and in WTC7, which brought down all three buildings on 9/11. A US military plane, not one piloted by al Qaeda, performed the highly skilled, high-speed 270-degree dive toward the Pentagon. . . ."

FBI Director Robert Mueller would tell CNN on September 20, 2002, that there was "no legal proof to prove the identities of the suicidal hijackers." As early as September 16, 2001, an article ran in the *Washington Post* that questioned the identities of the hijackers. "Two of 19 suspects named by the FBI, Saeed Alghamdi and Ahmed Alghamdi, have the same names as men listed at a housing facility for foreign military trainees at Pensacola," the paper reported. "Two others, Hamza Alghamdi and Ahmed Alnami, have names similar to individuals listed in public records as using the same address inside the base. In addition, a man named Saeed Alghamdi graduated from the Defense Language Institute at Lackland Air Force Base in San Antonio, while men with the same names as two other hijackers, Mohamed Atta and Abdulaziz Alomari, appear as graduates of the US International Officers School at Maxwell Air Force Base, Ala., and the Aerospace Medical School at Brooks Air Force Base in San Antonio, respectively." The BBC reported on September 23, 2001, in the story "Hijack 'Suspects' Alive and Well," that "*Asharq Al Awsat* newspaper, a London-based Arabic daily, says it has interviewed Saeed Alghamdi. He was listed by the FBI as a hijacker in the United flight that crashed in Pennsylvania . . . there are suggestions that another suspect, Khalid Al Midhar, may also be alive." They also noted, "Another of the men named by the FBI as a hijacker in the suicide attacks on Washington and New York has turned up alive and well."

The *Arizona Daily Star*, on September 28, 2001, declared, "An FBI notice to banks on Sept. 19 raised the possibility that Almihdhar might still be alive without speculating or explaining how that could be possible." CNN repeated this story on the same day. The *Boston Globe*, on September 25, 2001, reported, "Although a Brooklyn apartment lease from 1995–1996 bears Ziad Jarrah's name—and landlords there have identified his photograph—his family insists he was in Beirut at the time." Saeed Al-Ghamdi, Mohand Al-Shehri, Abdul Aziz Al-Omari, and Salem Al-Hazmi "are not dead and had nothing to do with the heinous terror attacks in New York and Washington," the Saudi Arabian Embassy told the *Orlando Sentinel*. The *Daily Trust*, on September 24, 2001, reported, in reference to suspected hijacker Walid Al-Shehri, "His photograph was released by the FBI, and has been shown in newspapers and on television around the world. That same Mr. Al-Shehri has turned up in Morocco, proving clearly that he was not a member of the suicide attack."

It seems quite clear that there are reasonable doubts about the identities of the men who allegedly hijacked four planes on September 11, 2001. There are strong indications that at least some of them are alive and well. It is very hard to ignore the historical fact that no steel-frame building had ever collapsed from fire prior to 9/11, and none have since. No evidence has been presented that the temperature inside the Word Trade Centers ever came close to being hot enough to melt steel. The analysis done by independent researchers—showing conclusively that the hole in the Pentagon wall, left by whatever crashed into it, was much smaller than a Boeing 757—cannot be refuted. The wings are the key here; if they hit the building, they left no mark, and if they were sheared off upon impact, they vanished into thin air.

Even without going deep down the rabbit hole and confronting frightening details about the passengers that simply don't add up, there is enough implausibility in the official account of events to make the most trusting, apolitical Americans skeptical. In light of all the unanswered questions about what really happened on September 11, 2001, it is impossible to avoid subscribing to those "outrageous conspiracy theories" President George W. Bush angrily promised not to tolerate.

CHAPTER TEN

MORE DUBYA

"I have a different vision of leadership. A leadership is someone who brings people together."

—George W. Bush

WAR AGAINST AL-QAEDA

"The truth is, there is no Islamic army or terrorist group called Al Qaida. And any informed intelligence officer knows this. But there is a propaganda campaign to make the public believe in the presence of an identified entity representing the 'devil' only in order to drive the TV watcher to accept a unified international leadership for a war against terrorism. The country behind this propaganda is the US. . . ."

—French Former Intelligence Officer Pierre-Henri Bunel

Most people probably don't know that "Al-Qaeda" roughly translates to "the toilet" in Arabic. As has been pointed out by critical thinkers, if you were forming any kind of group, would you give it such a demeaning name? During a 2011 interview with National Public Radio, author and *New York Times* reporter Thom Shanker admitted, "What the American military intelligence can do is forge the watermarks or certification of official al-Qaida postings. . . . American cyber technology is so advanced that they can have a near perfect re-creation of an al-Qaida message—and what they're doing from time to time is going on jihadi websites and posting conflicting and contradictory orders, statements that raise doubt about who the jihadis should follow and who is really in charge. . . . We've been told they've had some great success at that."

In a June 25, 2010, *Washington Post* article, the CIA acknowledged officially discussing the creation of a video of a fake Saddam Hussein having sex with a teenage boy in order to discredit him in the eyes of the Iraqi people. Evidently, the Agency did create a video of a fake Osama Bin Laden drinking liquor around a campfire with his cronies, bragging about their conquests of young boys. The article quoted an anonymous former CIA officer "chuckling" at the memory, and declaring that the actors used in the video were drawn from "some of us darker-skinned employees." These ridiculous clandestine ideas brought to mind the childish efforts to assassinate Fidel Castro forty years earlier.

The most curious senior official in Al-Qaeda is one Adam Gadahn. The FBI lists several Arabic-sounding aliases for Gadahn, but his real name is Adam Pearlman. Pearlman is the grandson of Carl Pearlman, a prominent urologist who also served on the board of directors for the Anti-Defamation League. Needless to say, it is difficult to believe that an American Jew could rise to such prominence in an organization supposedly devoted to the destruction of Israel. Another American Jew, Joseph Cohen, runs the radical website RevolutionMuslim.com, under the alias Yousef al-Khattab. The "islamo-fascist" who threatened the creators of the television show *South Park* using this same website was in reality an American named Zachary Adam Chesser.

On May 10, 2012, ABC News ran a report on a British intelligence mole who had infiltrated a recent Al-Qaeda bomb plot. At about the same time, reports surfaced admitting that the second so-called "underwear" bomber was actually an agent working for Saudi Intelligence and the CIA. (*New York Times*, May 8, 2012). American officials were said to be angry over the disclosure, since this might "discourage foreign intelligence services from cooperating with the United States." Have we become so jaded, so dumbed down as a people, that we can't understand how significant it is to have our leaders hire a "terrorist" to threaten such a horrendous act, and portray him as a real member of a shadowy group sworn to destroy us?

Former British House of Commons leader Robin Cook resigned in protest after the 2003 invasion of Iraq. In an article published in the July 8, 2005, *London Guardian*, Cook wrote, "Al Qaida, literally 'the database,' was originally the computer file of the thousands of mujahideen who were recruited and trained with help from the CIA to defeat the Russians." Cook had been a thorn in the side of the establishment for years; in March 1998, when he was serving as British foreign secretary, he had angered Israeli

Prime Minister Benjamin Netanyahu by meeting with Palestinians. Very shortly after writing the *Guardian* article, on August 6, 2005, Cook, fifty-nine, was on vacation with his wife in Scottish Highlands. While walking down a steep mountain ridge, Cook fell to his death. It took two days to determine the cause of death, but at length it would officially be reported that he died from "hypertensive heart disease." No head injuries were reported at the autopsy, yet early news stories had spoken of a broken neck sustained in the fall. The police issued this curious statement after Cook's death: "As this would appear to be a medical matter, there is no further police involvement."

By establishing what Alex Jones and others refer to as "Al CIAeda," the conspirators who misrule us have the perfect "enemy." Al-Qaeda "cells" are everywhere and anywhere, but ultimately nowhere to be found. They are an opponent that is unknowable and prepared for the long haul in this perpetual "war on terror." After what American forces have done in Iraq and Afghanistan for over a decade, it is inconceivable that this "powerful" group of radical Muslims has not plotted to retaliate against what they call the "Great Satan." They were able to outwit an unprepared sleeping giant on September 11, 2001, but apparently they have been totally inept ever since. Still, we must be constantly on the lookout for these "terrorists" and be willing to give up what remains of our civil liberties in order to be "protected" from them.

DEAD AND MISSING SCIENTISTS

On November 16, 2001, Memphis, Tennessee, police found the car of Harvard professor Don Wiley, one of America's foremost infectious disease researchers, sitting on a bridge with a full tank of gas and the keys still in the ignition. There was no indication of any depression or troubles in Wiley's life; he was, in fact, supposed to meet his family at the airport that morning to embark on a scheduled vacation to Iceland. On November 27, the *New York Times* reported that the FBI, in their usual manner, had found no evidence of foul play. Wiley was a noted expert in virology and immunology, although the flagship paper of the establishment, in that same article, made certain to quote fellow Harvard professor Gregory Verdine as saying, "If bioterrorists were to abduct Don Wiley, they'd be very disappointed." In January, the medical examiner inexplicably labeled Wiley's death as "accidental." Wiley's disappearance was only the beginning of an unexplained mystery, however.

On November 12, a few days before Wiley vanished, Dr. Benito Que, a biologist who specialized in infectious disease research, was found dead outside his Miami Medical School laboratory. *The Miami Herald* reported,

"The word among his friends is that four men armed with a baseball bat attacked him at his car." On November 23, the story became international, as Dr. Vladimir Pasechnik, a former microbiologist for a Soviet biological weapons facility was found dead. *The Times* of London described his career:

"The defection to Britain in 1989 of Vladimir Pasechnik revealed to the West for the first time the colossal scale of the Soviet Union's clandestine biological warfare programme. His revelations about the scale of the Soviet Union's production of such biological agents as anthrax, plague, tularaemia and smallpox provided an inside account of one of the best kept secrets of the Cold War. After his defection he worked for ten years at the U.K. Department of Health's Centre for Applied Microbiology Research before forming his own company, Regma Biotechnics, to work on therapies for cancer, neurological diseases, tuberculosis and other infectious diseases. In the last few weeks of his life he had put his research on anthrax at the disposal of the Government, in the light of the threat from bioterrorism." Oddly, his death was belatedly announced in the United States by Dr. Christopher Davis of Virginia, who as a member of British intelligence had been the one who had debriefed Pasechnik at the time of his defection.

On December 10, 2001, Dr. Robert M. Schwartz was found murdered in Leesburg, Virginia. Schwartz was a well-known DNA researcher and had founded the Virginia Biotechnology Association. On December 12, the *Washington Post* reported: "A well-known biophysicist, who was one of the leading researchers on DNA sequencing analysis, was found slain in his rural Loudoun County home after coworkers became concerned when he didn't arrive at work as expected. Robert M. Schwartz, fifty-seven, a founding member of the Virginia Biotechnology Association, was found dead in the secluded fieldstone farmhouse southwest of Leesburg where he lived alone. Loudoun sheriff's officials said it appeared that Schwartz had been stabbed." In a theatrical touch, the weapon used on Schwartz was a sword, and an X had been carved into the back of his neck.

On December 14, Set Van Nguyen, forty-four, a Victoria, Australia, microbiologist, died in a freak lab accident when he entered a room where biological samples were stored and was unaware that deadly gas had escaped from the liquid nitrogen cooling system. In January 2001, the magazine *Nature* had published a story about two scientists at this same facility developing an extremely virulent form of mousepox, a cousin of smallpox.

Two more Russian microbiologists died in January 2002. Ivan Glebov was killed in a "bandit attack," and Alexi Brushlinkski was murdered in Moscow. On February 9, 2002, Pravda.ru reported that Victor Korshunov, head of the microbiology sub-facility at the Russian State Medical University, had been killed. He was found dead in the entrance of his home with a head injury. *Pravda* reported that Korshunov's research had probably resulted in either the invention of a vaccine to protect against biological weapons or a weapon itself.

On February 12, the *Eastern Daily Press* in Norwich, England, reported the previous day's death of Ian Langford, a senior researcher at the University of East Anglia. The story indicated, not surprisingly, that the police "were not treating the death as suspicious." Two clerks who worked at a store near Langford's home were quoted as saying he would come there daily to buy "a big bottle of vodka." The next day, *The Times* reported that Langford had been found wedged under a chair "at his blood-spattered and apparently ransacked home." A February 14 follow-up story from the *Eastern Daily Press* reported that police believed Langford died after suffering "one or more falls."

Microbiologist and AIDS researcher Tanya Holzmayer was shot and killed "while taking delivery of a pizza" on February 28, 2002, by her ex-colleague Guyang Huang, who then shot himself a while later. Huang was allegedly still bitter after being fired by Holzmayer the year before. Dr. David Wynn-Williams was struck by a car and killed while jogging on March 24, 2002. He was an astrobiologist who'd been researching the way microbes reacted to environmental extremes. Dr. Steven Mostow, one of the country's leading infectious disease and bioterrorism experts, was killed in a plane crash on March 25, 2002.

British biological weapons expert Dr. David Kelly died on July 18, 2003. His case received widespread attention in America, and conspiracy theorists quickly surmised that, despite the official verdict, he had not committed suicide. Kelly had spoken off the record about his skepticism that Iraq had "weapons of mass destruction," and he was questioned by England's Foreign Affairs Select Committee only two days before his untimely death. Kelly was visibly upset over his treatment by the Committee. Suspicion was only further fueled by the fact that the postmortem report, along with photos of the body and other evidence, were classified and locked from public view for seventy years, purportedly to "protect" Kelly's daughters.

In a related death, the *Daily Mail UK* reported, on April 21, 2012, about the equally mysterious end of Kelly's associate, weapons expert Dr. Richard Holmes. Holmes's body was discovered in a field just a few miles away from the Porton Down defense establishment in Wiltshire, England. The paper referred to Porton Down as one "of the Government's most sensitive and secretive military facilities" and that "the site has long been the focus of controversy." Holmes had told his wife he was going for a walk on April 11, but he never returned. Predictably, police stated that there were "no suspicious circumstances" and revealed that Dr. Holmes had "recently been under a great deal of stress."

There was an intriguing connection between three of the five American scientists who had died. Wiley, Schwartz, and Benito Que had all worked for medical research facilities that received grants from Howard Hughes Medical Institute (HHMI). HHMI provided funding for a large number of research programs, and had long been alleged to be involved in "black ops" biomedical research for the CIA and other intelligence organizations. Biowarfare investigator Patricia Dole, Ph.D., claimed that there was a history of people connected to HHMI being murdered. In 1994, Jose Trias had met with a friend in Houston, Texas, and was planning to go public with his personal knowledge of HHMI "front door" grants being diverted to "back door" black ops bioresearch. The next day, Trias and his wife were found dead in their Chevy Chase, Maryland, home. Chevy Chase is where HHMI is headquartered. Police described the killings as a professional hit. Tsunao Saitoh, who formerly worked at an HHMI-funded lab at Columbia University, was shot to death on May 7, 1996, while sitting in his car outside his home in La Jolla, California. Police also described this as a professional hit.

In early October 2001, reports appeared indicating that British scientists were planning to exhume the bodies of ten London victims of the 1918 type-A flu epidemic known as the Spanish Flu. An October 7 article in the *Independent* (UK) stated that they had been victims of "the world's most deadly virus." British scientists, according to the story, hoped to uncover the genetic makeup of the virus, thereby making it easier to combat. Professor John Oxford of London's Queen Mary's School of Medicine, the British government's "flu adviser," acknowledged that the exhumations and subsequent studies would have to be done with extreme caution so the virus was not unleashed, causing another epidemic. This was the exact work Vladimir Pasechnik had been involved in. Pasechnik died six weeks after the planned exhumations were announced. MSNBC aired a story on September 6 that made the Frankenstein-like British exhumation plans seem even more maniacal. MSNBC referred to an article that would be published the following day in the weekly magazine *Science*, which disclosed that the 1918 flu virus had recently been RNA sequenced, as researchers had traced down and obtained virus samples from archived lung tissue of WWI soldiers.

256

These slew of deaths, most of them quite unnatural, began to occur in the mist of the post-9/11 anthrax scare. Independent researchers would later report that the anthrax that killed several Americans had come from US military sources connected to CIA research. There were known egregious security violations, for instance, at the notorious Fort Detrick, Maryland, biowarfare facility. While smallpox had been eradicated by 1977, according to the World Health Organization, *USA Today* reported on October 17, 2001, that the US government was ordering 300 million doses of smallpox vaccine from a British manufacturer.

DynCorp, a huge company handling data processing for many federal agencies—including the CDC, the Department of Agriculture, several branches of the Department of Justice, the Food and Drug Administration (FDA), and the NIH—was awarded a $322 million contract on November 12, 2001, to develop, produce, test, and store FDA-licensed vaccines for use by the Defense Department.

Investigative reporter Kelly O'Meara of *Insight* magazine, mentioned earlier in connection with the TWA Flight 800 case, reported on a massive US military investigation into how DynCorp employees in Bosnia had participated in a widespread child sex slave ring. O'Meara reviewed government documents and interviewed Army investigators looking into the activities. Videos and other evidence of the crimes were said to be in the Army's possession. In a February 23, 2002, story, journalist Al Giordano of www.narconews.com reported that a class-action suit had been filed in Washington, D.C., by more than ten thousand Ecuadorian farmers and a labor union against DynCorp for its rampant spraying of herbicides that had destroyed food crops, weakened the ecosystem, and caused more than eleven hundred documented cases of illness. DynCorp Chairman Paul Lombardi responded by sending intimidating letters in an attempt to get the plaintiffs to withdraw their claims. As frequently happens in these overlapping conspiracies, DynCorp had direct connections to both the PROMIS software from the Inslaw scandal and Enron.

While one would assume that scientists would be among the least likely occupations to be prone to violent, unnatural deaths, in the 1980s more than two dozen scientific experts associated in some way with the "Star Wars" defense research died under mysterious circumstances. There were the usual array of unnatural demises: car crashes, disappearances, gunshot wounds, falls from high buildings. The lists are widely available on the Internet and provide for some frightening reading.

THE PAUL WELLSTONE PLANE CRASH

One of the Bush administration's strongest critics was Minnesota Senator Paul Wellstone. Shortly before his death, Wellstone met with Vice President Dick Cheney, who was trying to garner support for an all-out invasion of Iraq. Wellstone graphically described the tenor of this meeting, in a speech to war veterans shortly thereafter, when he said that Cheney had warned him: "If you vote against the war in Iraq, the Bush administration will do whatever is necessary to get you. There will be severe ramifications for you and the state of Minnesota." On October 25, 2002, Wellstone faced those "severe ramifications."

Wellstone was killed, along with his wife and daughter, when his plane crashed in northern Minnesota while en route to a funeral. Questions immediately arose about the nature of the crash, especially considering that Wellstone had been the Senate's leading progressive voice. The NTSB would blame pilot error for the crash. However, critics uncovered some troubling questions. They alleged that the FBI's recovery team actually left to investigate the crash before the plane even went down. Professor James Fetzer spent a great deal of time investigating the case, and he claimed that emergency workers were denied access to the plane, which was still burning hours after the crash. Conspiracy researcher Michael Ruppert interviewed two Democratic members of Congress, who told him they believed Wellstone had been murdered. One of them disclosed, "I don't think there's anyone on the Hill who doesn't suspect it." A story in the *Duluth News Tribune*, published a few days after the crash, mentioned that "for some still unexplained reason, the plane turned off course and crashed." Carol Carmody, the NTSB's acting chair, was quoted in the article as saying, "We find the whole turn curious."

Megen Williams lived near the Eveleth airport, and she told the *St. Paul Pioneer Press* (October 26, 2002) that she heard "a diving noise and then an explosion" as she was preparing to leave her home, which was located near the crash site, for work. Don Sipola, a former president of the Eveleth Virginia Municipal Airport Commission, believed that "something" caused Wellstone's plan to veer off course. "This was a real steep bank, not a nice, gentle don't-spill-the-coffee descent," Sipola said. "This is more like a space shuttle coming down. This was not a controlled descent into the ground." Wellstone's pilots had contacted the airport, had the landing strip in sight, and were only two miles away at the time of that last communication.

President Dubya Bush, whose father Bush the Elder had once called Wellstone a "chicken shit," issued a few typically bizarre comments in response to his death. He referred to the articulate, former political science professor as "a plain-spoken fellow" and expressed his "condolences for the loss of the Senate." *The Nation* had described how anxious the Bush administration was to "get rid of" Wellstone. "There are people in the White House who wake up each morning thinking about how to defeat Paul Wellstone," a senior Republican aide was quoted as saying in a May 2012 story.

Whatever really happened to Wellstone's plane, his death was decidedly unnatural and a convenient boon for the establishment.

INVASION AND OCCUPATION OF IRAQ AND AFGHANISTAN

The "terrorist" attacks on 9/11 led inexorably to the second invasion of Iraq on March 20, 2003. Although no evidence was ever produced that linked former US ally Saddam Hussein to 9/11, and the "weapons of mass destruction" Bush warned about were never discovered, those were the reasons given for the invasion and subsequent decade-long occupation. Shockingly, this "war" was not given a colorful name like America's other recent global interventions. Saddam Hussein proved to be quite a benevolent fellow, as he didn't use those "weapons of mass destruction," even when his country was under assault by the world's greatest superpower. As some of us noted at the time, what exactly was Hussein waiting for? What kind of situation would have had to exist for him to use these "weapons" he'd been hoarding?

Former First Lady Barbara Bush, mother of Dubya, issued a remarkable comment during an interview with ABC's Diane Sawyer on March 18, 2003, only a few hours before Dubya delivered his dramatic, televised ultimatum to Saddam Hussein to step down from power and leave Iraq, or face US military action. In response to Sawyer's question about whether or not the senior Bushes found themselves watching more television than normal in the wake of the impending invasion of Iraq, Barbara stated, ". . . But why should we hear about body bags, and deaths, and how many . . . I mean, it's not relevant. So, why should I waste my beautiful mind on something like that?"

The performance of the American mainstream media during this second Iraq "war" was even more embarrassing than their coverage of Operation Desert Storm. The term "embedded journalist" became familiar, as professional journalists donned combat fatigues and sometimes literally entered the trenches with US troops. Well-known NBC reporter David Bloom died while "embedded" in Iraq, one of fourteen journalists who lost their lives there in that year alone. Obviously, if establishment reporters were cheerleading the war from their comfortable studios, they were going to give new meaning to the term *enthusiastic* when living with US occupying forces.

The dramatic capture of Saddam Hussein, followed by a show trial and summary execution, illustrated the growing immorality of US leadership. Americans would become accustomed to this official policy of brazen disregard for the lives of other human beings, and there was little outrage years later when President Obama, with loud and boisterous support, gleefully boasted about killing Osama Bin Laden. As was touched upon earlier, as recently as the 1970s, Americans were shocked at the notion that our government would sponsor the assassination of even the most reprehensible foreign figures.

The occupation of Iraq was an illegal, unprincipled, embarrassing failure. But Iraq wasn't the only country America invaded. Afghanistan was supposedly the home of the notorious Osama Bin Laden, who'd been a friend to the CIA and the American government during the Afghani battle against the Soviets in the 1980s, and thus came under American occupation as well. There were still enough morally sensitive Americans left to be mortified by the photographs that began to appear in 2004 of American soldiers abusing prisoners at a facility called Abu Ghraib. We all saw US soldiers shoving fluorescent lightbulbs up the anuses of male prisoners, attaching electric devices to their testicles, and a pretty female who posed next to a dead Iraqi body, with a warm, proud smile on her face.

But she wasn't the only soldier who looked happy; indeed, it seemed that, judging by the photos, a great many US soldiers were enjoying the experience of humiliating the Iraqis. There were pictures of a naked pile of male Iraqis, forced to contort themselves into a pyramid, with another smiling female soldier in front of them. There was another of a lovely American woman holding a male Iraqi on a leash, and still others featuring a female pointing in derision at a naked Iraqi's genitals, an Iraqi male forced to wear women's underwear, and soldiers using snarling dogs to intimidate still more naked male Iraqis. It was enough to make anyone blanch at the "support the troops" mantra.

President Bush and Secretary of Defense Donald Rumsfeld immediately sought to portray the soldiers in the photographs as "rogue" elements, nothing more than a few "bad apples." There were other, less talked about videos of more American "bad apples" torturing dogs, beating a defenseless sheep to death with a baseball bat, and other patriotic niceties. There were rumors of additional photos and videos, worse than anything publicly seen, that were alluded to by Rumsfeld, who said, "If these are released to the public, obviously it's going to make things worse."

Noted investigative reporter Seymour Hersh alleged, in a story first published by the *New York Sun* in July 2004, that American soldiers had raped little boys in Abu Ghraib and that there were tape recordings of it. In a speech shortly thereafter to the American Civil Liberties Union (ACLU), Hersh reiterated these charges. Hersh told the ACLU audience, "The boys were sodomized with the cameras rolling. And the worst above all of that is the soundtrack of the boys shrieking that your government has. They are in total terror. It's going to come out."

In May 2009, in a belated response to a 2004 Freedom of Information lawsuit by the ACLU, President Obama was about to release long-suppressed photos of abuse from Abu Ghraib when he reversed the decision at the last minute, allegedly because of pressure from military officials in Iraq and Afghanistan, who told him the photos would "endanger US troops deployed there," according to the *Washington Post*. The real reason was said to be because the photos depicted US soldiers raping boys in front of their mothers. Human rights groups and international legal observers had previously charged that Rumsfeld and other American officials condoned the rape of Iraqi boys in order to humiliate their parents into providing information.

During a 2006 debate on the subject of torture, Bush advisor John Yoo, deputy assistant to Attorney General John Ashcroft, was asked if the president had the right to do anything to somebody, "including by crushing the testicles of the person's child, there is no law that can stop him." Yoo responded, "I think it depends on why the president thinks he needs to do that." Yoo reasoned that, because the president is the commander in chief, no law could restrict any actions he took in prosecuting a war. Yoo was offended that some would compare the present-day American leaders to Nazis, protesting, "I think that to equate Nazi Germany to the Bush administration is irresponsible." Such is the world of moral ambiguity our dying civilization has entered, at the dawn of the twenty-first century.

The United States also came under critical scrutiny for the shameful treatment of prisoners at the US naval base Guantanamo Bay in Cuba. The Center for Constitutional Rights documented the abuses in a 2006 report. The indefinite detentions, and the absence of any due process of law for those sent to Guantanamo Bay, deeply troubled the few civil libertarians left in America. There was a great deal of doubt whether many, if any, of the prisoners were actually guilty of anything other than having Muslim names. As Brigadier General Martin Lucenti, deputy commander of the detention center, admitted, "Most of these guys weren't fighting. They were running." That didn't stop American officials from cavalierly "connecting" them to

Al-Qaeda or the Taliban in Afghanistan. Both former and present prisoners at Guantanamo Bay alleged they were systematically abused there.

For the first time in our nation's history, American officials responded to this criticism by defending the use of torture. The US government utilized the term "enemy combatants" to great effect, and claimed persons designated as such fell outside the traditional protections accorded individuals in US military custody. "Waterboarding," formerly known as "Chinese water torture" in the politically incorrect past, was an especially offensive form of torture. Vice President Dick Cheney and other leading neoconservatives defended it passionately, as did the so-called "liberal" *Washington Post*, which ran seemingly government-approved articles such as "How a Detainee Became an Asset," which appeared in the August 29, 2009, edition of the newspaper.

The CIA, in internal memos, steadfastly defended the use of controversial interrogation techniques that every previous generation of Americans would have labeled as torture and been horrified by. Several Republicans supported the use of torture, including Representative Allen West, who pointed out, "In the movie *G.I. Jane*, Demi Moore was waterboarded." Prominent Republican politicians Herman Cain and Michelle Bachmann publicly declared their support of waterboarding. In a December 21, 2005, column, wacky sensationalist right winger Ann Coulter wrote, "The government should be spying on all Arabs, engaging in torture as a televised spectator sport, dropping daisy cutters wantonly throughout the Middle East and sending liberals to Guantanamo." In a June 2, 2010, speech, former president George W. Bush defiantly declared, regarding the waterboarding of "terrorists," "I'd do it again to save lives." He also reiterated America's new morality regarding the assassination of foreign leaders by stating, "Getting rid of Saddam Hussein was the right thing to do. . . ."

In 2010, Wikileaks published nearly four hundred thousand secret war documents that revealed an extensive, shameful pattern of atrocities by US forces in Iraq. There were descriptions of bound, gagged, and blindfolded victims being whipped and sexually molested or raped. There was more of the familiar torture, with victims being burned with cigarettes, acid, and boiling water. The documents detailed previously unreported killings of civilians by private contractors such as Blackwater, as well as massacres of unarmed men, women, and children by US troops. One Apache helicopter crew, already notorious for a previously leaked video of them murdering civilians on the ground, was revealed to have also killed insurgents who were surrendering. The documents contained numerous accusations of US troops assaulting detainees, particularly marines; one soldier was described as choking a detainee and then pointing an unloaded gun at his stomach and pulling the trigger. Of particular interest was a 2004 "fragmentary order" that instructed Coalition troops not to investigate any alleged breach of the laws of armed conflict.

Mehmet Elkatmi, head of the Turkish Parliament's human rights commission, blasted US conduct in Iraq: "Never in human history have such genocide and cruelty been witnessed. Such a genocide was never seen in the time of the pharaohs nor of Hitler nor of Mussolini."

On March 4, 2007, US Private Joshua Key told the CBC (Canadian Broadcasting Corporation) that US soldiers had played soccer with the decapitated heads of Iraqi soldiers. An anonymous US soldier bragged, "While in Iraq we had a sport of killing dogs . . . it's pretty funny." Six American soldiers were charged with gang raping a fourteen-year-old Iraqi girl, then murdering her, her five-year-old sister, and their parents. Four other soldiers were accused of killing blindfolded Iraqi detainees for sport.

US troops used white phosphorus, one of the incendiaries banned by the United Nations, on the civilian population of Fallujah (killing two-thirds of the people there) as well as mustard gas and nerve gas. US forces opened fire on a vehicle in which Italian journalist Giuliana Sgrena, who'd been highly critical of US misconduct in Iraq, was riding. Sgrena survived, but Italian intelligence agent Nicola Calipari was killed. Sgrena openly charged the United States with knowingly firing on their convoy. American forces evidently were successful in getting rid of ITV news team members, who were assassinated. The prestigious medical journal *Lancet* estimated that the United States had killed more than one hundred thousand civilians in Iraq, most of them children. Americans bombed hospitals, mosques, and the water treatment plant in Basra.

In Afghanistan, US conduct was hardly better. There were the ugly photos of soldiers urinating on dead Afghani resistance fighters. Soldiers burned copies of the Quran. In response to visible evidence left behind on the bodies of Afghani children, General David Petraeus absurdly claimed that Afghan adults had "deliberately burnt" their children's arms and legs to make the US assault look bad. At least fifty women and children were killed in that particular attack by Apache helicopters. In 2009, US forces conducted a night raid on the residence of Brigadier Officer Awal Khan, who was away from home, killing his entire family, including his two teenage children and his infant son. That same year, US troops, purporting to be attacking a bomb factory, barged into a home where eight youths, aged eleven to eighteen, were asleep. They handcuffed the youngsters and summarily executed them.

Five US soldiers were charged with premeditated murder after staging killings to make it appear like they were defending themselves from Taliban attacks. Other soldiers were accused of removing body parts of Afghanis and keeping them as grisly "trophies." Afghan President Hamid Karzai begged the United States, "with honor and humbleness . . . to stop its operations on our soil." The photos and testimony from Afghanistan mirrored that of the American atrocities in Iraq, and in the prisons of Abu Ghraib and Guantanamo Bay. There was a clear pattern of barbaric behavior, and there was little about it that decent, upstanding Americans should "support."

The Jessica Lynch story bears special mention here. On March 23, 2003, the convoy carrying US Army Private Jessica Lynch became separated from their unit and wound up lost, coming under Iraqi attack thereafter. On April 1, 2003, the American people were inundated with mainstream press accounts of her dramatic rescue, during a daring night raid on Saddam Hospital. Lynch was initially referred to as a "prisoner of war," and on the day of the first reports of her rescue, the *New York Times* was stating that she "had been shot multiple times." Stories like the one that appeared in the April 2 *Washington Post* stressed how Lynch had "fought fiercely" and was determined not "to be taken alive." These accounts portrayed a Rambo-style shootout, with young Jessica Lynch in the middle of it, with some using this politically correct imagery as evidence that women belonged in the front lines.

The official fairy tale, however, began to dissipate quickly. By April 15, the *Washington Post* was questioning its own earlier account. On May 15, the *Guardian* (UK) deconstructed the original story completely, calling it "one of the most stunning pieces of news management yet conceived." On June 17, the *Washington Post* admitted that its previous reporting had been in error; Lynch had not been stabbed or shot, she had not become engaged in a gun battle and killed Iraqis, and Saddam Hospital had in fact been unguarded when US forces "raided" it. The real story would emerge when Lynch testified before Congress on April 24, 2007, and confessed that she never even fired a shot, because her rifle jammed, and she was knocked unconscious when her vehicle crashed. The convoy was in the position it was due to a series of wrong turns. Lynch was a victim herself, of the Pentagon's efforts to spin positive coverage of the Iraqi war. She told Diane Sawyer in an interview, "They used me to symbolize all this stuff. It's wrong."

Just as misleading were the official reports regarding the death of former NFL player Pat Tillman. The US Army originally stated that Tillman had been killed by enemy fire, in the mountains of Afghanistan, on April 22, 2004. It was later proven that Tillman was actually killed by friendly fire (shot three times in the head—quite a "mistake") and the Army was aware of it, but it still proceeded to award him the Silver Star and Purple Heart while promoting him posthumously to corporal. It was also discovered that Tillman's unit burned his body armor and uniform in an effort to conceal the facts about what had really happened. Tillman had in fact become strongly disillusioned with the military's presence in Afghanistan, and the notebook in which he had expressed his thoughts was also burned.

Kevin Tillman, brother of Pat, testified before Congress during the same hearing in which Jessica Lynch tried to set her own story straight. "The deception surrounding this case was an insult to the family," Tillman told Congress, "but more importantly, its primary purpose was to deceive a whole nation . . . we have been used as props in a Pentagon public relations exercise." Specialist Bryan O'Neal, who was the last known person to see Pat Tillman alive, also testified to Congress that day. He told them he'd been warned not to disclose that a US soldier had killed Tillman, especially to the Tillman family. The three shots to the head had indicated to many observers that Tillman's death was more likely a case of murder than friendly fire, and this was acknowledged by accounts that began appearing in the press, including an Associated Press report that quoted a doctor who'd examined Tillman's body as saying, "The medical evidence did not match up with the scenario as described."

The Associated Press was uncharacteristically diligent on this issue and filed a Freedom of Information lawsuit, resulting in the release of more than 2,000 pages of documents by the Defense Department. Among the information discovered was the fact that there was no evidence of enemy fire found at the scene of Tillman's death. There had been a provable cover-up of the facts surrounding Tillman's death, which extended to the highest levels of the military. Tillman's family was understandably bitter, and Americans were left to wonder if Oliver Stone had been accurate in his movie *Platoon*, when he portrayed US soldiers as not being above targeting their fellow compatriots for assassination and then lying about it.

GARY WEBB

One of the most important unnatural deaths that occurred during the Dubya years was that of journalist Gary Webb. Webb was a radical in the finest sense of the word. He summed up his credo in a 2003 speech to students at the Narco News School of Authentic Journalism in Mexico. "Journalists are revolutionaries. . . . You have to fight to change the world," Webb told the aspiring youngsters. In a 2004 BBC interview, Webb described himself as an "author and a responsible anarchist."

Before Webb became embroiled in his controversial research, a late 1980s congressional investigation chaired by John Kerry (the same future Democratic Party presidential nominee who had led the POW-MIA bogus inquiry) uncovered direct links between the Nicaraguan Contras and drug dealers. As Webb wrote in his book on the subject, *Dark Alliance*, "Kerry and his staff had taken videotaped depositions from Contra leaders who acknowledged receiving drug profits, with the apparent knowledge of the CIA." (*Dark Alliance* by Gary Webb, p. 14). Jack Blum, counsel for the Kerry Committee, told Webb that two Associated Press reporters, Robert Parry and Brian Barger, had investigated the Contra-drug story, "but they'd run into the same problems. Their stories were either trashed or ignored." (Ibid, p. 15). Webb spoke to Parry, who warned him of the ramifications of such a story. "The Justice Department was putting out false press releases saying there was nothing to this, that they'd investigated and could find no evidence." Parry recalled. "We were being attacked in the *Washington Times*." The rest of the Washington press corps scoffed at the whole thing, and Parry wound up quitting the AP.

Gary Webb's work on the issue that cost him his life began as a series of articles he wrote in 1996, as a reporter for the *San Jose Mercury News*. The articles exposed the connections between the CIA, the Contras, and the crack cocaine that had flooded into America's inner cities in the 1980s. Webb's own paper eventually turned against him, and his editor would publicly denounce the entire series. Webb turned his research into the book *Dark Alliance*, published in 1998. Webb's central thesis was that a drug ring, operating out of the San Francisco Bay area, had sold tons of cocaine to the violent Los Angeles street gangs the Bloods and the Crips, and funneled the millions in profits to Latin American guerillas run by the CIA. As Webb described it, "This drug network opened the first pipeline between Colombia's cocaine cartels and the black neighborhoods of Los Angeles, a city now known as the crack capital of the world."

The CIA reacted to Webb's charges as one might expect, calling them "ludicrous." Webb never directly accused the CIA of assisting the drug dealers, but he maintained that the Agency was well aware of the situation. Webb's exposé was all but ignored by the mainstream media, but thanks to the newly born Internet, it gained momentum and generated great public interest. Black activists such as Dick Gregory demanded an explanation from the CIA. Congresswoman Maxine Waters lobbied Attorney General Janet Reno for an independent investigation. CIA Director John Deutch even appeared at a November 1996 Watts, California, town meeting to denounce Webb's allegations. Thereafter, a slew of vicious attacks were launched on Webb by the usual suspects, the *Washington Post*, the *New York Times*, the *Los Angeles Times*, etc. While the mainstream media reacted in predictable fashion, many in the black community were outraged and alarmed by Webb's research that showed cocaine had been "virtually unobtainable in black neighborhoods" before the Contras started bringing it into South Central, Los Angeles.

Ex-CIA agent turned congressman Porter Goss, who would later be named CIA director by President George W. Bush, was instrumental in steering any inquiry into the Agency's role away from a full-scale congressional investigation toward a more limited one. The result was that the CIA was allowed to basically investigate itself, as the hearings were held in secret in conjunction with another private investigation by the Department of Justice. To no one's surprise, the CIA was cleared of any serious charges.

Curiously, the CIA inspector general would actually conclude, in the Agency's own final 1998 report, that there had indeed been a clandestine agreement between the CIA and the Justice Department that lasted from 1982 to 1995, which authorized them to ignore drug trafficking by CIA "agents, assets, and non-staff employees." The policy was known as MOU (Memorandum of Understanding). Gary Webb reacted to this disclosure by stating he now understood how the government could so easily deny the "evidence" of CIA/Contra drug trafficking, since "the CIA and the Justice Department had a gentleman's agreement to look the other way." The Justice Department's investigation concluded that the Reagan-Bush administrations had been aware of the situation but did nothing to stop the criminal activities.

Gary Webb not only suffered from professional abandonment, as he was forced to resign from the *San Jose Mercury News*, he had to deal with the breakup of his twenty-year marriage. Things began to look up a bit when he was hired by the *Sacramento News and Review* in the summer of 2004. Webb remained committed to his work and told *Counter Punch*: "To this day, no one has ever been able to show me a single error of fact in anything I've written about this drug ring, which includes a 600-page book about the whole tragic mess. But, in the end, the facts didn't really matter. What mattered was making the damned thing go away, shutting people up, and making anyone who demanded the truth appear to be a wacky conspiracy theorist. And it worked."

In the time period immediately before his death, Gary Webb spoke of strange figures seen outside his home, as well as receiving more death threats. On December 10, 2004, Webb allegedly shot himself in the face twice (!) and was found dead in his residence. The Sacramento County coroner attributed the death to suicide, despite the wild improbability of anyone shooting themselves twice in the head, and uttered the unintentionally hilarious line, "It's unusual in a suicide case to have two shots." There were supposedly two typed suicide notes found at the scene, and Webb's ex-wife appeared to provide the welcome information that Webb had been depressed for quite some time. Movers who were coming to Webb's house found a note on the door saying, "Please do not enter. Call 911 and ask for an ambulance." Filmmaker A. J. Booth, who was working on a documentary entitled *The American Drug War* at the time, told talk show host Alex Jones that Webb had been followed constantly before his death. Booth declared that everyone he'd spoken to "said there's no way this guy would have taken his own life—that he enjoyed life, he loved his kids." Webb was only forty-nine years of age.

Retired FBI agent Ted Gunderson would claim that "several days before Gary Webb's death [Michael] Riconosciuto had spoken with Webb on the phone." According to Gunderson, they were working together on the Hamlin case, which was associated with the Cabazon Indian Reservation, nefarious projects such as MK ULTRA, pedophile rings, drug trafficking—the usual conspiratorial goulash. Richard Hamlin, a former district attorney, had tried to call Riconosciuto to testify on his behalf during a 2004 trial, in which he alleged a satanic cult run by his father-in-law, Dr. Sid Siemer, had framed him for the torture of his wife. Evidently, Riconosciuto and Webb had been in communication for quite some time.

Riconosciuto's cousin, talk show host Anita Langley, verified that he had indeed been in communication with Gary Webb. Webb and Riconosciuto had exchanged letters for a three-month period prior to Webb's alleged suicide on December 10, 2004. Langley stated, "Riconosciuto still has the letters that Webb wrote to him, but they have been stashed away for safe keeping." She also claimed that they'd been working with attorney Harland Braun. Braun had been representing others involved with the Cabazon Reservation, which according to Riconosciuto was tied to a number of sordid intelligence activities. Mr. Braun had been forced to drop Riconosciuto as a client due to a conflict of interest, and Riconosciuto then gave Gary Webb power of attorney so that Webb could speak directly with Braun about Riconosciuto's case, as well as the Hamlin case. Webb was alleged to have been working on another book, which would have delved into all of this intriguing information.

Gary Webb provided his own epitaph: "In seventeen years of doing this, nothing bad had happened to me. I was never fired or threatened with dismissal if I kept looking under rocks. I was winning awards, getting raises, lecturing college classes, appearing on TV shows, so how could I possibly agree with people who were claiming the system didn't work, that it was steered by powerful special interests and corporations, and existed to protect the power elite? Hell, the system worked just fine, as [far as] I could tell. . . . And then I wrote some stories that made me realize how sadly misplaced my bliss had been. The reason I'd enjoyed such smooth sailing for so long hadn't been, as I'd assumed, because I was careful and diligent and good at my job. It turned out to have nothing to do with it. The truth was that, in all those years, I hadn't written anything important enough to suppress." (Gary Webb, *The Mighty Wurlitzer Plays On*, quoted in *Into the Buzzsaw: Leading Journalists Expose the Myth of a Free Press* (Kristina Borjesson, ed.), 2002, pp. 296–297).

Another embarrassing scandal for Dubya's administration may very well have tied into the earlier Franklin child sex atrocities (detailed later in this book). In early February 2005, stories broke about a conservative "journalist" named James Guckert, writing under the name Jeff Gannon, who had often been observed lobbing softball questions to Bush at press conferences. A little investigation revealed that Guckert was actually a gay escort, advertising his services on websites such as hotmilitarystud.com. Secret Service log records were obtained that showed Guckert had stayed overnight at the White House numerous times, even when there were no scheduled press conferences.

Noreen Gosch, mother of missing paperboy Johnny Gosch, suspected that Gannon might be her grown-up son. She thought that the facial features were the same and there were reports that Gannon shared an identical birthmark with Johnny. As Noreen declared in an interview, "It appears in all of the alias names Gannon has used that he kept the same initials as Johnny . . . JDG. Gannon also chose the last name of the *Des Moines Register* editor at the time Johnny was kidnapped." Rusty Nelson was familiar with the abducted youth Johnny Gosch, and he felt certain that Gannon and Gosch were the same person. Noreen had been in contact with several of the kids abused in the Franklin scandal, and they too had been familiar with Johnny and felt that Gannon was the same individual.

Nelson was the ex-photographer for Larry King (not to be confused with the talk show host), onetime director of the Franklin Community Credit Union in Nebraska and a rising Republican bigwig during the late 1980s. Noreen said that seven of the Franklin kids called Gosch "The Chameleon," because of his ability to disguise himself, and she claimed that Jeff Gannon also referred to himself as "The Chameleon." Noreen and Gannon went back and forth on whether or not he'd agree to a DNA test, but there is no available information that he ever did take it.

You don't have to be a "conspiracy theorist" to wonder why a gay escort, posing as a journalist, would *ever* be invited to stay overnight at the White House, let alone multiple times.

MORE BODY COUNT

More unnatural deaths were added to the Bush Body Count in the remaining years of Dubya's two terms in office. Milton William Cooper was a "conspiracy theorist" whose best-known book was *Behold a Pale Horse*. Cooper's theories tied aliens into everything, and some of his beliefs were outlandish; for instance, he thought that limousine driver William Greer had actually fired the head shot that killed JFK, and he maintained that real aliens were used in the television series *Alien Nation*. He was charged with tax evasion in 1998 and was labeled a "major fugitive" by the US Marshals Service. There was allegedly a Clinton White House memo that referred to him as "the most dangerous radio host in America." On November 5, 2001, in a fitting end for such an "extremist," Cooper was killed in a shootout with Apache County Sheriff's deputies at his Eagar, Arizona, home.

In February 2002, Tennessee Department of Motor Vehicles employee Katherine Smith was implicated in a scheme to sell driver's licenses to illegal aliens of Arab descent. Smith was released on her own recognizance, but on February 10, the day before she was scheduled to appear in court, her car was found resting against a utility pole at 12:15 a.m., totally engulfed in flames. According to the *Sierra Times*, state and federal investigators found gasoline on Smith's clothing. The FBI concluded that some kind of flammable accelerant had started the fire, and that Smith had not burned to death from crashing into the utility pole. FBI agent J. Suzanne Nash, in response to a question from a prosecutor about whether Smith's death had been the result of an accident, replied, "No, it was not." Prosecutors claimed there were "connections" between the illegal aliens and the World Trade Center, including a visitor's pass to the WTC dated September 5, 2011, issued to one of them.

Fairfax County, Virginia, police responded to a 911 call on September 29, 2003, for an accident that occurred at the home of Marvin Bush, brother of the president. Sixty-two-year-old Bertha Champagne, described as a longtime babysitter for Marvin and Margaret Bush's two children, was found crushed to death by her own vehicle in the driveway of the Bush home in Alexandria, Virginia, where she reportedly lived. How many babysitters have you ever heard of who were found run over by their own cars in their employer's driveway?

Like his predecessors in the White House, Ronald Reagan and Bill Clinton, George W. Bush was also accused of raping a woman. The alleged victim was Margie Schoedinger. Despite the sensational nature of the charges, only a small paper in her hometown saw fit to publicize them. Even the press in England, which had been noticeably active in reporting on the numerous scandals of the Clintons, ignored her story as well. Schoedinger became an entry in the Bush Body Count when she purportedly committed suicide on September 22, 2003. Even much of the Internet was lackadaisical about covering the story, and it wasn't until December 8, 2003, that the *New Nation*, which represents London's black community (Schoedinger was African American), ran a cover story on her charges and her untimely death. Schoedinger, of Sugar Land, Texas, was thirty-eight years old when she was found dead of a gunshot wound to the head. Schoedinger had earlier told American journalist Jackson Thoreau that Bush had contacted her and told her he wanted her killed. In the article, she was quoted as saying, "People have to be accountable for what they do and that is why I am pursuing this lawsuit."

Deborah Jeane Palfrey, nicknamed the "D.C. Madam" in the media, ran a Washington, D.C., escort service that reportedly catered to some of the nation's most powerful men. Her attorney claimed that Vice President Dick Cheney was among those on her client "list." On January 27, 2007, one of Palfrey's alleged prostitutes, former University of Maryland professor Brandy Britton, was found hanged to death in her apartment. Naturally, police instantly declared they did not suspect foul play. Palfrey herself was convicted of money laundering and racketeering in April 2008. On May 1, 2008, Palfrey was found hanged to death in a storage shed outside her mother's Florida mobile home.

Palfrey had been interviewed by talk show host Alex Jones shortly before her death, and she assured him that she wasn't going to kill herself. Journalist Dan Moldea, who was working on a book with Palfrey at the time of her death, conveniently recalled afterward that she had told him, "I am not going back to prison. I will commit suicide first." Moldea had a track record of whitewashing scandalous events, from his absurd book on the RFK assassination, *The Killing of Robert Kennedy*, in which he demolishes the lone-assassin theory and then incomprehensibly in the last chapter suddenly gets an epiphany that Sirhan acted alone, to his disinformation piece *A Washington*

Tragedy, which supports the untenable official explanation of Vince Foster's death. Like in Britton's case, police reported that there was no evidence of foul play.

When Dubya left the White House, the country was in dire straits. The era of greed had been solidified, as the very word *rich* now became anathema in polite society, replaced by the term *job creator*. In this vein, on April 20, 2005, Dubya had signed the New Bankruptcy Law, which made it much harder for average, debt-ridden people to wipe clean their financial slates by declaring bankruptcy. Elitists such as corporate tycoon Donald Trump, who declared bankruptcy on a routine basis, would still have that option, of course. "I've used the laws of this country to pare debt . . . ," Trump told ABC's George Stephanopoulos (an ex-aide to Bill Clinton, one of many mainstream "journalists" who came from the world of politics) in April 2011. "We'll have the company. We'll throw it into a chapter. We'll negotiate with the banks. We'll make a fantastic deal. You know, it's like on *The Apprentice*. It's not personal. It's just business."

Regarding Bush, it was hard to imagine that anyone could be worse than this much-less-funny version of Alfred E. Neumann, who'd referred to himself as "The Decider" and had been caught on tape making ridiculous gestures, even flipping the bird, before the cameras officially started rolling. However, as H. L. Mencken notably remarked, "No one never went broke underestimating the intelligence of the American people."

CHAPTER ELEVEN

OBAMA THE GREAT

"Obama's standing above the country, above the world. He's sort of
God. He's going to bring all different sides together."
— Evan Thomas, editor of *Newsweek*

"I can't stand to hear his voice anymore. He's a liar, and worse."
— Caroline Kennedy on Barack Obama

Barack Hussein Obama rose from relative obscurity in a rapid fashion. He
failed in his first run for elected office, to the House of Representatives
in 2000, yet just eight years later he was being treated as a revolutionary
figure who was going to transform America. Never has the power of the
mainstream media to make or break candidates been more evident than in
Obama's case. Intrepid Internet researcher Jeff Gold tabulated the number
of references to Obama in the press, and found that in 2003 he had 600
mentions, with not a single article about him, to 7,465 in 2004, when he won
election to the United States Senate from Illinois. Upon being elected to the
Senate, this decidedly inexperienced politician was almost instantly labeled
as future presidential material.

Obama's election to the presidency in 2008 was treated more like a
coronation, if not an intense religious ritual, by the establishment press and
a fawning, glassy-eyed majority of Americans. Anyone who questioned
anything at all about Obama was deemed to be a "hater" or, even worse,
a racist. One does not have to be a "birther" to acknowledge that there are
inexplicable gaps in Obama's personal history. In fact, we seem to know
less about him than any president in American history. Why are his medical
records, his birth records, his school records, and his passport records all

sealed? Why has he refused to release his college records from Harvard or Columbia or Occidental? Obama has even kept his Columbia College thesis from public view.

Apparently, his records from Punahou, the elite prep school he attended in Hawaii, cannot be found. Michelle Obama has claimed her husband never received any student loans while at Harvard, so how could he have afforded the prohibitive cost of tuition? Even the establishment organ the *Chicago Tribune* was curious about this, but their requests to see Obama's student loan records were denied. All his records from the Illinois State Senate are missing as well. What is going on here? Could any of these seemingly innocuous records be associated with national security?

We're not even sure about Obama's name. Evidently, he was known as Barry Soetoro, which was his Indonesian stepfather's name, while attending Occidental College. It has been alleged that he actually was considered a foreign exchange student at one time. But the biggest controversy has surrounded Obama's actual birthplace. Critics have alleged he was not even born in the United States, a basic requirement for the office of president, and thus should be declared constitutionally ineligible. The Obama administration finally released a "Certificate of Live Birth" for the president in April 2011, but independent document authentication experts concluded it was an obvious forgery. More than forty lawsuits were filed during Obama's first term in office, challenging his eligibility for the presidency. There were unsettling questions about his Selective Service card as well. Right wing blogger Debbie Schlussel discovered that the Document Location Number indicates that the card was issued in 2008, at the time the controversy was raised, and not when Obama was the proper age.

Was Obama actually born in Hawaii, as is officially claimed, or was he instead born in Kenya or Indonesia? The mystery of Obama's Social Security number is perhaps most baffling of all. A private investigator hired by attorney Orly Taitz, who filed numerous lawsuits against Obama that questioned the legality of his presidency, discovered multiple Social Security numbers associated with the individual residing in the White House. There were two different numbers for a Barack Obama at sixteen separate addresses he was known to have lived at. In California, where Obama attended Occidental College, there were three more differing Social Security numbers associated with his distinctive name, all located close to the college. Obama appears to have even used two varying Social Security numbers while serving in the US Senate. The Social Security number most often connected to Obama was issued in Connecticut in 1976–1977, yet he is not known to have ever lived or worked in that state. Even more strangely, researchers found multiple Social Security numbers for Obama's late mother, Ann Dunham. No one has been able to locate the marriage licenses for Dunham's two marriages, nor the marriage license for her parents. Researchers cannot find birth certificates for Dunham, her parents, or her grandparents. Obama has spoken proudly of his grandfather's military service, but there is no documentation for that either.

In May 2012, Breitbart News obtained a 1991 promotional booklet from Acton & Dystel, which was Barack Obama's literary agency at the time. The booklet boasted that Obama was "born in Kenya and raised in Indonesia and Hawaii." Edward Acton told Breitbart News that his clients "probably" approved the text about them in the booklet. Jane Dystel didn't respond to numerous requests for comment, and her assistant told Breitbart News that she "does not answer questions about Obama."

Henry Franklin Graff, a Columbia University professor emeritus of history, who taught at the university for forty-six years, declared in an interview with World Net Daily, "I have no recollection of Barack Obama at Columbia, and I am sure he never attended any of my classes. . . . For 46 years, I taught political history . . . and every future politician of note who went through Columbia in those years took one or more of my classes—every one, that is, except Barack Obama." Graff further supported rumors that Obama managed to remain implausibly invisible at the prestigious university, telling WND, "Nobody I knew at Columbia ever remembers Obama being there."

On September 11, 2008, the *Wall Street Journal* published the results of a Fox News survey; four hundred students who had attended Columbia from 1981 to 1983 had been contacted, and not a single one remembered Obama. *New York Times* reporter Janny Scott, hardly an anti-Obama partisan (she would subsequently write a favorable biography of Obama's mother), wrote in an October 30, 2007, story that Barack Obama had "declined repeated requests to talk about his New York years, release his Columbia transcript, or identify even a single fellow student, coworker, roommate or friend from those years." Ben LaBolt, an Obama spokesman, told Scott, "He doesn't remember the names of a lot of people in his life." The Associated Press reported on May 16, 2008, that the Obama campaign declined to comment on his time at Columbia "and his friendships in general."

Obama had connections to notable Sixties "radicals" (and husband and wife) William Ayers and Bernardine Dohrn. There are indications that Ayers's parents, Tom and Mary, put Obama through Harvard Law School. As most of the Sixties counterculture figures did, Bill Ayers came from an affluent background; his father, Tom, was the CEO of Commonwealth Edison. Despite

Tom Ayers's seemingly leftist leanings, he was close friends with Chicago Mayor Richard J. Daley, who was anathema to radicals in the Sixties.

In March 2012, retired postal carrier Allen Hulton told researcher Jerome Corsi that he'd encountered Obama while delivering mail to the Ayers from 1986 to 1997. Hulton swore that Mary Ayers told him that they were supporting a black "foreign" student. He couldn't remember the name, but he recalled it had a "strange," African ring to it. "I was taken aback by how enthusiastic she was about him," Hulton stated. One day, he met this young student in front of the Ayers's Glen Ellyn, Illinois, home. Hulton remembered his distinctive appearance, including his prominent ears, and felt certain it had been Barack Obama. The young man told the postman that he had come to thank the Ayers for having helped him with his education. "He looked right at me and told me he was going to be president of the United States," Hulton said.

Bernardine Dohrn also grew up in an upper-middle-class home. She was originally associated with the intelligence-connected Students for a Democratic Society, and she became a leader of one if its radical wings, the Revolutionary Youth Movement, which later became known as the Weathermen. She became the student director of the National Lawyers Guild, often accused by right wingers as being a legal bulwark for the Communist Party in America. Young Dohrn made these horrific comments in response to the murders of Sharon Tate and others by the Manson gang: "First they killed those pigs, then they ate dinner in the same room with them, then they even shoved a fork into the pig Tate's stomach! Wild!"

Future husband Bill Ayers would later claim, in 2008, that Dohrn was merely being "ironic" in her statement. By 1970, Dohrn went underground (the group would come to be known as the Weather Underground) and was apparently involved in violent bombing activities. She became one of the FBI's ten most wanted fugitives. Some charges against her and other members of the Weathermen were dismissed in 1974, but she would not completely reemerge into society until 1980, when she pled guilty to aggravated battery and jumping bail, for which she received probation.

Despite her dubious background, in 1984 Dohrn found work at the prestigious Chicago law firm Sidley Austin, with the apparent help of Thomas Ayers. By 1991, this "anti-establishment" crusader was a professor of law at Northwestern University. In a 2010 interview, Dohrn blasted the "right" in America, saying, "It's racist; it's armed; it's hostile; it's unspeakable." She specifically bemoaned the "white people armed."

Bill Ayers, like many good "radicals," attended a fancy prep school, the Lake Forest Academy. During his years with the Weathermen, Ayers participated in several bombings. Ayers coauthored the 1973 book *Prairie Fire*, and among the nearly two hundred people the book is dedicated to was RFK's alleged assassin, Sirhan Sirhan. Deftly adapting to the society he despised, Ayers worked with Chicago Mayor Richard M. Daley (remember, their fathers were great friends) in organizing city school reform. Despite this strong establishment position, he would tell an interviewer in 1995, "Maybe I'm the last communist who is willing to admit it." By 1997, he was awarded Chicago's Citizen of the Year honors. He was named to the board of directors for the Woods Fund of Chicago foundation. Ayers retired as a respected professor at the University of Illinois at Chicago. Although Obama would later claim Ayers was "just a guy in my neighborhood," the first organizational meeting for Obama's state Senate campaign was held in Bill Ayers's apartment.

OBAMA BODY COUNT

The usual dead bodies began to pile up around Barack Obama even before he was elected. Bill Gwatney was the state chair of the Arkansas Democratic Party. A strong supporter of Hillary Clinton's presidential candidacy, he was determined that she be treated fairly at the 2008 convention. Less than two weeks before the start of the Democratic National Convention, a gunman entered Democratic Party headquarters in Little Rock, Arkansas, on August 13, 2008, and shot Gwatney three times. Police killed the "lone nut" after a lengthy car chase. Incredibly, yet another Hillary Clinton super delegate, Representative Stephanie Tubbs Jones, who'd been an outspoken critic of the electronic Diebold voting machines that had become infamous during the 2000 Florida election imbroglio, was found dead in her car six days after Gwatney was killed, on August 19.

On December 31, 2010, the body of John Wheeler, who'd served as an aide to three different Republican presidents, was found in a Delaware garbage dump. Officials later determined that he'd been assaulted and died of blunt-force trauma. Accounts appeared of him seeming "unhinged" in recent days. He was caught on a parking garage video surveillance camera two days before his body was discovered, looking disoriented, without a coat on and holding one shoe in his hand. Oddly, Wheeler's last known message, on an Internet forum, was a rant against the corruption in NCAA football. His widow would come to publicly charge that Wheeler had been assassinated by a professional hit man, suggesting that his long work with the Pentagon had made him enemies. She accused the police of being "so bad" and "making my life miserable." She also charged that they had "treated us like criminals."

Donald Young, forty-seven-year-old choir director and deacon at Trinity United Church of Christ in Chicago, was found shot to death by his roommate on December 23, 2007. Trinity United had become renowned as Barack Obama's place of worship. Young was openly gay, and had supposedly been in contact with Larry Sinclair, who had long alleged he'd had a sexual relationship with Obama, and also did cocaine with him. Two other gay members of the Trinity congregation died during this same period. Larry Bland had been killed, execution-style, a month before Young, on November 17, 2007. Nate Spencer died, allegedly from pneumonia and HIV, right after Young, on December 26, 2007. Donald Young's elderly mother tried to speak out with her suspicions that her son was murdered to protect Barack Obama's reputation, but no one in the adoring mainstream media was about to listen to her.

Lobbyist Ashley Turton, wife of White House Director of Legislative Affairs Dan Turton, was found dead in her burning car on January 10, 2011, after she supposedly crashed into the garage of her family home. Turton was the former chief of staff to Representative Rosa DeLauro, who had permitted Obama's chief of staff, Rahm Emanuel, to live, rent free, in an apartment she had owned for five years. Steve Bridges, a comedian who had supposedly "deeply offended" Obama with his impersonation of him, was found dead in his home at age forty-eight on March 3, 2012, of "natural causes."

There were two separate unnatural deaths in the mansion of multimillionaire CEO of Medicis Pharmaceuticals Corporation Jonah Shacknai, only a few days apart from each other in July 2011. First, his six-year-old son, Max, fell from a flight of stairs and died the following week. Two days after the accident, Jonah's thirty-two-year-old girlfriend, Rebecca Nalepa (also referred to as Rebecca Zahau in some accounts), was found hanging naked from a second floor balcony of Shacknai's home, her hands and feet bound with electrical cord. She was also gagged, and blood was found on her body. The official story, as impossible as it sounded, held that Nalepa was despondent over the boy's fall, as she'd been watching him at the time. The police would initially acknowledge the obvious, that Nalepa's death was "very bizarre," but at the same time they would not rule out suicide, despite the fact she was nude and had both her hands and feet tied. Just as astonishingly, the authorities seemed unable to develop a connection between the two tragedies. I'm certain that if a poor or middle-class person wound up with two deaths like that happening in their home within days of each other, the police wouldn't establish any connection, either.

There was no real investigation of these unnatural deaths, and Jonah himself would tell ABC News, in September 2011, that he'd asked the

California attorney general to review the cases. In stating the obvious, Jonah said, "The circumstances of Rebecca's suicide were so unusual and upsetting that it was difficult to accept the hard facts that were presented." However, he also maintained he had no reason to dispute their findings. The establishment circled the wagons here, as they invariably do in such instances. Highly visible talking head criminal defense attorney Roy Black, calling the police's conclusions "inescapable," was willing to deliver the following ridiculous comments in support of the official suicide theory: "The chances of someone wrapping a rope around her neck, dragging her up and throwing her over the balcony without her fighting back, without a single piece of evidence with no evidence of a struggle is virtually impossible," Yeah, Roy, we can all picture your average suicide victim, undressing first in order to humiliate herself by being found naked, and then binding all four limbs, as well as gagging herself, before somehow flinging herself from the balcony. I guess she wanted to make herself look about as much like a quintessential murder victim as possible, but she didn't manage to fool the police, or apparently you.

Rebecca's family didn't buy the suicide theory, and their attorney hired renowned forensic pathologist Cyril Wecht, who'd achieved notoriety for disputing the lone-assassin thesis in the JFK assassination and had investigated many other high-profile cases, like the JonBenet Ramsey murder. "She has to get up on top of the railing and then fling herself over. Did she do that head first and then tumble and turn around?" Wecht asked. "Did she go over feet first, I don't know. I would like to see reenactments. To my knowledge, she was not a member of Cirque du Soleil." Wecht also noted that in his experience, it was very, very rare for a woman to take her own life while nude. It's hard to determine what exactly happened here; if it was foul play, was it directed against the powerful Jonah Shacknai, or was he somehow involved in Rebecca's death? At any rate, there is no doubt that the virtual non-investigation, as well as the preposterous suicide theory, were influenced by Shacknai's great wealth.

Andrew Breitbart was a well-known right wing journalist. In a speech he gave in Washington, D.C., before the Conservative Political Action Committee (CPAC) on February 21, 2012, Breitbart claimed to have obtained a damning videotape of young Barack Obama during his college days. "I've got video from his college days that show you why racial division and class warfare are central to what hope and change was sold in 2008 . . ." Breitbart teased the crowd. He specifically declared, "Wait 'til they see what happens March 1st." In true conspiratorial fashion, Breitbart was found dead on that very date,

March 1, of either "natural causes" or a sudden massive heart attack, at only forty-three years of age.

He'd spent a few hours with Arthur Sando of the *Hollywood Reporter* just prior to his unexpected death, and seemed perfectly fine. Breitbart left The Brentwood restaurant on foot, and apparently collapsed dead during the walk home. The video in question was subsequently released, but I found it hard to believe that it was the explosive one Breitbart had been so enthusiastic about. All it showed was Obama speaking as a student at Harvard, in support of controversial professor Derrick Bell. One thing about the video did intrigue me, however; unlike virtually any recorded speech I'd ever seen, this one didn't focus on the speaker. In fact, whoever was filming kept the video on the audience, especially professor Bell, for almost the entire time. The young Obama was shown only briefly, and never in a close-up.

Things grew even more sinister with the sudden death of Michael Cormier, the coroner in Breitbart's case, on April 20, 2012. For extra dramatic effect, Cormier dropped dead on the day Breitbart's autopsy results were released (officially, Breitbart died of "heart failure," and had only small traces of alcohol in his system). Police sources told the *Los Angeles Times* that they suspected he died from arsenic poisoning. Contradicting their standard operating procedure in these cases, the authorities did not immediately rule out foul play. "There are mysterious circumstances surrounding his death," reported Elizabeth Espinosa of KTLA-TV News. "We're told detectives are looking into the possibility that he was poisoned by arsenic." Oddly, there appears to have been an unexplained delay of about a week before news of the coroner's death was reported.

As if the coroner dying suddenly wasn't enough, on May 7, 2012, *World Net Daily* and other Internet sources reported that the only witness to Breitbart's death that night had vanished. Twenty-six-year-old Christopher Lasseter had been out walking his dog in Brentwood, California, when he saw Breitbart collapse suddenly "like a sack of potatoes" onto the sidewalk. A California private investigator discovered that Lasseter was no longer at his previous address, which was his parents' residence. No one answered the phone at the apartment number for the Lasseters, and the voicemail that came on indicated different first names for the people who lived there. A few days later, however, Lasseter was tracked down by private investigator Paul Huebl and interviewed. Lasseter claimed that he had done a "double take" when he saw a thick, white band around the top of Breitbart's forehead. He also described the strange, "bright red" color of Breitbart's face and skin.

THE KILLING OF BIN LADEN

In late March 2011, an unexpected new voice joined the "birthers" who'd been questioning Barack Obama's eligibility for office. Wealthy businessman Donald Trump focused national attention on the controversial topic, declaring on the March 23, 2011, television show *The View*, "There is something on that birth certificate he doesn't like." Predictably, the show's cohosts were indignantly offended about this, with Whoopi Goldberg saying, "That's the biggest pile of dog mess I have heard in ages." Even more predictably, Goldberg followed up by playing the race card, confronting Trump with, "It's not because he's black, is it?" At least enough pressure was finally brought to bear on Obama for him to address the subject at a news conference, on April 30, 2011. "We do not have time for this silliness," an obviously perturbed Obama told reporters. ". . . I've got better stuff to do. We've got big problems to solve . . . we're going to have to focus on them—not this." As if on cue, by a wonderfully fortuitous "coincidence," Obama managed to "solve" a very "big problem" the next day.

On May 1, 2011 (and yes, critics noted the date, important in the worlds of both communism and Satanism), the dreaded Osama Bin Laden, who'd been labeled by the establishment as the primary mover behind the events of September 11, 2001, was killed by, in the president's words, "a small team of Americans" (originally said to be some kind of joint special operations forces and the CIA, later changed to an elite team of Navy Seals) in his Pakistani hideout. President Obama, foregoing any pretext about humane and civilized behavior, bragged about it as if he'd just defeated the school bully on the playground. Calling the murder "the most significant achievement to date" in the effort to defeat Al-Qaeda (whom the United States was presently working *with* in Libya), Obama declared, "Justice has been done." "Sources" told ABC News and other mainstream media outlets that DNA testing had confirmed the victim was definitely Bin Laden.

Obama didn't even try to pretend that Americans had been forced to kill Bin Laden. On the contrary, he indicated that this had been a targeted assassination. ". . . I determined that we had enough intelligence to take action and authorized an operation to get Osama Bin Laden and bring him to justice," Obama stated. Revealing again that trusty bipartisan spirit, former President George W. Bush echoed the comments of his supposed political enemy, calling the murder "a momentous achievement" that "marks a victory for America, for people who seek peace around the world. . . ." Bill Clinton's words were almost identical to Bush's, and he called it "a profoundly important moment."

The official story of Bin Laden's death was frankly ridiculous. From the "spontaneous" crowds, some hanging in trees, that appeared outside the White House late that night, just after Obama's announcement, to the disposal of Bin Laden's body at sea, in "honor" of Muslim tradition (when, in reality, there is no such tradition among Muslims), the entire thing seemed scripted, and badly scripted at that. There was a photo released of Bin Laden, with a bloody wound on his face, which was widely disseminated throughout the establishment press, but was quickly proven to be a crude, Photoshopped forgery by Internet researchers. Forced to acknowledge this, Obama assured Americans that real photographs of Bin Laden's corpse did exist, but he wasn't going to release them. Presumably with a straight face, the president explained, "We don't trot this stuff out as trophies" and "We don't need to spike the football" (Obama relished sports analogies). In the next breath, however, it was back to the insensitive bragging; ". . . this is somebody who was deserving of the justice that he received." Then, laughably, Obama claimed that the release of the pictures "would create a national security risk."

The mainstream press released an astounding photo of President Obama, Vice President Joe Biden, Secretary of State Hillary Clinton (complete with hand over mouth, looking utterly aghast) and others watching something with great intensity, which we were told was "live coverage" of the shootout with Navy Seals that ended Osama Bin Laden's life. Detailed reports, such as the one appearing in the May 3, 2011, *Daily Mail (UK)*, claimed that one of Bin Laden's wives was used as a human shield as "he blasted away with an AK47 assault rifle." We were also told that the video had been relayed by satellite to the group, who were gathered together in the White House Situation Room. However, within days it was acknowledged by CIA Director Leon Panetta that the live feed to the White House had been cut off before the Navy Seals even entered the building. "A photograph released by the White House appeared to show the President and his aides in the situation room watching the action as it unfolded. In fact they had little knowledge of what was happening in the compound," the May 4, 2011, *London Telegraph* reported.

Steve Pieczenik, former deputy assistant secretary of state who worked for three different administrations, and was the figure whom novelist Tom Clancy's character Jack Ryan was based on, described the entire thing, in an interview with renegade talk show host Alex Jones, as "nonsense. . . . It's a total make-up, make-believe, we're in an American theater of the absurd . . . nine years ago this man was already dead. . . . Why does the government repeatedly have to lie to the American people?"

Pieczenik declared that Bin Laden had died in 2001. "Bush junior knew about it, the intelligence community knew about it," Pieczenik went on to say. "Osama Bin Laden was already dead, so there's no way they could have attacked or confronted or killed Osama Bin Laden." Pieczenik also told Jones that he was prepared to tell a federal grand jury the name of a top general who told him 9/11 was a false flag attack. The establishment press responded to any questioning of the whole affair in reliable fashion. In the May 4, 2011, issue of *Time* magazine, Adam Sorensen wrote, "Not releasing the image will surely agitate conspiracy mongers like talk radio hyperventilator Alex Jones, but evidence, photographic or otherwise, has never been much of an obstacle for Jones's black helicopter fantasies." Yes, Adam, it's certainly outrageous to question a government that brags about assassination, stages a photo purporting to be the president and his staff watching it unfold live, disposes of the body by dumping it into the sea, and then refuses to release photos of the corpse after being caught spreading an obvious forgery.

The murder of Osama Bin Laden, assuming it really happened, marked a watershed moment in American history. Here we had American leaders boasting about assassinating a foreign figure in no uncertain terms. From the president's comments to CIA Director Leon Panetta declaring, in seeming reference to perhaps someday releasing the alleged photos of his corpse, "we got Bin Laden, and I think we have to reveal to the rest of the world the fact that we were able to get him and kill him," our illustrious leaders engaged in disgraceful showboating. Am I the only American left who shudders at those kinds of sentiments? Either way, the public loses here. If, as seems likely, the entire thing was staged for political reasons, then we've gone deep down the rabbit hole and are confronting conspirators who can and will twist reality to suit their purposes. On the other hand, if they really assassinated Bin Laden, and aren't even bothering to construct a clumsy cover story that portrays them as being *forced* to do so, in self-defense, and the majority of citizens are okay with that, then our entire national moral compass is wildly askew, if not broken.

But if that was bad, several months later the Obama administration proved to be unfortunately capable of acting in an even worse manner. On September 30, 2011, American citizen Anwar al-Awlaki was killed in Yemen by a missile fired from an American drone aircraft. The missile also took the life of an American of Pakistani origin, Samir Khan, editor of Al-Qaeda's English-language Internet magazine *Inspire*. While the Bush administration had also killed an American citizen in 2002, at least they still bothered to claim they'd been targeting someone else. Awlaki, whatever his beliefs, had never been charged with or convicted of a crime.

However, President Obama made it clear that he was not bothered by constitutional niceties like due process any longer, as he basked in the aftermath of another "victory" with a jubilant speech before a military audience in Virginia right after the murder had been announced. "The death of Awlaki is a major blow to Al Qaeda's most active operational affiliate," the president boasted. With no evidence whatsoever, and certainly no previous indictment to base it on, Obama charged Awlaki with "planning and directing efforts to murder innocent Americans." Awlaki proved to be the first fatality from the Obama administration's "kill or capture" list, which they'd established in early 2010. The list, which was quite a bit more frightening than Richard Nixon's much ballyhooed "enemies list," targeted individuals for assassination who had been deemed to be "specially designated global terrorists." The Council on American-Islamic Relations protested the killing, calling on "our nation's leaders to address the constitutional issues raised by the assassination of US citizens without due process of the law."

As if all this wasn't morally outrageous enough, the next month, Anwar al-Awlaki's sixteen-year-old son, Abdulrahman, was killed by what even *Time* magazine characterized as a "CIA suspected" drone strike in Yemen. The boy had been born in Denver, and harbored no political inclinations at his tender age. The US government reacted to this cold-blooded murder of an American-born teenager by saying he'd been "in the wrong place at the wrong time," and that they had been trying to kill a "legitimate" terrorist (who also died in the blast). Again, no shame, no apologies, and a ready acknowledgment that the United States is trying to kill individuals. The only words of sanity in this whole mess were expressed by the boy's grieving grandfather, Nasser al-Awlaki, who said, "In addition to my grandson's killing, the missile killed my brother's grandson, who was a 17-year-old kid, who was not an American citizen but is a human being, killed in cold blood . . . killed my son Anwar without a trial for any crime he committed. . . . They killed him just for his freedom of speech. . . . I urge the American people to bring the killers to justice . . . to expose the hypocrisy of the 2009 Nobel Prize laureate. To some, he may be that. To me and my family, he is nothing more than a child killer." (*Time* magazine, October 27, 2011).

The American Civil Liberties Union and the Center for Constitutional Rights both condemned the killing. The two organizations joined in a federal court case challenging on constitutional grounds the White House's claim that it had the right to target US citizens for assassination. Columnist Jonathan Turley expressed the absurdity of the situation well: "Previously, the Administration succeeded with an almost mocking argument that al-Aulaqi's family could not file a lawsuit seeking review of the power to assassinate because al-Aulaqi himself should appear to ask for review. Thus, after saying that it would kill al-Aulaqi on sight, the Justice Department insisted that he should walk into a clerk's office and ask for declaratory judgment. Even if his family were to sue for wrongful death, the Administration would likely use the military and state secrets privilege to block the lawsuit." *Salon* opined, "Without a shred of due process, far from any battlefield, President Obama succeeds in killing Anwar al-Awlaki." Even the *New York Times* was a bit outraged, stating, "It is extremely rare, if not unprecedented, for an American to be approved for targeted killing."

As the one-year anniversary of Bin Laden's alleged death approached, Obama overtly exploited it for maximum political value. Again, even the *New York Times* was somewhat repulsed by the president's behavior. In the April 27, 2012, edition of the establishment's flagship newspaper, an article headlined *Obama Trumpets Killing of Bin Laden, and Critics Pounce,* began with, "Presidents running for reelection typically boast of programs they created, people they helped or laws they signed. They talk about rising test scores or falling deficits or expanding job rolls. President Obama is taking the unusual route of bragging about how he killed a man." The article went on to say, "Mr. Obama has made a concerted, if to some indecorous, effort to trumpet the killing as perhaps the central accomplishment of his presidency. . . . Vice President Joseph R. Biden gave a speech saying the reelection slogan would be 'Bin Laden is dead and General Motors is alive.'" The epitome of a mainstream media outlet, the *Times* bluntly stated, ". . . few presidents have talked about the killing of an individual enemy in such an expansive way."

The immorality of the entire subject was surprisingly summed up perfectly by former high-ranking CIA official Jose A. Rodriguez Jr., who had been a vociferous defender of the harsh interrogations of prisoners during the Bush years, when he contrasted those methods with Obama's apparent relish for the new drone technology, by asking, "How could it be more ethical to kill people than to capture them?"

Barack Obama sounded reasonable in most of his speeches. However, like so many other politicians, his record didn't live up to his rhetoric. Obama actually expanded on Bush's disastrous foreign adventurism, launching additional "peacekeeping" missions in Libya, Pakistan, Somalia, Uganda, South Sudan, the Congo, and Yemen. In Libya, Reagan's onetime primary bogeyman Muammar Gaddafi (curiously, the name had been consistently spelled Qadaffi or Kaddafy during the 1980s), provided the impetus for our invasion. Although he'd apparently reformed his act, and been almost our friend for more than twenty years, now Gaddafi—armed with a deadly new spelling of his last name—burst back into the headlines again, as someone who "must be stopped."

One of the most outlandish lies told by the US government in recent memory occurred in 2011 when Obama's secretary of state, Hillary Clinton, informed the compliant establishment press that Gaddafi had supplied Viagra to his troops to incite them into mass rapes of Libyan dissidents. The former first lady breathlessly disclosed that there were also "virginity tests" being forced on the hapless female population. This was even more over the top than the hackneyed propaganda normally employed in order to prime the sheeple for war; for example, the first sentence in a story from the April 25, 2011, *Daily Mail* declared, "Children as young as eight are being raped in front of their families by Gaddafi's forces in Libya."

The mainstream media dutifully passed along these absurd claims, but they paid much less attention to Amnesty International's report debunking Clinton's assertions. In the words of Amnesty International, "Not only have we not met any victims, but we have not even met any persons who have met victims." Even US military and intelligence officials had to admit that "there is no evidence that Libyan military forces are being given Viagra and engaging in systematic rape against women in rebel areas." However, at the same time, Susan Rice, US ambassador to the United Nations, "told a closed-door meeting of officials at the UN that the Libyan military is using rape as a weapon in the war with the rebels and some had been issued the anti-impotency drug. She reportedly offered no evidence to back up the claim." (NBC News, April 29, 2011).

The "strongman" formerly known as Qadaffi or Kadaffy was killed, along with his son, on October 20, 2011. They were both captured alive, and video surfaced of them being mocked and beaten by their captors, with the public treated to footage of their dead bodies decaying in a meat locker. Their bodies were buried in a secret location, lest the people (who supposedly despised them) try to make it into a shrine. The "rebel" forces the United States supported in Libya turned out to be, as noted before, largely elements of Al-Qaeda, the alleged new number one collective bogeyman and the supposed reason why America was engaged in a perpetual "war against terror."

Operation Fast and Furious was another embarrassment to the Obama administration. Although it had been ongoing since 2008, this operation wasn't exposed until 2011. The scandal involved the FBI, ATF, and DEA engaging in an illegal gun-trafficking ring. The brilliant strategy behind this operation was that by using undercover government agents to sell weapons to the

Mexican drug cartels, US authorities would be able to track their movement and identify the higher-ups in the cartel. Shockingly, none of the higher-level cartel figures were ever apprehended, and barely a third of the firearms were recovered. The firearms sold by the US government were discovered at the scene of numerous violent crimes in both Mexico and America, and resulted in the deaths of an untold number of Mexicans.

Attention was finally focused on the operation when a US Border Patrol agent was murdered with one. President Obama would move to distance himself completely from Fast and Furious, claiming, "There may be a situation here in which a serious mistake was made, and if that's the case then we'll find out and we'll hold somebody accountable." Attorney General Eric Holder denied any knowledge of the fiasco as well. A congressional investigation revealed that individual agents had been told to stand down instead of confiscating illegal weapons, and that Fast and Furious had unquestionably led to more deaths and violence in Mexico.

In October 2011, a series of emails between ATF Special Agent Bill Newell and White House National Security Director Kevin O'Reilly went public. Although Holder had specifically denied knowledge in testimony before Congress, Newell admitted that he had discussed Fast and Furious with O'Neill, who met regularly with Obama, Vice President Biden, and other high-ranking cabinet members. The emails linked Newell to other important National Security advisors in the Obama White House. While continuing to cling to the pretense that Obama had no knowledge of, and in fact had never even heard of, Fast and Furious, the president's chief counsel announced that the White House was "withholding an unspecified number of internal emails exchanged among three National Security staff aides." This attorney, Kathryn Ruemmler, went on to declare that the president "has significant confidentiality interests" in these communications. CBS News and Fox News both reported, also in October 2011, that Attorney General Eric Holder was informed of the plan and had been sent documents about it as far back as July 2010.

Obama raised the war against "conspiracy theorists" to new levels. In a 2008 Harvard law academic paper, Obama's regulatory "czar" Cass Sunstein, along with coauthor Adrian Vermeule, proposed that "conspiracy theorizing" should be banned by the US government. A less draconian alternative to this, Sunstein suggested, would be to impose some kind of special tax "on those who disseminate such theories." Sunstein also argued for "cognitive infiltration of extremist groups," as if that hadn't been standard government policy for decades. Sunstein specifically mentioned the utilization of agents on social networks and Internet forums to "undermine percolating conspiracy theories . . . ." Of course, regular posters on many Internet forums would argue that such "trolls," as they are called, have existed since the early days of the Internet. Sunstein is typical of the people around Obama; he even proposed some Orwellian nightmare called the "First Amendment New Deal," which would establish a panel of "nonpartisan experts" to monitor debate. It is difficult to imagine a more obvious admission that there *are* indeed conspiracies than this outrageous, censorious suggestion.

Courageous, young Luke Rudkowski, whose organization We Are Change has done yeoman's work confronting our corrupt and incompetent leaders, was able to raise this topic with Sunstein during a question and answer session following a May 1, 2012, speech at NYU law school. Clearly embarrassed by the reference to his indefensible views, Sunstein unconvincingly responded, "I don't remember that article very well." He went on to ignore Luke's relentless attempts to get him to expound upon the subject.

TAX SCAMS, NDAA, AND OTHER ASSORTED NICETIES

With the endorsement of the Obama administration, Warren Buffett, one of the world's richest men, began campaigning for the government to tax people "like him" at a higher rate. Once again, the puppet masters behind the scenes orchestrated a phony "debate," with Obama cast in the role of shining crusader, attempting to make the "rich" pay their "fair share." In reality, Buffett and his mega-wealthy ilk don't pay much "income" tax because their portfolios are purposefully designed to shield them from the taxes they are so publicly enamored with.

Buffett's "income" is subject to the usual loopholes the wealthy have always taken advantage of. Meanwhile, the *New York Post* revealed, in its August 29, 2011, edition, that Buffett's firm, Berkshire Hathaway, owed back taxes going back to 2002. So much for Buffett's affinity for being taxed. Buffett admitted that he'd paid only 7 percent of his income in taxes the previous year, but that is a reflection of the cockeyed system and would not change if "income" tax rates were raised, because most of his "income" will always be categorized as dividends and other classifications not subject to the same taxes the common riffraff have to pay.

While Obama and his pal Buffett begged the sheeple to make him pay more taxes, Buffett has fought tooth and nail to avoid paying what he owes. Not only does his firm owe an estimated *$1 billion* in back taxes, but Buffett engaged in a fourteen-year battle with the IRS over dividend deductions, which was finally settled in 2005. Buffett, Bill Gates, and others are also in favor of the estate tax, but they make certain to shelter their huge fortunes in their foundations so that they aren't subject to any estate tax. Obama, in the best tradition of Bill Clinton, used Buffett's secretary, Debbie Bosanek, as a stage prop for his tax "fairness" policy during his 2012 State of the Union address. The claim was that Buffett's secretary had paid a higher tax rate than her immensely wealthy boss. However, critics pointed out that judging by Bosanek's reported income tax rate, she must have earned between $200,000 and $500,000 that year. This hardly put her in the "average Joe" category.

Bill Gates is just as adamant about the rich "paying more" as Buffett is. Gates's father, William Gates Sr., felt so strongly about the estate tax that he cowrote the book *Wealth and the Commonwealth; Why America Should Tax Accumulated Fortunes*. Bill Gates and his wife, Melinda, have publicly proclaimed they are not leaving anything in their wills to their children, which on the surface seems even more hard-hearted than Buffett's refusal to lend minimal assistance to his loved ones; it had been widely reported that Buffett refused to help his daughter pay for the remodeling of her kitchen or even to assist with his granddaughter's college tuition. However, current tax laws will permit Gates to channel any appreciation on his Microsoft stock to his children without anyone being taxed. His children will therefore almost certainly bypass the estate tax that both he and his father are so much in favor of.

On January 2, 2012, Obama signed perhaps the most draconian, dangerous piece of legislation in American history—the National Defense Authorization Act (NDAA). The law appears to permit the indefinite military detention of American citizens, without charge or trial. Obama pretended to be reluctant to sign it, but sign it he did. This was just another step in the "war on terror" and the extension of the concept of "battlefield" into nearly anything.

Another dastardly piece of legislation, the Stop Online Piracy Act (SOPA), was defeated thanks to a strong grassroots effort. However, an identical and even more diabolical bill, the Cyber Intelligence Sharing and Protection Act (CISPA), was passed by the House of Representatives in April 2012. Obama, of course, is in favor of any efforts to overturn the freedom of the Internet, so that the only uncontrolled means of communication can be subject to the same strictures that have made television the wasteland it is.

Obama supports all the worst abuses of the Bush years, from the Patriot Act to the perpetual "war on terror." The Transportation Security Administration (TSA) has seen its powers increased under Obama so that travelers (even small children) now are forced to submit to obscene groping and naked body scans. With "liberals" like Obama, who needs "conservatives?"

On April 20, 2010, BP Oil executives held a party to commemorate Deepwater Horizon having gone seven years without an accident. Incredibly, the party was being held onboard *Deepwater Horizon* at the exact moment a natural gas explosion occurred, sinking the rig and killing eleven crew members. The BP Oil spill turned out to be one of the greatest environmental disasters of all time. What was even more curious than the inexcusable negligence that allowed it to occur was the inept, plodding response on the part of authorities.

The Obama administration practically gave BP carte blanche to oversee the cleanup, and nearly everyone criticized their lackadaisical efforts. Why were toxic chemicals, which were probably more harmful than the oil itself, used in the cleanup process? A report from the American Medical Association entitled *Health Effects of the Gulf Oil Spill* described how the use of toxins like Corexit had caused innumerable cases of disease in local residents. On July 4, 2010, *Salon* reported that the US Coast Guard, which has no legislative authority, had issued an edict indicating that journalists who came closer than sixty-five feet to BP cleanup operations in the Gulf of Mexico without permission would be punished by a $40,000 fine and one to five years in prison. The *New York Times* and other mainstream media outlets reported that BP, the US Coast Guard, Homeland Security, and local police were prohibiting journalists from even photographing the massive damage from the continuing flow of oil and toxic chemicals into the Gulf.

In a report titled *Questioning EPA Fraud*, a group of Gulf residents compiled what they claimed was proof that the Environmental Protection Agency had lied about the health impact on Gulf residents and downplayed the significance of the contaminated beaches, water, and seafood. According to the report, there was an alarming difference between the levels of exposure to toxic chemicals considered as "safe" back in 1999 and those listed more recently by the EPA, which were "thousands of times higher." While George W. Bush had rightfully been criticized for his carefree reactions to the Katrina tragedy, Obama dodged any real media scrutiny for his similar tepid responsiveness to the BP oil spill. FEMA, meanwhile, had proven conclusively during Katrina that they simply weren't effective at dealing with real emergencies, and in the BP Oil spill they were a total nonfactor.

MORE OBAMA BODY COUNT

Robert F. Kennedy's second oldest son, Robert F. Kennedy Jr., began to show signs of becoming a political force to be reckoned with during the first decade of the twenty-first century. RFK Jr. ventured into the dangerous waters inhabited by the dreaded "conspiracy theorists" with his public posture that big medicine was covering up the rather obvious links between vaccines and autism, and on the general issue of vote fraud, inspired by the 2000 presidential election fiasco. In June 2005, Kennedy wrote an article about the vaccine-autism link that was published in *Rolling Stone* magazine and by Salon.com. Under pressure from powerful forces, the article was eventually retracted and deleted by both media organizations, supposedly because of numerous "factual errors." Rumors abounded that RFK Jr. was inevitably going to seek political office. He told Oprah Winfrey, in a January 2007 interview in her *O: The Oprah Magazine*, that he'd consider seeking the open New York Senate seat of Hillary Clinton if she were elected president.

Despite the fact that Hillary Clinton's seat was vacated when she was named secretary of state by President Obama, RFK Jr. opted not to run for the Senate, using the Ted Kennedy standby excuse that he needed to concentrate on his wife and children. JFK's lone remaining child, Caroline Kennedy Schlossberg, was considered a shoo-in to be named as a replacement for Senator Clinton, but a last-minute media campaign derailed her chances completely. During an interview with the establishment flagship the *New York Times*, Caroline, like many famous people, wasn't superbly articulate. Unlike most famous people, however, she didn't get the usual grammatical cleanup, and there ensued a media firestorm in which she was compared to Alaska Governor Sarah Palin. A December 29, 2008, article in the *London Telegraph*, quaintly titled "Caroline Kennedy repeats 'you know' 142 times in interview," exemplified the powerful forces aligning against her. To the supposed "shock" of the political world, Caroline withdrew her name from consideration.

On July 15, 2012, the *New York Times* would demonstrate just how unusual this kind of pristine accuracy is when it admitted to censoring stories at the whim of the government. When dealing with public figures, the paper acknowledged, "The quotations come back redacted, stripped of colorful metaphors, colloquial language and anything even mildly provocative." Evidently, the daughter of an ex-president of the United States wasn't granted this standard courtesy.

On May 16, 2012, RFK Jr.'s second wife, Mary Kennedy, was found hanged to death in a barn on her Mount Kisco, New York, property. While Mary had exhibited some unstable behavior for quite some time, this was yet another in a seemingly endless series of unnatural deaths in the Kennedy family. One thing was certain; RFK Jr. no longer appeared to be in any position to run for higher political office.

Nancy Hamilton, eighty-two-year-old wife of former Representative Lee Hamilton, who'd been instrumental in seeing that Congress didn't look deeply into the October Surprise scandal, and later served as vice-chairman of the 9/11 Commission, died in a very strange manner. On August 11, 2012, she was outside a veterinarian's office when her car rolled backward and ran her over. It was reminiscent of the way Marvin Bush's nanny had died. However you look at, it was a decidedly unnatural way for someone to leave this world.

MEDIA AND CELEBRITY FAWNING

Celebrity and journalistic fawning over Obama was so embarrassing that it made the Teflon coverage Bill Clinton had received look mild in comparison. Beginning with his inauguration, during which ABC's Bill Weir gushed, "Never have so many people shivered so long with such joy. From above, even the seagulls must have been awed by the blanket of humanity," the always biased press corps acted like unofficial members of Obama's cabinet. Following Obama's election, CBS's veteran liberal curmudgeon Andy Rooney declared, ". . . I'm not hearing anyone who hates Barack Obama." *USA Today* headlined, "Americans go gaga over First Lady's inaugural gown."

Obama's unprecedented appearance on *The Tonight Show with Jay Leno* in March 2009 resulted in the president launching a tasteless, offensive comment about the Special Olympics that would have caused mere mortal politicians a great deal of embarrassment. Obama, however, received no strong criticism of his politically incorrect "joke." In reality, the establishment press treated Obama like the "rock star" they'd often claimed he was. The mainstream media goes absolutely livid over any of the reasonable questions that need to be asked about Obama's background, smearing those who raise them derisively as "birthers."

Hollywood has been even more obsequiously pro-Obama. The Black Eyed Peas created a campaign video titled "Yes We Can," with an array of celebrities participating, from Kareem Abdul-Jabbar to Scarlett Johansson. "He is 'The One,'" declared Oprah Winfrey. George Clooney called Obama "the best candidate I've ever seen." Halle Berry said she would "collect paper cups off the ground to make his path clear." Tom Hanks gushed, "He has the integrity and the inspiration to unify us as did FDR and Harry Truman and John F. Kennedy. . . ." Hanks, who is intending to make a miniseries devoted to Vincent Bugliosi's book claiming that Oswald acted alone in assassinating

Kennedy, has become renowned in recent years for acting as if he'd served in WWII and/or been an actual participant in NASA's Apollo program.

At the 2012 BET Soul Train awards, Jamie Foxx actually referred to Obama as "our Lord and Savior." Comedian Chris Rock uttered these syrupy comments at a 2013 Capitol Hill press conference: "I am just here to support the president of the United States. President of the United States is our boss, but he is also . . . you know, the president and the first lady are kinda like the mom and the dad of the country. And when your dad says something you listen, and when you don't it will usually bite you on the ass later on. So, I'm here to support the president." There was no ridicule directed Rock's way, and it is impossible to accept that there wouldn't have been any if, say, a country music star such as Brad Paisley had said the same things about George W. Bush.

"Libertarian" Bill Maher, who was noticeable for defending Bill Clinton 100 percent of the time on his horribly mistitled television show *Politically Incorrect*, donated a widely publicized $1 million to Obama's 2012 campaign, explaining to Chris Matthews, "These Republicans scare me." "Cutting edge" comedian Denis Leary uttered the following assessment of Obama, presumably with a straight face, on the May 30, 2009, *Larry King Live*: "I do have to say that I think that President Obama is the greatest president in the history of all of our presidents, and that he can do no wrong in my book."

There are plenty of people outside Hollywood who think otherwise.

CHAPTER TWELVE

THE FRANKLIN COVER-UP/ CHILD SEX SCANDALS

"I'm just going to tell you at this point that we will not participate
with you. . . . It's something that we don't even care to delve into."
—Public Affairs officer for Boys Town, refusing an interview with
the makers of the suppressed film *Conspiracy of Silence*

On June 29, 1989, the *Washington Times* ran an explosive, front-page story headlined "Call Boys Took Midnight Tour of White House." The paper revealed that a homosexual prostitution ring, featuring often underage males, was connected to "key officials of the Reagan and Bush administrations" and other powerful people "with close social ties to Washington's political elite." When questioned about these odd midnight tours of the White House, First Lady Barbara Bush expressed no concerns about them and stated she was glad the *Washington Post* hadn't covered the story. One of the busiest clients in the ring was Craig J. Spence, a very influential Republican lobbyist and Washington, D.C., party host.

In the August 9, 1989, *Washington Times*, there were damning excerpts from a recent interview with Spence. "How do you think a little faggot like me moved in the circles I did?" Spence was quoted as saying. "It's because I had contacts at the highest levels of this government." At another pertinent point, Spence declared, "They'll deny it. But how do they make me go away, when so many of them have been at my house, at my parties and at my side?"

Not surprisingly, Spence was found dead in a room at Boston's Ritz-Carlton Hotel on November 10, 1989. Near his body was a newspaper story regarding proposed legislation to protect CIA agents testifying before Congress. On the mirror in his hotel room's bathroom, written in a black felt-tip marker, was: "Chief, consider this my resignation, effective immediately. As you always said, you can't ask others to make a sacrifice if you are not ready to do the same. Life is duty. God bless America." Spence had told the *Washington Times* that if he testified, he would provide damaging information into the call boy ring, bribery of Japanese and US officials, and other sordid matters.

Showing that these scandals were a bipartisan affair, on August 25, 1989, the *Washington Times* broke a story about a prostitution ring run out of Democratic Congressman Barney Frank's Capitol Hill residence. Frank quickly threw the "male escort" involved under the bus and claimed that while he was aware his former lover, whose professional name was Greg Davis, had been a prostitute, he hadn't known he was involved in a prostitution ring. Maryland's Chevy Chase Elementary School Principal Gabriel A. Massaro was a notable client of Davis, who introduced him to Representative Frank. Davis claimed Frank was fully aware of the situation. Frank explained his curious lack of awareness about what was going on thusly: "I was emotionally vulnerable at that time. I guess I was still coming to terms with being gay. . . ." The newspaper went on to report that Davis had actually used Chevy Chase Elementary School in late 1987 to run his prostitution ring, after the principal began paying him for sex. Principal Massaro admitted that he'd provided Davis with a guidance counselor's office and his own telephone line at the model "magnet school," which he used even when children were elsewhere in the building.

Both Davis and Massaro denied that any children were involved in the ring, but in light of what was to come out of Franklin, Nebraska, one can't help but wonder. Davis would be identified by his real name, Stephen L. Gobie, in subsequent news accounts. In a September 1, 1989, *Washington Times* story, it would be stated that Craig Spence had been one of Gobie's clients. Unsuccessful efforts to expel and censure Frank were led by Republican Representative Larry Craig, who would make headlines in 2007 when he was arrested for soliciting gay sex in an airport restroom.

Attorney John DeCamp, a former Nebraska state senator, would write an important book on this subject, *The Franklin Cover-Up*. DeCamp discovered that the aforementioned Republican Party insider Larry King had organized a child sex ring, to service politicians and powerful business figures, during his tenure with the Franklin Credit Union in Omaha, Nebraska. DeCamp client Paul Bonacci claimed that as a youth he'd been transported all over the country, forced to have sex, deliver drugs, and appear in snuff films, at Larry King's behest. Without any knowledge of Bohemian Grove, the northern California spot where powerful leaders gather every summer to worship a giant owl and participate in occult rituals with no females allowed to attend, Bonacci described the ceremonies perfectly. Later, when talk show host Alex Jones would sneak inside Bohemian Grove and film the frightening "cremation of care" ritual, which revolves around the supposed "mock" sacrifice of a child, Bonacci's testimony that a *real* child was murdered there became even more chilling. Bonacci also specifically alleged that he'd had sex with Representative Barney Frank in the basement of his Washington, D.C., home.

Powerful local figures in Omaha were implicated by Bonacci, including Police Chief Robert Wadman and newspaper publisher Harold Anderson. The FBI refused to investigate the allegations of child abuse. A grand jury labeled the charges a "hoax," and one witness, Troy Boner, retracted his statements but later claimed he was threatened into doing so by the FBI. Victim Alisha Owen told the Nebraska Senate's Franklin Committee that the FBI had informed her lawyer that if she recanted her story, "no charges would ever be brought against me." She also claimed to have seen President George H. W. Bush himself at one of these parties, accompanied by a young black male companion. Incredibly, this young lady who had testified before a federal grand jury about being sexually abused as a minor by a Nebraska District Court judge, and Larry King himself, among others, was sentenced on August 8, 1991, to serve nine to twenty-seven years in prison on charges of perjury. You read that right: The child victim of sexual abuse was thrown into prison for an absurdly long period of time because she dared to report the outrageous crimes of powerful figures. Alisha Owen stuck by her story, even after her seventeen-year-old brother Aaron was found hanged to death in a correctional center cell on November 9, 1990. She was finally released from prison in 2001.

DeCamp quoted one professional reaction to this excruciatingly harsh sentence in the introduction to his book: "'This is unprecedented, probably in the history of the United States,' commented Dr. Judianne Densen-Gerber, a lawyer, psychiatrist and nationally prominent specialist on child abuse, during her visit to Nebraska in December 1990. 'If the children are not telling the truth, particularly if they have been abused, they need help, medical attention. You don't throw them in jail!'"

The Nebraska State Senate's chief investigator for the Franklin Committee, Gary Caradori, died in a highly suspicious plane crash on July

11, 1990. A deputy sheriff who first arrived at the crash scene reported there was child pornography scattered all over the farmer's field where the plane went down. The farmer claimed that he'd seen the plane explode in midair. In an odd coincidence, Caradori's wife, Sandie, reported receiving several phone calls from witness Troy Boner on the day her husband's plane crashed. "I am familiar with his voice," Sandie Caradori said. "Gary wasn't lying. He didn't tell me what to say." Boner told her, and she could hear him fighting back tears. "What I told him was the truth. They made me take it back. They threatened me." (*The Franklin Cover-Up* by John Decamp, pp. 186–187).

Boner had good reason to be frightened; on January 17, 1991, his brother Shawn had been killed while allegedly playing "Russian Roulette." In a 2005 updated edition of his book, DeCamp revealed what later happened to Troy Boner. In late 2003, Boner walked into a New Mexico hospital screaming, "They're after me. They're after me because of this book." He was waving a copy of *The Franklin Cover-Up*. After being mildly sedated, Boner was placed in a private room for observation. "When nurses came back to check on him early the next morning, Boner was sitting in a chair, bleeding from the mouth and quite dead," DeCamp wrote. "No news stories were published on Boner's death despite his 'notoriety' in the Franklin case."

A powerful documentary about this entire subject, *Conspiracy of Silence*, was produced by England's Yorkshire Television. An investigative team worked on the project for ten months, locating new witnesses and uncovering new evidence in the process. The program stressed how Nebraska's Boys Town, immortalized in the classic 1938 film starring Spencer Tracy as Father Flannigan, was used by Larry King and others from Franklin to recruit youths from troubled backgrounds. When the program was first sent to the United States, custom officials tried to label it as "pornographic material." Pressure from key US politicians caused the show to be pulled at the last minute. *Conspiracy of Silence* was scheduled to air on the Discovery Channel on May 3, 1994, and was even listed in *TV Guide*. After it was pulled, all copies were supposed to be destroyed. Fortunately, a copy soon began circulating all over the Internet, even though the picture quality was decidedly subpar.

DeCamp described speaking with Monsignor Robert Hupp, who had been executive director of Nebraska's Boys Town from 1973 through 1985. In Decamp's words, again from his Introduction: "When I asked Monsignor Hupp how this ever could have happened at Boys Town, he looked at me and told me, so apologetically, 'I am like the wife who did not know, and was the last to find out. And when I finally did suspect something and tried to act, the Archbishop [Daniel Sheehan] elected to do nothing about it, when I asked him to help. And then, when I came upon something horribly evil, I found public officials and the Church would do nothing—apparently terrified at the damage it would do to the Church and to the entire city of Omaha. . . .'" Hupp told DeCamp that he was pressured relentlessly and eventually had to leave Boys Town. Hupp would go on to appear in the censored *Conspiracy of Silence* documentary.

But there was still more to this grisly story. Renowned "gonzo" journalist Hunter Thompson had been identified by Paul Bonacci (Bonacci remembered hearing his name) as directing a snuff film at Bohemian Grove. Thompson was also supposedly looking into the alternative theories of what really happened on September 11, 2001, and was even rumored to be coming clean about his association with the pedophile ring, at the time he "committed suicide" on February 20, 2005.

There were more unnatural deaths associated with this story; DeCamp provided a list in his book, though unfortunately he didn't include most of the dates. Omaha restaurant owner Bill Baker, a purported partner of Larry King in his pornographic business, was found shot in the back of the head. Newt Copple, a confidential informant for investigator Gary Caradori, died suddenly at the age of seventy in March 1991. DeCamp points out he was an ex-wrestler with no known health problems, and that his parents had lived into their late eighties or nineties. Another alleged King crony, Joe Malek, died from a gunshot wound that was ruled a suicide. Charlie Rogers, described as Larry King's lover, was found with his head blown off. Dan Ryan, another King associate, was found strangled or suffocated in a car. Kathleen Sorenson was an outspoken activist against Satanism, and had been the foster parent for two of the child victims after they fled the home of Larry King's relatives. She was killed in a suspicious car crash in October 1989. Sorenson was highly visible; she had appeared on Geraldo Rivera's memorable, sensationalistic television special on Satanism. Curtis Tucker, yet another King comrade, fell or jumped from the window of a Holiday Inn in Omaha.

DEATH OF WILLIAM COLBY

Franklin Cover-Up author John DeCamp had an intriguing mentor and friend in former CIA director William Colby. Colby encouraged him to write about the hideous child sex scandal but cautioned him with these words: "What you have to understand, John, is that sometimes there are forces and events too big, too powerful, with so much at stake for other people or institutions, that you cannot do anything about them, no matter how evil or wrong they are and no matter how dedicated or sincere you are or how much evidence you have. This is simply one of the hard facts of life you have to face." Those words became more poignant when Colby himself died under very mysterious circumstances on April 29, 1996. Colby went missing and was the victim of an apparent boating accident. His body was ultimately discovered in Maryland's Wicomico River minus his life jacket, which his family and friends insisted he always wore while boating. To no one's surprise, the authorities attributed his death to a heart attack or stroke, concluding he fell into the water and drowned as a result.

Christopher Ruddy, before finding a publisher for his important book about the Vince Foster case, had considered the idea of asking William Colby to write the foreword. Colby had danced all around the political spectrum; in recent years, he had advocated unilateral disarmament and became affiliated with the "liberal" Institute for Policy Studies. Colby had been a contributing editor to James Dale Davidson's investment newsletter, and Davidson wasn't shy about publicly proclaiming that Foster had been murdered. The newsletter, *Strategic Investment*, covered all the sordid Clinton shenanigans in full detail.

Ruddy looked into the death of Colby and found some glaring inconsistencies. For instance, the Associated Press had run an initial story prematurely declaring Colby "missing and presumed drowned," and quoted a source close to his wife as saying he'd told her that day he wasn't feeling well "but was going canoeing anyway." A week later, Colby's wife assured the *Washington Times* that her husband had been well and had not mentioned canoeing. When police arrived at Colby's home, they found both his computer and radio left on. There were dinner dishes still on the table. Friends reported this was unusual behavior for a meticulous man like Colby. While the coroner attributed his death by drowning to a heart attack or stroke, the autopsy found no evidence of either. Colby always wore shoes when boating, and the late April day had been blustery, but his body was found without them. Colby had headed the dreadful Operation Phoenix for the CIA in Vietnam; perhaps a guilty conscience finally caused a sea of change within him.

SATANIST/MILITARY CONNECTIONS

The Franklin scandal would tie into the larger question of whether or not Satanist groups, associated with powerful US officials, were involved in these child sex rings. Lieutenant Colonel Michael Aquino was a strange individual. High-ranking military officers are not usually easily connected to Satanism, but Aquino admittedly founded the Temple of Set in 1975 while he was in the Special Reserves. Aquino, who wrote his doctoral dissertation on the neutron bomb and also produced a widely circulated paper titled "From Psy Ops to Mind War," had a long affiliation with government mind-control programs.

One of the most celebrated missing children cases in recent times was the previously noted 1982 disappearance of Des Moines, Iowa, paperboy Johnny Gosch. John DeCamp, Paul Bonacci's lawyer, alleged that Larry King and others were guilty of ritualistically abusing children, including Bonacci. Bonacci testified that the mastermind behind the Gosch kidnapping, of which he was well aware, had been someone referred to as "The Colonel." Bonacci described a nationwide pedophile network that involved powerful military, CIA, political, and corporate powers.

In his book, DeCamp refers to a May 21, 1989, *Omaha World-Herald* article linking Larry King and the Franklin Credit Union to the Iran-Contra affair. DeCamp wrote that "rumors have persisted that money from the credit union somehow found its way to the Nicaraguan contra rebels." (*The Franklin Cover-Up* by John DeCamp, p. 171). Photographer Rusty Nelson, mentioned earlier, took many of the obscene photos of Larry King's underage sex slaves. In a June 22, 2000, written statement Nelson declared, "Another dark villain was Colonel Akino [Colonel Michael Aquino] to whom King paid off with a suitcase of bearer bonds and cash earmarked for covert Contra operations." King told Nelson that Aquino was part of the Contra guns and drug trafficking program, run by Colonel Oliver North.

The July 24, 1988, issue of the *San Jose Mercury News* ran a story with the alarming headline "Child Abuse at the Presidio, The Parents' Agony, the Army's Coverup, the Prosecution's Failure." The article told how Aquino had been implicated in a nationwide Satanic pedophile ring, where children had been procured from day care centers on military bases like the Presidio. "The criminal case [Presidio] is closed, but by June, the parents of 23 children had filed $55 million in claims against the Army . . . ," the paper reported.

The Presidio Child Development Center in San Francisco was run by the US Army. Allegations of abuse at the center first emerged in November 1986. A concerned parent had her three-year-old son medically examined, based upon his accusations, and the exam confirmed that the boy had been anally raped. No one was ever prosecuted at the Center because of what Aquino and his defenders would cite as a "lack of evidence." More scandals began to cross over here, as the US Attorney in San Francisco, who failed to prosecute the charges, was Joseph Russoniello, identified by journalist Gary Webb as being involved in Contra cocaine drug trafficking. In May 1989, Aquino was questioned again in regard to child abuse, as five children in three different cities had made accusations against him.

Noreen Gosch would give sworn testimony in a Nebraska courtroom on February 5, 1999, linking Aquino to a nationwide pedophile ring. She connected the disappearance of her own son with Aquino. Gosch testified: "Well, then there was a man by the name of Michael Aquino. He was in the military. He had top Pentagon clearances. He was a pedophile. He was a Satanist. He's founded the Temple of Set. And he was a close friend of Anton LaVey. The two of them were very active in ritualistic sexual abuse. And they deferred funding from this government program to use [in] this experimentation on children. . . . They used these kids to sexually compromise politicians or anyone else they wish to have control of. This sounds so far out and so bizarre I had trouble accepting it in the beginning myself until I was presented with the data. We have the proof. In black and white." Under questioning from DeCamp, Gosch declared: "I know that Michael Aquino has been in Iowa. I know that Michael Aquino has been to Offutt Air Force Base [a Strategic Air Command base, near Omaha, which was linked to King's activities]. I know that he has had contact with many of these children."

Even as Aquino was being investigated by Army Criminal Investigation Division officers for possible involvement in these child abuse cases, he was retaining the highest-level security clearances. On August 14, 1987, San Francisco police raided Aquino's home in response to allegations that the house had been the scene of a brutal rape of a four-year-old girl. The primary suspect in the rape, a Baptist minister named Gary Hambright (who was also named by the previously mentioned three-year-old boy as the "teacher" at the Presidio who had raped him), was indicted in September 1987. He was charged with committing "lewd and lascivious acts" with six boys and four girls, ranging in age from three to seven years. At the time of the alleged crimes, Hambright had been employed at a child care center on the US Army base at Presidio. In fact, the San Francisco police charged that he had been involved in at least fifty-eight separate incidents of child sexual abuse.

The October 30, 1987, *San Francisco Examiner* reported that one of the victims had identified Aquino and his wife as participants in the child rape. According to this victim, the Aquinos had filmed scenes of the child being fondled by Hambright in a bathtub. The child's description of the residence, which was also the headquarters of Aquino's Satanic Temple of Set, was so detailed that police were able to obtain a search warrant. They found thirty-eight videotapes, photo negatives, and other evidence indicating that the home had been the center of a pedophile ring, operating in and around US military bases.

Despite all this, Aquino and his wife were never indicted or charged with anything. The public furor over Hambright's indictment did prompt the US Army to transfer Aquino from the Presidio, where he was the deputy director of reserve training, to the US Army Reserve Personnel Center in St. Louis. On April 19, 1988, the ten-count indictment against Hambright was inexplicably dropped by aforementioned US Attorney Joseph Russoniello. On April 22, 1989, the US Army sent letters to the parents of at least fifty-six of the children believed to have been molested by Hambright, urging them to have their children tested for the HIV virus, because Hambright was reported to be a carrier. The *San Jose Mercury News* of January 5, 1990, would report that Hambright had died of AIDS the previous November, at the age of thirty-six. The paper reported that Hambright had denied he was sick when they'd tried to interview him in the spring of 1989, but his death certificate indicated he'd had the disease for "years." The paper also stated that the Army was refusing to discuss how many children had been tested for the disease, or what the results of those tests were, due to "confidentiality laws."

The Pentagon's spokesman told the press, in defense of Aquino, "The question is whether he is trustworthy or can do the job. There is nothing that would indicate in this case that there is any problem we should be concerned about." The US military's seeming tolerance of a Satanist who had been connected to the worst imaginable offenses against children was disturbing, to say the least.

MCMARTIN PRESCHOOL SCANDAL

The McMartin Preschool scandal, which concerned allegations that those who ran the California day care center committed numerous acts of sexual abuse on children, began in 1983 and culminated in a high-profile trial that ran for three years until all charges were dropped in 1990. However, archeological excavation at the site in May 1990 disclosed a startling fact; the "tunnels" so many of the children had described indeed did exist. In fact, two elaborate underground complexes were discovered under the preschool. Later, the tunnels were filled in with dirt and concrete by unknown parties before the building was demolished.

Apologists would try and explain that the tunnels were merely a "rubbish pit." Even now, there is more debunking of the claims of abuse, which resulted in hundreds of families filing police reports, than supportive information to be found on the Internet. In a related unnatural death, Judy Johnson, the woman whose initial complaint eventually led to the McMartin teachers being arrested, was found dead in her home at age forty-two on December 20, 1986. Online accounts claim she had been the recipient of several threats and had been followed in public.

The press was overtly biased against the children and parents who made claims against the McMartin teachers. Journalist Alexander Cockburn, another of those alleged "leftists" who despised the Kennedys, wrote one of the most blatant hit pieces, an op-ed that appeared in the February 8, 1990, *Wall Street Journal* and was charmingly titled, "The McMartin Case: Indict the Children, Jail the Parents." It didn't matter to Cockburn or anyone else in the mainstream media that the Children's Institute International had concluded "a full eighty percent displayed physical symptoms, including vaginal or rectal scarring." There were also former McMartin students, now young adults, who corroborated the stories of these children. Powerful Hollywood figure Abby Mann became oddly involved in the case, overtly defending the accused McMartin officials to the extent of convincing CBS to air a *60 Minutes* episode that was basically a brief for the defense. Mann was one of many progressives whom eccentric researcher Mae Brussell labeled as disinformation agents working for the government.

There were other deaths associated with the case. KABC reporter Wayne Satz had broken the McMartin preschool scandal in 1984, and unlike most of his peers in the mainstream media, strongly believed the allegations were true. He died of a heart attack in January 1993, at the very young age of forty-seven. Then there was Robert Winkler, whom the children claimed was a frequent guest at the preschool and was referred to as the "Wolfman." Winkler would be subsequently arrested for running a babysitting service in Torrance, California, that was allegedly a front for a sexual abuse ring. Winkler turned up dead of an alleged drug overdose just before his trial. Also, former Hermosa Beach police officer Paul Bynum, who'd been hired by the victims' parents as a private investigator, died before his scheduled testimony could be delivered, supposedly from a self-inflicted gunshot wound.

Los Angeles District Attorney Robert Philibosian announced, just after the story was broken by Satz, that the 1976 murder of Karen Klaas was going to be reexamined for possible connections to the McMartin scandal. Klaas was the ex-wife of famed singer Bill Medley of the Righteous Brothers. She had been murdered about an hour after dropping off her five-year-old son at the McMartin preschool. Her husband, Gerald Klaas, died in March 1984, shortly after the first indictments in the case, when he drove off a mountain road one afternoon in Oregon. There are numerous accounts from various sources in the mainstream media, easily accessible online, reporting that the Klaas rape and murder was "about to be reopened" in mid-2009. Bill Medley was said to be hopeful that new DNA technology could help solve the case. Interestingly, Paul Bynum had been assigned the Karen Klaas murder case in 1976 by the Hermosa Beach police department. I contacted Bill Medley's manager as this book was going to the editor, and he informed me that Medley had "nothing to add" on the subject.

It is difficult to believe that all those children invented the same identically "outrageous" allegations, and that all those parents were so fooled by them. Ted Gunderson, renegade ex-chief of the Los Angeles division of the FBI, told *Executive Intelligence Review* in a May 25, 1990, interview, "In the McMartin case, for example, before any criminal charges were filed against anyone, 460 complaints were filed with the Manhattan Beach police. Are we to believe that 460 families fed their children the same story of ritualistic sexual abuse, animal sacrifices, etc.?" In the July 1982 issue of *Reader's Digest*, an article estimated that "approximately 100,000 children are unaccounted for" every year. Believe it or not, the FBI doesn't bother to keep count of the number of missing children.

As Gunderson noted, "The FBI has an accurate count of the number of automobiles stolen every year. It knows the number of homicides, rapes, and robberies, but the FBI has no idea of the number of children who disappear every year. They simply do not ask for the statistics. Every month, every major police department in the United States files its uniform crime statistics with the FBI. It would be simple for the bureau to add one more column to the statistics and get a breakdown of every reported case of missing children—not to even mention children who are kidnapped for ritualistic purposes—and, in some cases, murdered. I am convinced that the FBI does not ask for these statistics because they do not want to see them. They would be confronted with an instant public outcry for action, because the figures would show a major social problem. That problem would demand action." (From the foreword to *The Franklin Cover-Up* by John DeCamp).

I exchanged emails with Jackie McGauley, one of the McMartin parents and the individual who had personally hired the archeologist that found, as she described it in her online article "It's Time to Set the Record Straight Regarding McMartin Preschool Satanic Abuse," "3 sections of tunnels directly under the preschool building foundation." McGauley further wrote, "A year later I commissioned a formal report. I arranged to pay the archaeologist $3,000 to write the formal report, $1,000 in donations, $1,000 from Gloria

Steinam and $1,000 from me. I contacted many publishers. No one would publish it."

McGauley sounded like a passionate advocate, and I wanted to see if she would share some further details. When I emailed her, I questioned the involvement of Gloria Steinem, because I found that a bit puzzling. I was surprised by the curt, brief tone of her emails. She had no further information to provide and explained away the Steinem connection thusly: "Needed to raise money to have the report written so a mutual friend suggested I call Steinam. I did, she was behind the idea and helped. Very nice lady." I then received another short reply to my follow-up, in which she corrected me about Judy Johnson's death, saying, "Judy died from alcohol poisoning. She was allergic to alcohol and that was her only way of coping." I found the tone of her emails to be far different from that of her online article, for whatever reason.

THE FINDERS, CHILD PROTECTIVE SERVICES, AND MORE

A few reports appeared in the mainstream media (*US News and World Report*, December 27, 1993, and January 3, 1994; *Washington Post*, February 7, 1997) about a strange group called the Finders. On February 4, 1987, Tallahassee, Florida, police were alerted to the fact that six ill-clad, extremely dirty young children had been sighted in a nearby park. Two adults with them were subsequently arrested and found to be connected to the Finders, an organization based in Washington, D.C. The children were all under seven, and only one could speak. They didn't seem to understand what everyday items like toilets and telephones were.

Metropolitan Police Department along with the Customs Service, raided a warehouse, which a police detective had been told was used for orgies and blood rituals. Information was discovered revealing that the children had been transported around the world, and there were photographs of naked children, along with others of both children and adults dressed in white robes, participating in the ritualistic slaughtering and obscene mutilation of goats. They found what appeared to be an altar, numerous jars of feces and urine, and documents containing "detailed instructions for obtaining children for unspecified purposes." The Metropolitan Police immediately dropped the matter "like a hot rock," in the words of the Tallahassee police. According to a Metropolitan police official, the case "had become a CIA internal matter." The FBI, along with the Customs Service, ordered any further investigation stopped on the grounds of "national security," and the Metropolitan police case files were sealed.

The leader of the Finders was retired Air Force officer Marion Pettie. His wife had worked for the CIA, and his son was employed by Air America, known as the "CIA's airline." One would think that an organization found to be in possession of such reprehensible material would no longer exist; on the contrary, the Finders presently have facilities in both Washington, D.C., and Culpepper, Virginia. As *US News and World Report* described it, "The group's practices, the police said, were eccentric—not illegal." Also noted by the mainstream media organ were the "allegations that the Finders are somehow linked to the Central Intelligence Agency." Not surprisingly, CIA officials were quoted as calling these allegations "hogwash." Florida Republican Congressman Tom Lewis expressed concern that ". . . there is a lot of evidence. I can tell you this: We've got a lot of people scrambling, and that wouldn't be happening if there was nothing here."

On January 23, 2010, reports broke in the mainstream media about "several dozen Pentagon officials and contractors with high-level security clearances who allegedly purchased and downloaded child pornography, including an undisclosed number who used their government computers to obtain the illegal material, according to investigative reports." (*Boston Globe*, January 23, 2010). A year later, in January 2011, stories in the mainstream media recounted how an unfathomable fifty-two hundred Pentagon employees had purchased child pornography in 2006.

Some researchers into these child sex scandals have been very critical of state Child Protective Services agencies, and allege they are connected to the corruption. One highly vocal critic of CPS was former Georgia State Senator Nancy Schaefer. Schaefer made numerous allegations against the Georgia CPS and the Department of Family & Child Services, including that they had permitted children to be left in foster homes with known pedophiles and had refused to remove children from situations in which they were being abused and tortured.

Controversial talk show host Alex Jones interviewed Schaefer in depth about the subject of CPS corruption nationally. Schaefer had come to believe that CPS was involved in basically kidnapping children for profit and sexual exploitation. In one article she wrote, entitled "The Corrupt Business of Child Protective Services," published on the Kidjacked.com website, Schaefer concluded that, based on her firsthand research, financially poor parents were frequently targeted by CPS because they couldn't afford proper legal services; that case workers and social workers often fraudulently withhold or fabricate evidence; that National Center on Child Abuse and Neglect statistics reveal that six times as many children die in foster care as in the general population; that once removed to the "safety" of the system, children were far more likely to suffer sexual and other abuses than they were in the general population; and the Adoption and Safe Families Act, signed by President Clinton, was in reality a perverted slush fund, with cash "bonuses" awarded to states for every child adopted from foster care. Some local CPS agencies, according to Schaefer, provided an extra bonus for "special needs" children, and additional funds for children placed in mental health facilities.

On March 26, 2010, Schaefer and her husband, Bruce, were found shot to death in their Habersham County home. It was impossible for those who knew the Schaefers to accept that either of them would have committed suicide or murder. They had five children, more than a dozen grandchildren, and were faithful Christians who valued the sanctity of life. In typical fashion, the mainstream media covered the story of Schaefer's death dishonestly. The *Atlanta Journal-Constitution* quoted State Senator Don Thomas, indicating he was a "close friend" of Schaefer's, when in reality he was diametrically opposed to most of her beliefs. Thomas also supported the predictable (and instantaneous) "murder suicide" theory of the police. Several people posted on Facebook that they had recently spoken with Schaefer, and everything had seemed fine. Police claimed to have found a four-page suicide note from Bruce at the scene and vaguely alluded to financial problems, as well as his "terminal" cancer. The autopsy revealed no such "terminal" illness, and their children were not aware of any financial difficulties.

CPS agencies seem to be a part of the problem, not the solution. There are horror stories to be found all over the Internet regarding CPS officials forcing children as young as three years old to take powerful psychotropic drugs. During an October 4, 2004, Texas State Committee hearing on Psychotropic Drugs and Foster Children, Joe Burkett, chairman of the Texas Society of Psychiatric Physicians, shocked many with his statement that foster children needed medication because "they are very sick, from a bad gene pool." This pseudo-eugenicist line of thinking has permeated officialdom at all levels for a very long time.

The website Kidjacked.com published an article, on March 24, 2005, about gruesome medical experimentation being done on foster children in New York City. The children were under the guardianship of the City's Administration of Children Services, and the experiments were sponsored by the National Institutes of Health in conjunction with various big pharmaceutical companies. These poor children were given up to seven different drugs and vaccines at a time, in multiple combinations, and they had all been previously diagnosed as being HIV positive. The government agencies never released information about the results of these experiments or how many children died or were adversely affected by them. A powerful documentary on this issue, called *Guinea Pig Kids*, aired on the BBC in England and other parts of Europe, but no part of the American mainstream media covered the story of these inhumane experiments being done inside their country, funded by their government.

In November 2011, a new child sex scandal made headlines across the country. Former Penn State football defensive coordinator Jerry Sandusky was accused of sexually molesting several young boys, including a particularly graphic assault in the Penn State university locker room showers, which was personally witnessed by an ex-player turned grad student. The story brought head coach Joe Paterno's long and illustrious career to an end, as he was fired by the university only days after the news broke, on November 9. The elderly Paterno died in January 2012. In June 2012, Sandusky was found guilty on forty-five counts of sexual abuse over a fifteen-year period.

While the media covered the scandal extensively, as usual their reporting left a lot to be desired. There was little mention, for instance, about the mysterious disappearance of Centre County, Pennsylvania, District Attorney Ray Gricar on April 15, 2005. Gricar had investigated Sandusky on the same kinds of allegations that would ruin him six years later, and he curiously chose not to prosecute. This is all the more inexplicable when one considers Gricar's "tough as nails" reputation and the fact that his nephew told reporters that his uncle was left with "a bitter taste in his mouth for the Penn State program and its coach." Gricar's body was never found, but his laptop was discovered in the Susquehanna River, with the hard drive conveniently removed.

I emailed ESPN, asking them why they failed to note Gricar's connection to Sandusky during all their hours of saturation coverage of the scandal, but they never replied. Gricar's disappearance brought back memories of Assistant United States Attorney Jonathan P. Luna, who was found dead in a stream outside Lancaster, Pennsylvania, stabbed thirty-six times, on December 4, 2003.

The NCAA is corrupt to the core, with tons of money being made off players who masquerade as "students." While the establishment would love to portray Sandusky as a "lone nut" type of "predator" whose actions shocked the sensibilities of all the fine, upstanding people who run college athletics, I'm dubious that he was the only one involved, or that Penn State was the only college plagued by this sordid behavior. How would Sandusky have felt secure, for instance, in raping a ten-year-old boy in full view of anyone who entered the Penn State locker room? Doesn't that indicate he knew no one was going to object to his vile act?

Sandusky had formed his Second Mile Foundation, a nonprofit program designed for "at-risk" youths, in 1977. Senator Rick Santorum (R-PA), a sanctimonious arbiter of morality, presented Sandusky with a Congressional Angels in Adoption Award in 2002. The Second Mile Foundation was listed as one of President George H. W. Bush's "Thousand Points of Light." Bush's son Marvin (President Dubya's brother) sits on the NCAA's board of directors.

Predictably, the establishment trotted out a tried and true trooper, Louis Freeh, ex-FBI director during the Clinton years, to "investigate" the Penn State scandal. Freeh wasn't about to venture near the sordid underbelly of college athletics and contained the inquiry to Sandusky and a few other Penn State officials. Unfortunately for Paterno's family, the mainstream press coverage of the Freeh report "revelations" focused primarily on him, and what was now almost certain to be a dramatically tarnished legacy.

There are some curious crossover connections here, as the Second Mile Foundation was considered both a "charity" and part of the "foster care" system. The ugly reality is that there are shameful organizations within our society that appear to cater to the perverted whims of the rich and powerful. Some maintain that there is a literal pedophile network, with fresh victims doled out to the wealthy at their request. The entertainment industry appears to be full of these people, too. Former child actor Corey Feldman memorably told ABC's *Nightline*, "I can tell you that the No. 1 problem in Hollywood was and is and always will be pedophilia." Feldman discovered as a child that pedophiles were "everywhere" in Hollywood. However one looks at it, the problem is all too real and clearly hasn't been adequately addressed by our mainstream media or political leaders.

CHAPTER THIRTEEN

WORLD GOVERNMENT/
THE NEW WORLD ORDER

"There is no salvation for civilization, or even the human race, other
than the creation of a world government."

—Albert Einstein

THE COUNCIL ON FOREIGN RELATIONS (CFR)

"The Council on Foreign Relations is the American Branch of
a society which originated in England [and] believes national
boundaries should be obliterated and one-world rule established."

—Professor Carroll Quigley

The idea of a World Government, in and of itself, was probably born out of misguided idealism. My favorite film director, Frank Capra, based his 1948 feature *State of the Union* on this concept. Woodrow Wilson's goal of a League of Nations, which eventually resulted in the United Nations, seemed like a noble idea. But would any of us truly want to have the kind of remote representation a World Government would offer? Think of how difficult it is to talk to a member of your local school board, let alone your district's congressional representative, and imagine what it would be like trying to communicate with your World Government representative. What kind of monstrous bureaucracy would be born with such a massive government? What kind of taxes? What kind of conflicting policies, that almost assuredly would be to the detriment of millions of humans somewhere on the planet, would there be?

The Council on Foreign Relations is like an establishment country club—a veritable Who's Who of American policy making. The mainstream press has historically given scant coverage to exactly what it is that the CFR does. The "Foreign Relations" part of the name would seem to indicate a group devoted to the study of foreign policy objectives. Indeed, on the rare occasions that the CFR is mentioned in the mainstream media, it is inevitably referred to as "an influential foreign policy think tank"—makes it even more curious that so many celebrated figures decidedly lacking in "foreign policy" experience are or have been members.

Presently, Warren Beatty, David Geffen, Jimmy Iovine, Tom Brokaw, George Clooney, Katie Couric, Joan Didion, Barry Diller, Jeffrey Katzenberg, Steven Spielberg, Angelina Jolie, Dan Rather, Paul Tagliabue, and Barbara Walters are all members of the CFR. Obviously, mainstream journalists like Brokaw, Couric, Rather, and Walters should have no role to play in deciding foreign policy. Diller is a media executive—what does he have to do with any "foreign relations?" Didion is a novelist. Geffen and Iovine are music industry powers—what possible "foreign policy" experience do they have? The presence of actors such as Beatty, Clooney, and Jolie, and movie industry powers like Katzenberg and Spielberg, on their membership rolls should detract from the credibility of the CFR, as should the membership of Tagliabue, former commissioner of the National Football League.

However, the CFR is also full of assorted Rockefellers and other loyal members of the inner sanctum. "Right" and "left" labels mean nothing in organizations like this, as ideological enemies Dick Cheney, Jesse Jackson, Newt Gingrich, and Caroline Kennedy (yes, sadly, the Kennedy family is now represented in the CFR) all belong to the same club when it comes to "foreign relations." The blue-blood nature of the American elite is represented by the likes of Theodore Roosevelt IV and William H. Taft IV.

THE BILDERBERGERS

"We are on the verge of a global transformation. All we need is the right major crisis."
—David Rockefeller, Club of Rome executive manager

More secretive and potentially even more powerful is the shadowy group known as the Bilderbergers. The group derived its name from the location of their first annual meeting, at the Bilderberg Hotel in the Netherlands in 1954. At Bilderberg meetings, politicians, corporate leaders, and members of royalty from around the world gather in secrecy once a year, to the complete silence of the mainstream press. This is the same mainstream media that will send helicopters loaded with paparazzi to snap photos of some decadent celebrity wedding. However, when the world's movers and shakers come together behind closed doors, the same "journalists" aren't the least bit curious. This may be in part because usually there are a handful of establishment favorites from the media that are invited to attend the Bilderberg meetings. In the spirit of eugenics, no one from developing countries is ever invited.

Bilderberg is one of the organizations, which also includes the CFR and the Trilateral Commission, that critics allege are engaged in a conspiracy to overthrow US sovereignty and promote a one-world government. There are abundant indications that our leaders do desire such a world government. Denis Healey, one of Bilderberg's founders, stated in 2001, "To say we were striving for a one world government is exaggerated, but not wholly unfair."

In a 1999 appearance at the United Nations to accept the Norman Cousins Global Governance Award from the World Federalists Association, "liberal" icon newsman Walter Cronkite reveled in the globalist creed. Cronkite declared, "It seems to many of us that if we are to avoid the eventual catastrophic world conflict we must strengthen the United Nations as a first step toward a world government patterned after our own government with a legislature, executive and judiciary, and police to enforce its international laws and keep the peace," he said. "To do that, of course, we Americans will have to yield up some of our sovereignty. That would be a bitter pill. It would take a lot of courage, a lot of faith in the new order." Cronkite added, "Pat Robertson has written in a book a few years ago that we should have a world government, but only when the Messiah arrives. He wrote, literally, any attempt to achieve world order before that time must be the work of the devil. Well, join me. I'm glad to sit here at the right hand of Satan." Cronkite also served as the longtime voice of the giant owl in the bizarre, occult rituals at the yearly Bohemian Grove gatherings. (*Spy* magazine, November 1989).

During a February 17, 1950, appearance before the US Senate Committee on Foreign Relations, establishment stalwart banker James Warburg told them bluntly, "We shall have world government, whether or not we like it. The question is only whether world government will be achieved by consent or by conquest." Strobe Talbot, Bill Clinton's fellow Rhodes scholar and roommate at Oxford, who went on to become his secretary of state, predicted, "In the next century, nations will be obsolete; all states will recognize a single global authority and realize national sovereignty wasn't such a great deal after all." When Talbot received the Norman Cousins Global Governance Award in 1993, Clinton sent him a congratulatory message that lauded him for his work toward "world government."

Nelson Mandela, Mikhail Gorbachev, and even Robert Kennedy mentioned the "new world order" in speeches. Many people mistakenly believe the term "new world order" was the exclusive property of "conspiracy theorists" until President George H. W. Bush brought it out of the closet in his March 6, 1991, speech. In another bit of classic irony, of the many references Bush made to the "new world order," his best remembered speech is the one he gave to congress on September 11, 1990, eleven years to the day before one of the most seminal events in American history.

Henry Kissinger, one of the establishment's top figures, laid out the globalist agenda with perfect candor: "Today America would be outraged if UN troops entered Los Angeles to restore order. Tomorrow they will be grateful. When presented with this scenario, individual rights will be willingly relinquished for the guarantee of their well-being granted to them by the World Government." Kissinger, it may be recalled, notoriously used the odious term *useless eaters* to describe the unfortunate masses who suffer under the misrule of his ilk (and who, of course, would be strongly discouraged from reproducing by the eugenicists). During the "debate" over NAFTA, Trilateralist and former CFR president Winston Lord told a town hall meeting in Los Angeles, on September 29, 1992, "To a certain extent, we are going to have to yield some of our sovereignty, which will be controversial at home. . . . [Under] the North American Free Trade Agreement [NAFTA] . . . some Americans are going to be hurt as low-wage jobs are taken away."

David Rockefeller, dean of the world's elite, has been more frank than most regarding this clear-cut agenda. He supposedly made the following remarks at the June 1991 Bilderberg meeting in Baden-Baden, Germany: "We are grateful to the *Washington Post*, the *New York Times*, *Time Magazine*, and other great publications whose directors have attended our meetings and respected their promise of discretion for almost forty years. It would have been impossible for us to develop our plans for the world if we had been subject to the bright lights of publicity during those years. But, the world is now much more sophisticated and prepared to march toward a world government."

In his 2002 memoirs, he literally copped a plea: "We wield over American political and economical institutions. Some even believe we are part of a secret cabal working against the best interests of the United States, characterizing my family and me as 'internationalists' and of conspiring with others around the world to build a more integrated global political structure, one world, if you will. If that's the charge, I stand guilty, and I am proud of it." Giving the lie to the contention that super capitalists like himself were ideological enemies of communism, Rockefeller sang the praises of China's communist dictator Mao Tse-Tung: "The Social experiment in China under Chairman Mao's leadership is one of the most important and successful in human history." (*New York Times*, August 10, 1973).

BOHEMIAN GROVE

"Did you say Bohemian Club? That's where all those rich
Republicans go up and stand naked against redwood trees, right?
I've never been to the Bohemian Club, but you ought to go. It'd be
good for you. You'd get some fresh air."
—Bill Clinton, responding to a heckler

Every July, approximately 2,000 of the most powerful men on earth gather in the woods of northern California for two weeks. It is an exclusive male fraternity, with no women permitted, even as employees (although in recent years, the ban against female workers has apparently been lifted). According to insider accounts, the men drink heavily from morning to night (*Spy* magazine described "the traditional 7:00 a.m. gin fizzes served in bed by camp valets. . ."), revel in urinating against the giant redwood trees there (in fact, they defended themselves in a sex-discrimination suit by maintaining that women would be offended because this is all they'd see), and frequently engage in homosexual activity. The pagan "Cremation of Care" ritual is performed in front of an altar under a gigantic, forty-foot stone owl, during which members don red-hooded robes and chant occult dogma. The Old Testament God Moloch is associated with both owls and child sacrifice, two obvious themes of the rituals at the Grove. As noted earlier, talk show host Alex Jones managed to sneak into the super-secretive gathering at the Grove in 2000. The resulting video, *Dark Secrets: Inside Bohemian Grove*, provided great insight into these bizarre activities.

Past attendees include presidents Nixon (who later called the Grove "the most faggy goddamned thing you could ever imagine"), Ford, Carter, Reagan, both Bushes, and Clinton, as well as such luminaries as Henry Kissinger, Alan Greenspan, Dick Cheney, Newt Gingrich, John Major, Tony

Blair, Arnold Schwarzenegger, Chris Matthews, various members of the rock group The Grateful Dead, Harry Shearer (voice of numerous characters on *The Simpsons*), David Rockefeller, and Colin Powell, to name just a few. Farther back, Teddy Roosevelt, legendary "radical" writer Mark Twain (also close friend of plutocrat and should-be enemy J. P. Morgan), and socialist author Jack London were all members. In July 2004, the *New York Post* reported that gay porn star Chad Savage had been flown in to service the notable figures at the Grove. In 2011, reporters for Alex Jones's radio show interviewed workers at the Grove, who indicated that actor Tom Cruise and ex-Major League Baseball player Mark McGwire were among the attendees.

While the motto of the Grove is "Weaving Spiders Come Not Here," as long ago as 1927 Herbert Hoover would remember in his memoirs that, within an hour of Calvin Coolidge's announcement that he would not run for president again, "a hundred men—editors, publishers, public officials and others from all over the country who were at the Grove, came to my camp demanding that I announce my candidacy." The often elaborate "talent" shows put on at the Grove are considered vitally important by attendees, and are allegedly planned years in advance. Merv Griffin and Art Linkletter were among those who organized past performances. As would be expected, there is always a great deal of drag material, since all female roles must be played by male actors. (*The Truth About the Bohemian Grove* by Alexander Cockburn, online article, June 16, 2001).

Whether important policy decisions are made at Bohemian Grove or not, it is at the very least disturbing to know that our leaders are gathering together to worship a massive owl, dress in robes, and recite occult incantations.

CHAPTER FOURTEEN

THE FEDERAL RESERVE AND FRACTIONAL BANKING

"It is well that the people of the nation do not understand our banking and monetary system, for if they did, I believe there would be a revolution before tomorrow morning."

—Henry Ford

"I believe that banking institutions are more dangerous to our liberties than standing armies."

—Thomas Jefferson

"Let me issue and control a nation's money and I care not who writes the laws."

—Mayer Amschel Rothschild

Nefarious robber baron J. P. Morgan supposedly issued the following statement in a private communication with the leading bankers of his era: "Capital must protect itself in every way. . . . Debts must be collected and loans and mortgages foreclosed as soon as possible. When through a process of law the common people have lost their homes, they will be more tractable and more easily governed by the strong arm of the law applied by the central power of leading financiers. People without homes will not quarrel with their leaders. This is well known among our principle men now engaged in forming an imperialism of capitalism to govern the world. By dividing the people we can get them to expend their energies in fighting over questions of no importance to us except as teachers of the common herd."

The Federal Reserve System, created in 1913, while promulgated as a way of taking power out of the hands of bankers, did precisely the opposite. Congressman Charles A. Lindbergh Sr., father of the noted aviator, was a strong opponent and argued, "This [Federal Reserve Act] establishes the most gigantic trust on earth. When the President [Wilson] signs this bill, the invisible government of the monetary power will be legalized . . . the worst legislative crime of the ages is perpetrated by this banking and currency bill." Congressman Louis McFadden tried for years to get the Federal Reserve audited, without success. He called the Fed "one of the most corrupt institutions the world has ever known." McFadden died suddenly on October 3, 1936, supposedly of heart failure, but he had previously been shot at and an attempt had been made to poison him.

Congressman Wright Patman accurately observed, "The Federal Reserve bank buys government bonds without one penny." The Fed is the basis for our entire corrupt banking system. The Boston Federal Reserve Bank has freely acknowledged the legal counterfeiting that goes on within their organization: "When you or I write a check there must be sufficient funds in our account to cover the check, but when the Federal Reserve writes a check there is no bank deposit on which that check is drawn. When the Federal Reserve writes a check, it is creating money." (*Putting It Simply*, Boston Federal Reserve Bank).

Thomas Jefferson was not only the man John F. Kennedy would acknowledge as having more talent than all the greatest artists he could possibly assemble in the White House; he understood this particular subject better than almost any other leader in American history. "If the American people ever allow private banks to control the issue of their currency, first by inflation, then by deflation, the banks . . . will deprive the people of all property until their children wake-up homeless on the continent their fathers conquered," Jefferson declared. "The issuing power should be taken from the banks and restored to the people, to whom it properly belongs."

However, with the creation of the Federal Reserve, and the installation of a fractional lending system, the already shady banking industry became corrupt to the core. Imagine if private citizens had the right to "lend" out money they didn't possess. Under fractional lending, banks are only required to have 10 percent in reserve, which means they can "lend" out $100 for every $10 they actually possess. This is why all economic debates between Republicans and Democrats are meaningless;

they don't address the core issue, which is that 90 percent of all *principal* in circulation from various loans is counterfeit and was created out of thin air. Obviously, as such, it can never be retrieved, and every penny of the usurious interest rates on every loan is imaginary, again conjured up out of nothing.

The "Fed" in Federal Reserve is purposefully misleading; the Federal Reserve is a private corporation, not a government agency. Of course, most people don't even know that, let alone understand the concept of fractional banking, which is legal counterfeiting. How many people in the course of history have been sentenced to prison for doing what every bank does routinely? When you hear the candidates, and their mouthpieces in the mainstream media, bemoaning the "debt" we *must* pay, remember how our system really works. That debt is not the responsibility of the taxpayers; why should the public assume the incomprehensible loans that bankers brokered from Communist China, for instance? In reality, we need to repudiate the interest on the national debt and force the banks to manage their own faulty business transactions.

When individuals suffer financial hardship, even in an economy as precarious as the present one is, they are advised to "pull up their bootstraps" and be willing to "sacrifice," as the "American people" have seemingly always been asked to do. However, when banks or huge corporations lose some of their astronomical profits, through incompetence and greed, every leading politician of both major political parties falls all over themselves to write a blank check from the taxpayers to bail them out. Well over 90 percent of Americans opposed the banker bailout of 2008, but our two "choices" for president, Barack Obama and John McCain, were fully in support of it.

One reporter had the audacity to actually sue the Federal Reserve. In late 2008, Mark Pittman, who worked for Bloomberg News, filed a Freedom of Information Act request with the Fed, regarding records of taxpayer-financed loans that are routinely withheld from public scrutiny. Predictably, the Fed denied his request, and Pittman appealed. The Fed denied him again. Saying, "It's not Ben Bernanke's money, it's our money," Pittman turned to the Federal Courts. In August 2009, a judge ruled that the Federal Reserve had "improperly withheld" the information and ordered the Fed to turn over the information within five days to Bloomberg News. A few months later, on November 25, 2009, Pittman died suddenly at age fifty-two. Pittman was said to suffer from "heart related illnesses," but according to reports, "the precise cause of death wasn't known." On August 27, 2010, the US Court of Appeals granted the Fed's request for a delay so that it could appeal to the US Supreme Court. In March 2011, some of the data Pittman and Bloomberg had requested was belatedly released.

There have been no further updates regarding the exact nature of Pittman's death at such a relatively young age. Pittman's daughter, Maggie, assured the public that there was "no conspiracy" behind her father's death. The Big Picture Report and other websites tried to delve into the matter, but as thebigpicturereport.com noted in an update on August 6, 2011, "Despite a long search, I could not find any new information about his cause of death." Both of Pittman's parents were alive at the time of his death, suggesting a pretty strong set of genes. Whatever the true cause, the fact remains that the only reporter to sue the Fed died shortly afterward, of officially undetermined causes.

CHAPTER FIFTEEN

THE BIG CHARITY BOONDOGGLE

"Organized charity itself is the symptom of a malignant social disease."
—Margaret Sanger, founder of Planned Parenthood

In 1992, the charity giant United Way garnered unwanted headlines. The mainstream media reported that longtime CEO William Aramony had been paid $390,000 in salary the previous year, plus $76,000 in bonuses. During his tenure, Aramony had filled United Way's board of directors with corporate scions from IBM, American Express, etc. A few years later, Aramony was sentenced to seven years in prison on twenty-five counts of conspiracy and fraud, as well as sexual misconduct.

Aramony, however, was hardly alone in using well-intended contributions to line his pockets. Elaine Chao, who succeeded Aramony as CEO, resigned in 1996, and the organization, which clearly hadn't changed its culture one bit, tried to give her a $292,500 "appreciation" bonus. Oral Suer, who was United Way's National Capital Area's CEO for nearly thirty years, eventually spent more than two years in prison for the same sorts of offenses; things like collecting retirement while still employed, abuse of leave time, misreporting expenses, etc. In 2006, Ralph Dickerson, CEO of United Way, was caught stealing $227,000 for his personal use. Revealing the extent of our justice system's double standard for the wealthy and powerful, Dickerson "volunteered" to pay the money back and thereby avoided jail time. I'm sure there are thousands of convicted thieves in prison who would have gladly accepted that kind of deal.

In 2010, despite the horrific economic conditions, Americans gave more than $290 billion to their favorite causes. It's important to check out exactly how much of each individual donation is utilized for the cause, as opposed to how much is spent on overhead. The Alzheimer's Foundation of America, for instance, pays their CEO nearly $300,000, according to Charity Navigator. Many charities waste donated money on fund-raising to a ridiculous degree; the Cancer Survivors' Fund, National Vietnam Veterans Foundation, Firefighters Charitable Foundation, Children's Charity Fund, and many others spend more than fifty cents out of every dollar raised on promotional activities.

During her tenure as head of the Red Cross, Elizabeth Dole, wife of powerful Republican Senator Bob Dole, received not only a $200,000 salary but was paid $35,000 per speech to urge lobbyists to *volunteer for charities*. The Red Cross, while not an actual charity, certainly shouldn't be paying celebrity figureheads like Dole such an extravagant salary. They also might want to look up the definition of "irony" before they give someone such an elaborate sum to lecture others about the virtues of volunteerism. And Elizabeth Dole was a pro at milking the talk circuit; from 1994 to 1996, she raked in nearly a million dollars in speaking engagement fees. There was a bit of an uproar over Dole's Red Cross salary, so she didn't accept it during her first year at the helm. Instead, she deferred it into contributions to the Red Cross itself—and enormous amounts to her own retirement fund.

Dole even established her own "charity," but the Elizabeth Dole Charitable Foundation, financed primarily through her lucrative speaking fees, gave away barely $29,000 of over $1 million in assets in 1998. In January 1996, the *Los Angeles Times* ran a critical story on her paltry personal contributions to charity. An embarrassed Dole blamed it on her accountant and quickly donated an additional $75,000. The Red Cross continues to reward its management in a most "charitable" way; in 2005, for instance, President Marsha Evans was paid $651,957. By contrast, the Salvation Army pays its head a nominal amount (in 2002, $13,000 plus housing for Commissioner Todd Bassett).

Invariably, whenever a natural disaster strikes, the mainstream media emphasizes the roles of the Red Cross and United Way, and makes certain to provide regular contact information for citizens to send them their donations. This occurs despite the fact that the Red Cross has been caught not releasing funds to desperately needed disaster situations. For instance, after the 1989 San Francisco earthquake, the Red Cross kept $40 million out of the $50 million donated to them. Because of this, they were actually sued by San Francisco Mayor Art Agnos, which resulted in an out-of-court settlement. (*New York Times*, March 6, 1990, and others). The Red Cross attempted to abscond funds donated to Minnesota flood victims, and it was taken to task by Minnesota Attorney General Hubert H. Humphrey III. ". . . the Red Cross, by withholding millions of dollars in donations, has failed in its responsibility to donors, to survivors and to the public at large," Humphrey was quoted as saying. "When people gave the Red Cross their hard-earned money, they expected it would promptly get to those whose lives were devastated by the floods, not sit in a bank account for a year and a half." (*New York Times*, December 16, 1998).

The Red Cross apparently even pocketed money sent directly to family members who'd lost loved ones in the Oklahoma City (OKC) bombing. *Insight* magazine quoted a family member as saying, "People from all over the country were sending checks in lieu of flowers and we were getting a lot of checks and cash every day. . . . Then the Red Cross went down to the post office and made arrangements to collect the mail and they would deliver it to us in bulk. All the mail had been opened, and from that point on, there never was a dime, even in letters that said money was enclosed."

Formal complaints were lodged with the Postal Service. Red Cross Senior Vice President for Communications and Marketing Bill Blaul told *Insight* that the organization had "cooperated with the US Attorney and he found no inappropriate handling of the matter, and it was closed." Blaul responded to allegations that money had been removed from envelopes clearly intended for a specific family by saying, "The families may feel that way. I'm not sure what their memories and recollections are." Further pressed on this issue, Blaul became "defensive," in the words of the reporter, and snapped, "I don't know what more I can say about it." (*Insight on the News*, November 5, 2001).

Another OKC bombing survivor, the aforementioned Edye Smith, who lost two little boys in the blast, told host Tom Valentine during an August 16, 1995, appearance on *Radio Free America* that money sent to her via the Red Cross by sympathetic Americans never made it to her family. Following 9/11, the Red Cross collected $564 million in donations, yet months later they'd released only $154 million of it. Even mainstream media outlets focused attention on the controversy. Red Cross President Bernadine Healy was hammered by New York Attorney General Eliot Spitzer (later to resign after a sex scandal), who declared, "I see the Red Cross, which has raised hundreds of millions of dollars that was intended by the donating public to be used for the victims of September 11—I see those funds being sequestered into long-term plans for an organization." Healy dismissed criticism of her organization by telling a US House Congressional Committee that the funds were going to the "war on terror," and stated, "The Liberty Fund is a war fund. It has evolved into a war fund."

The Red Cross was harshly criticized by several members, including Louisiana Republican Billy Tauzin, who wondered why "a special fund established for these families" was being closed, while, "by the way, we're going to give two-thirds of it away to other Red Cross needs." At least one 9/11 widow was frustrated over the "red tape" that was seemingly preventing "a quicker way for families to receive these funds." (CNN, November 6, 2001).

Doug Copp, rescue chief and disaster manager of the American Rescue Team International, was told by the president of 3M Company that after 3M donated $750,000 worth of life-saving respirators to the Red Cross, for use by the first responders after 9/11, they were instead stored in a warehouse by the Red Cross to be sold later. Predictably, the mainstream media went after Copp for his attack on the Red Cross, with a four-part hit piece in the *Albuquerque Journal*, starting on July 11, 2004. Incredibly, in 2005, the Canadian Red Cross was caught knowingly shipping out blood infected with HIV and hepatitis C. And this organization does it all out of an ornate national headquarters in San Francisco, that the *San Francisco Chronicle* dubbed the "Marble Palace."

I exchanged a few emails with Doug Copp in late May and early June 2012. Copp clearly is at odds with the establishment, and is on a mission to expose official corruption. According to Copp, Thompson Lang, owner of the *Albuquerque Journal*, is an empowered rich kid who was described by prominent attorney F. Lee Bailey as a "power hungry bully." Copp accused one of Lang's gang of punching the corpse of an NYFD firefighter while searching through the World Trade Center rubble. His emails were a bit over the top, and his allegations were all over the place. Still, he certainly seemed to be on the side of good, and at this point there is very little I would put past the kinds of forces he describes.

While the largest, most publicized charities are woefully uncharitable in steering donations where they can actually do some good, the wealthiest Americans are also often the least charitable with their personal contributions. Al Gore, for example, gave a miserly 0.18 percent ($353) of his 1997 income of $197,729 to charity. Joe Biden donated an average of only $369 a year during the period from 1998 to 2008. In 1999 Biden gave $120, only 0.1 percent of his yearly income. While wealthy "leftists" like Gore and Biden were donating only a few hundred dollars of their huge incomes to charity, Americans on average donated some 3 percent of their income, or about $2,047 in 2004. (*USA Today*, September 12, 2008).

An updated study, by the *Chronicle of Philanthropy*, produced an even more damning indictment of the wealthiest Americans. Using data from the IRS, the group found that while households earning between $50,000 and $75,000 gave some 7.6 percent of their income to charity, those earning more than $100,000 donated only 4.2 percent. In some of the wealthiest neighborhoods, with incomes averaging over $200,000, the giving rate dipped to a paltry 2.8 percent (CNBC and others, August 20, 2012).

Barack Obama gave less than 1 percent of his income to charities until he became a presidential aspirant, when he increased the amount to a more politically palatable figure. Peter Schweizer, in his book *Makers and Shakers*, disclosed the fact that 2004 Democratic presidential nominee Senator John Kerry, who married Teresa Heinz, widow of super-wealthy Senator John Heinz, donated *nothing* to charity in 1995. That same year, however, he had $500,000 discretionary cash to spend on a seventeenth-century Dutch painting. This was not unusual behavior for Kerry; he also donated zero money to charity in 1991 and only $175 in 1993. Jesse Jackson averages less than 1 percent in charitable donations as well. His "charitable" organization, the Jackson Foundation, is controlled by family members. In 2004, the Foundation collected nearly $1 million in donations. They spent $84,172 on a gala celebration to "honor" Jesse Jackson, and they listed "none" under "Direct Charitable Activities" on their 2004 tax return.

The award for the most gall in this area, however, has to go to U2 band leader Bono. Bono has carved out a second career by pontificating on political issues, and certainly seems to take himself very seriously. Bono, like all clever multimillionaires, established a tax-free foundation as a tax shelter, and he has received the typical fantastic publicity from the fawning mainstream media in return. In 2010, however, it was discovered that Bono's ONE antipoverty foundation gave only *1.2 percent* of its donations to those in need. Well over half of the money well-meaning people sent in, in fact, went to salaries alone. The *New York Post* reported receiving gifts such as leather notebooks, bags of coffee, and water bottles prior to a ONE-sponsored event. A spokesman for ONE actually attempted to defend this legalized theft by declaring, "We don't provide programs on the ground. We're an advocacy and campaigning organization." ONE also claimed it got most of its funding from the Bill and Melinda Gates Foundation. (*Daily Mail UK*, September 23, 2010).

Bono's fellow pretentious, one-namer rock star, Sting, wasn't quite as stingy with his own Rainforest Foundation, but he still directed only 41 percent of the donations toward those in need. As the *New York Post* reported on September 4, 2008, "the local arm of Sting's Rainforest Foundation is rated one of New York City's worst charities, according to Charity Navigator." The paper went on to state that Charity Navigator had given the Rainforest Foundation a zero rating for the previous four years.

Understand how this works: When an earthquake wreaks destruction somewhere, the mainstream media trumpets the efforts of the Red Cross and basically serves as publicity agent for donations. They rarely report, and even when they do the public soon forgets, how little of the money goes toward directly alleviating the crisis. When Bono or Sting or some other mega-rich celebrity gives a "benefit" concert and implores the decidedly nonwealthy audience members to "give" in order to eradicate hunger in Africa, or whatever, only a small percentage of that money actually goes toward the cause. As many have noted before, why don't Bono, Sting, and the other multimillionaire celebrities simply give their own money directly to people in need? Doesn't that make a lot more sense than demanding their nonwealthy fans fork out contributions? Even after the stories about Sting's foundation giving an embarrassingly low percentage of the proceeds collected toward the cause it was supposed to be serving, high-profile New York Mayor Michael Bloomberg declared May 2008 "Rainforest Awareness Month" and directed that the Empire State Building glow green in tribute, on the evening of Sting's benefit concert.

Warren Buffett, one of the world's richest men, created a big public stir a few years back when he gave a huge chunk of money to the foundation run by Bill Gates, often ranked as *the* richest man in the world. Buffett is symbolic of the super-wealthy, and reminds us of the eternal truth in F. Scott Fitzgerald's declaration that "the rich are different from you and me." As noted earlier, Buffett had notoriously refused to financially assist his own daughter and granddaughter. In another of those wild interconnections, Buffett's wife Susie had been a volunteer for the Franklin Credit Union in Nebraska and became close to the notorious Larry King. As author John DeCamp described it, in his book *The Franklin Cover-Up*, "For years, it has been part of Larry King lore in Omaha, that the Buffetts hosted a tenth wedding anniversary party for him and Alice." Buffett is also predictably concerned with "over-population" and has been a generous financial supporter of groups like Negative Population Growth, the Association for Voluntary Sterilization, Planned Parenthood, and many others.

While Buffett wouldn't lend a hand to his loved ones, he had $30 billion to give to the Bill and Melinda Gates Foundation, which is primarily intent upon vaccinating Africans in another twisted, back-door eugenics program.

The Bill and Melinda Gates Foundation employs staff that were formerly with agricultural and pharmaceutical conglomerates, including Rob Horsch, a former vice president with Monsanto, a multinational corporation that manufactures herbicides. Thanks in large measure to Buffett's humongous contribution, the Bill and Melinda Gates Foundation endowment is now larger than the gross domestic product of more than a hundred countries. (*Stanford Social Innovation Review*, Summer 2009). A perusal of Gates Foundation salaries on glassdoor.com listed thirty-two positions being paid more than $100,000 annually, and eighteen others paid between $77,000 and $95,000. Gates Foundation CEO Jeffrey Raikes was paid an incredible $990,000 in 2008.

Gates and Buffett teamed up in 2010 to promote the "Giving Pledge," whereby they urged their fellow multibillionaires to give at least half of their money to "charity." I think we can rest assured that the charities will all be the "right" kind, and the "pledge" will result in fantastic tax breaks and wonderful publicity for the contributors, albeit not much real assistance for those truly in need of it. Familiar names like Michael Bloomberg and Ted Turner quickly jumped on board. They couldn't have expected to count on Apple's Steve Jobs for support; he was long notorious for donating almost nothing to charities.

Bill Gates is already on record as anticipating that the widespread vaccination programs he funds and endorses will result in a significant *reduction* in population. He also issued some "controversial" remarks about the so-called "death panels" many opponents of Obamacare had grown alarmed about during the health-care "debate." At a 2010 Aspen Ideas Festival in Colorado, Gates seemed to imply that elderly patients ought to be killed rather than "wasting" resources on keeping them alive. Gates bemoaned the "lack of willingness" on the part of society to confront the choice between "spending a million dollars on that last three months of life for that patient" or laying off ten teachers. "But that's the death panel and you're not supposed to have that discussion," Gates declared. These hideous comments define the driving force behind the Gates Foundation far more accurately than any fluff pieces in the establishment press ever could.

The American Cancer Society is, according to the feisty website disinfo.com, the largest nonreligious charity in the world. It is run in the familiar, irrational way that the others we've examined are. While it collects over $6 million in yearly donations, and has an unbelievable $1 *billion* in cash reserves, only about 16 percent of the money collected actually goes toward directly helping cancer patients. The board of directors is full of the typical suspects from pharmaceutical and processed-food backgrounds, who obviously have a conflict of interest. Why would any charity need "cash reserves," especially such an incomprehensibly large amount? Just as Abbie Hoffman wondered why the government called its antidrug agency Drug *Enforcement*, I wonder why an organization supposedly dedicated to eradicating the scourge of our times would not be called the Anti-Cancer Society.

The other large group collecting money in this disease's name is the National Cancer Institute. Again, both names sound as if they are *supportive* of the disease, not like organizations dedicated to wiping it out. According to a 2006 Better Business Bureau report, American Cancer Society CEO John R. Seffrin was paid over $1.1 million in annual compensation. Its 2006 tax returns also indicated it had some seven hundred employees being paid more than $50,000 per year. For the same year, American Cancer Society records revealed it paid out more than $100 million in total to employees. The National Cancer Institute isn't any better. According to the Think Before You Pink website, only about 5 percent of its annual $1.8 billion budget goes to cancer prevention. That doesn't leave a whole lot of money for the people they're allegedly "helping," does it?

Another huge charitable organization, the American Heart Association (AHA), paid their CEO Nancy A. Brown $646,000 in 2010, according to the Better Business Bureau. Moreover, an article on Yahoo! (April 13, 2010) reported that the AHA's previous CEO, M. Cass Wheeler, had been paid more than $1 million in 2009. The same Yahoo! article highlighted some other outrageous salaries from the charity world: Houston's YMCA CEO was paid more than $661,000 (remember, there are YMCA's in cities all over the country, so just imagine how much the organization collectively spends on salaries); the normally well thought of St. Jude's Research Hospital gave their CEO John P. Moses $589,833; Race for the Cure CEO Hala G. Moddelmog earned $459,406 in 2009; the American Society for the Prevention of Cruelty to Animals (ASCPA) paid its CEO Edwin J. Sayres just under $474,000 in 2008; and World Vision, dedicated to eradicating poverty, paid CEO Richard E. Steams $376,399 in 2008. Even the Make a Wish Foundation, which I thought was doing great work, gave more than $350,000 in 2008 to CEO David A. Williams.

Muscular Dystrophy Association (MDA) President and CEO Gerald C. Weinberg earned nearly $380,000, according to a July 2010 report by the Better Business Bureau. MDA took in more than $190 million, not to mention an additional million in federal matching funds, in 2009. While MDA does claim to spend more of a percentage of its donations on actual research than many other charities, the fact remains that all those Jerry Lewis telethons and the billions that were raised during them appear not to have brought us any closer to wiping out this horrible disease. Yahoo! reminded its readers that all these extravagant executive salaries do not include bonuses and other perks.

The Salvation Army, alone among the biggest charities, really is devoted to good works with insignificant overhead expenses, and about ninety-three cents out of every dollar donated goes toward actually helping people. *Forbes* and other establishment media outlets, along with the institutions themselves, vigorously disputed most of these claims. In light of what we know about the mainstream media, and what has already been exposed about the sordid finances of these charities, do they really have more credibility than anonymous sources on the Internet? While the figures vary from source to source, there is no question that these huge charities are spending far too much on salaries, and not nearly enough on worthy causes.

I contacted the American Red Cross about the specific charge that their CEOs are given lifetime 100-percent free medical coverage, and a representative from their Public Inquiry department informed me, ". . . I checked with our Human Resources staff and they are unaware of any retired national paid staff member (including former CEOs) that has 100% American Red Cross paid benefit coverage." The spokesperson went on to add, "You may also be interested that one of the Better Business Bureau's standards for accountability is that a charity should spend at least 65 percent of total expenses on program activities. The American Red Cross vastly outperforms on this measure, spending an organization-wide average of 91 percent of every dollar raised on humanitarian services." (Private email from Public Inquiry at American Red Cross, June 5, 2012).

These statistics fly in the face of the reports we cited earlier. On its website, Charity Navigator has a page full of prescient comments from those who've had firsthand experiences with the Red Cross. Most of the comments are quite negative, and they certainly don't reflect the claim that 91 percent of donations go to humanitarian services. Charity Navigator does indicate that 91 percent of donations go to "program expenses," but that hardly translates into specific funds for relief efforts. As we've seen, these "program expenses" seem to involve withholding huge amounts of donations in reserve funds. During the relief efforts in Haiti following the massive 2011 earthquake, ABC News asked the Red Cross why it was sitting on a few hundred million dollars of funds, and the organization responded that it was better to dole out the money slowly for best impact. There is a clear pattern here of the Red Cross withholding huge portions of donated money that could be helping people.

I found another informative article online, published in the March/April 1998 edition of Electric Edge (the digital version of *Ragged Edge* magazine). Working with 1995 figures, researcher Keith Storey reported that the National Easter Seal Society had a top salary of nearly $300,000 and paid five other executives over $150,000 that year. Twenty-nine other Easter Seal employees made more than $50,000. The Arthritis Foundation paid its president, Don Riggin, more than $220,000 in 1996, six other employees over $100,000, and thirty-one more over $50,000. United Cerebral Palsy Executive Director Michael Morris was paid $175,000 in 1996. Special Olympics CEO Sargent Shriver, in the tradition of all Kennedy family members, did not accept any salary. Overall, their salaries, while still too much in my opinion, were a bit more reasonable than the other charities we've examined. Keep in mind, these numbers are from the mid-1990s and should be adjusted accordingly.

The article also focused on the incredibly inefficient nature of charity fund-raising. The commercial fund-raiser My Favorite Charities, for instance, was paid $3,399 by Easter Seals to raise $101, and $3,350 by the Arthritis Foundation to raise $150. While Sergeant Shriver was paid nothing by Special Olympics, the organization lavished over $600,000 on direct mail consultant Epsilon and over $550,000 on telemarketing consultant Meyer Associates.

Feed the Children was formed by Oklahoma's Larry Jones and his wife in 1979. In 2011, the organization was investigated by Oklahoma's attorney general for "possible violations of law during Jones's tenure as president of Feed the Children." Jones had been fired by the group in 2009 and filed a lawsuit against them. The organization filed a counter lawsuit alleging that Jones took bribes, accepted kickbacks, and misused the charity's funds. Feed the Children, resorting to the standard business practice of recycling the same executive "talent," named the aforementioned ex-American Heart Association CEO Cass Wheeler as its interim president. (*Huffington Post*, January 26, 2011). The American Institute of Philanthropy called Feed the Children America's "most outrageous charity." Jones had overseen the purchase of a $1.2 million home in Los Angeles in 2008, which his daughter conveniently lived in. After the fallout with the charity he founded, Jones would accuse his daughter of treating a business residence as her personal residence. (*Daily Bellwether*, October 1, 2010). Jones was paid more than $230,000 annually by the organization.

With "charities" like these, is it any wonder that the untold fortunes donated by caring individuals haven't resulted in a single cure, or often even any significant improvements?

CHAPTER SIXTEEN

OUR INJUSTICE SYSTEM

"Judges . . . are picked out from the most dextrous lawyers, who
are grown old or lazy, and having been biased all their lives against
truth or equity, are under such a fatal necessity of favoring fraud,
perjury and oppression, that I have known several of them to refuse
a large bribe from the side where justice lay, rather than injure the
faculty by doing any thing unbecoming their nature in office."
—Jonathan Swift, *Gulliver's Travels*

According to the most recent statistics from the Death Penalty Information
Center, 140 people have been released from death row since 1973 because
of belatedly discovered exculpatory evidence. DNA evidence first became
available for use in forensics in 1986, and it really exposed the extent of the
injustice in our legal system. The Innocence Project recently reported that there
have been 289 post-conviction DNA exonerations since 1989, and that the
average length of time served by those wrongfully convicted was 13.5 years.
Faulty eyewitness identification is usually to blame for these situations, but
in January 2012, the US Supreme Court, in an 8–1 decision, refused an appeal
from a wrongfully convicted man to adopt new constitutional safeguards
against witness testimony being obtained under suggestive circumstances.
Giving the lie to those "left" and "right" labels again, and how important
it is for a Democrat or Republican president to appoint particular justices,
was the near unanimity of this absurd decision. However they are labeled
ideologically, Supreme Court justices have rarely voted as civil libertarians.

A new national database was set up jointly by the University of Michigan
Law School and the Center on Wrongful Convictions at Northwestern

University School of Law to tabulate the number of wrongful convictions in America. According to their initial research, more than two thousand people were falsely convicted of serious crimes and subsequently exonerated from 1989 to 2012. "We know there are many more that we haven't found," declared Samuel Gross, editor of the National Registry of Exonerations. The registry excluded at least 1,170 additional cases in which police corruption was involved. In most of those, police had fabricated evidence, planting drugs or guns on innocent individuals. (Associated Press, May 21, 2012).

What is truly astonishing about all this is that even when DNA evidence is found to rule out an individual who's already been convicted of a crime, the legal authorities usually respond slowly and often still refuse to rectify things. In a 2007 case in Alabama, where Darrell Grayson requested DNA testing that could prove his innocence in the murder he'd been convicted of committing twenty-seven years before, the state attorney general released a statement that said the state should not "delay justice" this way. Prosecutors in this case had, in fact, vigorously fought testing of the biological evidence left behind at the murder scene. Grayson was executed, without the DNA test ever being performed, on July 27, 2007.

Innocent people have served as long as thirty-five years in prison (James Bain in Florida) before being exonerated by DNA evidence. Groups like The Innocence Project and Truth in Justice detail the heart-wrenching tales on their websites. Josiah Sutton spent more than four years in prison for a crime that DNA evidence finally showed he couldn't have committed. First, the Texas Board of Pardons and Paroles stalled, reviewing his clemency petition for nearly a year. Texas Governor Rick Perry granted him a full pardon in 2004, but Sutton was still waiting years later for his $100,000 check from a state fund especially established to compensate wrongfully imprisoned Texans. The reason: Sutton wasn't able to get the required letter from Houston prosecutors admitting that he'd been mistakenly convicted. Richard Danziger was wrongfully convicted of rape but released on DNA evidence in 2001 after serving eleven years. During his incarceration period, he suffered permanent brain damage when his head was bashed in by another inmate.

The Associated Press studied the first 110 cases of those released on DNA evidence and discovered that almost half of them had no prior convictions, and only slightly more than a third had received any financial remuneration for the huge chunks of their lives that had been stolen from them by the injustice system. And, of course, this doesn't take into account the untold numbers of innocent people who have no one advocating for them, and no available DNA evidence to exonerate them. Can we even venture a reasonable guess at how many pathetic souls have already served an unjust sentence and died, or how many wrongly convicted prisoners are presently behind bars?

In 1968, Peter Limone was convicted in Boston, along with four other men, for the 1965 murder of Edward Deegan. Limone spent four years on death row and a total of thirty-three years in prison for Deegan's murder. Before Deegan was murdered, an informant told the FBI that he would be killed and identified who would kill him. This informant, mob hit man Joseph "The Animal" Barboza, was the one who actually killed Deegan and then framed Limone and his associates in the killing, even testifying against them. Declassified documents would subsequently show that FBI agents were fully aware that Limone and his friends were innocent, wrongly convicted, and sitting in prison for a crime their informant had committed, but they did nothing. Limone was finally exonerated and released from prison in January 2001, based on information known to the FBI since 1965. One of Limone's codefendants, Joseph Salvati, was released from prison a few years earlier, in 1997. Two of his innocent codefendants, Henry Tamlo and Louis Greco, died in prison. Who knows if the truth would ever have come to light if not for the fortunate fact that Limone and his codefendants had attorneys committed to their cause, who fought for justice. (*Actual Innocence: Five Days to Execution and Other Dispatches from the Wrongly Convicted*, by Barry Scheck, et al., pp. 34–35).

Nothing can make up for losing years of one's life. Justin Brooks of the California Western Innocence Project, observed, "Innocent people do some of the hardest time. They never reconcile themselves to why they're in prison. They feel their lives have been taken away. We expect them to just start functioning in the workforce. But there's a stigma to having been incarcerated." It's bad enough that our injustice system fails so often when human lives are at stake, but it's unconscionable that so many officials appear unwilling to acknowledge mistakes and quickly rectify them. What kind of authority figures are given definitive proof of someone's innocence and still conspire to keep them imprisoned and delay justice as long as possible?

The justice system has always been biased against the poor. Prisoners tend to come overwhelmingly from poor backgrounds and are often unemployed at the time of their arrests. A 1973 Philadelphia study, for instance, found that police referred juveniles from lower-class backgrounds to court much more frequently than they did those from the upper class. In the rather unlikely event a wealthy individual is charged with a serious crime, he or she has a tremendous advantage, in simply being able to afford top-notch legal services. *Criminal Justice: Law and Politics* found, on the other hand, that the public defenders to whom almost all poor defendants are assigned spend an average of only five to ten minutes with their clients, and this minimal time is usually devoted to devising plea bargaining strategies.

If someone is charged with a federal offense, guilt is almost assured; Bureau of Justice Statistics for the year 2000 showed that 90 percent of federal defendants were convicted, regardless of what type of attorney they had. But then again, the prosecution normally doesn't have to prove anything in these trials, since 95 percent of federal defendants plead guilty. (*Pittsburgh Tribune-Review*, July 31, 2006). Nationally, only 6 percent of those charged with murder in urban areas win acquittal. (*Boston Phoenix*, August 19, 2005).

The insanity defense, while popular on television, is almost nonexistent in the real justice system. Only used in about 1 percent of all court cases, the insanity defense is only successful 26 percent of the time. Pleas of temporary insanity are even rarer. Overall, juries vote for conviction about two-thirds of the time in all cases. If a defendant is wealthy and/or famous, the odds of acquittal are significantly higher. Dominick Dunne's *Justice: Crimes, Trials and Punishments* documented this clearly. While many bemoan that the law is "racist," in fact the one telling factor in determining possible imprisonment is class. This is inherent in the way society instantly looks to "get tough" with poor drug offenders of all races but just as passionately wants rich celebrities of all races to "get treatment" for the same offenses. As Paul Wright observed in *Prison Legal News*, "After more than 16 years in prison I have yet to meet anyone who was wealthy when they were convicted."

None of this is new, of course. One of the most incredible examples of "justice" produced by our judicial system in the past was the case of Stephen Dennison. Dennison was sent to the New York state reformatory in 1925 after the sixteen-year-old shoplifted a $5 box of candy from a store. He was transferred to the state penitentiary two years later, and over the years he broke a number of minor rules there. For these infractions, extra time was added to his sentence. Apparently forgotten by the alert prison officials, this pathetic creature served thirty-four years behind bars for stealing that precious $5 box of candy before finally being released in 1959.

In 1933, Leonard Hankins was convicted of robbing a bank and murdering two policemen and a passerby in Minneapolis, Minnesota. Two years later, the FBI arrested one Jess Doyle, who confessed that he'd committed the crimes that Hankins had been convicted of. In an unbelievable display of bureaucratic bungling, the FBI informed the Minneapolis police of Doyle's confession, but the local authorities refused to release Hankins because the FBI would not give them its file on Doyle. Bureaucratic knots take a long time to untangle, and Hankins, although pronounced innocent by the FBI itself, served another fifteen years in prison before being pardoned in 1951.

In 1931, Julius Krause and another man were convicted and imprisoned for robbery and murder in Ohio. Four years later, the other man made a deathbed confession in which he informed prison officials that Krause was innocent and named his real accomplice. This named accomplice, Curtis Kuermerle, was evidently of no interest to the authorities, but Krause was, understandably, very interested in him. After spending nine years behind bars, Krause escaped, tracked down Kuermerle, persuaded him to confess, and reported back to the authorities with the real guilty party in hand. Kuermerle was convicted of the same crimes Krause had been, but our illustrious courts refused to review Krause's case. He spent another eleven years in prison before being pardoned in 1951. (*The Book of Lists 2* by Irving Wallace, David Wallechinsky, Amy Wallace, and Sylvia Wallace, pp. 60–61).

The Supreme Court, as envisioned by the Founding Fathers, is supposed to have a very limited function: to interpret the Constitution and be the final arbiter in the appeals process. Unfortunately, over time it has evolved into a lawmaking body, and at this stage it is more powerful than the legislative branch. The arrogance of those serving on the highest court was best expressed by the Great Depression–era chief justice Charles Evans Hughes when he declared, "The Constitution is what the judges say it is." In recent years, the Court has outdone itself in terms of upholding tyrannical laws and restricting civil liberties. In a particularly outrageous 1996 decision, the Court ruled against a woman whose husband had been caught with a prostitute in a car *she* owned, and under the draconian asset forfeiture laws, the car was still seized by the authorities. This woman had broken no laws but still lost her property because of an offense her husband committed, and the supposed brightest legal minds in our nation saw nothing wrong with that.

Most citizens are unaware of just how much personal property is confiscated by the police every year, as long as they can connect it to a crime in some way. In 2005, the Supreme Court upheld the right of law enforcement officers to physically detain even obviously innocent citizens, and destroy their personal property, if it assists them in "taking command of the situation." In 2012, the Obama administration cited this ludicrous 2005 decision as justification for DEA agents roughly handcuffing eleven- and fourteen-year-old girls during one of their all-too-frequent "wrong door" raids.

Those who have been unfortunate enough to have to depend on our courts for justice have far too often been disappointed, heartbroken, or even ruined by the experience. Corruption reigns everywhere, from the lordly judges, in whose glorious presence the audience must stand and pay homage to, to the ambitious, unconscionable prosecutors to the power-mad police who frequently start the entire sorry process off dishonestly with their own misdeeds and brutality. A simple perusal of YouTube videos on any given day will reveal fresh examples of police misconduct caught on camera. It's a surreal experience to watch these public servants—entrusted with more power than anyone should ever have—threatening and bullying skateboarder kids, old people, and individuals in wheelchairs. Shockingly, there are no filmed examples of them giving this rough treatment to members of violent gangs like the Bloods and Crips and the Hells Angels, or real-life "Goodfellas." Despite the impressive visual evidence available to them, an inordinate number of Americans remain enthralled with our police forces—until they are forced to interact with them, of course. Anyone who manages to avoid all contact with our injustice system is very, very lucky.

CHAPTER SEVENTEEN

WHERE DO WE STAND NOW?

"The case for government by elites is irrefutable . . . government by
the people is possible but highly improbable."
—Longtime US Senator J. William Fulbright

So what hope is there? Will the mass of Americans, what George Orwell
aptly dubbed the "Proles" in his classic *1984*, ever be able to take control of
their destinies away from these demented and destructive leaders? I'd like to
answer optimistically, but that's simply very difficult to do. Perhaps we have
more of a chance than the insects, as they scurry across the pavement hoping
that a gigantic foot doesn't stomp on them.

Our society has come to adopt many of the draconian measures Orwell
tried to warn us about. Cameras monitor citizens from nearly every street
corner in the United Kingdom, and there are a steadily growing number
of them mounted on traffic lights in America. The fact that Orwell's *1984*
remains a part of the required reading curriculum in many high schools
across the country is laughably ironic. What is truly sad is how many readers
acknowledge the brilliant foresight of Orwell yet fail to grasp how closely
present-day America (and England) resemble Winston Smith's Oceania.

We have far less personal freedom now than we did even thirty years
ago. When the seemingly "hard ass" World War II generation was in
charge, Baby Boomers complained about too many rules and regulations.
Now that the former hippies and members of the "Me" generation run
things, the restrictions on personal liberty they've established would have
been unimaginable in 1970 or even 1980: "Click It or Ticket" campaigns for
compulsory seatbelt use. Smoking banned almost everywhere, despite the

fact that tobacco products continue to be legally sold. Electronic time cards that compel workers (of course, those with really good jobs are exempt) to stay for virtually every second of their eight-and-a-half-hour job shifts. FDA raids on health food stores. Restrictions against "hate speech." Free-speech "zones." The threat of sexual harassment charges over the most innocuous comments or gestures. "Sensitivity training" to compel the unwary offender, and even uninvolved coworkers, to obey the tenets of political correctness. Americans have grown to accept unconstitutional roadblocks as a regular activity in their communities. The examples are endless, and made all the worse by the fact that so many dumbed down Americans heartily approve of them.

Recently, former New York City Mayor Michael Bloomberg proposed a ban on "supersized" soft drinks in restaurants. His proposal illustrates, in microcosm, why our "system" doesn't work. "Conservatives" do not want to harm big business interests in any way, and thus would be aghast at this kind of idea. "Liberals" come up with these sorts of "solutions" that do nothing but restrict personal choice. In reality, soft drinks are deadly poison, and public scrutiny should be focused on the ingredients in them. Simply switching back to sugar—from the nefarious high-fructose corn syrup, which soda companies began using in the early 1980s—would be a big help. But you won't hear any politician, Democrat or Republican, talk about that, nor about banning the harmful chemicals and preservatives that are unnecessarily in so many of the foods we consume on a daily basis. Instead, the Bloombergs of the world devise these kinds of pointless proposals, and the mainstream media trumpets them as some kind of meaningful reforms.

It's all about inconveniencing and punishing individuals, instead of targeting the root of the problem. Thus, "illegal downloading" becomes a tool for the huge record companies to crack down on individual file sharers, but no one mentions Dell or HP or Gateway and the CD and DVD burners they manufactured and sold to consumers for just this purpose. And no one questions why it is "theft" for someone to use a legal product to download a song or film that someone else wants to share. My generation used to tape-record songs from the radio, and we all swapped records to create our own cassette mix tapes. And what was the point of VCRs, if not to record and keep copyrighted movies and television shows? Why was all that legal, while file sharing is not? Don't we teach our children it's good to share?

To cite another example, "air pollution" results in Al Gore–inspired state emission inspections, which target those from lower socioeconomic backgrounds, who must of necessity drive older vehicles that have a much greater chance of failing them. These often financially strapped car owners are forced to pay for repairs, but only up to a certain limit. So, it's obvious those who designed this law are not concerned about pollution, because after the car owner pays the required amount, even if the car still fails inspection, a waiver is granted. Meanwhile, the huge factories that spew out real pollution into the air are left untouched. No "inspections" for them.

In many parts of this country, America is beginning to *look* like a Third World nation. Median strips and other public areas are overgrown and unkempt, with authorities in even the wealthiest counties claiming they can't mow the grass on a regular basis due to financial constraints. Even twenty years ago, this simply was not the case. It's either tragic or comical—depending on one's perspective—to see the high-income neighborhoods juxtaposed against the poverty-stricken appearance of the common areas around them. Our culture has voluntarily frittered away much of its aesthetic appeal. Snow removal is similarly inefficient; twenty-five to thirty years ago, the state authorities responsible for upkeep of the roads used to plow even the smallest side streets during snow storms. Over the past decade or so, citizens have come to accept that "side streets don't get plowed," and too many of them who lived through a different reality seem incapable of remembering it.

Perpetual road construction is everywhere, yet the roads seem to remain in abysmal shape. Power outages of days, not hours, after violent thunderstorms are now routine all across America. That never happened fifty years ago. How could we have been better equipped to deal with natural disasters then than we are now? Our power grids are woefully outdated. The cost of essential services such as electricity and water—like the cost of local, state, and federal government—continues to rise dramatically while the services received in return diminish each year. Why are Americans satisfied with continually paying more for less?

The 2012 Republican primaries provided demonstrable proof that voting fraud is alive and well. Everywhere renegade candidate Ron Paul went, he was swarmed by huge, enthusiastic crowds. Meanwhile, mainstream right winger Rick Santorum was drawing small groups at every rally, and yet we were supposed to believe that somehow he was "surging" while Paul, who was often literally ignored by the media, continued to lag behind him. The "irregularities" in Iowa, Nevada, Maine, Arizona, and other Republican primaries and caucuses were transparent and bold. At last, the normally unflappable and good-natured Paul was exasperated enough to publicly question the official vote totals. "Quite frankly, I don't think the

339

other candidates get crowds like this, and we get them constantly," Paul told Missouri reporters in early March 2012. "You would get the perception that we would be getting a lot more votes. Sometimes we get thousands of people like this and we'll take them to the polling booth, yet we won't win the caucus. A lot of our supporters are very suspicious about it." Critics on the Internet claimed that, in some instances, Paul drew more people at one particular rally in a given area than the total amount of official votes he was recorded as receiving there.

When the dust had settled from the dubious primary and caucus process, establishment blue blood W. Mitt Romney was the Republican nominee. Son of former Michigan governor and onetime GOP presidential hopeful George Romney, his first name, Willard, was in honor of a family friend, hotel magnate J. Willard Marriott. Romney was involved in a little publicized automobile accident as a youth; in 1968, while serving as a Mormon missionary in France, he was driving a car that crashed into a vehicle being driven by a Catholic bishop. Romney would claim for years that a drunken priest was actually behind the wheel of the other car, and that he'd died in the accident. In reality, the "priest" was a bishop, and he wasn't killed. The only person to die in the wreck was a female passenger in Romney's car. While the mainstream media dutifully reported the inaccurate "drunken priest" story in the minor coverage it allotted the incident, intrepid Internet researchers exposed the truth. According to them, the other survivors in the car were urged not to speak to reporters during Romney's unsuccessful 2008 presidential campaign.

The American people don't think much of Congress as an institution, as witnessed by recent polls indicating it has about a 12 percent approval rating from the public. Despite this, nearly all incumbents are routinely reelected. While the 2010 elections weren't quite as absurd as the 1998 elections, when 98 percent of all incumbents won reelection, there was still an incredibly high return rate of 86 percent. More than 60 percent of all incumbents face no primary challenge within their party. Too many incumbents actually run unopposed. Could anything be more ridiculous than the sight of allegedly free citizens trudging to the polls to cast a vote for someone who has no opponent?

Back in the late 1980s and early 1990s, there was a strong campaign for term limits, and it did result in the ousting of a few entrenched congressional veterans such as Dan Rostenkowski and Thomas Foley. However, the handful of new congressmen who'd made term limits an issue and pledged not to stay beyond a few terms themselves quickly changed their minds once they became spoiled by the superlative benefits and perks our elected officials receive. There were simultaneous movements to "throw all the bums out," with catchy bumper stickers that read, "Clean House, Senate, Too." As can be seen by the 98-percent reelection rate in 1998, a figure that was actually higher than the percentage of Politburo members being returned to office at the height of the Soviet Union, they weren't successful. With what we know of election fraud, it's hard to determine what would be worse—our votes not really being counted or the voters actually casting ballots for these disastrous, Snidely Whiplash–like snake oil salesmen.

The Internet remains the great hope for those who crave liberty and freedom, and a more fair and just world. The powers that be are surely frustrated beyond all measure at their utter failure to control the Internet, as it represents the first form of mass communication they haven't been able to monopolize and twist to suit their purposes. As long as we have this free means of imparting information to each other, all is not lost. Every day, more and more people are turning away from the dinosaur establishment news outlets in favor of the truly alternative sources found on the Internet.

I've delineated the basic details of conspiratorial activity over the past fifty years in this book. The cocktail of corruption and incompetence among our leaders, at every level of society, would be humorous if we weren't all so adversely affected by it. Those who have influence over our affairs appear to be, to quote Charles Dickens, experts in "how not to get it done." Where vital reforms are necessary, they cling to antiquated notions that persistently fail. Where rich traditions should be preserved or celebrated, they push for unnecessary and damaging changes. Whatever they do, the wealthiest benefit, and the large masses of people continue their perpetual "sacrifices."

When "investigations" are conducted into an obvious problem, investigators rely almost exclusively on the advice of those who should be investigated themselves. For instance, health-care initiatives utilize the input of doctors and administrators, banking committees utilize the input of bankers, anti-bullying efforts rely on the input of teachers and school officials, etc. This is only a minor step away from the hilarious practice of professionals monitoring themselves. Does anyone really think the police, for instance, examine the myriad of accusations of wrongdoing against their officers fairly and without bias?

What I can't say is what the underlying purpose behind all the chicanery and skullduggery is. Winston Smith, Orwell's protagonist in 1984, expressed the dilemma best when he wrote, "I understand how, but I don't understand why." That is the great question—the unfathomable *why*? The inequity of wealth, the total consolidation of power—what else do they want? Exactly what is it that they're after?

In 2011, a frightening new economic fact was widely reported. Thanks to decades of wealth transfer from what was the middle class to the elite at the top, the richest four hundred people in the United States now possess more wealth than the bottom *half* of all Americans combined. Now that's a stat to ponder; four hundred people having more than 50 percent of the public. Even more incredibly, according to Chrystia Freeland, author of *Plutocrats: The Rise of the New Global Super-Rich and the Fall of Everyone Else*, just *two* individual billionaires alone, Bill Gates and Warren Buffett, have more aggregate wealth than the bottom 40 percent of the American population combined.

In one sample study, a report by the Citizens for Tax Justice, compiled in 1996 during the midst of the "liberal" Clinton presidency, showed that poor and middle-income families in Virginia paid 2.5 percent more of their income in state and local taxes than did the richest families in the state. The report found that families earning less than $28,000 a year paid approximately 9.6 percent of their income in state and local taxes, while families earning between $28,000 and $80,000 paid 8.8 percent in taxes. Not surprisingly, the study revealed that the richest 1 percent of Virginians, with an average income of $731,000 annually, paid just 7.1 percent in state and local taxes. When the families were broken down another way, the unfairness was even more glaring: Virginia families with incomes exceeding $391,000 a year paid only about 5 percent in state and local taxes, 2.1 percent less than the poorest families in the Old Dominion. Nationwide, the disparities were greater. The study found that the average state and local tax burden on the richest families in the country amounted to 7.9 percent, but "middle-income" people (undefined) paid 9.8 percent and the poorest people, unbelievably enough, paid 12.5 percent (*Burke Times*, July 4, 1996, p. A5). The situation is no different all across this country.

Thanks primarily to the tax cuts instituted by President George W. Bush in 2003, the average tax rate the four hundred wealthiest Americans pay dwindled from 30 percent to 18 percent. (*Forbes*, July 25, 2011). Giving new meaning to the concept of a "graduated" income tax, according to the IRS, 1,470 of the richest Americans paid *no* taxes in 2009. (*LA Weekly*, August 8, 2011). According to author David Cay Johnston, early on in his business career, billionaire Donald Trump—who had the decided advantage of starting out his investment career as a multimillionaire—paid *no* taxes in two different years. Frank and Jamie McCourt, former owners of the Los Angeles Dodgers, paid *no* taxes from 2004 to 2011. The misleadingly titled

2004 American Jobs Creation Act cut the tax rate that corporations paid for foreign profits they brought home from 35 percent to 5.25 percent (*Willamette Week*, April 13, 2011).

That's the reality of our cockeyed world. Those who have continue to be given more benefits as well as more perks that they don't need. Meanwhile, those who are desperate for help are called "deadbeats" and are ostracized for whatever meager "handouts" they are grudgingly given. This odd inversion of common sense is best exemplified by the standard banking practice of raising credit card interest rates on those who can't pay, while giving those who can pay lower rates and easier terms. What kind of minds, faced with situations where people can't make payments, penalize them and raise the payments? Who devises the notion that those who can't pay a lesser amount will somehow magically be able to pay more? Why does our society have such a strong impulse to keep rewarding those who don't need rewards?

But while poor and working-class Americans receive almost no benefits from their government, they do pay the costs of a true nanny state. The money is not directed toward national health care or mass transit or living-wage measures. Instead, it is funneled into huge bureaucracies, some of them much like the charities we examined earlier—supposedly designed to offer specific types of assistance, but in reality only a small percentage of the revenue is utilized to help anyone.

The CIA, DIA, NSA, and other intelligence agencies don't even have a public budget; the taxpayers have no idea how much of their money is being spent there, or what it's being spent on. Rather shockingly, one of the few sound suggestions of the 9/11 Commission Report was that the budgets of the individual intelligence agencies should be made available to the public. As the Grace Commission discovered in the 1980s, a huge chunk of taxpayer money is simply wasted. There is little to suggest that things have improved in this area since then. If our money system was reformed, we would simply repudiate the national "debt," thereby solving that problem. So, it would be possible, if resources were allocated logically and even semi-fairly, for all Americans to start benefiting from government services while at the same time paying fewer taxes and reducing the actual size of the government.

When I was a child, in the 1960s, virtually every full-time job in America afforded workers a chance to live in a single-family home, own a car, and have as many children as they wanted. It was extremely rare for a wife to have to work out of economic necessity. Stores like Sears, Montgomery Ward, and Woodward & Lothrop employed many respectable husbands and fathers (and a smaller number of women in those pre-"liberated" times) in basic retail positions. Viable unions permitted employees in grocery store chains to have a very good standard of living. Now, of course, these kinds of jobs wouldn't permit a single person to live in their own apartment in most areas of the country. We are the first generation to have a lower standard of living than our parents, as Ross Perot astutely predicted back in the early 1990s. Many Americans now work two jobs, and one spouse must make an exceptional salary in order for the other one to stay at home and raise children.

Republican presidential nominee Mitt Romney's wife, Ann, expressed the elite's view of the unwashed masses with unintentional candor, in a speech to Connecticut Republicans in April 2012. "I love the fact that there are women out there who don't have a choice," declared this deluded, privileged lady, "and they must go to work and they still have to raise the kids. Thank goodness that we value those people too. And sometimes life isn't easy for any of us." But even she wasn't quite as out of touch as President George W. Bush, who once marveled at a divorced mother who was forced to work *three* jobs to support her family, telling her, "You work three jobs? . . . Uniquely American, isn't it? I mean, that is fantastic that you're doing that." I think we can rest assured that this is another unenviable category America leads the world in; most citizens working more than one job.

Harvard Professor Juliet B. Schor wrote an excellent book called *The Overworked American*. She found that the amount of time Americans spend at their jobs had risen steadily from the 1970s to the 1990s. She concluded, "Working hours are already longer than they were forty years ago." This book was written in 1993; there is no question that this unfortunate pattern has continued unabated. At the time her book was published, Schor's research revealed that US manufacturing employees worked about 320 more hours—the equivalent of more than two extra months—than their counterparts in West Germany or France. What makes this trend so tragic is that with the huge advances in technology and productivity, Americans ought to be enjoying more leisure time than ever before. Schor measured the 1993 productivity rate of American workers versus the rate in 1948 and concluded that Americans could have taken every other day off from work and matched the 1948 level. If our leaders had the wisdom and common decency of a Huey Long, then we would have adopted a four-hour workday, or a six-month work year, long ago. Instead, Americans must now work longer and harder than ever, for less pay, with fewer benefits, and a continuously lowered standard of living.

The vast majority of Americans now struggle to meet the ever-rising costs of living, on wages that are not raised annually at the same rate that costs increase (when they are raised at all). The utterly clueless nature of present-day corporate America, the sinful greed that reigns everywhere, is exemplified by *Washington Post* publisher Katharine Weymouth. Like Donald Trump, Mitt Romney, and countless other present-day scions of wealth, Weymouth did nothing to attain her position except be born the granddaughter of longtime *Post* publisher Katharine Graham. Despite the fact that the *Post* had laid off lots of workers, adopted austere cost-cutting measures, and asked the remaining staffers to sacrifice under her leadership, Weymouth granted herself an unconscionable 2010 bonus of $483,750 based on "performance goals." Considering that the *Post's* circulation, like that of all newspapers and magazines, continues to dwindle every year, exactly what "goals" could she have reached? She also saw that her base salary of $537,000 was raised 10 percent. She received over a million more dollars for meeting something called "pre-established goals" under a vague "incentive" plan and then another $72,000 for reasons I could not decipher from news accounts. Topping that, Weymouth gave herself an even bigger raise in 2011, some 16.5 percent. The performance of the *Post* during her tenure has been anything but impressive, yet this typical corporate executive is using her power to make certain that, even though her company is collapsing, *she* is profiting handsomely.

In boardrooms across America, this sorry scenario is being played out. CEOs who are failing miserably, their companies a complete wreck, are frequently given huge "buyouts" to get them to leave. They are rewarded for failure, and yet these same people are often the first to lash out at "welfare queens" and deride the notion of giving those most in need any kind of assistance. When you factor in the whole mess of benefits big business receives from government, what critics refer to as "corporate welfare," then it becomes obvious that the private sector, dominated by these unprincipled multinational corporations, is at least as bad as anything big government can devise.

MSNBC reported, on September 1, 2010, the case of Hewlett-Packard's CEO Mark Hurd, who in 2009 eliminated more than six thousand jobs and was given an incredible compensation package of more than $24 million. MSNBC found that the CEOs for the fifty firms that had laid off the most workers since 2008 received 42 percent more in pay in 2009 than their peers at other large companies. That's quite an "incentive" plan.

But inevitably the government never fails to be just as corrupt as the private sector. For years, numerous outrageous examples of government officials receiving lucrative pensions, especially those who have no business getting one, have been recounted, even in the mainstream media. On July

26, 2012, the *Boston Globe* ran a story about former Massachusetts state police commander Marian J. McGovern being approved for a tax-free disability pension due to a previously unreported heart condition. McGovern will receive about $163,000 in annual retirement pay. Another state commander, Thomas Foley, had previously retired in 2004 with a heart condition. Typical of "double dippers," Foley's heart condition did not prevent him from serving as governor's councilor or running unsuccessfully for sheriff after retirement.

Bloomfield, New Jersey, detective John Sierchio is a strong advocate of disability pension reform. He wrote a column for the *Star-Ledger* on May 27, 2012, recounting his own experiences with this issue. He noted the following examples of egregious abuse: "A 38-year-old is ruled disabled after tripping over a raised door seal. A 40-year-old receives a check for life after striking a car bumper with his knee. A firefighter falls out of bed while sleeping and is judged totally and permanently disabled." Siercho bemoaned an awful decision by the State Supreme Court in 2007, which made it incalculably easier to qualify for a disability pension. Disability claims rose 30 percent after the decision, as the change meant, "Basically, if you're injured at work and it's not a pre-existing condition, you qualify for an accidental disability pension. It's that easy."

It's a certainty that *Soprano* wannabe Chris Christie, the governor of New Jersey, isn't going to do anything to reform this odious system. The obese bully governor sponsored predictable Republican-style pension "reform" that penalized lower-level government employees by increasing the amount they were forced to contribute to the system while simultaneously cutting benefits and stopping cost-of-living raises. Meanwhile, Christie's "reform" somehow managed to overlook the despicable "double dipping" issue. Perhaps this was due to the fact that Christie's own deputy chief of staff was not only being paid a $130,000 salary but was collecting an $89,000 annual state pension. In addition, Christie's running mate, New Jersey Lieutenant Governor Kim Guadagno, made false statements as county sheriff in 2008, permitting her chief officer to collect nearly $85,000 yearly in retirement in addition to an $87,500 annual salary.

Illustrating the extent of the problem, twenty-three supervisors and investigators in the state Attorney General's Office were using legal loopholes themselves to collect both salaries and pension pay, *New Jersey Watchdog* discovered. As NBC's local Open Channel reported on May 14, 2012: "Most 'retired' for just one night. Those officers left their positions with the Attorney General's Office only to return to the same employer the next morning with new job titles—and two paychecks instead of one." *New Jersey Watchdog* found similar "double dipping" abuses with 125 officers employed by prosecutors, eighteen officials from a state Homeland Security unit, and forty-four county sheriffs and undersheriffs. Democratic State Senator Fred Madden won the title of "triple dipper," with a $241,000 yearly haul: a $49,000 salary as a legislator, $106,983 as a police academy dean, and an $85,272 pension from the State Police. Madden's response to the exposure of his "triple dipping" was to nonchalantly declare, "I don't have a problem with it at all."

In New York alone, the state Civil Service Commission inexplicably approves hundreds of special retirement waivers every year, permitting government workers to receive a pension for one position while receiving a second salary for working another government job. Mirroring the ludicrous situation in New Jersey noted previously, the New York State Attorney General's Office alone had eighty-eight such "double dippers" working for them, many of them as investigators. (*Albany Times Union*, July 2, 2012).

Presently, twenty-five states plus the District of Columbia do not have a pension forfeiture provision regarding any crimes committed by the recipient. Theoretically, an ex-government official convicted of a felony in those states could still continue to receive a hefty retirement income courtesy of the taxpayers. Thus, former Penn State assistant coach Jerry Sandusky continues to be paid an annual pension of nearly $60,000 despite his conviction for atrocious sex crimes against young children.

CBS News reported on December 23, 2009, that only two members of Congress had pledged not to accept their generous taxpayer-funded pension; North Carolina's Howard Coble and, as might be expected, Ron Paul of Texas. Some four hundred former congressional representatives now receive pensions, totaling more than $26 million, in addition to the $7.4 million shelled out by taxpayers to present members of Congress. Like other representatives convicted of various crimes and sent to prison, odious longtime Democrat Representative Dan Rostenkowski collected a six-figure pension during his fifteen months of incarceration and was receiving more than $176,000 at the time of his death in 2010. Unlike the vast majority of taxpayers, these retired politicians get automatic annual increases; in 2009, CBS reported that Rostenkowski was awarded a $9,000 cost-of-living raise. CBS reporter Sharyl Attkisson noted, regarding Rostenkowski: "According to public records, he owns three homes and waterfront property on San Marco Island in Florida." CBS found more than two dozen congresspersons still eligible for pensions, despite being convicted of serious offenses, including ex-Louisiana Representative William Jefferson, a Democrat, who was caught accepting a bribe on tape in 2005 but still qualifies for "a roughly $674,000 nest egg."

An August 15, 2012, report in *USA Today* explored the problem of excessive government pensions in general. According to the article, "More than 21,000 retired federal workers receive lifetime government pensions of $100,000 or more per year. . . . Retired law enforcement is the most common profession receiving $100,000-plus pensions, including three hundred twenty-six Drug Enforcement agents, two hundred thirty-seven IRS investigators and one hundred eighty-six FBI agents." The story also states that 714 retired Postal Service employees are getting six-figure pensions. Mercatus Center economist Veronique de Rugy was quoted as saying, "Government pensions are vastly more generous than those in the private sector. . . ." *USA Today* analyzed Census data revealing that the average federal pension was $32,824 annually, the average state and local government pension was $24,373, and the corporation having one of the best remaining private pensions, Exxon-Mobil, paid an average of only $18,250 to its retired workers.

Only 18 percent of Americans working in the private sector now receive a traditional pension, which is a dramatic and telling drop from the nearly 80 percent that had such pensions twenty-five years ago. As we have shown, greedy corporate leaders have grossly slashed benefits, salaries, and pensions for the huge majority of workers while enriching themselves and their upper-management cronies to an almost unfathomable degree. Meanwhile, our elected officials and other well-paid "public servants" seem to be engaged in enriching themselves, too, through "double dipping" and other distasteful practices.

It is hard to remain optimistic about the future. With corruption rooted into place throughout every organ of the establishment, and a population distracted by reality shows and potty humor "comedies," making the country look more and more like an Idiocracy every day, one struggles to find a silver lining anywhere. There is still a possibility, however, that enough people will be left to eventually become aroused from their stupor by harsh financial austerity measures and awake to the reality that, unless they do something to counteract it, the future is hopeless.

Let's trust that our fellow citizens will draw on some inner resource, some recessed gene from several generations back, and realize that they have the power to regain their birthright. No group of elitist plutocrats can contend with an aroused mob of millions. Tell everyone you know to turn off the television. Talk with each other. Demand accountability from those with power. Despite the risks involved, become a whistle-blower. And above all else, when someone scoffs at you countering their spoon-fed propaganda with real facts, look them straight in the eye and say, "Yes, Virginia, there *is* a conspiracy."

POSTSCRIPT

"Yes, we did produce a near perfect republic. But will they keep it? Or will they, in the enjoyment of plenty, lose the memory of freedom?"
—Thomas Jefferson

During the period between completion of the original draft of this book and its eventual publication, the corrupt behavior on the part of our leaders continued unabated. Bradley Manning, a courageous soldier in the US Army, was incomprehensibly convicted of "espionage" and other offenses and sentenced to thirty-five years in prison. Manning's "crime" was leaking classified documents to the public, which exposed the extent of the barbarity US troops had been guilty of in Iraq and Afghanistan. Another brave whistle-blower was Edward Snowden, who sacrificed a lucrative career by releasing some two hundred thousand classified documents to the press, which revealed the extensive surveillance program engaged in against American citizens by the National Security Agency (NSA). It has come to be routinely accepted by the majority of Americans that those who expose wrongdoing are to be scrutinized and reprimanded, instead of those who are doing wrong.

The tragedy at Sandy Hook Elementary School in Connecticut provoked an enormous amount of skepticism among "conspiracy theorists" on the Internet. These intrepid souls, doing the work professional "journalists" wouldn't, produced some thought-provoking articles and videos that raised doubts about every aspect of the story. A few months later, a similar tragedy, which took place during the running of the Boston Marathon, was dissected in a like manner on the Internet, and again the narrative being spun by the mainstream media and shameless politicians simply didn't add up. The authorities literally locked down the city of Boston in the aftermath, as they searched for the alleged suspects. It was disconcerting to watch the videos

351

online, recorded by people who were there, of tanks and militarized police forces pointing guns at American citizens as they conducted warrantless door-to-door searches. Ron Paul was among those appalled at this scene. "The Boston bombing provided the opportunity for the government to turn what should have been a police investigation into a military-style occupation of an American city," Paul observed. "This unprecedented move should frighten us as much or more than the attack itself."

In addition to the NSA spying scandal, the public learned that the Obama administration had used the IRS to target its political opponents, to a far greater degree than Richard Nixon ever dreamed of. The Benghazi attack in Libya, on the meaningful date of September 11, 2012, was added to the list of Obama's scandals. The mysterious death of *Rolling Stone* reporter Michael Hastings still hasn't been satisfactorily explained. On June 18, 2013, Hastings was driving a car that crashed into a tree in Los Angeles and killed him on impact. Hastings had grown increasingly radical, publicly charging the Obama administration with "waging a war" on journalists. Just prior to his accident, Hastings had expressed the belief that he was being investigated by the FBI. In a gloriously conspiratorial email sent to some of his peers in the media, Hastings claimed to be "onto a big story," and that he needed to "go off the radar" for a while. Predictably, new establishment "journalist" Cenk Uygur, host of television's *The Young Turks*, was there to issue a public statement, explaining that many of Hastings's friends had been concerned that he was in "a very agitated state" and that his work had led him to become "paranoid."

Robert Kennedy Jr. continued his recent drift toward political "extremism" with his daring comments during an interview with PBS talk show host Charlie Rose. Kennedy spoke about "very convincing evidence" that Oswald wasn't a lone assassin. He told Rose that his father thought the Warren Report was "a shoddy piece of craftsmanship" and that "In private, he was dismissive of it." (*Dallas Morning News*, January 12, 2013).

Oddly, a year later, the video from that particular Charlie Rose program was still unavailable. RFK Jr. would subsequently praise James Douglass's excellent book *JFK and the Unspeakable*. On November 20, 2013, in time for the fiftieth anniversary of JFK's assassination, RFK Jr. penned an article for *Rolling Stone* magazine in which he described JFK's war against the national security state. RFK Jr. quoted Kennedy aide General Maxwell Taylor as declaring, "I don't recall anyone who was strongly against sending troops to Vietnam except one man, and that was the president." He also shared Assistant Press Secretary Malcolm Kilduff's recollection of JFK's passionate tirade on the morning of November 21, 1963, just prior to leaving for his fatal trip to Texas.

"It's time for us to get out . . . ," JFK said, reacting to a new casualty report that showed more than one hundred Americans had died in Vietnam to date. "We're the ones doing the fighting. After I come back from Texas, that's going to change. There's no reason for us to lose another man over there."

The mainstream media coverage of the fiftieth anniversary of President Kennedy's assassination was even more pathetic than most of us could have imagined. Every single television program, with the exception of a decent, balanced one on the Travel Channel, drummed home the lone-nut, official story relentlessly. One troubling new aspect of the coverage was the persistent use of declarative statements such as "when Lee Harvey Oswald shot him" and "Oswald the sniper." There wasn't any "alleged" in these programs; to each and every "journalist" involved in these identical productions, there was no doubt about who killed JFK, despite the fact that an overwhelming majority of Americans still reject the official story.

Even long-discredited myths, such as "Oswald was the only employee missing during a post-assassination roll call," were trotted out on a few of these awful programs. This "roll call" almost certainly never took place; Texas School Book Depository Manager Roy Truly said in his Warren Commission testimony that he never made a "complete check" of the employees, but merely "saw a group of the employees over there on the floor and I noticed this boy wasn't with them." (*Hearings and Exhibits*, Vol. 7, pp. 382–383). Even if a "roll call" had been taken, Oswald would hardly have been the only employee "missing." FBI statements from seventy-three Book Depository employees revealed that seventeen of them never went back inside the building after shots were fired. In his Warren Commission testimony, Oswald's coworker Bonnie Ray Williams specifically noted the absence during this time of another TSBD employee, Charles Givens, who had a criminal history. (*Hearings and Exhibits*, Vol. 3, p. 183).

In the print press, there was more character assassination of the Kennedys, and reinforcement of the previously mentioned "Bobby was responsible" or "felt responsible" types of theories. For instance, a story in the November 24, 2013, *Boston Globe*, while promisingly headlined "Robert F. Kennedy Saw Conspiracy in JFK's Assassination," focused on the "blame Bobby" theme. Former US Attorney Robert Morgenthau, who was lunching with RFK when he received the news his brother had been shot from J. Edgar Hoover, was quoted thusly, in terms of what thoughts were racing through Bobby's mind at the time, "Was there something I could have done to prevent it? Was there something I did to encourage it? Was I to blame?" Former Kennedy aide and future US senator Harris Wofford echoed these sentiments, saying, "I think he carried a lot of potential guilt." The article also repeated the inaccurate allegation that RFK had been "determined" to oust Fidel Castro. The *Boston Globe* story did, however, describe RFK's campaign speech at San Fernando State Valley College, and strangely reported that he had told the crowd he would open the Warren Commission archives "at the appropriate time." As noted earlier in this book, I listened to that speech but missed this; it is possible it came near the end, after I'd heard the first exchange about the assassination.

Obama's reelection, over the typically inept Republican nominee Mitt Romney, guaranteed four more years of dishonest debate over issues such as Obamacare, which appeared to have done the impossible: making our bloated, expensive medical care system worse than ever. It was hard to find the "affordable" part of the Affordable Care Act, as the law mandated that everyone buy insurance or pay a penalty—which increases yearly—for opting out. Such a nonsensical proposal is identical to the Uninsured Motorists fee, which permits drivers who can't afford insurance to remain on the road. Obama would tell ABC News in a December 2013 interview that because some might "freeload" the system, he refused to rule out *jail sentences* as a potential penalty for not purchasing health insurance.

Needless to say, forcing those least able to pay for health insurance to purchase it is about as far away from providing free health care for the needy as anyone could imagine. Still, the phony two-party "debate" went on, as the Republicans ranted about Obama giving away free health insurance at taxpayer expense. There will be a great deal of taxpayer expense, but no one is getting free insurance, with the possible and incomprehensible exception of illegal immigrants, under this "affordable" legislation. Left unasked by any of our politicians was the obvious question: How are the unemployed and those working low-paying jobs supposed to fit health insurance into their budgets? Most of these people are barely making ends meet, and now they face the prospect of jail time if they can't find a way to buy this mandatory product?

As far as the 2016 presidential campaign goes, the mainstream media is already beating the drums for two more disastrous "choices," former first lady Hillary Clinton and New Jersey's obnoxious Chris Christie. If Christie can't recover from his recent "Bridgegate" scandal, where lanes were closed in Fort Lee, New Jersey, inconveniencing lots of motorists, after the mayor there refused to endorse the governor's reelection bid, other establishment Republican favorites include Marco Rubio and Bobby Jindal.

The Bureau of Alcohol, Tobacco and Firearms (ATF) was discovered to have engaged in some truly heinous behavior, in a story that broke all over the mainstream media in December 2013. The *Milwaukee Journal Sentinel* reported, on December 7, 2013, that AFT agents had used mentally disabled young people, in a plan even more demented than their "Fast and Furious" fiasco, for the supposed purpose of getting guns and drugs off the street. The ATF set up a "smoke shop" in Portland, Oregon, and forced some of these individuals to get tattoos (in one case cited, the tattoo was of a giant squid smoking a joint) on their necks, among other things. The paper also reported that the ATF had been caught earlier that year using a brain-damaged man to promote another of their undercover storefronts. In a rare bit of real investigative journalism, the paper revealed that it had read thousands of pages of court records and police reports involving ATF operations nationwide, interviewed dozens of those associated with them, and found that agents had used questionable, rogue tactics in every case. Among their numerous misdeeds were buying known stolen items at their fake pawn shops, damaging buildings, and then charging the landlords for the repairs and urging individuals to saw off shotguns to an illegal degree (shades of Ruby Ridge).

The Body Count kept growing. Twenty-six-year-old digital rights activist Aaron Swartz allegedly killed himself on January 11, 2013. Swartz was facing an unbelievable thirty-five years in prison for downloading thousands of articles from a database connected to the Massachusetts Institute of Technology. His girlfriend would assure *Atlantic Wire* that Swartz was not depressed.

FBI agents who were "interrogating" twenty-seven-year-old Ibragim Todashev, friend of dead Boston Bomber suspect Tamerlan Tsarnaev, shot and killed him on May 22, 2013. Todashev had been questioned in his apartment for more than five hours by the federal agents and Massachusetts State Police before he was inexplicably killed. Needless to say, it is extremely rare for interrogation sessions of unarmed citizens to end up in a homicide. Friends of the deceased Chechen would later accuse the FBI of harassing and threatening them, according to the Council on American-Islamic Relations. (*Russia Today*, September 26, 2013).

Anders Ebbesen, sixty-eight-year-old husband of former Florida secretary of state Katherine Harris, who played an instrumental role during the 2000 presidential election fiasco, was found dead from a self-inflicted gunshot wound on November 19, 2013. On December 9, 2013, sixty-five-year-old Milton Everett Olin Jr., former CEO of the pioneering online file-sharing service Napster, was struck and killed by a Los Angeles County, California, sheriff's patrol car while riding his bicycle. On December 13, 2013, the mainstream media reported that Hawaii State Health Director

Loretta Fuddy, who had verified what many considered to be a fraudulent birth certificate for Obama, had been killed in a plane crash. Donald Trump chimed in on Twitter about the suspicious death, tweeting, "How amazing, the State Health Director who verified copies of Obama's 'birth certificate' died in plane crash today. All others lived."

There were a slew of suspicious, unnatural deaths associated with the financial world in early 2014. When thirty-three-year-old Li Junjie leaped to his death from the roof of JP Morgan's Hong Kong office tower on February 18, it marked the third mysterious death of a JP Morgan banker. Autumn Radtke, CEO of the bitcoin exchange firm First Meta, was found dead in her Singapore apartment on February 28, 2014, a supposed suicide. (*New York Post*, March 5, 2014). Although an "investigation" into Radtke's death was said to be ongoing, there were no further updates before this book went to publication, although police instantly and predictably indicated there was no evidence of foul play.

Liberal Alabama blogger Roger Shuler was actually thrown in jail, in October 2013, for writing allegedly "libelous" things about high-profile Republicans in the state. As of January 2014, he was still behind bars. Shuler published a photo of a former Alabama attorney general, now a US Circuit Court judge, posing naked for a gay magazine, and he made scandalous allegations about former Bush aide Karl Rove, among others. He also claimed that former Alabama governor Don Siegelman had been framed and imprisoned for political reasons. It is hard to imagine how all this would warrant incarceration, but in the present climate of the United States, it seems par for the course.

In this same vein, the American Civil Liberties Union found that there are presently more than three thousand inmates in US prisons serving *life sentences* for nonviolent offenses. The Obama administration has been at least as hard in prosecuting nonviolent drug cases as his ideological "opponent" Bush was. And following President Obama's 2014 State of the Union address, New York Republican Representative Michael Grimm was caught on tape threatening to throw local reporter Michael Scotto off a balcony after Scotto told the audience, "So Congressman Michael Grimm does not want to talk about some of the allegations concerning his campaign finances." This thug mentality is spreading throughout the body politic. Is it conceivable that any congressman would have made such a threat fifty years ago? Forty? Thirty?

One of the worst of all the unjust decisions the Supreme Court has rendered in recent years occurred in January 2013. The Organic Seed Growers and Trade Association (OSGATA) had initially filed a 2011 lawsuit against corporate giant Monsanto because its deadly seeds had sometimes been carried onto their farms by insects, wind, etc. One might perhaps argue that farmers didn't necessarily have the right to sue Monsanto for this inadvertent poisoning of their soil, but our esteemed justices ruled that *Monsanto actually has the legal right to sue the farmers* when their seeds show up in organic fields. This is akin to ruling that, if someone spray-paints their car and gets some paint on a neighbor's siding, he would be able to sue the neighbor for having his paint on their house. Jim Gerritsen, president of OSGATA, described the Court's mind-boggling decision this way: "We don't think it's fair that Monsanto can trespass onto our farm, contaminate and ruin our crops and then sue us for infringing upon their patent rights."

American voters demonstrated how ignorant they can be by voting down two separate proposals to demand mandatory labeling of genetically modified (GMO) food. Californians rejected Proposition 37 in 2012, and Washington state voters followed suit in 2013 by voting against Initiative 522. In both cases, many millions of dollars were spent by powerful corporations such as Monsanto, DuPont Pioneer, Dow AgroSciences, and Bayer CropScience to oppose giving consumers this kind of essential nutritional information. (*USA Today*, November 6, 2013).

Further demonstrating how corrupt and unfair our justice system is, during the same month a jury found two police officers not guilty of beating a homeless man to death in Fullerton County, California. On July 5, 2011, Kelly Thomas had been savagely beaten for more than twenty minutes by a group of officers, with the entire thing caught on videotape. He can clearly be heard on the video begging for mercy and crying for his father, a retired police officer. There was no doubt here, let alone reasonable doubt. The moronic jury sent a clear message out to all Americans that, no matter how well documented the brutality is, police officers are above the law. (*Los Angeles Times* and others, January 14, 2014).

On October 3, 2013, unarmed mother Miriam Carey was shot to death by federal officers a block from the Capitol Building in Washington, D.C. The incident was apparently precipitated by Carey's unfamiliarity with the incredibly confusing layout of the roads in our nation's capital. The thirty-four-year-old mother's one-year-old daughter witnessed the shooting from the backseat of the car. The following day, the US Congress, at the behest of Minority Whip Steny Hoyer of Maryland, gave the Capitol police a *standing ovation* that lasted over a minute in appreciation of this "performance."

Representative Eric Cantor declared that the lawmakers "really appreciate" these brave officers.

In February 2013, even the Islamic Republic of Iran cited this particular incident as one of the examples of grave abuses occuring in the United States. Meanwhile, our own mainstream media has maintained its typical silence, even in the face of Carey's family lodging a $75 million lawsuit. Carey family lawyer Eric Sanders commented, "We criticize other countries about their record on human rights, yet our own liberties are trampled upon just as Miriam's." Constitutional lawyer John Whitehead, president of the civil liberties organization Rutherford Institute, was much bolder, stating, "They [the Iranians] recognize something a lot of Americans don't—that we live in a police state." (*World Net Daily* and others, February 4, 2014).

The Heritage Foundation and the *Wall Street Journal* released their annual Index of Freedom Report for 2014, and after several years of declining in the rankings, the United States finally dropped out of the top-ten list of the most economically free countries in the world. The index measures such things as fiscal soundness, government size, and property rights. (*Wall Street Journal*, January 13, 2014). And as further illustration of how far America has sunk, a January 2014 snowfall of *two* inches literally shut down the city of Atlanta. Children were forced to spend the night at schools, motorists were somehow stranded on the interstates, and the city became what CNN called "a laughingstock to the country."

During the broadcast of the 2013 Academy Awards ceremony, the line between government and media became even more indistinguishable. As Jack Nicholson was seemingly about to announce the nominees for Best Picture, he instead informed the audience that a special guest was joining him. A huge screen appeared behind him, with First Lady Michele Obama beaming from the Diplomatic Room of the White House, surrounded by members of the military. Shockingly, the Best Picture turned out to be *Argo*, Ben Affleck's syrupy tribute to the CIA. We've already seen an increasingly overt military presence at many sporting events in recent years, so this is really just a logical extension of that, and another earmark of a Third World country.

Meanwhile, out-of-control police forces all across America continue to wreak havoc on what is left of our liberties, with the outrageous murder of Kelly Thomas being just one glaring example. The excuse that this is just a case of "a few bad apples" doesn't hold water. In every instance, we see the police departments in question defending their officers, no matter how much video evidence of wrongdoing there is. Honest police departments would want to make examples of these "bad apples" and banish them from the force. When there are multiple instances of law enforcement officers harassing little children running lemonade stands, and still no peep of protest about it from any politician in either major party, it should be obvious to everyone that this is no longer the country we grew up in.

In April 2014, Ralph Nader gave a powerful speech at Yale University, in which he charged that America was teetering on the verge of being a police state. Nader slammed the Obama administration for its spying, secrecy, and further curtailment of civil liberties, and he concluded that the country was "on the road to tyranny and collapse." Nader's comments were made before a panel titled "Showdown for Democracy: Obama's Prosecution of Whistleblowers, Lawyers and the National Security State." Another member of the panel, former Reagan administration official Bruce Fein, declared, "We have, maybe, 30 years. It's our job to save the country from destruction."

It was revealed in the new book *Double Down: Game Change 2012* that President Barack Obama had been overheard bragging "I'm really good at killing people" to his aides, in reference to the deadly US drone program. The administration's response to this story was hardly reassuring, as White House advisor Dan Pfeiffer told ABC's *This Week*, "I haven't talked to him about the book. . . . But he hates leaks." The Bureau of Investigative Journalism in London reported that since 2004, drones had killed between 2,500 and 3,600 people, 950 of whom were considered civilians. (*Washington Times*, November 4, 2013). At least one soldier who was tasked with killing civilians is bothered by it. Brandon Bryant told *Der Spigel* that his gruesome "work" left him feeling "disconnected from humanity." In a later article about Bryant, *The Atlantic* quoted from the Bureau of Investigative Journalism's finding that there were at least 168 credible reports of *children* being killed by drones, just in Pakistan's tribal areas alone. Both Presidents Bush and Obama actively prevented human rights observers from accessing the full data on casualty reports from these still top-secret drone-strike programs. (*The Atlantic*, December 19, 2012).

The atrocities left behind in the wake of this unconscionable drone warfare is endless; in one incident, an entire wedding party in Afghanistan was killed in order to get one alleged Al-Qaeda member. Barack Obama, much like George W. Bush, seems unable to recognize the concept of tasteful boundaries. During a recent White House Correspondents Dinner, the president of the United States "joked": "The Jonas Brothers are here—they're out there somewhere. Sasha and Malia are huge fans. But boys, don't get any ideas. I have two words for you: predator drones. You will never see it coming. I'm not joking." (*The Examiner*, February 7, 2013).

Incumbents in the US Congress continued to be reelected at an unfathomable rate, especially given the fact that polls consistently showed an overwhelming lack of support for their performance (in November 2013, Congressional approval sunk to 9 percent nationally in the latest Gallup poll). In the 2012 elections, 90 percent of the House and 91 percent of the Senate was reelected. This is incomprehensibly high for any free society, even if our representatives hadn't failed so miserably at their jobs, and if every poll didn't tell us how dissatisfied the vast majority of Americans are with them.

On every front, those tasked with leading us continue to make the wrong choices, bringing closer the inevitable collapse of our once great civilization.

ACKNOWLEDGMENTS

I would like to thank my wife, Jeanne, for her years of encouragement and support, and her eternal optimism. I want to especially express my appreciation to the editors at Skyhorse Publishing, for helping me wade through all this material. The following individuals deserve thanks for their help; Dean Andrews III, Scott Buckley, Doug Copp, Scott Forbes, Linda Ives, Mark Lane, Anita Langley, David Lifton, Wayne Madsen, Edward Meyer, Barr McClellan, Robert Morrow, Scott Myers, Mark Oakes, Vince Palamara, Steve Sbraccia, Linda Tripp, Frankie Vegas, and Owen White. William Law deserves a special thank you for his work on my behalf. Finally, I owe a tremendous debt of gratitude to David Wayne, whose efforts were instrumental in getting this book published.

BIBLIOGRAPHY

Gary Allen; *None Dare Call it Conspiracy*. San Pedro, CA: GSG Associates, 1972

John Armstrong; *Harvey and Lee: How the CIA Framed Oswald*. Arlington, TX: Quasar Books, 2003

Meg Azzoni; *11 Letters and a Poem: John F. Kennedy, Jr. to Meg Azzoni*, New York, NY: Self-Published, 2012

Richard Blow; *American Son: A Portrait of John F. Kennedy, Jr.* New York, NY: Henry Holt and Co., 2002

Kristina Borjesson, editor; *Into the Buzzsaw: Leading Journalists Expose the Myth of a Free Press*. Amherst, NY: Prometheus Books, 2004

Walter Bowart; *Operation Mind Control*. New York, NY: Dell Publishing, 1978

Michael Canfield and A.J. Weberman; *Coup D'etat in America*. New York, NY: The Third Press, 1975

James F. Collier and Kenneth F. Collier; *Votescam: The Stealing of America*. New York, NY: Victoria House Press, 1992

Milton William Cooper; *Behold a Pale Horse*. Flagstaff AZ: Light Technology Publishing, 1991

Jesse Curry; *JFK Assassination File*. Dallas, TX: Self-Published, 1969

R.B. Cutler; *In Re: Chappaquiddick*. Danvers, MA: Bett's & Mirror Press, 1973

John DeCamp; *The Franklin Cover-Up: Child Abuse, Satanism, and Murder in Nebraska*. Lincoln, NE: A.W.T. Incorporated, 2011 (2nd edition)

James DiEugenio; *Destiny Betrayed*. New York, NY: Skyhorse Publishing, 2012 (2nd edition)

James DiEugenio; *Reclaiming Parkland*. New York, NY: Skyhorse Publishing, 2013

James Douglass; *JFK and the Unspeakable: Why He Died and Why it Matters*. New York, NY: Touchstone, 2010

Ambrose Evans-Pritchard; *The Secret Life of Bill Clinton: The Unreported Stories.* Washington, DC: Regnery Publishing, 1997

James H. Fetzer, editor; *Assassination Science.* Chicago, IL: Open Court, 1998

James H. Fetzer, editor; *Murder in Dealey Plaza.* Chicago, IL: Open Court, 2000

Mary Barelli Gallagher; *My Life With Jacqueline Kennedy.* Philadelphia, PA: David McKay Company, 1969

Jim Garrison; *A Heritage of Stone.* New York, NY: Berkley Publishing, 1972

Jim Garrison; *On the Trail of the Assassins.* New York, NY: Warner Books, 1991

Barbara Garson; *Mac Bird!* New York, NY: Grove Press, 1967

J.H. Hatfield and Mark Crispin Miller; *Fortunate Son: George W. Bush and the Making of an American President.* London, UK: St Martins Press, 1999

Seymour Hersh; *The Dark Side of Camelot.* New York, NY: Back Bay Books, 1998

Abbie Hoffman; *Steal This Book.* New York, NY: Pirate Editions, Grove Press, 1971

David Hoffman; *The Oklahoma City Bombing and the Politics of Terror.* Los Angeles, CA: Feral House, 1998

Barbara Honneger; *October Surprise.* New York and Los Angeles: Tudor Publishing Company, 1989

Webb Hubbell; *Friends in High Places.* New York, NY: William Morrow and Company, 1997

Henry Hurt; *Reasonable Doubt; An Investigation Into the Assassination of John F. Kennedy.* New York, NY: Holt, Rinehart & Winston, 1986

Lee Israel; *Kilgallen.* New York, NY: Delacorte Press, 1979

Penn Jones, Jr.; *Forgive My Grief I-IV.* Midlothian, TX: Midlothian Mirror, 1966

Seth Kantor; *Who Was Jack Ruby?* Pune, India: Everest House, 1978

Michael Kazin *The Populist Persuasion.* Ithaca, NY: Cornell University Press, 1998

Jim Keith; *Black Helicopters Over America.* Atlanta, GA: Illuminet Press, 1995

John Kelin; *Praise From a Future Generation.* San Antonio, TX: Wings Press, 2007

Kitty Kelley; *Nancy Reagan: The Unauthorized Biography.* New York, NY: Pocket Books, 1992

William Klaber and Philip H. Melanson; *Shadow Play: The Murder of Robert F. Kennedy, the Trial of Sirhan Sirhan, and the Failure of American Justice.* London, UK: St Martins Press, 1997

William Law; *In the Eye of History.* Walterville, OR: Trine Day, 2015 (2nd edition)

Mark Lane; *Rush to Judgment.* New York, NY: Holt, Rinehart and Winston, 1966

Mark Lane; *A Citizen's Dissent.* New York, NY: Holt, Rinehart and Winston, 1968

Mark Lane; *Code Name "Zorro:" The Murder of Martin Luther King, Jr.* Upper Saddle River, NJ: Prentice-Hall, 1977

Mark Lane; *Plausible Denial.* New York, NY: Thunder's Mouth Press, 1991

Timothy Leary; *Flashbacks.* New York, NY: Tarcher, 1997

Evelyn Lincoln; *My Twelve Years with John F. Kennedy.* Philadelphia, PA: David McKay Co., 1965

David Lifton; *Best Evidence.* New York, NY: Macmillan Publishing Company, 1980

Harrison Livingstone and Robert J. Groden; *High Treason.* New York, NY: Berkley Reissue edition, 1990

Jim Marrs: *Crossfire: The Plot That Killed Kennedy.* New York, NY: Carroll and Graf, 1989

Phillip Marshall; *False Flag 9/11.* Booksurge (self-published), 2008

Phillip Marshall; *The Big Bamboozle: 9/11 and the War on Terror.* Createspace (self-published), 2012

Jason Mattera; *Hollywood Hypocrites.* New York, NY: Threshold Editions, Reprint edition, 2013

Sylvia Meagher; *Accessories After the Fact.* New York, NY: Bobbs-Merrill, 1967

Barr McClellan; *Blood, Money & Power: How LBJ Killed JFK.* Springdale, AR: Hannover House, 2003

Gerald McKnight; *Breach of Trust; How the Warren Commission Failed the Nation and Why.* Lawrence, Kansas: University Press of Kansas, 2005

David McGowan; *Weird Scenes Inside the Canyon; Laurel Canyon, Cover Ops and the Dark Heart of the Hippie Dream.* London, UK: Headpress, 2014

Dan E. Moldea; *The Killing of Robert F. Kennedy.* New York, NY: W.W. Norton & Company, 1995

Michele Marie Moore; *Oklahoma City: Day One.* Eagar, AZ: Harvest Trust, 1997

Kenneth P. O'Donnell and David F. Powers; *Johnny, We Hardly Knew Ye: Memories of John Fitzgerald Kennedy.* New York, NY: Pocket Books, 1972

Barbara Olson; *Hell to Pay: The Unfolding Story of Hillary Rodham Clinton.* Washington, DC: Regnery Publishing, Revised Edition, 2013

George O'Toole; *The Assassination Tapes.* New York, NY: Penthouse Press, 1975

Vincent Palamara; *Survivor's Guilt: The Secret Service and the Failure to Protect President Kennedy.* Walterville, OR: Trine Day, 2013

Terry Reed; *Compromised: Clinton, Bush and the CIA.* New York, NY: S.P.I. Books, 1994

George Reedy; *Lyndon B. Johnson: A Memoir.* Riverside, NJ: Andrews McMeel Publishing, 1985

Dr. John A. Richardson; *Laetrile Case Histories: The Richardson Cancer Clinic Experience*. Boca Raton, FL: American Media, 1977

Howard Roffman; *Presumed Guilty*. New York, NY: A.S. Barnes, 1976

Mike Rothmiller; *L.A. Secret Police: Inside the LAPD Elite Spy Network*. New York, NY: Pocket Books, 1992

Christopher Ruddy; *The Strange Death of Vincent Foster*. New York, NY: Free Press, 1997

Dominic Sandbrook; *Eugene McCarthy: The Rise and Fall of Postwar American Liberalism*. New York, NY: Anchor, 2005

James Sanders; *The Downing of TWA Flight 800*. New York, NY: Zebra Books, 1997

Arthur Schlesinger, Jr.; *A Thousand Days*. Boston, MA: Houghton Mifflin, 1965

Arthur Schlesinger, Jr.; *Robert Kennedy and His Times*. New York, NY: Mariner Books. 2012

Arthur Schlesinger, Jr.; *Journals*. New York, NY: Penguin Books, Reprint edition, 2007

J. Gary Shaw and Larry Ray Harris; *Cover-Up: The Governmental Conspiracy to Conceal the Facts About the Public Execution of John Kennedy*. Cleburne, TX: Self-Published, 1976

Barry Scheck, et al; *Actual Innocence: Five Days to Execution and Other Dispatches From the Wrongly Convicted*. New York, NY: Doubleday, 2000

Richard E. Sprague; *The Taking of America,1-2-3*. Woodstock, NY: Rush Harp and Barbara Black, 1976

R. Harris Smith; *OSS: The Secret History of America's First Central Intelligence Agency*. Guilford, CT: Lyons Press, 2005

Oliver Stone and Zachary Sklar; *JFK: The Book of the Film*. New York, NY: Applause Theater & Cinema Books, 2000

David Talbot: *Brothers: The Hidden History of the Kennedy Years*. New York, NY: Free Press, Reprint edition, 2008

Webster Tarpley; *George Bush: The Unauthorized Biography*. San Diego, CA: Progressive Press, Reprint edition, 2004

Josiah Thompson; *Six Seconds in Dallas*. New York, NY: Bernard Geis / Random House Inc., 1967

John Kennedy Toole; *A Confederacy of Dunces*. New York, NY: Grove Weidenfeld, Reissue edition, 1987

Noel Twyman; *Bloody Treason*. Miller Place, NY: Laurel Publications, 1997

Gary Webb; *Dark Alliance: The CIA, the Contras, and the Crack Cocaine Explosion*. New York, NY: Seven Stories Press (2nd edition), 1999

Harold Weisberg; *Whitewash*. New York, NY: Dell Publishing, 1966

Harold Weisberg; *Whitewash II: The FBI-Secret Service Cover Up*. New York, NY: Dell Publishing, 1967

Harold Weisberg; *Photographic Whitewash*. Frederick, MD: Privately Published, 1967

Harold Weisberg; *Oswald in New Orleans*. New York, NY: Canyon Books, 1967

Harold Weisberg; *Post Mortem*. Frederick, MD: Privately Published, 1975

Harold Weisberg; *Case Open*. New York, NY: Carroll & Graf, 1994

Kathleen Willey; *Target: Caught in the Crosshairs of Bill and Hillary Clinton*. Medford, OR: WND Books, 2007

INDEX

INDEX

INDEX

INDEX

INDEX

Boston Ritz Carlton Hotel, 295
Boys Town, Nebraska, 298
Burkett, Joe, 308
Bynum, Paul, 304
Capitol Hill, 296
Caradori, Gary, 297
Caradori, Sandie, 298
Chevy Chase Elementary School, 296
Child Protective Services, 307
Children's Institute International, 304
Conspiracy of Silence, 298
Copple, Newt, 299
Customs Service, 306
Davidson, James Dale, 300
Davis, Greg, 296
Densen-Gerber, Judianne, 297
Department of Family and Child Services, 307
Discovery Channel, 298
ESPN, 309
Father Flannigan, 298
Feldman, Corey, 310
Finders, The, 306
Freeh, Louis, 310
Gobie, Stephen L., 296
Gricar, Ray, 309
Guinea Pig Kids, 309
Hambright, Gary, 302
Hermosa Beach, 304
Hupp, Monsignor Robert, 298
Institute for Policy Studies, 300
Johnson, Judy, 304
KABC, 304
Klaas, Gerald, 304
Klaas, Karen, 304
LaVey, Anton, 302
Lewis, Tom, 307
Luna, Jonathan P., 309
Malek, Joe, 299
Mann, Abby, 304
Massaro, Gabriel A., 296
McGauley, Jackie, 305
McMartin Preschool, 303
Medley, Billy, 304
National Center on Child Abuse and Neglect, 307
NCAA, 309
Nebraska Senate Franklin Committee, 297
Neutron Bomb, 301
New York City Administration of Children Services, 308
Omaha World-Herald, 301
Owen, Aaron, 297
Owen, Alisha, 297
Paterno, Joe, 309
Penn State, 309
Philibosian, Robert, 304
Presidio Child Development Center, 301
Reader's Digest, 305
Righteous Brothers, 304

Rogers, Charlie, 299
Russoniello, Joseph, 301
Ryan, Dan, 299
San Francisco Examiner, 302
Sandusky, Jerry, 309
Satanism, 300
Satz, Wayne, 304
Schaefer, Bruce, 308
Schaefer, Nancy, 307
Second Mile Foundation, 310
Sheehan, Archbishop Daniel, 298
Sorenson, Kathleen, 299
Special Reserves, 301
Spence, Craig J., 295
Strategic Investment, 300
Temple of Set, 301
Texas Society of Psychiatric Physicians, 308
Thompson, Hunter, 299
Thousand Points of Light, 310
Tracy, Spencer, 298
Tucker, Curtis, 299
TV Guide, 298
US News and World Report, 306
Wadman, Robert, 297
Washington D.C. Police, 306
Wicomico River, 300
Winkler, Robert, 304
Yorkshire Television, 298

WORLD GOVERNMENT/ THE NEW WORLD ORDER
Beatty, Warren, 312
Brokaw, Tom, 312
Couric, Katie, 312
Club of Rome, 312
Didion, Joan, 312
Diller, Barry, 312
Geffen, David, 312
Gingrich, Newt, 312
Gorbachev, Mikhail, 314
Iovine, Jimmy, 312
Jolie, Angelina, 312
Katzenberg, Jeffrey, 312
Oxford University, 313
Quigley, Carroll, 311
Roosevelt, Theodore, IV, 312
Spielberg, Steven, 312
Taft, William H., IV, 312
Tagliabue, Paul, 312

THE BILDERBERGERS
Bilderberg Hotel, 313
Healey, Denis, 313
Lord, Winston, 314
Mandela, Nelson, 314
Cousins, Norman, 313
Robertson, Pat, 313
Talbot, Strobe, 313
U.S. Senate Committee on Foreign Relations, 313
Warburg, James, 313
World Federalists Association, 313

BOHEMIAN GROVE
Blair, Tony, 315–316
Coolidge, Calvin, 316
Cremation of Care, 315
Cruise, Tom, 316
Grateful Dead, The, 316
Griffin, Merv, 316
Hoover, Herbert, 316
Linkletter, Art, 316
London, Jack, 316
Major, John, 315
McGwire, Mark, 316
Moloch, 315
Morgan, J.P., 316
Powell, Colin, 316
Savage, Chad, 316
Schwarzenegger, Arnold, 316
Shearer, Harry, 316
Spy Magazine, 315
Twain, Mark, 316

THE FEDERAL RESERVE AND FRACTIONAL BANKING
Bernanke, Ben, 319
Bloomberg News, 319
Ford, Henry, 317
Lindbergh, Charles A., Sr., 318
McFadden, Louis, 318
Patman, Wright, 318
Pittman, Maggie, 320
Pittman, Mark, 319
Rothschild, Mayer Amschel, 317
U.S. Court of Appeals, 320
U.S. Supreme Court, 320

THE BIG CHARITY BOONDOGGLE
Agnos, Art, 322
Albuquerque Journal, 324
Alzheimer's Foundation of America, 322
American Cancer Society, 327–328
American Express, 333
American Heart Association, 328, 330
American Institute of Philanthropy, 330
American Red Cross, 329
American Rescue Team International, 324
American Society for the Prevention of Cruelty to Animals, 328
Apple, 327
Aramony, William, 321
Arthritis Foundation, 330
Aspen Ideas Festival, 327
Association for Voluntary Sterilization, 326
Bailey, F. Lee, 324
Bassett, Todd, 322
Better Business Bureau, 328-329